This book develops an integrated approach to u[...] [...]the American economy and national elections. Economic policy is generally seen as the result of a compromise between the president and Congress. Because Democrats and Republicans usually maintain polarized preferences on policy, middle-of-the-road voters seek to balance the president by reinforcing in Congress the party not holding the White House. This balancing leads, always, to relatively moderate policies and, frequently, to divided government.

The authors first outline the rational partisan business cycle, where Republican administrations begin with recessions, and Democratic administrations with expansions, and next the midterm cycle, where the president's party loses votes in the midterm congressional election. The book argues that both cycles are the result of uncertainty about the outcome of presidential elections. Other topics covered include retrospective voting on the economy, coattails, and incumbency advantage. A final chapter shows how the analysis sheds light on the economies and political processes of other industrial democracies.

PARTISAN POLITICS, DIVIDED GOVERNMENT, AND THE ECONOMY

Editors
James E. Alt, *Harvard University*
Douglass C. North, *Washington University in St. Louis*

PARTISAN POLITICS, DIVIDED GOVERNMENT, AND THE ECONOMY

ALBERTO ALESINA and HOWARD ROSENTHAL

Harvard University   *Princeton University*

CAMBRIDGE
UNIVERSITY PRESS

Published by the Press Syndicate of the University of Cambridge
The Pitt Building, Trumpington Street, Cambridge CB2 1RP
40 West 20th Street, New York, NY 10011-4211, USA
10 Stamford Road, Oakleigh, Melbourne 3166, Australia

First published 1995

Printed in the United States of America

Library of Congress Cataloging-in-Publication Data

Alesina, Alberto.
Partisan politics/Alberto Alesina, Howard Rosenthal.
p.   cm. – (Political economy of institutions and decisions)
Includes bibliographical references and index.
ISBN 0-521-43029-1 (hard). – ISBN 0.521-43620-6 (pbk.)
1. Business cycles – Political aspects – United States –
History – 20th century. 2. Presidents – United States – Election –
History – 20th century. 3. United States – Economic policy – Decision
making. 4. Representative government and representation – United
States – History – 20th century. I. Rosenthal, Howard, 1939–   .
II. Series
HB3743.A45 1994   93–48512
338.5′42–dc20   CIP

A catalog record for this book is available from the British Library

ISBN 0-521-43029-1 hardback
ISBN 0-521-43620-6 paperback

To Marianne and Margherita

Contents

Tables, figures, and boxes

Tables, figures, and boxes

BOXES

Series editors' preface

The Cambridge series on the Political Economy of Institutions and Decisions is built around attempts to answer two central questions: How do institutions evolve in response to individual incentives, strategies, and choices, and how do institutions affect the performance of political and economic systems? The scope of the series is comparative and historical rather than international or specifically American, and the focus is positive rather than normative.

For two decades, a – perhaps the – central emphasis of the empirical study of political economy in industrial societies has been on one interaction, the relationship between the impact of the economy on electoral outcomes on the one hand and, on the other, the incentives and abilities of elected politicians to affect, and maybe manipulate, macroeconomic policy in ways which depend critically on the institutional context. In this book, Alberto Alesina and Howard Rosenthal provide by far the richest model of this interaction yet developed, along with a battery of supporting, and generally supportive, empirical evidence. Their model incorporates an explicit theory of voting, in which ideologically moderate voters divide their votes over elected representatives in a political regime in which there are multiple elections and executive and legislative powers reside in separate institutions. By doing so voters achieve significant moderation of economic policy, enforcing a balance between politicians' desires to stimulate output and restrict inflation. A number of observable features, including post-election partisan-inspired cycles in output and the regular midterm loss of votes by the executive's legislative partisans, are derived from the model and shown to be regular features of the American political economy. The book's sweeping synthesis, encompassing a wide range of observable phenomena while unifying explicitly rational approaches to both political and economic behavior, makes it a benchmark achievement in the field and a focus for further theoretical development and empirical investigation.

Acknowledgments

Our collaboration was initiated in the fall of 1987 at Carnegie Mellon University, when we realized that electoral uncertainty might be the fundamental force between two empirical regularities. One regularity, that the economy expands after a Democratic victory in a presidential election and contracts following a Republican win, pertains to the economy. The other, that the president's party inevitably loses vote share in midterm congressional elections, pertains to politics. Research on these two cyclical phenomena – the rational partisan business cycle and the midterm electoral cycle – led to this book. In the following six years we moved to Harvard (Alesina in 1988) and to Princeton (Rosenthal in 1993). In addition, both of us went on leave to other institutions, but we managed to collaborate despite a hectic travel schedule which usually kept us apart. (Each of us accuses the other of travelling too much!)

As our work progressed, we received suggestions, help, and encouragement from many friends and colleagues. First of all we were fortunate to have been joined at Carnegie Mellon by John Londregan, whose econometric skills were essential to the empirical analysis of the political economy of the United States. The results of chapter 9 are based on collaborative work with him which appeared in an article in the *American Political Science Review* in 1993.

We owe much to Guido Tabellini. He introduced the two authors to each other; subsequently, both during his visit to Carnegie Mellon University in 1987/88 and in later years he was a source of comments and intellectual stimuli. We have a major intellectual debt to Yossi Greenberg, who clarified our analysis of the voter equilibrium through concepts presented in another Cambridge University Press volume, *The Theory of Social Situations*. Yossi's initial insights came during a superb conference he organized in Haifa in 1988. Several participants in the conference, particularly Alex Cukierman, Melvin Hinich, Richard McKelvey, Thomas Palfrey, and John Roemer, have had a major influence on our work. The development of the uncertainty model in chapter 4 was influenced by key insights offered by Geir Asheim. Another important source of direction has come from Keith Poole, whose emphasis on ideological politics resulted in much of the empirical work summarized in section 2.6. James Alt was very important for us. First he encouraged us to write this book and then greatly helped us in getting it published by Cambridge University Press. Finally he provided very useful comments on the first draft of the manuscirpt.

We have also benefitted from comments from numerous other individuals including John Ferejohn, Morris Fiorina, Gregory Hess, Thomas Romer, Mathias Dewatripont, Henry Chappell, William Mishler, Timothy Feddersen, Daniel Ingberman, Susanne Lohman, Kenneth Shepsle, and many others whom we have neglected to mention. Special thanks are owed to William Keech, who read early drafts and provided detailed feedback. He visited Harvard and M.I.T. in 1992/93 and he was an invaluable source of challenging conversations.

Many useful comments were also provided by students in Government 2062 at Harvard. Additional thanks go to our research assistant, Gerald Cohen, who carried out some initial data analysis that resulted in chapter 6.

Our own spatial mobility as authors and the very low typing skills of one of the two authors have resulted in our reliance on a legion of typists. Joy Lee, an exceptionally gifted secretary, typed our early papers. The word processing pools at the Center for Advanced Study in the Behavioral Sciences, the Graduate School of Industrial Administration at Carnegie, and the National Bureau of Economic Research completed the typing and assembled the manuscript.

Our collaborative research was initiated while Alesina was a Political Economy Fellow at Carnegie Mellon under the auspices of the Center for Public Policy headed by Allan Meltzer. Thomas Palfrey is also largely responsible for our opportunity to collaborate at Carnegie Mellon. In 1989/90 Alesina was an Olin Fellow at the National Bureau of Economic Research. The first draft of most of the book was written while Rosenthal was a Fellow at the Center for Advanced Study in the Behavioral Sciences. The Center's attraction as a research environment and the hospitality of the directors, Philip Converse and Robert Scott, are most deservedly widely recognized in the social sciences. Work on the book continued while Rosenthal was a Fellow at the International Centre for Economic Research in Torino, Italy. Further support for this research was provided by the National Science Foundation and the Sloan Foundation.

PARTISAN POLITICS, DIVIDED
GOVERNMENT, AND THE ECONOMY

1

Introduction

1.1 GENERAL OVERVIEW

Economics and politics deeply interconnect. On the one hand, incumbents are likely to benefit from an expanding economy and challengers to thrive on misery. On the other, the outcomes of elections influence economic policy and the state of the economy. This book studies the joint determination of political and macroeconomic outcomes. It focuses on the United States, but we also briefly discuss how our work sheds light on the political economy of other industrial democracies.

A few basic ideas underlie our work. The first one is that the American political system is "polarized". Contrary to the widely held view, particularly in the "rational choice" framework, that a two-party system generates convergence of party platforms (Downs (1957)), we posit that, when in office, the two American parties follow different policies. The degree of polarization has varied greatly in American history (Poole and Rosenthal (1991a, 1993b)), but the two parties have never fully converged. What is important for us is not that polarization is constant, but simply that it does not vanish.

The second idea is that policy polarization leads to macroeconomic cycles. The two major parties follow sharply different macroeconomic policies. Whereas the Republicans are relatively more concerned with inflation, the Democrats emphasize reducing unemployment.[1] These distinctive objectives, coupled with uncertainty about the outcome of elections, make macroeconomic policy not perfectly predictable. The actual outcomes of elections then generate economic recessions and expansions even though predictable macroeconomic policies should not influence growth in an economy with

---

[1]Hibbs (1987) grounds these preferences in the economic interests of the social groups supporting the Democratic and Republican parties. Although we adopt this "partisan" approach pioneered by Hibbs (1977, 1987), we differ from him substantially about the impact of political polarization on the macroeconomy. See chapter 7.

rational agents. Our emphasis on the role of expectations and of electoral uncertainty strongly distinguishes our work from previous research (Hibbs (1977, 1987)) on partisan macroeconomic cycles. Hence, we dub our cycle the "rational partisan business cycle".

The third basic idea is that the institutional process leading to policy formation is very important. Specifically, we emphasize that policy outcomes depend not only on which party holds the presidency but also on how strong each party is in the legislature. For instance, the policy outcome with a Republican president and a Republican majority in Congress is more conservative than the policy outcome with the same president and a Democratic majority in Congress. The actual form of this interplay between the executive and legislative branches of government is determined by institutional details. The crucial point is, however, that policy emerges from an *interaction* between the executive and the legislature.

The fourth idea is that voters take advantage of "checks and balances" implicit in the executive–legislative interaction to bring about moderate policies. Even though the American electorate faces two polarized parties, the voters can achieve "middle-of-the-road" policies. Since policy must reflect compromise between the executive and legislative branches, the voters may moderate a president from one party by handing Congress to the opposing party. Alternatively, if the voters are aware that the incumbency advantage is likely to assure continued control of Congress by one party, they may tilt toward the other in presidential elections. In either scenario, middle-of-the-road voters, who are the bulk of the electorate, may prefer to divide power between the two parties rather than to hand complete control of both branches of government to the same party. Thus "divided government", where one party holds the presidency and the other has a majority in Congress, is not an accident, but the result of the voters' desire for policy moderation. Even so, divided government is not a necessary condition for moderation. Some voters always engage in moderating behavior, but this behavior may not produce divided government if middle-of-the-road voters prefer one of the two parties. Thus, we do not predict that we should *always* observe divided government. Nonetheless, since policy depends upon the composition (i.e., relative shares) of Congress, even minority opposition in Congress can provide some balance to a president of the opposing party.

Finally, the fifth idea is that the midterm cycle is part of this institutional balancing. The electorate has two opportunities to balance the president: first in the on-year congressional election, and second at midterm. The on-year congressional elections take place with uncertainty about the identity of the next president. This uncertainty is removed in midterm: in midterm congressional elections the voters know which president the next Congress will have to face. We will show how this difference in the uncertainty concerning the president leads to a midterm loss for the party

2

holding the White House. Thus uncertainty about presidential elections is the fundamental cause of both the midterm cycle and the rational partisan business cycle.

The purpose of this volume is *not* to build theory *per se*. On the contrary, we develop a theoretical framework with the explicit goal of deepening our substantive understanding of the American political economy. Therefore we use the theory to generate specific empirical predictions,which are explicitly tested.

From a methodological standpoint, we use the rational choice approach without making an orthodox, full-fledged commitment to it. In fact, as we outline below, we temper rationality in the economy with a rigidity in economic contracting to which the purest exponents of the rational choice school would take exception. These rigidities and frictions account for empirical regularities in the relationship between economic growth and the outcomes of elections. In addition, we find little empirical support for recent attempts to provide a rational choice explanation of the phenomenon of retrospective voting, where recent economic performance affects the incumbent president's electoral fate. In spite of these caveats, the rational choice perspective is enormously useful in that it permits us to develop a formal model that has testable propositions about empirical observations. In a sense, we explore how far we can go with rational choice in explaining the American political economy of this century. We feel that we have succeeded to a very great extent.

Within the rational choice framework, utility-maximizing voters make decisions, based both on their preferences and information and on political constraints. In addition, when forecasting the future, both voters and economic agents behave rationally; that is, they form "rational expectations" defined as the best possible forecasts of future events, given the amount of information available at the time the forecast is made. Rational expectations are not perfect foresight: the amount of information available to a forecaster (say, a voter) may be very limited; thus his best forecast (i.e., "rational expectation") may be very imperfect. The point is *not* that rational expectations are always correct, but a deeper methodological one: the assumption of rational expectations is the natural extension of the basic rational choice ideas to a dynamic context where the future matters. If agents are assumed to behave rationally when making static decisions, why should they not behave rationally when making forecasts? The rational expectation assumption, as is shown in this book, has important implications for both the polity, via voting behavior, and the economy, with regard to the "real" effect of macroeconomic policies, via economic agents' behavior.

A second important methodological aspect of this monograph is that we develop a stylized, parsimonious model to capture rather complex institutional interactions. Although we introduce a much richer institutional structure than usual in the rational choice model of two-party elections, we abstract from many important features of American institutions.

We do not apologize for this choice , which we have made for two good reasons. First, the simplicity of a "bare-bones" model provides the analytical tractability needed to generate sharp empirical predictions that can in turn be tested. These tests allow one to evaluate the usefulness of the model itself. Second, by being sufficiently general on the specification of the institutions, we capture basic relationships and mechanisms that can shed light on several different political systems. Therefore the assumptions needed to construct an analytically tractable model should not be judged by whether they are a completely realistic characterization of American institutions. The point is *not* whether what is ignored is "important", but whether such an omission just simplifies an argument or, instead, distorts it.

Using this simple rational choice approach, we look at the American political economy as a system in which both the economy and the polity are jointly endogenous. This feature of our work will make it possible to encompass in a general equilibrium framework several phenomena that have heretofore been analyzed in isolation. Previously, separate strands in the literature examined (1) the effect of economic conditions on general elections;[2] (2) partisan macroeconomic policies;[3] (3) the absence of a pre-electoral "surge" in economic growth;[4] (4) "divided government";[5] and (5) congressional elections and the midterm cycle.[6] We build a general model that will account for the following regularities identified by this literature:

(i) Presidential elections are strongly influenced by the business cycle. The vote share of the incumbent president's party's presidential candidate increases with the rate of GNP growth in the election year.

(ii) Congressional elections are less sensitive to economic conditions.

(iii) There is a midterm cycle; the party holding the White House loses plurality in midterm congressional elections.

(iv) There is a "rational partisan business cycle". Specifically, in the first half of Republican administrations, economic growth tends to decelerate, reaching its minimum during the second year of each term; the economy grows more rapidly during the first half of Democratic administrations. In the last two years of each term, there are no significant differences between growth rates for Democratic and Republican administrations.

(v) The rate of GNP growth in election years is *not* systematically higher

[2] See Kramer (1971), Fair (1978, 1982, 1988), Fiorina (1981), Lewis-Beck (1988).
[3] See Hibbs (1977, 1987), Alt (1985), Alesina (1987, 1988b), Alesina and Sachs (1988), Chapell and Keech (1988), Beck (1992).
[4] See McCallum (1978), Golden and Poterba (1980), Hibbs (1987), Alesina and Roubini (1992), Alesina, Cohen, and Roubini (1992, 1993).
[5] See Fiorina (1988, 1992), Alesina and Rosenthal (1989, 1991).
[6] See Erikson (1988, 1990), Alesina and Rosenthal (1989).

4

than average: there is no evidence of a systematic pre-electoral economic boom.

These observations may not appear, at first sight, consistent with each other, in particular (i) and (v) and (i) and (ii). One of the strengths of our approach is that we can explain all of them within the same logically consistent framework.

Our analysis begins by studying voting in the context of an executive–legislative interaction in policy formation. Policy is, in our model, a function of which party holds the presidency and of the composition of Congress. In rational choice models of two-candidate elections where the winner takes all, the candidates propose the same platform to the electorate in order to win. In these models, the candidates are the strategic actors: they choose policy positions in order to attract voters. The voters simply vote for their preferred candidate, since they face a forced choice between the two platforms proposed by the candidates.

In many respects, we take the exactly opposite view. Our basic premise is that the candidates of the two major parties represent polarized positions. The voters, who are the strategic actors in our model, have to make the best of the situation. Even though they face two polarized parties, they manage to bring about moderate policies by virtue of the checks and balances created by the Constitution: the party not holding the presidency is made relatively strong in the legislature. Whereas in the standard rational choice model policy moderation is achieved because the two candidates move toward the political center, in our framework moderation is created by the voters who take advantage of the institutional complexity in policy formation. Both divided government and the midterm cycle are explained as phenomena of institutional balancing.

In the second part of the book, we examine, using our model of the polity, an important public policy problem: the macroeconomic management of the economy, with specific reference to the trade-off between inflation and either unemployment or GNP growth. Our model of the economy draws on recent macroeconomic theory by incorporating two key assumptions: rational expectations and wage–price rigidities.

The application of the rational expectation idea in macroeconomics (Lucas (1972), Sargent and Wallace (1975)) led to a dramatic shift in views concerning the role of economic policy. Contrary to the traditional Keynesian wisdom, the rational expectation theorists argued that aggregate demand policies targeted to reduce unemployment are ineffective, both in the short and in the long run. After this critique was digested, neo-Keynesian models were developed to incorporate rational expectations in macroeconomic models with some forms of short-run wage and price rigidities. These types of models predict, generally speaking, real effects (non-neutrality) from the government's aggregate demand policy in the short run (in the Keynesian mode) and medium to long-run neutrality (in the rational expectations mode). This eclectic spirit very much reflects our views; we believe that both rational expectations and short-run wage–price rigidities are critical elements in a realistic macroeconomic model.

We test our model using a simultaneous estimation of a system of equations in which the endogenous variables are the rate of growth of the gross national product and the results of presidential and congressional elections. Our sample begins in 1915 and extends to the present. This beginning date was dictated by important political and economic events. In politics, Theodore Roosevelt's Bull Moose candidacy in 1912 split the Republican party and generated a three-candidate race. After 1912 (but until 1992!) American politics, despite the occasional appearance of third-party candidates, has approximated the two-party system that we model in the theoretical part of the book. In the area of economic policy formation, the Federal Reserve was created in 1914, leading to a significant regime shift in key macroeconomic time series.[7]

Our empirical analysis is largely successful. Our model is broadly consistent with the evidence and can explain important features of the American political economy. Nevertheless, we will not be shy in pointing out aspects of the real world that seem to escape our formalization.

In particular, rational choice theorists have tried to explain the strong correlation between economic performance just before elections and the incumbent's fate at the polls. Should rational voters be influenced by the past performance of the economy? How should rational voters distinguish the effect of an administration's ability in managing the economy from events that are unrelated to government actions but may, for better or for worse, deeply affect the economy?

These questions have been explored theoretically by other researchers; we have blended their work into our model. We provide the first empirical test of this approach. The basic idea is that different administrations may have different degrees of "competence" in handling the economy. *Ceteris paribus*, more competent administrations achieve higher growth and lower unemployment than less competent ones.[8] Thus the electorate votes on two grounds: "partisanship" and competence. For example, moderate Democrats may be easily convinced to vote Republican if the incumbent Democratic administration is perceived as incompetent. (The reader may identify the

---

[7]On this point see Mankiw, Miron, and Weil (1990). A third reason not to begin before 1914 is that the reliability of economic data before the First World War is much lower than for the subsequent period. See Romer (1989).

[8]The original proponents of this idea of competence are Rogoff and Sibert (1988). Our model of competence builds upon, but is quite distinct from, Persson and Tabellini (1990, chapter 5).

"Reagan Democrats" of the 1980s in this example.) On the other hand, a hard-core liberal may never be persuaded to vote Republican, even in the presence of a highly incompetent Democratic incumbent. The voters gather information about an administration's competence by observing the state of the economy: thus the voters are retrospective, and good pre-electoral economic conditions increase the chances of reappointment for the incumbent. We fail, however, to find any empirical linkage between economic growth and the competence of administrations, at least within our formalization of the concept of "competence". If this finding were correct, rational voters should entirely disregard recent economic performance in making their voting decisions. Thus we are unable to reconcile retrospective voting on the economy with our rational choice model. Our rejection of rationality on this point suggests a question for further research: why are short-run economic conditions in the 9 to 12 months before an election so important?[9]

Before we proceed, it is useful to explain, with an example, how our model of the American political economy works. Suppose that a Democratic president who was a slight favorite is elected. This presidential outcome is associated with a reasonably strong showing of the Republican party candidates in congressional elections, since the voters balanced the favored presidential candidate. The Democratic administration follows expansionary macroeconomic policies, which lead to an upsurge of growth in the first half of the term and an increase in inflation. At midterm, the electorate further balances the Democratic administration by reinforcing the Republican party in Congress. In doing so, the voters seek to insure themselves against excessive inflation. Note that this pattern implies a non-obvious correlation: strong economic growth in the first half of a Democratic administration is associated with a political *loss* by this party in midterm. In the second half of the Democratic administration, growth returns to its average level; because the economy has had time to adjust to the Democrats holding the White House, the "real" effects of expansionary policies fade away. Thus, growth

---

[9]The results of the 1992 presidential election may, at first glance, indicate a weakening of this relationship. In fact, given the "not so bad" growth performance of the American economy in the second and third quarters of 1992, the incumbent president should have won, not only according to the model presented in chapter 9 but also according to the widely cited forecasting model of Fair (1988). The prediction of a Bush victory stems from the high weight both models place on incumbency and the rate of economic growth in the 9–12 months before the presidential election. Nevertheless, several observations suggest that this relationship between GNP growth and presidential elections has not disappeared. First and foremost, the 1992 election is only one data point in a statistical relationship. Only incompetent forecasters think that they should always be right! Second, it is not clear how Perot's campaign affected the result. Third, for several reasons, probably rather specific to this particular period, voter perception of the state of the economy was grimmer than the actual measures usually emphasized, such as GNP growth. Finally, had the recovery started only a few months earlier than it did, Bush might still have made it.

decreases in the third and fourth years of the term. In addition, unfavorable economic shocks hit the economy, leading to a particularly poor growth performance in the second half of this hypothetical administration. The electorate cannot perfectly distinguish the effects of these unfavorable events from lack of administrative competence in handling the economy. As a result, the Republican challenger wins. The new Republican administration reduces inflation, leading to a downturn in growth. In midterm, the electorate balances the Republican president by reinforcing the Democratic party in Congress. In the second half of this hypothetical Republican administration, the growth downturn is over, and the economy returns to its "natural" level of growth. Lacking unfavorable economic shocks, and with an acceptable perception of the administration's competence, the Republican incumbent president is re-elected. The Democratic party remains relatively strong in Congress.

This story, which flows directly out of our model, reads as a fairly accurate description of the period 1976–1984 with Jimmy Carter followed by Ronald Reagan. We will show in this volume, that, in fact, the American political economy of the last 80 years, as manifested in the time series of gross national product and national election results, is largely consistent with our model.

One issue that this book will *not* address in much detail is the possibility that divided government may lead to inaction and deadlock in policy formation. Researchers have indeed found convincing evidence that fragmented coalition governments in parliamentary democracies have been unable to act promptly and decisively, particularly in the case of budget policies.[10] The point is not that coalition governments create budget deficits but that, when budget deficits emerge because of some economic shock, coalition governments are slow in implementing stabilization policies. Alt and Lowry (1992) and Poterba (1992) present similar evidence for American states: divided state government reduces the speed of adjustment to fiscal shocks. However, the impact of such delays is clearly smaller than the effect of, say, the fragility of Italian coalitions on the size of that country's public debt.

While we find this evidence on parliamentary democracies and American states intriguing and convincing, we do not believe that divided government at the Federal level has had similar gridlock effects on fiscal policies. We agree with Fiorina (1992), who argues that the evidence of legislative inaction caused by divided government at the Federal level is questionable. Indeed, Mayhew (1991) finds that major legislative initiatives have been as frequent under divided government as under unified government.

[10]See, for instance, Roubini and Sachs (1989a,b) and Grilli, Masciandaro, and Tabellini (1991). For a formalization of these ideas, see Alesina and Drazen (1991) and Spolaore (1992).

We do not deny that divided government may, occasionally, slow down the legislative process. Perhaps divided government in the eighties is partially responsible for the accumulation of debt (McCubbins (1991)).[11] In general, however, because of the evidence discussed by Fiorina (1992) and Mayhew (1991), we feel that the costs of legislative inaction in periods of divided government are not likely to be large.

In any case, an extension of our model could incorporate the costs of divided government. Suppose that policymaking became less efficient with divided government. Then the middle-of-the-road voters would have to trade off moderation against inefficiency. That is, the benefits of institutional balancing may come at some costs of legislative slowdown. The larger the costs, the less frequently, everything else constant, one should observe divided government. The higher the inefficiency costs of divided government, the more voters would collectively prefer unified and polarized governments, and vice versa.

Finally, it should also be noted that, in some cases, inaction and moderation might be indistinguishable. Divided government may achieve moderation by preventing changes of a middle-of-the-road status quo toward one of the two extremes. In other words, moderates might prefer the status quo. Cries of "inaction" or "gridlock" might be more expressive of the unfulfilled preferences of extremists than of social costs that would be inherent in divided government.

1.2 THE PLAN OF THE BOOK

This book is divided into two parts. In chapters 2 to 6 we model politics and study the executive–legislative interaction in policy formation. This part of the book considers a generic policy issue and derives our explanation for the occurrences of divided government and the midterm cycle. The second part of the book, chapters 7 to 9, studies, using the model of the polity developed in the first part, the specific problem of economic policy represented by the trade-off between inflation and growth. We build and test a general equilibrium model in which both the economy and voting behavior are endogenous. The last chapter of the book, chapter 10, discusses how the ideas put forward in this volume and developed with explicit reference to the American political system can be useful in studying the institutional framework of other democracies.

We now briefly review the content of each chapter, so that the reader may have a sense of how the book unfolds.

Chapter 2 is concerned with two-party elections, in which the candidates care not only about winning *per se* but also about the public policies

---

[11]McCubbins's results were severely criticized on methodological grounds by Barro (1991).

implemented as a result of the election. First, we consider how the candidates face a trade-off between being truthful to their ideological motivation and choosing platforms that increase their changes of victory (Wittman (1977, 1983), Calvert (1985), Roemer (1992)). We then analyze the problem of credibility of campaign platforms (Alesina (1988a)). If the voters know the true preferences of individual politicians, the latter have a hard time in moving toward the political middle in order to appeal to the "median voter": the voters mistrust the promises of moderation of well-known extremists. In a nutshell, this chapter justifies two basic ideas of the entire construction of this book. The first is that politics is low dimensional; that is, little is lost by assuming that a "liberal–conservative" ideological line summarizes voters' and politicians' preferences. The second is that politicians are relatively immobile at their ideological positions. We conclude this chapter by reviewing the empirical work that has explored these two important issues and, in particular, the work by Poole and Rosenthal (1984a,b, 1985, 1991a). We argue that the empirical evidence from American politics strongly supports those two assumptions.

Chapter 3 analyzes the executive–legislative interaction in policy formation. We begin by noting that policy depends on which party holds the presidency and on the composition of Congress. The voters take advantage of this institutional provision of checks and balances to bring about middle-of-the-road policies. In particular, by splitting their tickets, the voters can create divided government. Whether divided government occurs depends on various characteristics of the process of executive–legislative interaction and the preferences of the parties and the electorate. We will discuss which of these characteristics are more or less conducive to a divided-government outcome. This chapter develops the simplest possible version of our model of executive–legislative interaction; the following several chapters build upon it.

Chapter 4 introduces a simple but realistic and important form of uncertainty. Voters are uncertain of the preferences of other voters. In some elections, the mood of the electorate may take a leftward swing. In others, the pendulum swings to the right. These swings make electoral results *ex ante* uncertain; even though the policies proposed by the two parties are known in advance, electoral results cannot be predicted with complete certainty. This form of uncertainty leads to the midterm voting cycle: voters have to hedge against the swings in on-year elections but can fully moderate the sitting president at midterm. Some voters who hedge by voting for the party of the future president in the on-year choose to support the opposition at midterm. We also discuss how our model of the midterm cycle relates to and, in a sense, encompasses other theories of this phenomenon.

Chapter 5 studies several important additional issues, by extending the model of chapters 2, 3, and 4. We first consider the realistic situations in which the president and the congressional representatives of the same party have different preferences over policy. Our basic results of balancing apply here as well, but the model is enriched. Next, we address the problem of staggered terms of office, namely the fact that in every legislative election, only one-third of the Senate is at contest. Finally, we study how the executive–legislative interaction influences the choice of presidential platforms, which were considered fixed in chapters 3 and 4. We demonstrate that since a presidential candidate knows that, when in office, she will be balanced by Congress, she has an incentive to be less moderate than otherwise, as moderation will be imposed on her by a Congress in which the opposing party is relatively strong. This result shows that the fixity of party platforms is *not* a necessary ingredient in our model. We *can* have the parties choosing their platforms without any change in the message of this volume.

Chapter 6 addresses directly, and empirically, a question that, at this point, has probably arisen in the reader's mind. What about the "incumbency advantage", which, as is well known (Fiorina (1989), Gelman and King (1990)), is an important determinant of congressional races? How does a predilection for reelecting incumbents interact with the moderating role which our model posits for congressional elections? We examine the evidence from a large sample of congressional races.

Chapter 7 focuses on how politics affects the economy. We introduce a model of the macroeconomy that borrows from both the rational expectation literature and the neo-Keynesian "wage rigidity" approach. Building on earlier work by Alesina (1987, 1988b), we spell out the "rational partisan theory" of business cycles. In this chapter, we assume that policy is made solely by the executive, deferring the executive–legislative policy interaction to the succeeding chapter. We also compare this theory with its main alternatives, the "political business cycle" model of Nordhaus (1975) and the "partisan theory" of Hibbs (1977, 1987). We conclude by showing that macroeconomic fluctuations in the United States since World War II are consistent with the implication of the rational partisan theory.

Chapter 8 integrates rational partisan theory of the economy with the model of policy formation via the executive–legislative interaction developed in the first part of the book. We show that the midterm cycle, produced by voter behavior, and the absence of fluctuations in economic growth in the second half of administrations, produced by economic agents' behavior, both result from the resolution of the uncertainty in presidential elections. In addition, we introduce an element of "competence", which differentiates various administrations in their ability to achieve good economic outcomes. We show how administrative competence generates a role for rational retrospective voting in presidential elections. In summary, *this chapter presents our general model of the political economy of the United States.*

11

In chapter 9 we test the model of chapter 8 using the data from the United States for the period 1915–1988. From the theoretical model of chapter 8 we derive four equations which are then jointly estimated: one for the rate of GNP growth, one for presidential elections, and two for congressional elections, in "on" and "off" years. The estimation not only provides a test of our specific model, but also permits reconsideration of several important empirical issues in a general equilibrium framework. The literature in the field has previously dealt with these issues one at a time, in isolation. Chapter 9 also provides a test of the "rationality" of retrospective voting based on recent economic performance.

Chapter 10 discusses how the ideas of this book can shed light on the political economy of other western democracies. The application of our ideas to countries, such as France, where the president is directly elected is relatively straightforward. Nevertheless, even in other parliamentary democracies, different forms of institutional moderation may appear. Coalition governments, which are very common in parliamentary democracies, may be a form of moderation. Furthermore, local governments may be used as a moderating device against national governments. If a federalist Europe ever materializes, national governments and the Federal European Government may provide an additional balancing device for the European electorate.

1.3 HOW DOES THIS BOOK COMPARE WITH OTHERS?

The field of "politics ánd the macroeconomy" has grown rapidly in the last decade, with several contributions by political scientists and economists. What is new in this book? After having outlined the substance of our contribution in the previous section, we now complete our answer to this question by briefly comparing this book to the most nearly related volumes and to our own previous work.

A widely cited and influential book by Tufte (1978) has a much more specific purpose than ours. Tufte wanted to present evidence in favor of the "opportunistic political business cycle" formalized by Nordhaus (1975), whereas we emphasize partisan concerns. Tufte focuses on many more economic variables than we do, but he does not provide an original theoretical model.

Hibbs (1987) adopts the same view as we do on party motivations in macroeconomic policy. His book is much richer than ours in details concerning party platforms, discussion of specific episodes, and the actual policy-making process. On the other hand, he has no formal model of voting behavior, nor does he consider the presidential–congressional interaction in any detail. Furthermore, our model of the economy, based on rational expectations, is different from his (see chapter 7) and leads to different predictions.

Three recent books by economists also deal with related topics. Persson and Tabellini (1990) survey and extend recent developments in the positive theory of economic policy. In doing so, they cover the literature that has introduced voting into these models. Their book is much wider than ours in coverage. On the other hand, it is exclusively theoretical, and their model of voting is, for the most part, an application of the median voter theorem to various economic problems. There are no political institutions in their models.

Cukierman (1992) and Havrilesky (1993) have recently published two books on the politics of monetary policy. Their contributions are much more concerned with monetary institutions, on the relationship between the Federal Reserve and the president and Congress, on the decision-making process leading to monetary policy decisions, on political pressures over the Federal Reserve, and so on. Our book has no direct role for the Central Bank: we assume that macroeconomic policy is under the control of the president and Congress. This simplifying assumption is supported by the viewpoint of scholars (Weingast (1984), Moe (1985)) who argue that regulatory agencies are responsive to elected officials.[12]

Alt and Chrystal (1983) cover not only political business cycle models, but many other topics such as the determinants of the size of government and budget deficits. The executive–legislative interaction in policy formulation is not at the center of their attention, nor do they present original evidence on voting in the United States.

Divided government has received much attention in political science in recent years, particularly by Fiorina (1988, 1990, 1991, 1992) and Jacobson (1990a). Fiorina's (1992) book is related in spirit to the first part of our volume. But he does not consider the connection between divided government and the business cycle. In addition, his (1988) view of both policy formation and voter behavior differs sharply from ours; the distinctions are covered in detail in chapter 3. Jacobson (1990a) provides a detailed empirical examination of the electoral processes which sometimes lead to divided government. His work, which emphasizes incumbency, relates most directly to our chapter 6. Jacobson does not have either a model of the economy or a formal "spatial" model of elections.

Finally, Cox and Kernell (1991) have edited a series of papers on divided government. Those papers, with the exception of one by Fiorina, do not emphasize balancing as an explanation of divided government. Instead, the authors consider a variety of alternative explanations such as voters'

---

[12]The degree of Central Bank independence from elected officials may, however, be a powerful explanatory variable in cross-country differences. Even though completely independent Central Banks do not exist, the degree of autonomy varies considerably across countries. On this point see Grilli, Masciandaro, and Tabellini (1991) and Alesina and Summers (1993).

preferring a Democratic Congress in order to obtain constituency services and a Republican president in order to reduce total expenditures.

With reference to our own previous work, the reader will find a substantial amount of new material in this volume, which is definitely not a collection of published papers. None of the material in chapters 5 and 6 has previously appeared in print. Although chapters 3 and 4 relate to work in Alesina and Rosenthal (1989), and especially, Alesina and Rosenthal (1992), the voter equilibrium is better motivated by use of the concept of conditionally sincere voting. In addition, sections 3.10 and 4.6 contain entirely new material. Chapter 7 presents a model, with updated empirical results, previously developed in Alesina (1987) and Alesina (1988b). Chapters 8 and 9 are largely based on Alesina, Londregan, and Rosenthal (1993) with some new material. Some work that each of us has done apart from our joint research effort enters the discussion in chapters 2 and 10.[13] In both chapters, this work and the work of other authors is integrated with the basic themes of this volume. In integrating approaches to politics and economics in this volume, we hope to have provided perspectives that would not be evident in reading individual papers. This objective and the goal of making the work accessible to a wider audience than that of professional journals have in fact led us to write virtually the entire book from scratch.

1.4 TIPS FOR THE READER

This book is organized in a way that makes it "user friendly" for readers with different interests and backgrounds.

First, even though the material is, in part, fairly technical, we have made an effort to keep technical derivations and proofs at a minimum. Generally, we first present an argument intuitively with the help of pictures and simple algebra. Sometimes we then derive the same results more formally, either in sections that can be omitted by readers who want to avoid the formal presentation or in appendices to each chapter. The technical sections (or subsections) that can be skipped are indicated. In any case, a full grasp of the technical aspects of the book is never crucial for an understanding if its basic message.

Chapters 2, 3, and 4 build on each other and cannot be skipped. On the

[13]Some parts of our work do not appear in this volume. The appendices to Alesina, Londregan, and Rosenthal (1993) contain the technical development of conditions where our model extends to two-dimensional environments and of the estimation methods for the empirical work in chapter 9. Alesina and Rosenthal (1989) contains empirical work for Senate elections that accords with the analysis of the House of Representatives in this volume. It also reports results for the impact of the economy on congressional voting when income rather than gross national product is used as the measure of economic performance. Alesina, Fiorina, and Rosenthal (1991) analyze balancing of each state's delegation in the United States Senate.

other hand, chapters 5 and 6 can be skipped by either the quick readers interested only in the general message of the book or the readers interested mainly in the more economic aspects of our analysis.

On the contrary , the readers interested mainly in voting issues will find chapters 5 and 6 important. The same readers may want to skip, instead, chapters 7 and 8 and focus on the empirical results on voting behavior presented in chapter 9. The readers mainly interested in the economic aspects of our politico-economic model will find chapters 7, 8, and 9 the most relevant.

Finally, chapter 10, which is more speculative than the previous nine, can be ignored by the strict "Americanists". We believe, however, that much can be learned from comparisons with other countries in this as in many other fields.

Despite these tips for selective reading, we do believe that the strength of this volume lies in the *joint* determination of economic and political events. A selective reading of the book may miss this fundamental theme.

2

Models of policy divergence

2.1 INTRODUCTION

According to a widely held view about American politics, the two parties are indistinguishable and both located in the middle of the political spectrum. We emphatically disagree.

The notion of convergence of party platforms emerges from the initial rational choice models of two-party electoral competition in the contributions of Hotelling (1929), Black (1958), and Downs (1957). These seminal works assumed that although voters care about public policy, candidates care only about winning. In this situation, the candidates propose identical platforms: one should observe complete convergence of policies toward the middle. Which policy is actually chosen by a candidate depends on the specification of the electoral process: the number of issues involved, the dissemination of information within the electorate, the nature of voters' preferences, and the ability of voters to make decisions consistent with their preferences.

The most famous convergence result is the "median voter theorem" (Black (1958)). It implies that, under a certain specification, the candidates converge to the policy most preferred by the median voter.[1] For other specifications, Hinich (1977), Coughlin and Nitzan (1981), Ledyard (1984), and Tovey (1991) analyze cases of convergence *not* at the median.[2] For our purposes, the important point is not so much "where" the candidates converge (at which particular point of the political "middle") but the fact that they *fully converge*.

---

[1] A number of technical assumptions are needed for this theorem to hold; furthermore, the multiplicity of relevant policy dimensions creates substantial technical problems. For a discussion of the median voter theorem, see Ordeshook (1986) and the references cited therein.

[2] The literature cited shows convergence or near convergence in multi-issue contexts.

16

A different view of party competition holds that political parties, as well as the voters, care about *policy outcomes*, in addition to winning *per se* (Wittman (1977, 1983), Calvert (1985), and Roemer (1992)). According to this view, political parties represent the interests and values of different constituencies. In a Downsian model (where parties care only about winning), the parties choose policy in order to win elections, whereas in a partisan model the parties want to be elected in order to choose policies. Each party has an incentive to adopt a platform that is truthful to its policy preferences. However, since these preferences can't be translated into policy unless the party wins, each party also has an incentive to move toward the middle in order to increase its chances of winning. These conflicting incentives (policy goals and electoral needs) generate the basic insight of the partisan model: there should be only "partial convergence"; the two parties propose platforms that are closer to each other than their most preferred policies, but that are, nevertheless, distinct.

Calvert (1985) interprets the partial convergence result as an endorsement of the basic message of the convergence literature, since even when parties care about policies, they should propose similar platforms; convergence is "almost" complete, even with partisan politics. The intuition of the "almost complete" result is provided by considering the case where the parties have complete information about voter preferences including, most importantly, knowledge of the median voter's bliss point. In this case, a party knows victory is guaranteed if it is even slightly closer than its opponent to the median voter (who is known). The ability to ensure victory against any non-median position generates complete convergence even for parties with policy preferences (see Calvert (1985) and Roemer (1992)). The need to win provides a competitive pressure toward convergence even when information is incomplete. With a "small" amount of uncertainty, convergence is nearly complete, even with policy-motivated parties. Divergence is substantial only when parties have little control over their electoral destinies; that is, when there is a large amount of incomplete information.

In summary: non-convergence of platforms results with policy preferences *and* uncertainty about the distribution of voter preferences; these two assumptions are the most realistic scenario, compared to alternatives. Table 2.1 indicates the convergence or divergence outcome as a function of different assumptions about party behavior and information.

The tendency toward policy divergence and polarization in a partisan model is much stronger than it appears in Calvert's work if, as seems most likely, candidates are unable to make credible commitments to carry out their campaign promises (Alesina (1988a)). Before an election, the candidates (or parties) would like to appear moderate in the eyes of the voters. But the winner, once in office, has an incentive to renege on campaign promises and implement her most preferred policy. Not being fooled by campaign

17

Table 2.1. *Equilibrium position of parties*

Party Objectives

		Electoralist	Policy-Oriented
Party Information About Voter Preferences	Complete	*Convergence to Median Voter's Ideal Point*[1]	*Convergence to Median Voter's Ideal Point*[2]
	Incomplete	*Convergence*[3]	*Possible Divergence*[3]

Notes:

1. See Black (1958).
2. See Calvert (1985), Roemer (1992).
3. See Wittman (1983), Calvert (1985), Roemer (1992).

promises of moderation, voters will perceive this incentive and vote knowing that whichever party wins, it will implement its truly most preferred policy. Thus there is *no* convergence: the two parties follow their most preferred policies when in office. The lack of credibility of campaign promises greatly reinforces the tendency to diverge in a two-party election.

Credibility and reputation for not reneging on promises can, however, be built with time. If one considers the *repeated* interaction between the same two parties and the voters, then an incentive to maintain promises of moderation may reappear, generating partial convergence. For this incentive to be effective, voters must believe that parties and candidates are relatively "patient" – that they care substantially about the long term as well as current outcomes. Although a long-term perspective is diminished not only by the finite political lives of politicians but also by the 22nd Amendment, which limits presidents to two terms, it is possible (see section 2.5) that party organizations maintain incentives that induce individual politicians to take a long-term perspective. More generally, when we examine dynamic settings we find that the credibility of campaign promises of moderation is a complex issue with no simple theoretical answer.

The absence of a conclusive theoretical answer to the question of credibility makes it important to look at the choice between an "electoralist" model with full convergence and a "partisan" model without convergence

18

as an empirical question. Which of the two models is more consistent with the evidence of the American system? The empirical evidence reviewed in section 2.6 suggests that American politics *is* polarized. Therefore, models that imply full (or nearly full) convergence of party policies are not an appropriate tool for analyzing American politics.

We proceed as follows. Section 2.2 describes the basic partisan model with partial convergence. Section 2.3 covers the same model more formally, and can be skipped by the reader less interested in formal modelling. Section 2.4 discusses the problem of credibility of party platforms and shows how such problems greatly reinforce polarization. Section 2.5 addresses the consequences of repeated elections on the degree of policy convergence. Section 2.6 summarizes the empirical evidence on the polarization of American politics. Finally, section 2.7 discusses the origin of party preferences and also reviews other models of policy divergence, in which even though the two parties care only about winning, they choose separate platforms.

2.2 A MODEL OF "PARTIAL CONVERGENCE"[3]

Let us consider electoral competition between two parties, labelled, with obvious reference, D and R. In the formal analysis, no distinction is made between a "candidate" and a "party": a party and its candidates have identical preferences. Thus, we do not consider internal heterogeneity within the party, at least for the moment. Discussion of this issue is postponed to chapter 5. The parties have preferences defined on policy outcomes; thus we can think of the parties as representatives of two different constituencies with different preferences. We illustrate the policy implications of partisan competition under the assumption that the election is on a single issue.[4] In section 2.6 we argue that this assumption does not do too much injustice to the American political system.

How the two parties evaluate policy is illustrated by figure 2.1. Each party likes one policy best; this ideal policy is represented by the highest point on its curve. The party is worse off as actual policy gets farther from its

---

[3]This section is based on work by Wittman (1977, 1983) and Calvert (1985). For a survey of partisan models, see Wittman (1990). There are many alternative models that lead to polarized candidate positions. In particular, see Bernhardt and Ingberman (1985), who find that even purely office-motivated candidates diverge when incumbents have reputational advantages, and Londregan and Romer (1993), who find that candidates diverge in policy positions when voters are incompletely informed about candidates' capabilities in providing constituency services.

[4]Several of the results of this chapter generalize to the multi-issue case (Calvert (1985)), but similar generalizations are far from immidiate for what follows in chapters 3, 4, and 5. These multi-dimensional issues are not formally analyzed in this book, except in chapter 8.

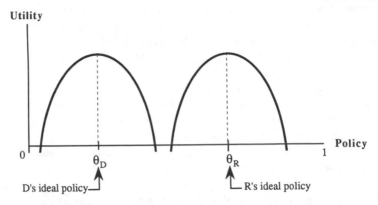

Figure 2.1. Quadratic utility functions for the two parties

ideal point. Formally, the preferences of party D depend on x, the policy outcome and θ_D, the party's ideal policy. This dependence is represented by the following utility function:

$$u_D = u(x, \theta_D) \tag{2.1}$$

This function is strictly concave. Consequently, it is single-peaked; that is, it exhibits a single maximum at $x = \theta_D$. An example of such a function is the quadratic one shown in figure 2.1:

$$u_D = - (x - \theta_D)^2 \tag{2.2}$$

Analogously, party R has preferences represented by the same concave utility function, but with a different bliss point:

$$u_R = u(x, \theta_R) \tag{2.3}$$

This function has a maximum at $x = \theta_R$.

We assume that party D is to the left of party R, namely:

$$\theta_D < \theta_R \tag{2.4}$$

Policy preferences alone do not suffice to determine a party's platform. A party prefers to be in office rather than out. When in office, and *regardless* of the policy chosen, a party receives a "reward", which we indicate with $\hat{u}$. We can think of $\hat{u}$ as the prestige and personal satisfaction associated with officeholding.[5] For simplicity, we assume that this reward of officeholding is the same for both parties, but the nature of the results of this chapter does not hinge on this simplification. Thus, the total utility for party R

[5] A more cynical view would link officeholding with pecuniary gains.

when in office is $\hat{u}$ plus the utility, given in (2.3), from the public policy x. An analogous argument applies to party D.

The voters also care about policy. The generic voter, indicated by i, has a utility function identical to that of the two parties, except for the bliss point; θ_i is the bliss point of the generic voter i:

$$u_i = u(x, \theta_i) \tag{2.5}$$

Thus the only possible difference in the preferences of the parties given in (2.1) and (2.3) and those of the voters given in (2.5) is in the location of the respective bliss points. Each voter evaluates the alternative policies proposed by the two parties according to the utility function given in (2.5) and votes for the party offering the policy that produces a higher utility. For instance, if voter i has to choose between a policy of $\frac{1}{3}$ and $\frac{3}{5}$, he will vote for the party delivering the policy $\frac{1}{3}$ if $u(\frac{1}{3}, \theta_i) > u(\frac{3}{5}, \theta_i)$, namely if the utility of $\frac{1}{3}$ is higher than the utility of $\frac{3}{5}$.[6]

It is often helpful to assume that the utility function of the voters is symmetric, as in the case of the quadratic function shown in figure 2.1 and in equation (2.2). Symmetric single-peaked utility functions, like the one in figure 2.2a, exhibit a useful property: each voter always prefers the policy closest to his own bliss point. Thus, all one needs to know to determine voting behavior is the distance between the voter's bliss point and the policy of party R and the corresponding distance for party D. This is not the case for non-symmetric utility functions. In figure 2.2b, preferences are asymmetric in the sense that the voter is "more tolerant" of policies to the right of his ideal than of policies to the left. All of the results of this chapter and most of the results of the entire book can be obtained without imposing symmetry of the utility functions, but it will often be easier to develop the intuition using the symmetric case.

Finally, note that the concavity of the utility functions of both voters and parties implies risk aversion. Both voters *and* parties prefer a sure policy outcome of, say, $x = \frac{1}{2}$, to a lottery with an expected value of $\frac{1}{2}$.

With no loss of generality and as customary in the formal literature, we normalize the range of possible policy choices to an interval that runs from zero to one. That is, $0 \leqslant x \leqslant 1$. The bliss points of the voters (θ_i) are distributed on this interval, and the bliss points of the two parties are such that the following inequalities hold:

$$0 < \theta_D < \theta_R < 1 \tag{2.6}$$

The bliss points of the voters are also contained in this interval. Our model applies to electorates composed of a very large number of voters. Consequently,

---

[6]An indifferent voter may flip a coin or follow some other arbitrary voting rule. The behavior of indifferent voters is never important for any of the results of this book.

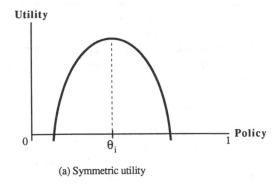

(a) Symmetric utility

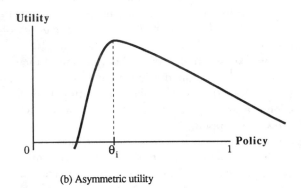

(b) Asymmetric utility

Figure 2.2.   Voter utility functions

it is convenient (but not essential) to assume that the electorate is a continuum with an infinity of voters. That is, there is a distribution of bliss points. Figure 2.3 illustrates three possible distributions of voter bliss points. The first one is uniform; the second one is unimodal, with the median at $\frac{1}{2}$. The third one is bimodal, with the two peaks coinciding with the party bliss points, and with the median still at $\frac{1}{2}$. Most of the results of this book can be derived with no restrictions on the distribution of voter bliss points, even though, for illustrative purposes, it will be easiest to assume the uniform case, particularly in chapters 4 and following.

The parties D and R simultaneously choose policy platforms, labelled respectively x^D and x^R. In this section we study the case in which the two parties are irrevocably committed to implementing these policies, if elected. Thus, there is no distinction between policy platforms and actual policies. The importance of this assumption will become apparent in section 2.4.

Throughout this chapter and the rest of the book we will always assume that party preferences are known by the voters, who will thus know which policies will be chosen by the two parties.

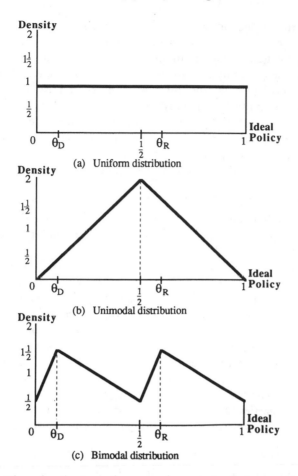

Figure 2.3.   Three distributions of voter preferences. In all three cases, the median voter is at 1/2. In the uniform case, the ideal policy of a randomly chosen voter is equally likely to be at any position between 0 and 1. Many voters have ideal policies more extreme than those of the parties, whose ideal policies are located at θ_D and θ_R. In the unimodal case, moderate voters predominate. In the bimodal case illustrated, voters are concentrated near the ideal policies of the parties.

The positions chosen by the parties depend critically on the information available about voters' preferences – that is, about the distribution of the voters' bliss points, θ_i. Results differ substantially depending on whether the information about voters' preferences is *complete* or *incomplete*. Complete information means that the parties know for sure the distribution of voter bliss points. With complete information, the choices of party platforms completely determine the election results. Either one of the two parties wins with certainty or there is a tie; in fact, given the two party platforms, and given the knowledge of the distribution of voter preferences, one can compute which one of the two platforms is preferred by a majority of voters.

Clearly, the assumption of complete information is unrealistic. A more compelling case is that of incomplete information where the distribution of voter preferences (i.e., the distribution of the voter bliss points θ_i) is not known with certainty by anybody. In this more realistic case, for given party platforms, both the parties and the voters are uncertain about the results of the election.[7] For the purposes of this chapter, it is sufficient to posit the existence of a function that captures this uncertainty as the probability of one of the outcomes. We define the following function:

$$P = P(x^D, x^R) \tag{2.7}$$

as the probability that party R wins the election. This probability depends, of course, on the policy platforms, x^D and x^R. The probability of a D victory is, therefore, $[1 - P(x^D, x^R)]$.

The function $P(\cdot)$ embodies the idea that if one party moves its position toward that of the other party, it increases its chances of winning by capturing a larger fraction of "middle-of-the-road voters" (i.e., voters with preferences in between the two platforms). For instance, consider two platforms, x^D and x^R with $x^D < x^R$. Suppose that party D now proposes a more right-wing platform; that is, it proposes $(x^D + \varepsilon)$, with ε positive. Then the probability of a D victory increases, and thus $P(\cdot)$ falls. Analogous considerations apply to changes in x^R. Finally, if $x^D = x^R$, $P(\cdot) = \frac{1}{2}$. That is, there is no "bias" in favor of one of the two parties.[8] The function $P(\cdot)$ and the preferences of parties D and R (i.e., θ_D and θ_R), as emphasized above, are known to everybody; in the language of game theorists, they are "common knowledge".

Figure 2.4 illustrates the function $P(x^D, x^R)$ for symmetric preferences when the median voter is equally likely to be anywhere in the interval [0.4, 0.6]. The position of party R is held constant and party D's position is varied. In the top panel, party R is at the expected median. As D moves toward the expected median from the left, D's chances of winning improve. When D matches R, the probability is $\frac{1}{2}$. In the bottom panel, R is very much to the right of the expected median. As D moves toward the expected median from the left, D's probability of winning increases. In fact, as D

---

[7]There can be a range of party platforms for which the electoral result becomes certain; for instance, if one of the two parties adopts an extreme position and the other maintains a middle-of-the-road policy. In what follows it is assumed that electoral results remain uncertain for the relevant range of policies, i.e., for the range of policies that includes all the possible electoral equilibria.

[8]This assumption can be easily generalized, but we do not pursue this issue here. For a derivation of this type of probability function from individual preferences, see Alesina and Cukierman (1990) for some special and intuitive cases and Roemer (1992) for a more general treatment.

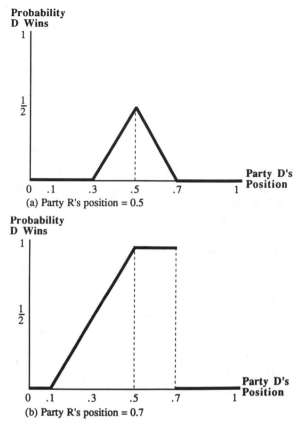

Figure 2.4. The probability D wins. In this example, the median voter is equally likely to have an ideal policy at any point between 0.4 and 0.6. When, in panel (a), R locates at the center, D's changes of winning are never above 1/2, but the chances do improve as D gets closer to R. When, in panel (b), R takes an extreme position, D can win for sure by taking a position between the center and R.

passes 0.5, this probability goes to 1.0 since D is closer than R to the *rightmost* (0.6) possible location for the median voter. The probability stays at 1.0 as long as D is to the left of R. But as soon as D "jumps over" R, D's probability of winning goes to zero.

We are now ready to examine the policy platforms chosen by the two parties in the *Nash equilibrium* of this game. Each party faces a trade-off between the cost of moving to a policy away from its most preferred policy (i.e., θ^D or θ^R) and the benefit of increasing the probability of victory as a result of the same move. Note that the benefits of an increase in the probability of winning are twofold. First, it makes it less likely that a less

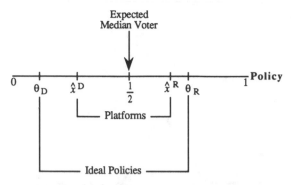

Figure 2.5. Equilibrium platforms with policy oriented parties. While the parties do not take identical positions, they do move away from their ideal policies toward the center of the distribution of voters.

preferred policy will be implemented by the opponent. Second, it increases the likelihood of achieving office and receiving the benefit $\hat{u}$.

In equilibrium both parties equalize the marginal cost of a further move in their platform to the marginal benefits of the same move, taking the opponent's platform as given. One can show (Calvert (1985)) that this equilibrium is, in fact, unique. An important feature of this equilibrium is partial convergence: the platforms of the two parties are closer to each other than their ideal policies, but need not be identical. Denoting the equilibrium platforms by $\hat{x}^D$ and $\hat{x}^R$, the following inequalities, illustrated in figure 2.5, hold, assuming that $\hat{u}$ is not too large;

$$\theta_D < \hat{x}^D < \hat{x}^R < \theta_R \tag{2.8}$$

It is instructive to review the basic intuition of this result. Let us first examine why full convergence cannot be an equilibrium. Consider the following case: $\theta_D < \hat{x}^D = \hat{x}^R < \theta_R$. Also assume for a moment that the parties are purely partisan – they do not attribute any "reward" to winning *per se* (i.e. $\hat{u} = 0$). Suppose that party D moves just a bit to the left, say to $(\hat{x}^D - \varepsilon)$, with ε very small. In this situation, if party D loses the election, the policy $\hat{x}^R = \hat{x}^D$ is implemented by party R. If instead party D wins, it implements $(\hat{x}^D - \varepsilon)$, which is a *better* policy for party D. Thus party D has to be *better off* with this move: either the previous policy is implemented, *or* a better one is chosen. The analogous argument applies for a rightward move by party R.

If the two parties also value winning *per se*, this argument is slightly complicated by the additional consideration that D moving left to $(\hat{x}^D - \varepsilon)$ reduces the party's probability of winning. Since party D cares about the "reward" of victory, this loss of probability induces a discrete "electoralist" loss in party D's utility, unrelated to the choice of policy. If this electoralist component is sufficiently large (i.e., $\hat{u}$ is very high) then in equilibrium we may even have full convergence, although, in general, convergence is not complete.[9]

The case of no convergence, $x^R = \theta_R$, $x^D = \theta_D$, is also not an equilibrium of this game. In fact, consider a small move to the right for party D, from θ_D to $x^D = \theta_D + \varepsilon$, with ε positive but small. The loss in utility from this move is small (in technical terms, "second order"), since the policy $\theta_D + \varepsilon$ is still very close to party D's bliss point and its utility function is concave (see figure 2.1). But there is a gain in the probability of victory (which in technical terms is "first order") that more than compensates for the first effect. The increase in party D's probability of winning has two beneficial effects described above: first it reduces the likelihood that the policy θ_R will result (the "partisan" motivation); second, it increases the likelihood of obtaining the "reward" of victory. The first, "partisan", effect is sufficient alone to rule out this case as a possible equilibrium. Using similar arguments it is easy to show that policies such as $x^D > x^R$, $x^D < \theta_D$, or $x^R > \theta_R$ cannot be equilibria.

We have established that the two platforms have to lie between θ_D and θ_R; additional observations help to characterize their location more precisely.

(*i*) The higher the "reward" $\hat{u}$ placed on holding office, the smaller will be the distance between the two policies ($\hat{x}^D$ and $\hat{x}^R$). That is, more "electoralist" parties converge more. In the extreme case in which the two parties care *only* about winning, convergence is always complete: $x^D = x^R$.[10]

(*ii*) If there is no uncertainty about voters' preferences, convergence is complete, $x^D = x^R$. In fact, suppose $x^D < x^R$. Since there is no uncertainty, it is known who wins with such policies. If, say, D is the loser, this party will want to "move in" closer to x^R until it becomes the winner. At this point party R will want to "move in", and so on. In this model, a platform that implies a sure defeat cannot be optimal, even for a purely partisan party! With certainty about voters' preferences we do *not* have a well-defined trade-off between the probability of winning and ideology.[11]

In summary, substantial lack of convergence emerges only if parties are sufficiently "partisan" and there is enough uncertainty about voters' prefer-

---

[9]Complete convergence is more likely to occur when the function $P(x^D, x^R)$ is discontinuous along the diagonal (i.e., for $x^D = x^R$ in figure 2.4b). See Alesina and Spear (1988) for more discussion of this technical point.

[10]The proof of this result is immediate. If $\delta = 0$ in equations (2.9) and (2.10), then the problem faced by the two parties is simply one of maximizing their probability of winning. Suppose $x^D < x^R$; then if x^D moves to the right, it increases its chances of winning. Thus this party will keep moving until $x^D = x^R$.

[11]Roemer (1992) has formally established the continuity of this result. He shows that the equilibrium policies are closer to each other the smaller the amount of uncertainty on voter preferences.

ences. Good polling techniques and a fair amount of "lust for office" keep parties' platforms very close together. For these reasons Calvert (1985) concludes that the full convergence result is robust.

2.3 A FORMAL ANALYSIS OF PARTIAL CONVERGENCE

In this section, which can be skipped by the reader not interested in formalization, we characterize analytically the equilibrium illustrated in the preceding section.

We look for a (Nash) equilibrium to the simultaneous choice by party D of its policy platform x^D and by party R of x^R. Each party maximizes its utility given its preferences, the function $P(x^D, x^R)$, and the policy position of the other party. The equilibrium policy $\hat{x}^D$ maximizes D's utility given $\hat{x}^R$ and vice versa.

The expected utility maximization problem solved by party R is:

$$\text{Max}_{x^R} \delta[P(x^D, x^R)u(x^R, \theta_R) + (1 - P(x^D, x^R))u(x^D, \theta_R)] + (1 - \delta)P(x^D, x^R)\hat{u}$$

$$(2.9)$$

The term in the square brackets represents the expected policy utility for party R. In fact, $u(x^R, \theta_R)$ is the utility for party R if it wins and thus chooses policy, whereas $u(x^D, \theta_R)$ is the utility for party R if party D chooses policy. The expected utility is just the weighted average of these two utilities, the weights being, respectively, the probability of an R victory and the probability of a D victory. The second term represents the benefit of an electoral victory. The parameter δ captures the weight attributed by the party to its policy preferences relative to its reward for winning, $\hat{u}$. If $\delta = 0$, the party is completely electoralist; it cares only about winning. If $\delta = 1$, the party is only partisan; it cares only about policy. If $0 < \delta < 1$, the party cares about both.

Equation (2.9) can be rewritten as follows:

$$\text{Max}_{x^R} \delta\{P(x^D, x^R)[u(x^R, \theta_R) - u(x^D, \theta_R)]\} + (1 - \delta)P(x^D, x^R)\hat{u} + \delta u(x^D, \theta_R)$$

$$(2.10)$$

Equation (2.10) highlights the two reasons why an increase in $P(\cdot)$ makes party R better off: (i) the first term (in curly brackets) reflects the fact that if $P(\cdot)$ goes up, party R is more likely to be the one that chooses policy; this makes this party better off, given that, in equilibrium, $u(x^R, \theta_R) > u(x^D, \theta_R)$; (ii) the second term reflects the benefits of the pure electoralist objective. (Note that the last term, which is unaffected by the choice of x^R, does not influence the solution.)

The analogous problem for party D is as follows:

$$\text{Max } \delta\{P(x^D, x^R)u(x^R, \theta_D) + (1 - P(x^D, \theta^R))u((x^D, x_D)\}$$
$$x^D$$
$$+ (1 - \delta)(1 - P(x^D, x^R))\hat{u} \qquad (2.11)$$

With the help of a few innocuous mathematical assumptions (see Calvert (1985)) one can show that problems (2.9) and (2.11) have a unique solution pair $(\hat{x}^D, \hat{x}^R)$ such that (for $\hat{u}$ below a certain cutoff point):

$$\theta_D < \hat{x}^D < \hat{x}^R < \theta_R \qquad (2.12)$$

For the pair (illustrated in figure 2.5) that solves the equations, each party is giving an optimal response to the other. In other words, we have found the unique Nash equilibrium with *partial convergence*: party platforms are closer to each other than the parties' ideal policies. Nevertheless, party platforms are not identical.

2.4 NO CONVERGENCE[12]

A crucial assumption underlying the model described in the previous two sections is that the parties can make an irrevocable commitment before the election to implement, if elected, their announced platforms. The lack of credibility of electoral promises, and, more generally, the difficulty of tying policymakers' hands to follow announced policy plans, is evident in mass media reports ("Read my lips!"). The academic literature, particularly in the context of macroeconomic policy, has recently devoted a substantial amount of attention to problems of "credibility" of policy announcements.[13]

If policy commitments cannot be made, then the results of the previous two sections change substantially. Suppose that party D has won the election. When in office, party D, unconstrained by its electoral platform, chooses policy to maximize its utility function. That is, this party solves the following problem:

$$\text{Max } u(x^D, \theta_D) \qquad (2.13)$$
$$x^D$$

Clearly, the solution is $x^D = \theta_D$. The same argument applied to party R implies that $x^R = \theta_R$. This result holds even if the parties care very much about winning *per se*, as long as they maintain even a small "partisan" motivation. In fact, after the election, the "electoralist" motivation is

---

[12]This section is largely based on Alesina (1988a).
[13]See Kydland and Prescott (1977), Barro and Gordon (1983), and the recent survey by Persson and Tabellini (1990).

irrelevant: once in office, the winner may as well go for his most preferred policy, even though his main motivation might have been, *ex ante*, to win!

Let us now consider the voters' problem. Aware of what will happen after the election, the voters will not believe any policy platforms other than the parties' ideal policies, θ_D and θ_R. In fact, as argued above, the two parties have no incentive, when in office, to implement any policy other than θ_D and θ_R. Thus the voters cast their ballots knowing that they are choosing between the policies θ_D and θ_R. As a result, party R wins with probability $P(\theta_D, \theta_R)$ and party D with probability $[1 - P(\theta_D, \theta_R)]$.

It is worth repeating that this result of complete divergence holds regardless of how much the parties care about their partisan motivation relative to the "reward" of winning, as long as they have even a minimal amount of ideological preference.[14]

This very simple, almost trivial, result has, however, vast substantive and methodological implications, since it questions the robustness of the convergence result in two-party elections: *even a very small amount of ideological commitment breaks down convergence completely*. This is in sharp contrast with Calvert's comments on the "robustness" of the convergence results.

From a substantive standpoint, this result of policy divergence implies that candidates (and parties) who have relatively well-known policy preferences (for example, because of a track record established by roll call voting) have very little ideological mobility. A candidate who is well known for being, say, left-leaning, will have no chance of credibly moving her platform toward the right to capture middle-of-the-road voters. It follows that campaign activities might have relatively little influence on voters' views about the candidates' preferences.

The methodological implication of this result is that a proper analysis of both spatial mobility in a partisan model and the credibility of campaign promises requires an explicit consideration of repeated elections. A good reputation for maintaining campaign promises can arise only in the context of repeated political competition.

2.5 PARTISAN POLITICS IN REPEATED ELECTIONS

The formal theory of social choice typically is "static": each election is studied in isolation, with no connection with past or future contests (see Ordeshook (1986) and the references cited therein). Recently, however, several researchers have moved toward modelling repeated elections.[15]

---

[14]This result holds for *any* positive value of δ. Note that, strictly speaking, the case of purely electoralist parties is indeterminate. Such parties may want to converge completely in platforms, but the model cannot explain how the elected party chooses policy. In fact, it is not committed to its platform and has no preferences over policy.

[15]An incomplete list includes Ferejohn (1986), Alesina (1988a), Alesina and Spear (1988), Alesina and Cukierman (1990), Banks and Sundaram (1993).

Models of policy divergence

This section briefly reviews some results obtained in repeated-election models with parties with policy preferences, as in the previous section. The main point is that when the parties face each other (and the voters!) in more than one election, promises of moderation may become credible. In fact, reneging on a promise today would lead to costs in lost reputation in future elections. Irrelevant in the one-shot case, these costs are important in repeated elections. In being truthful to campaign promises, the two parties gain in credibility and, consequently, regain some "spatial mobility". They can credibly announce and follow more moderate policies than θ_D and θ_R.

The simplest way of examining this issue is to consider an infinite sequence of repetitions of the same electoral game described in the previous section (Alesina (1988a)). As before, there is uncertainty about voters' preferences, captured by the function $P(\cdot)$; the parties' preferences are known by the electorate. The fully divergent outcome described in section 2.4 remains an equilibrium in the repeated electoral game. In fact, that outcome is the unique Nash equilibrium of the one-shot game, and this equilibrium can simply be repeated in every election. But the use of "tit for tat" platform strategies supports other equilibria, with partial or even full convergence. These strategies work as follows. A party promises moderation; for instance, party D promises a policy to the right of θ_D. The voters believe the promise. If, when in office, party D implements the policy promised, the voters (and the other party) keep believing party D's promises in the future. If party D does not implement its promise, the voters (and the other party) will forever (or for a certain number of elections) expect θ_D from party D, that is, its ideological position. Analogous arguments apply to party R's promising to follow a policy to the left of θ_R.[16]

When in office, a party has to balance a "temptation" and an "enforcement". A party is "tempted" to follow its most preferred policy (θ_D or θ_R) rather than the promised, moderate policy. Clearly, following its most preferred policy, the party in office is better off in the current period. The "enforcement" is that if the party breaks the promise, nobody will believe its future promises; it will be expected to implement its most preferred (and extreme) position in the future. This expectation will imply a loss of moderate votes for that party. If the "enforcement" is greater than the "temptation", the parties can adopt identical, or, at least, relatively centrist policies; that is, they can converge.

The question then is the following: would the two parties *prefer* to adopt fully convergent policies when they are credible, namely, when the "enforcement" is greater than the "temptation" as defined above? The following numerical example provides an affirmative answer. Suppose that $\theta_D = \frac{1}{4}$,

[16]See, for instance, Fudenberg and Tirole (1991), chapter 4, for a more detailed theoretical discussion of this type of strategy.

$\theta_R = \frac{3}{4}$, and $P(\frac{1}{4}, \frac{3}{4}) = \frac{1}{2}$. That is, if the two parties implement their most preferred policies they are equally likely to win. Suppose, instead, that a fully convergent equilibrium is achieved. For instance, say $x^D = x^R = \frac{1}{2}$; and $P(\frac{1}{2}, \frac{1}{2}) = \frac{1}{2}$. In both cases, with complete convergence or no convergence, each party is in office, in the long run, half of the time. But in the first case, policy fluctuates between $\frac{1}{4}$ and $\frac{3}{4}$, depending upon which party is in office. In the second case, policy is always at $\frac{1}{2}$. Because of risk aversion, a sure outcome of $\frac{1}{2}$ is preferred by both parties to the "lottery" $(\frac{1}{4}, \frac{3}{4})$ where the two outcomes are equally likely.[17]

For this game to result in complete or even partial convergence, one needs an infinite horizon and low time discounting on the part of two parties. That is, parties have to think that they are always "at the beginning of a beautiful relationship" and have to care a great deal about the future. If there is a finite number of elections, the strategies described above are not feasible. In the last period, there is no convergence because there is no future "enforcement" of promises of moderation. In the period before the last, the parties know that in the last period there is no convergence, no matter what they do; thus they may as well go for their preferred policy if in office, and so forth. Therefore the convergent equilibrium unravels from the last period to the first. Even with an infinite horizon, with high discounting, the future "enforcement" has little bite relative to the current "temptation".

Both assumptions are obviously problematic. Even though we may think of political parties as permanent institutions, actual politicians have finite political (and biological) lives; an obvious last-period problem emerges. A politician in her "last period" (say a "lame duck" president) may not be particularly sensitive to future concerns of her own party; thus the enforcement has no bite. This effect may create a conflict of interest between politicians at the end of their career and "young" members of the party, who care more about future elections.

The "overlapping generations" model, developed for studying intergenerational transfers in economics (Diamond (1965)), can be usefully applied to transfers (in kind, services, or money) from "young" to "old" members of the party. Alesina and Spear (1988) show that these redistributions within a party can overcome the last-period problem by making the transfers to lame duck politicians a function of their behavior when in office. A lame duck receives her transfer only if she behaves in a way that does not compromise the "reputation" (that is, the future electoral prospects) of her own party. These transfers can be seen as a pension system within the party in which the retiring politician's "pension" is made contingent on her behavior in office.

A different way for a party to acquire spatial mobility emerges if the voters

---

[17]Note that since in both scenarios the two parties are in office half of the time, the "reward" for holding office, $\hat{u}$, does not influence the comparison of the two cases.

are not perfectly informed about the party preferences – if they do not know with certainty the position of θ_D and θ_R. In this case, some degree of convergence may occur even with finitely repeated elections. Alesina and Cukierman (1990) show that an incumbent party may choose moderate policies and compromise on its ideological position in order to increase its chances of re-election. Rational voters are aware of this incentive and take that into account in forming expectations about future policies, that is, what will happen if they re-elect the incumbent. In equilibrium, the incumbent chooses a moderate policy (say, x_R on the left of θ_R if the incumbent is Republican) in order to influence voters' beliefs and make them think that the party is actually moderate so as to win the following election. Such an incentive completely disappears only in the politician's "last period", when there are no more elections ahead. The point is that since the voters are unsure about the incumbent's preferences, their beliefs can be strategically influenced by the incumbent's choice of policy.[18]

In this model, voters gather information by observing the incumbent's policies. They are *rationally retrospective*: they use efficiently all the available information, including their knowledge of the incumbent's incentive to be strategic, in order to form expectations about what the incumbent will do if re-elected. In contrast, in the model of section 2.2 in which the voters know party preferences with certainty, the incumbent cannot influence voters' beliefs.[19]

Note that the incumbent may also have an incentive to choose policy procedures that increase ambiguity, that is, procedures that make it more difficult for the voters to pinpoint with precision the party preferences (Alesina and Cukierman (1990)). This ambiguity grants the incumbent more latitude in her strategic choice on the trade-off between moderate and ideological policies. The incentive to be ambiguous about policy contrasts with earlier results by Shepsle (1972), who had shown that candidates who care only about winning and facing risk-averse voters would always try to reduce the uncertainty associated with their policy position. In fact, purely electoralist candidates do *not* face this trade-off between a partisan and an electoral motivation.

At this point a legitimate question may be asked: given that various mechanisms operating in a repeated-election framework support some amount of convergence, should we take the Calvert–Wittman model of sections 2.2 and 2.3 as an approximation of actual political systems and dismiss the model of complete divergence of section 2.4?

---

[18]The voters may also be uninformed about the challenger's preferences; in the model by Alesina and Cukierman (1990) the challenger cannot do anything to influence voters' beliefs since it is out of office and cannot choose policy.

[19]The issue of "rational retrospective voting" will reappear as an important topic in chapters 8 and 9.

We believe that the answer to this question is "not quite". It is true that both the repeated partisan election model and the Wittman–Calvert model predict partial convergence, but the variables that influence the degree of partial convergence are very different in the two models. The length of the horizon and the amount of discounting of the distant (or not so distant) future, the party structure, the amount of voters' information about "true" party ideology are variables that do not enter into the Wittman–Calvert model but are crucial in models of repeated elections. Second, the empirical implication, particularly of Calvert's paper, is that one should always observe a large amount of convergence. On the contrary, the model of section 2.4 emphasizes polarization and relative immobility of party platforms. One way of judging the different emphases of the two models is to look at the available evidence, to which we now turn.

2.6 POLARIZATION IN AMERICAN POLITICS

The theoretical discussion of this chapter holds that politics is "low" dimensional, namely, that not much is really lost by considering models in which the parties choose a position on a unidimensional line, from "left" to "right". In fact, throughout this book, we use a one-dimensional model. In American politics, this is equivalent to assuming that policy can be captured on a classical liberal–conservative ideological continuum (Converse (1964, 1966)). We begin by examining the available evidence on this point. We then consider whether American politics is "polarized" in the sense that politicians adopt distinct policy positions. These two issues, dimensionality and polarization, are independent; that is, one could have high or low dimensionality and high or low polarization.

Our evidence on dimensionality comes largely from roll call voting. In this context, a one-dimensional model claims that there is an ordering of legislators from liberal to conservative. For example, Kennedy–Byrd–Specter–Danforth–Helms might be part of the ordering for the Senate in 1992. If these five senators always voted in a manner that conformed to the ordering just given, we would see only the five following voting patterns: unanimity; Kennedy voting on one side, all the others on the other; Kennedy and Byrd against the other three; Kennedy, Byrd, and Specter against the other two; Kennedy, Byrd, Specter, and Danforth against Helms. Other patterns, such as Kennedy and Helms on one side and the "moderates" on the other, would be ruled out. Of course, among the thousands of actual roll call votes in which these five senators have participated, there will be some that do not fall into the five patterns consistent with the one-dimensional ordering. A variety of techniques exist for ascertaining the *degree* to which the actual data corresponds to a one-dimensional model.

A widely used[20] method is the Poole and Rosenthal (1991a) D-NOMINATE scaling procedure. Heckman and Snyder (1992) have recently developed an alternative scaling model that replicates the Poole and Rosenthal findings. The two procedures give virtually identical orderings of legislators. Moreover, the procedures produce estimates of legislator bliss points in addition to an ordering. The estimated bliss points are highly correlated with the ratings of the Americans for Democratic Action and other ideological interest groups. The methods can also estimate models where legislators use more than one dimension in voting. Poole and Rosenthal (1991a) find that, except for brief periods before the Civil War when total "chaos" prevailed, at most two dimensions are needed to account for the roll call voting behavior of members of Congress. Indeed, in recent times, particularly in the 1980s and 1990s, voting is largely unidimensional. A one-dimensional scaling that aims at optimal classification can correctly classify more than 90 percent of the individual decisions, even on close votes.

Snyder (1991) has recently applied the D-NOMINATE algorithm to the Assembly of California and reached a similar conclusion. Moreover, scaling citizen preferences using aggregate returns on initiatives and referenda by Assembly district, Snyder again found a low-dimensional structure. He argues, in light of this finding, that voting is low-dimensional because legislators perceive, through aggregate data, constituent preferences to be low-dimensional.

A low-dimensional result was also found by Poole (1981) and Poole and Daniels (1985), who applied an alternative method, least squares metric unfolding, to the ratings produced by various ideological interest groups. Although the interest groups spanned labor, farm, industry, small business, environmental, and public interest organizations, the interest groups, as well as the politicians, fit into a low-dimensional space.

In short, *even though politics is full of nuances and complexities that we will not address in this volume, there is now overwhelming evidence that low-dimensional models are appropriate simplifications.*

We now turn to the issue of "polarization". Substantial evidence of policy divergence is found within the estimated one-dimensional space. For our purposes, the positions of presidential candidates are most important. Many candidates, particularly in the postwar period, have previously served in Congress. Where did they stand ideologically? Figure 2.6 shows the Poole–Rosenthal positions of the candidates in their last period of service before running, the mean position in the Senate, and one-standard-deviation bands for the Senate.

What is striking is not just that these candidates, including the successful ones, were distant from the overall median in many cases, but that they

[20]See Cox and McCubbins (1993), Kiewiet and McCubbins (1991), Kiewiet and Zeng (1993), Snyder (1991), Romer and Weingast (1991), Weingast (1993).

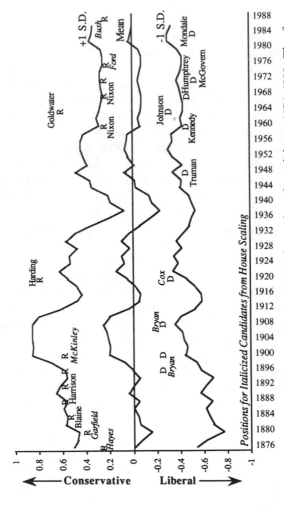

Figure 2.6. Liberal–conservative positions of presidential candidates, 1876–1988. The figure compares the Poole–Rosenthal (1991a) estimates of the positions of presidential candidates who served in the Senate or House to the mean and one standard deviation bands for the entire Senate.

often represented relatively extreme positions *within their own parties*. This scaling procedure is obviously not available for presidential candidates who did not serve in Congress. Even so, a casual observation of the candidates who had not served in Congress would suggest that although Dewey, Eisenhower, and Carter were moderates, Stevenson, Dukakis, and Reagan were not.[21]

In summary, moderate, middle-of-the road politicians are underrepresented as presidential candidates. Moreover, analysis of survey data (Brody and Page (1973), Rabinowitz (1976), Cahoon, Hinich, and Ordeshook (1978), Poole and Rosenthal (1984a)) has shown that voters perceive substantial differences in candidate positions. Moreover, Poole and Rosenthal (1984a) show that most voter ideal points are more moderate than the positions of the candidates. The evidence is clear: even though, once selected, candidates must compete for the presidency in a general election, they fail to adopt convergent positions, consistent with our analysis (in section 2.4) of the credibility problem.

Very similar results on political polarization are available for legislators. Poole and Rosenthal (1984b) examine the ideological positions of the two senators from each state. If a state's two senators are from the same party, they tend to be quite similar, but if one senator is a Democrat and the other a Republican, their positions are highly distinct. For example, see figure 2.7, which graphs the D-NOMINATE positions of the California Senate delegation. Although, in the initial postwar period, Senator Thomas Kuchel was a moderate, the two senators have subsequently been at opposite ends of the spectrum when they were from different parties.[22] This opposition pertains not only to questions of national policy but also, consistent with our view that almost everything fits into a low-dimensional space, to policies that pertain strictly to California, as illustrated by the recent squabble between senators Cranston and Seymour over the California Desert Protection Act (*San Francisco Chronicle* (Feb. 17, 1992)).

Each congressional district has a single representative, so the comparisons that Poole and Rosenthal (1984b) carried out for the Senate are not possible for the House of Representatives. Nevertheless, Fiorina (1974) found, in comparing the ADA ratings of representatives and their successors, that a change in party control of a district led to a dramatic change in the ADA rating of the district's representative, a change much too great to ascribe to demographics, which evolve slowly, or to changes in individual voter preferences.

[21]Figure 2.6 shows that Bush had a relatively moderate record in the House. Once he joined Reagan as vice-president, however, he had to endorse Reagan's relatively extreme positions. When Bush became president he could not easily turn around and become a moderate again. For the kind of credibility argument discussed above, Bush was stuck in a conservative position within the Republican party.

[22]For a discussion of split Senate delegations, see Alesina, Fiorina, and Rosenthal (1991).

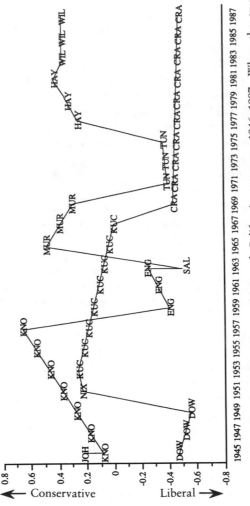

Figure 2.7. Liberal–conservative positions of California senators, 1946–1987. When the two senators are not from the same party, their positions are very different. Lines connect senators holding the same seat. *Key*: JOH = H. Johnson, KNO = W. Knowland, ENG = C. Engle, SAL = P. Salinger, MUR = G. Murphy, TUN = J. Tunney, HAY = S. Hayakawa, WIL = P. Wilson; DOW = T. Downey, NIX = R. Nixon, KUC = T. Kuchel, CRA = A. Cranston.

Fiorina's work has recently been extended, and replicated for more current data, by Loomis and Poole (1992) and Poole and Romer (1993), now using D-NOMINATE scores. These authors find that when a representative is succeeded by another member of his party, the D-NOMINATE scores are significantly correlated. Within party, relatively liberal districts tend to elect relatively liberal representatives, but the correlation is not strong. Indeed, the successor's position ranges over about half the range of positions within the party. Thus each representative, rather than representing a middle-of-the-road position in the constituency, is afforded considerable latitude in crafting an electoral coalition congruent with his own position (Fenno (1978)). Again, these findings suggest an important role for policy motivation.[23]

An additional implication of the "partisan" model is that if politicians are mainly driven by policy preferences, positions should not change much over time: this is exactly the finding of Poole and Rosenthal (1991a). Members of Congress generally do not adjust their relative positions: they enter and die with their ideological boots on! Annual movements per senator or representative average less than 1 percent of the range of the liberal–conservative continuum.[24]

Interestingly, although Poole and Rosenthal (1984b, 1991a) report polarized positions of elected politicians and presidential candidates, at the same time they report (1984a) a unimodal distribution of preferences in the mass public, with the middle of the road predominating. This finding implies that a large mass of the electorate is "in between" the two parties; they would prefer more moderate policies than either of the two parties alone can deliver.

In summary, the evidence surveyed in this section supports three basic assumptions on which this book is built: First, policy has one or, at most, two dimensions. For all practical purposes, not much is lost by positing that political conflict is summarized by movements along a liberal–conservative line. Second, candidates and, more generally, politicians are polarized and show strong signs of policy motivation. Third, a large mass of the electorate is "moderate", that is, less polarized than the average candidate of the two parties.

---

[23]The findings of Loomis and Poole (1992) are echoed by those of McCarty and Poole (1992). These authors extended the Poole–Rosenthal method to the analysis of Political Action Committee campaign contributions. This allowed them to scale incumbents, challengers, and PACs in a common space. They find considerable polarization of the contestants for House seats.

[24]Similarly, Loomis and Poole (1992) and Poole and Romer (1993), echoing Lott and Bronars (1993), find that members of Congress about to retire do not "shirk". Shirking might occur if a representative took a "constituency" position as long as he was interested in running for re-election but then turned toward his personal preferences in a last term. But according to these authors there are no important last-term effects.

2.7 WHY ARE PARTIES POLARIZED?

The preceding section summarized overwhelming empirical evidence of a polarized two-party system in the United States, but two basic theoretical questions remain. Why are the two parties polarized? Why are there only two parties?

One explanation for polarization emphasizes party activists, who, typically, are *not* middle-of-the-road voters and have more extreme views than the mass electorate. Activists are also influential in forming party platforms, which, as a result, tend to reflect relatively extreme views.

A related explanation focuses on the primary system (Coleman (1971), Wittman (1983, 1990)). A presidential candidate needs to appeal to the "median" of her party to win the nomination. Then, in the presidential race, she is committed to such a position and cannot easily move toward the overall median of the population. (Remember our discussion of the credibility issue in section 2.4.) Forward-looking voters should account for this effect and recognize the trade-off between choosing the candidate who is really representative of their views and somebody who can win. These choices, in both parties, lead to the selection of two candidates with different preferences. Again, once the candidates have made their preferences known, both in the primaries and in their previous records, they cannot change them without a loss of credibility. This effect of the primary system is reinforced if, as appears to be the case, the actual participants in primary elections tend to be relatively extreme voters. Furthermore, the uncertainty about the process is augmented by the complicated system whereby primaries and caucuses take place at different times in different states.

A third explanation establishes a connection between polarization of policies and voter participation. Feddersen (1992) develops a model that predicts policy polarization. He allows for plurality voting directly over policies, rather than over candidates, and anyone who votes incurs a cost. The (multiple[25]) equilibria to Feddersen's model all have two realistic properties: first, there is positive participation even with a large electorate; second, only two *separated* positions are picked. Feddersen's results reflect the implication that political participation disappears when the choices are identical and voting is costly.[26]

"Participation" is especially costly to people who do more than vote, by contributing money or canvassing voters. Not surprisingly, when the ideal points of interest groups (Poole and Daniels (1985), Poole and Rosenthal (1985)) or Political Action Committees (McCarty and Poole (1992)) are estimated jointly with those of the members of Congress, many interest

[25]Interestingly, Feddersen (1993) has recently shown that the game-theoretic refinement of *Coalition Proof Nash*, which we apply in our analysis in the appendices to chapters 3 and 4, greatly mitigates the multiple-equilibrium problem.
[26]See also Ledyard (1984).

groups are more extreme than the legislators. Since these interest groups are providing essential services to campaigns, even a candidate who cares only about winning needs to trade off appealing to voters in the center for the resources provided by the more active extremists and pressure groups.[27]

An important theoretical question that concerns any model with two polarized parties (and polarized policies) is what prevents entry of a third party in the middle. Why are Ross Perot types not more frequent and more successful? As a matter of fact, the formal literature on entry is, unfortunately, limited. Shepsle and Cohen (1990) provide a general assessment of the research on entry.

For the case of purely electoralist candidates, Palfrey (1984) actually shows that the threat of entry of a third party induces the two established parties to adopt separate, rather than convergent, positions. The difference between the established parties and the potential entrant is, in Palfrey's model, that the former can pick their positions *before* the latter.

Suppose the two established parties both locate at the median. Then imagine that a third party positions itself just to the left of the median. The consequence is that the new entrant captures all the electorate on the left of the median, and the other two parties split the other 50 percent of the electorate between them. The entrant gets roughly 50 percent of the vote, the other two parties roughly 25 percent each. The entrant wins the election. If, instead, the two established parties separate (one on the left and one on the right of the median), they can prevent a successful entry by not leaving enough "space" either in the middle or in the extremes. Thus because of the threat of entry, even two parties that care *only* about winning may choose platforms on opposite sides of the median.

Greenberg and Shepsle (1987), however, criticize Palfrey's result by arguing that a potential entrant may aim not at winning, but at finishing second. By doing so, the new entrant becomes an "established party" and can displace one of the previous two in the next election. In this scenario, in which coming in second may lead to an advantage in the next election, Palfrey's equilibrium does not survive. More generally, Greenberg and Shepsle (1987) show that no stable equilibria exist.

2.8 CONCLUSIONS

American politics is polarized. In this chapter we developed theoretical arguments backed by empirical evidence that reject the notion of convergence of party platforms and policy outcomes.

Polarization is crucial for the entire construction of the book; this chapter has laid down the foundations of everything that follows in several ways.

---

[27]On campaign contributions, see Austen-Smith (1981), Baron and Mo (1993), Ingberman (1994), and Snyder (1991).

First, without polarization of party platforms the concept of "moderation" by means of checks and balances would not make sense. Furthermore, without party polarization the macroeconomic effects due to uncertainty about future policies following an election would disappear. One critical element linking the polity and the economy would be missing, and our model of the political economy of the United States (chapters 7, 8, and 9) would collapse.

Second, our argument about credibility of party platforms suggests that the candidates have limited mobility in the policy sphere. Politicians cannot adopt very different positions to please the electorate in different elections without incurring costs of lost reputation. The idea that the two parties have fixed positions underlies the balancing model of the next two chapters. In chapter 5, however, we will also discuss the case in which the two parties have mobility, as in the Wittman–Calvert model discussed in this chapter. The choice of party platform is discussed there in the context of the executive–legislative interaction in policy formation.

The idea that the two parties have relatively stable positions on economic policy is also important for our politico-economic model. This relative stability implies that voters and economic agents know what economic policy to expect from the two parties.

3

A *theory of institutional balancing*

3.1 INTRODUCTION

A primary purpose of this book is to understand how politics affects public policy. In the previous chapter, we considered two possible scenarios. One had politics leading to middle-of-the-road policies as the result of electoral competition between electoralist parties. This approach was refuted both theoretically, because of the inability of candidates to make credible campaign promises, and empirically, because of widespread observations of party polarization. The other scenario had partisan politics with alternation between the relatively extreme policies pursued by two polarized parties.

This second scenario is also likely to be inaccurate because it ignores the institutional structure that leads to policy formation. In the United States, the Constitution provides for "checks and balances". Legislation, including measures that affect economic policy, requires congressional majorities and a presidential signature. Regulatory agencies, important in policymaking (like the Federal Reserve), are subject to congressional oversight. The need for some degree of concurrence between the executive and legislative branches of government contributes to policy moderation.

In this chapter, we consider the effect of institutional "checks and balances" on policy moderation in a highly stylized manner that is, nonetheless, empirically descriptive. We build on the case of fully divergent and "immobile" parties of section 2.4: if the executive has full control of policy, the two parties implement their ideal policies. We posit, however, that the influence of the executive in policymaking is mediated by the legislature: policy depends on which party holds the presidency *and* on the composition of the legislature. We view policy as a compromise between the executive and the legislature. We further mimic the American electoral system by considering a scenario in which the president remains in office for two periods and the legislature is elected every period; this feature, obviously, captures the midterm congressional election.

Middle-of-the-road voters – that is, voters with policy preferences in between the two parties' ideal policies (θ_D and θ_R) – take advantage of this legislative–executive interaction in policy formation to bring about moderate policy outcomes, policies in between θ_D and θ_R. They achieve this goal by favoring one party in the legislative election and the opposite party in the presidential election. As a result, "divided government" becomes a possibility: the *electorate may choose to give the majority in the legislature to the party not holding the presidency*. Divided government does not occur for every configuration of voters and party preferences in our model; we discuss which factors are more or less likely to produce this outcome.

Divided government does not happen by accident: it is not an undesired result of a cumbersome electoral process, nor is it the result of a lack of rationality or of well-defined preferences of the electorate. Divided government occurs because moderate voters like it, and they take advantage of "checks and balances" to achieve moderation. In dividing government, the voters force the parties to compromise: divided government is a remedy to political polarization.

Public opinion polls do, in fact, suggest that the American voters like divided government. A strong majority expresses a preference for divided government over one party controlling both branches. An NBC News/Wall Street Journal poll taken before the 1988 election showed that 54 percent of the voters preferred divided government while only 32 percent preferred unified government. Later polls taken by the same organization gave similar results. In October 1990, the split was 63–23; in January of 1994, even with the national government unified, the split was 56–33 in favor of divided government. The American voter therefore does not appear particularly concerned with the possibility of legislative immobility associated with divided control.[1] For the theoretical and empirical reasons discussed in chapter 1, we do not focus here on the possibility of legislative deadlocks. In other words, we assume that the institutional "compromise" between executive and legislature is costless; namely, no inefficiencies or costly delays are introduced by their bargaining.

In this chapter we use the simplest possible model to make our point; in particular, we posit that every voter knows the distribution of voters' preferences. This unrealistic assumption of complete information precludes the emergence of the "midterm cycle". In chapter 4, we consider the more

---

[1] There are at least two other reasons why divided government might not be desired by some voters. One is simply that their utility is not concave, so they prefer a lottery between left and right to getting the middle of the road for sure. The other reason may arise from left voters who believe in "ratcheting". That is, during the periods when the left is in power, it enacts reforms that are not undone by the right. We don't give much credence to either reason. Most voters are likely to be risk averse. The presence of ratcheting is dubious: as both Reagan and Thatcher showed, the real value of previous transfer programs can be reduced sharply.

realistic situation in which voter preferences are not known with certainty and show how the midterm cycle as a balancing device results from this kind of uncertainty.

This chapter is organized as follows. Section 3.2 describes the process of policy formation with the interaction between an executive and a legislature. Section 3.3 covers the basic strategic problem that confronts voters faced with the process of executive–legislative interaction. A box with a summary of the model (box 3.1) appears after section 3.3. Some readers may find it useful to jump ahead and skim the box before proceeding. Section 3.4 provides the intuition behind how we arrive at a political equilibrium. After section 3.5 treats midterm elections, section 3.6 presents the overall equilibrium result. The conditions that determine whether there is a unique equilibrium or two equilibria are discussed in section 3.7. Section 3.8 highlights the results concerning divided government. Section 3.9 indicates several possible generalizations, and section 3.10 compares our model of divided government with a specific alternative approach developed independently by Fiorina (1988) and, more generally, with "majoritarian" models. The last section concludes. The appendix to the chapter presents a more formal, game-theoretic analysis of the model.

Consistent with the plan set forth in chapter 1, this chapter, except for the appendix, relies only on simple algebra. Even so, some readers may prefer not to work through the numerical examples that illustrate the points of section 3.7.

3.2 EXECUTIVE–LEGISLATIVE INTERACTION AND THE ELECTORAL PROCESS

Policy in the United States depends on an interaction between the executive and the legislature. To capture this interplay in a formal model, one necessarily must adopt a simple model that abstracts from many of the details of the "real" world. How can this be done in a manner that best captures important aspects of the policy process?

Some scholars have focussed on the "majoritarian" aspect of political decision-making. This approach is found in a set of writings that view policy as dependent only on which party controls the presidency and which party has a majority in Congress. Fiorina (1988) has proposed a model with only four possible policies, corresponding to unified Democratic government, unified Republican government, and the two possible divided governments. Stewart (1990), in analyzing late 19th-century politics, has emphasized the consequences of Democratic control of the House of Representatives while the Republicans controlled the presidency and the Senate. Ingberman and Villani (1993), Kernell (1991), McCubbins (1991), and Cox and McCubbins (1991) look at the impact of the executive veto on policy formation in models where the executive is confronted by an "agent" who represents the majority in Congress.

Our approach is non-majoritarian and, we believe, more realistic. Although majority control is important, one additional seat does not turn day into night in Congress. In particular, in the Senate, a simple majority gains control of committees and passes legislation, but a minority retains the power to block legislation with the filibuster, which can be ended only with a three-fifths vote. More generally, the legislative process reflects the diversity of positions of members of Congress. Indeed, there are very few pure party-line roll calls in Congress. This is why political scientists have developed expressions such as "conservative coalition" votes for alliances between Southern Democrats and Republicans and why a "three-party" (Northern and Southern Democrats, Republicans) was preferable to a two-party model as a benchmark for roll call studies (Hammond and Fraser (1983)). It is also why ideological or spatial models are preferable to party models (Poole and Rosenthal (1987, 1991a)). We capture this diversity in a very rough way: Congress becomes more "liberal" as the proportion of Democrats increases. The rate at which it becomes more "liberal" can be allowed to increase sharply as the proportion passes 50 percent; this extension is developed in section 3.9. In fact, we show that the "majoritarian model" is a special case of our more general formulation.

Just as the position of Congress lies intermediate between that of the two parties, the overall policy is intermediate between the position of Congress and that of the president. That is, the interaction between the executive and the legislature is viewed as a bargain between the executive's position and that of Congress. A parameter of the model captures how strongly the bargain tilts to the executive's preferences. We think this approach is preferable to a focus on executive vetoes. In executive veto models, the status quo (Romer and Rosenthal (1978)) is critical. But policy is best thought of as the outcome of a series of bills, all of which may have different status quo points.

Executive veto models are one example of agenda control models of policy formation (McKelvey (1976), Romer and Rosenthal (1979b)). In recent years, such models have been extensively used in the analysis of decision-making in the American governmental system.[2] These applications typically depend on various assumptions about the order in which players move and information conditions. Often, as Krehbiel (1988) indicates, the results are sensitive to assumptions that are difficult to evaluate empirically. Consequently, we have chosen to avoid the fine detail of such models. Moreover, recent developments on budget and tax legislation, social security, minimum wage, and civil rights (Poole and Rosenthal (1991b, 1993b))

[2]Denzau and Mackay (1983), Gilligan and Krehbiel (1989), Ferejohn and Shipan (1990), Matthews (1989), Ingberman and Yao (1991), Hammond and Miller (1987).

suggest that, in many cases, bargaining may be more crucial than the intricacies of agenda setting. In these situations, the final legislation was hammered out in direct negotiations between the White House, the Speaker of the House of Representatives, the majority leader of the Senate, and a few other key actors. The basic logic of our argument concerning balancing behavior of voters applies, however, equally well to "majoritarian" as to "shares" models, as we show in section 3.10.

We now proceed to the description of our model. The two parties have exactly the same preferences as in chapter 2. Since we consider a one-shot game, the parties cannot make credible commitments to platforms but must adopt policies that are identical to their bliss points. Thus, abstracting from the role of the legislature, party D implements θ_D and party R, θ_R. But we posit an institutional structure in which policy is determined by a compromise between the president and the legislature. For analytical tractability, we assume that both the legislature and the president are elected in a single national district. The president is elected by majority rule, and a fair coin is tossed to decide a tie. In contrast, the legislature is elected by proportional representation.

This setup obviously differs significantly from American institutions, where the president is chosen by the Electoral College and the Congress is elected by plurality in geographically based constituencies. In chapters 5 and 6, we consider extensions to our basic model that move us closer to actual institutions. Nonetheless, even in this chapter we capture what are perhaps the two most crucial features of American elections. First, a single party (individual) is awarded the presidency. Second, Congress has representatives from both parties. Furthermore, even with these drastic simplifications, the model of this chapter generates empirically testable and realistic results that explain important regularities of American politics.

Let us define V_D and V_R as the proportion of votes in the legislative election obtained by party D and party R respectively. Given the strict proportionality of the voting rule we have assumed, they also represent the share of seats in the single legislative body. We further assume full turnout, so that $V_R = 1 - V_D$.[3] When D is president, we posit that the policy x^D is as follows:

$$x^D = \alpha\theta_D + (1 - \alpha)[V_R\theta_R + (1 - V_R)\theta_D] \qquad (3.1)$$

with $0 \leqslant \alpha \leqslant 1$.

The parameter α represents the weight of the president in policy formation. If $\alpha = 1$ the legislature has no role; as in the model of section 2.4,

[3]Clearly, the assumption of full turnout is not realistic for the American electorate. But the theoretical question of "why people vote" and the empirical question of what affects participation rates are beyond the scope of this volume and would require a separate research project.

$x^D = \theta_D$. The term in the square bracket represents the policy position of the legislature; it is an average of the ideal policies of the two parties weighted by the vote shares (V_R and $V_D = 1 - V_R$). Thus the policy x^D is itself a linear combination of the president's position and that of the legislature. If $V_R = 0$, the legislature is fully Democratic and the policy is θ_D. Instead, the higher is V_R, the further away the policy x^D is from θ_D: the stronger is the Republican contingent in Congress, the more right wing is the policy outcome.

Analogously, if R is president we have:

$$x^R = \alpha\theta_R + (1 - \alpha)[V_R\theta_R + (1 - V_R)\theta_D] \qquad (3.2)$$

The interpretation of equation (3.2) parallels that of equation (3.1).

Equations (3.1) and (3.2) imply that the parties are homogeneous: the president and her party's congressional representatives have the same preferences. A discussion of the heterogeneous case, in which the president and her party's congressional delegation may disagree about policy, is postponed to chapter 5.

For expositional purposes it is convenient to rewrite (3.1) and (3.2) as follows:

$$x^D = \theta_D + KV_R \qquad (3.3)$$

$$x^R = \theta_R - K(1 - V_R) \qquad (3.4)$$

where:

$$K \equiv (1 - \alpha)(\theta_R - \theta_D) \qquad (3.5)$$

These equations make clear that for any fixed value of V_R, the policy outcome with a D president is always to the left of the policy outcome with an R president. That is:

$$0 < x^D < x^R < 1 \qquad (3.6)$$

As in chapter 2, the voter bliss points, θ_i, are distributed on the segment [0, 1], which is the range of possible policies. The formal analysis in the appendix is facilitated by assuming a continuum with an infinite number of voters, even though our results are substantively identical if we assume a large but finite number of voters. For simplicity, we posit that the distribution of voter bliss points is uniform on the interval [0, 1], so that the median voter has a bliss point of $\frac{1}{2}$. The appendix to this chapter shows that the assumption of uniformly distributed ideal points is inessential for the qualitative features of our results, but it is easier to illustrate the results with this assumption. Finally, throughout this chapter we assume that the distribution of voters' bliss points is known by everybody (parties *and* voters); that is, we assume complete information.

We consider two periods, labelled periods 1 and 2, which together represent a four-year presidential term. In the first (two-year) period both the executive and the legislature are simultaneously elected. In the second period, the executive remains in office while the entire legislature is re-elected. Rational voters will, when voting in period 1, take into account the implications of their decisions in period 1 for their utility in period 2. In particular, in period 2, they will be "stuck" with the president elected in period 1. A rational voter might well have an even longer horizon, looking beyond a single presidential term. But since our setup allows for complete replacement of the executive and legislature every two periods, voters need not plan beyond two periods. Our analysis, therefore, need consider only a two-period game, that is, one presidential term.

3.3 THE VOTING GAME: AN INFORMAL DISCUSSION

Unlike the two-candidate models of chapter 2, where policy depended only on the platform of the winner, we let policy outcomes depend on vote shares: in fact, the policy outcome is a function of the share of votes received by the two parties in the legislative election. This realistic feature of our model implies that the decision of each middle-of-the-road voter (i.e., of each voter with ideal policy in between θ_D and θ_R) depends on his beliefs about the behavior of other voters. It follows that the voters in our model need to be "strategic" in the following sense. Suppose that, say, a center-right voter believes that a Republican president will be elected *and* that the composition of the legislature will be tilted in party R's favor. Then he may vote D in the legislature to "balance". But, if the same voter believes that many other fellow voters in the center right and center left are doing this balancing, he may choose to vote R for the legislature; his vote cannot be independent of what he believes the relative shares in the legislature will be, since these shares determine which policy will result from the election.[4] The linkage between a voter's own decision and his beliefs about other voters' choices means that we must analyze a coordination game between the voters who are responsive to the executive–legislative interaction in policy formation.

In this game the choice of each voter includes two votes in the first period and one vote in the second.[5] One possible simple strategy would be: "*Vote R in every election, no matter what!*" Many voters, however, may use richer strategies: they may either split their ticket in the first period or make their second-period legislative vote contingent on who is president. An example is the following strategy:

---

[4]Note that relative shares do not matter in the presidential election, which is decided by majority rule. This implies that we do not consider mandate effects on the presidency; nevertheless, such an extension is feasible in the context of our model. See Chilton (1989) for some work in this direction.

[5]We rule out randomization by voters. This simplification does not affect results

"Vote R for the presidency and D for the legislature in period 1; vote D for the legislature in period 2 if R is president, otherwise, if D is president, vote R."

We will show that some voters with bliss points between those of the two parties will adopt these strategies. The reader may be skeptical that voters can solve this coordination problem. It turns out that the co-ordination has a simple form, which we term *conditional sincerity*.

Conditional Sincerity Condition: A voter equilibrium occurs only if no voter would prefer a decrease in the expected vote for the party he has voted for in an electoral contest,[6] either the presidential or the legislative election.

It is almost self-evident that the condition should hold in equilibrium: if a voter would like a decrease in the expected vote for the party voted for, he is voting the "wrong" way, given his expectations and preferences.[7]

Consider how a voter should vote in the presidential election assuming that the legislative result (V_R) was fixed. The voter would face a choice between x^D and x^R as given by (3.3) and (3.4): a rational voter should vote as if she were pivotal between these two outcomes. Since there are only two outcomes, the voter should vote for whichever of the two she sincerely prefers. That is, *conditional* on the legislative vote, voters should be voting sincerely for the executive.

Now consider how a voter should vote in the legislative elections assuming the presidency was determined. If voters are sincere in their legislative votes, they will be voting for the party whose legislative vote they would like to see increased. Given the presidential outcome, there is only one way in which all voters can be voting sincerely. This gives the *pivotal* voter his most preferred outcome, as shown in section 3.5.

Conditional sincerity is intuitive and obviously a necessary condition for voter equilibrium. Can *conditional sincerity* be simultaneously satisfied in both contests? It turns out that the condition can hold simultaneously in two ways, one corresponding to an R presidential victory, the other to

---

[6]The term "expected" is somewhat redundant in the perfect information model discussed in this chapter, i.e., when the distribution of voter ideal points is known with certainty. Expectations are not perfect foresights in the incomplete information version of the model described in chapter 4.

[7]The "almost" refers to the fact that a voter might just as well vote "the wrong way" if his vote isn't going to make a difference. That is, if one isn't *pivotal*, it doesn't matter how one votes. The arbitrary behavior of non-pivotal voters is, however, an uninteresting technical matter and arises only in the case of the presidential vote. Basically, voters must vote "the correct way" in both contests.

Box 3.1

THE TWO-PERIOD COMPLETE INFORMATION MODEL

Information Conditions

Voters know the distribution of voter preferences and the ideal points of the two parties, θ_D and θ_R.

Period 1

Election held. Simultaneous choice of executive and legislature. Each voter votes either D(president)D(legislature), DR, RD, or RR. Presidency awarded to D or R by majority rule. Party R receives share of legislature equal to its vote share, V_R. Party D receives $1-V_R$.

If D president, policy is given by:

$$x^D = \alpha\theta_D + (1-\alpha)[V_R\theta_R + (1-V_R)\theta_D]$$

If R president, policy is given by:

$$x^R = \alpha\theta_R + (1-\alpha)[V_R\theta_R + (1-V_R)\theta_D]$$

Period 2

Midterm election held. Only legislature chosen. Each voter votes either D or R. First period president continues in office. Party R receives share of legislature equal to its vote share, V_R. Party D receives $1-V_R$. (The first period and second period vote shares are allowed to differ, but they turn out to be identical in equilibrium.)

If D president, policy is given by:

$$x^D = \alpha\theta_D + (1-\alpha)[V_R\theta_R + (1-V_R)\theta_D]$$

If R president, policy is given by:

$$x^R = \alpha\theta_R + (1-\alpha)[V_R\theta_R + (1-V_R)\theta_D]$$

---

a D victory.[8] Therefore, there can be at most two voter equilibria. We now turn to discuss how these two possible equilibria are determined and under which conditions only one of the two survives. Before proceeding, the reader may consult box 3.1, which summarizes the structure of our model.

3.4 AN INTUITIVE VIEW OF EQUILIBRIUM

With respect to the benchmark of the two-candidate election model, we are standing the methodology for modelling elections on its head. In the

---

[8] Technically, conditional sincerity can be satisfied in a third way corresponding to an exact tie for the presidency. We later show that this knife-edge result does not represent an equilibrium.

standard model, the voters are passive players, simply voting for whichever of the two parties they prefer; the candidates are the active players, adapting their positions to what they know about the preferences of voters. In the model of this chapter and the next, the candidates or parties are passive players, with fixed, immutable positions. The only passive voters are those who desire policies to the left of party D's position or to the right of party R's position; these "extremists" always vote for their preferred party in every election.[9] On the contrary, the "middle-of-the-road" voters (i.e., those with bliss points between θ_D and θ_R) are the active players. Collectively, they must make the best of the bad situation represented by the fixed party positions, which are more extreme than their ideal points.[10]

The voters must choose subject to equilibrium conditions closely related to the basic premise of rational choice. Although our formal model has a continuum of voters, for expositional purposes, it is more natural if we think of a finite (but very large) number of individual voters. The basic (Nash) equilibrium concept is that no single voter would like to change his strategy given the strategy of others. That is, no one can unilaterally do better for himself given what others are doing.

When we consider *simultaneous* voting in the two electoral contests, we need to extend this basic notion of equilibrium to study which conditionally sincere outcomes are "sensible". We allow an electoral outcome to represent an equilibrium if no group of voters would like to create a "defection" by changing its vote to bring about an outcome that makes every member of the group better off *provided that it does so in a credible fashion*. What makes a defection credible is that no sub-group of the original group would want to change its vote further.

The first part of the equilibrium concept deals with whether an outcome can be challenged by a defection to another outcome that is "profitable" to the defectors. The second part requires that this "profitable" defection also be *credible* in that further defections will not arise. In the terms of the voting game of this chapter, the role of credible defections can be expressed as follows:

No Credible Flip Condition: Given that the conditional sincerity condition is satisfied, no group of voters can better themselves by flipping the outcome of the presidential election while continuing to satisfy conditional sincerity (defined above) in their legislative votes.

That is, in defecting from a certain electoral outcome by flipping the result of the presidential election, no voters can "promise" to vote in the

---

[9]In the language of game theory, these voters have a "dominant strategy".

[10]In chapter 5 we discuss the case in which parties have "mobility", as in the Wittman–Calvert models reviewed in sections 2.2 and 2.3.

legislative elections in a manner that would not be in their interest once the presidency has been switched.

Even though the definition employs the collective term "group", we do not require any active communication or coalition organization among voters. We do not pursue here a "group theory" of voting. Indeed, any single voter can compute, acting alone, all the necessary conditions to be satisfied in equilibrium and act accordingly. As for any other notion of equilibrium, like the Nash one, we see the one adopted here as an "as if" construction. As the next sections will show, our notion of equilibrium generates intuitive and sensible results.

More discussion of these game-theoretic issues and a more formal characterization of our notion of equilibrium can be found in the appendix to this chapter.

3.5 VOTING AT MIDTERM – THE PIVOTAL-VOTER THEOREM

Our analysis begins with the legislative elections of the second period, when the identity of the president is obviously known, since she was elected in period 1.

One of the most important theoretical results of this book is the "pivotal-voter theorem". This result, which will come up over and over again, implies that in legislative elections we have a pivotal voter who corresponds to a *cutpoint*, that is, one voter, illustrated in figure 3.1, who separates the D voters (on his left) from the R voters (on his right), and the policy outcome equals the bliss point of this pivotal voter.

As in chapter 2, we assume that the voter ideal policies are distributed on the interval from 0 to 1. Because our exposition uses a uniform distribution of ideal points, when there is a legislative cutpoint, denoted $\tilde{\theta}$, the expressions

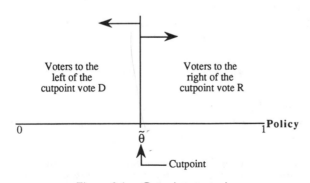

Figure 3.1. Cutpoint strategies

for the vote shares are very simple:[11]

$$V_D = \tilde{\theta}$$
$$V_R = 1 - V_D = 1 - \tilde{\theta}$$

The first expression states that the D voters are those with bliss points between 0 and $\tilde{\theta}$; the second highlights that the R voters are those with bliss points between $\tilde{\theta}$ and 1. Thus we can now define a configuration of voter strategies, which we label "cutpoint strategies".

Definition

Voters use *cutpoint strategies* for the legislative elections if there is a unique voter, denoted $\tilde{\theta}$, such that voter i votes D if $\theta_i < \tilde{\theta}$ and votes R if $\theta_i > \tilde{\theta}$.

Since extremists (i.e., voters with bliss points below θ_D and above θ_R) always vote for their more preferred party, we must have $\theta_D < \tilde{\theta} < \theta_R$; that is, the cutpoint voter is always between the two party bliss points.

This definition and the specification of vote shares are used in establishing the following important result:

Pivotal-voter theorem

When R is president, $\tilde{\theta}_R$ is the ideal policy of the pivotal voter *and* is equal to the policy outcome x^R. When D is president, $\tilde{\theta}_D$ is the ideal policy of the pivotal voter *and* is equal to the policy outcome x^D. In equilibrium the voters adopt cutpoint strategies, with the ideal point of the pivotal voter being the cutpoint. Voters to the left of the cutpoint vote D; voters to the right vote R. Furthermore, the following inequalities hold:

$$\theta_D < \tilde{\theta}_D = x^D < \tilde{\theta}_R = x^R < \theta_R \tag{3.7}$$

Equation (3.7) implies that the cutpoint when R is president is to the right of the cutpoint when D is president. Furthermore, policy is more conservative under an R president, given that the theorem implies that the bliss point of the cutpoint voter is equal to the policy outcome. Given our specific functional forms, it follows that:

$$\tilde{\theta}_D = \frac{\theta_D + K}{1 + K}; \qquad \tilde{\theta}_R = \frac{\theta_R}{1 + K} \tag{3.8}$$

where K is defined as in equation (3.5).

A formal proof of the pivotal-voter theorem and of equation (3.8) is given in the appendix to this chapter. The intuition is quite simple, however,

[11]We should stress, once again, that the assumption of uniformity is used purely for expositional purposes. The pivotal-voter theorem does not require any restriction on the distribution of voter preferences, other than continuity.

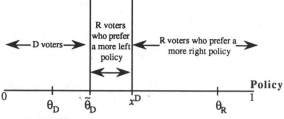

(a) Voters in $(\tilde{\theta}_D, x^D)$ vote inconsistently.

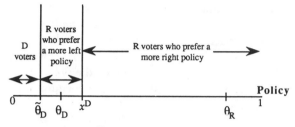

(b) Voters in $(\tilde{\theta}_D, x^D)$ vote inconsistently. $\tilde{\theta}_D < \theta_D$ cannot be an equilibrium because it is always true that $x^D \geq \theta_D$.

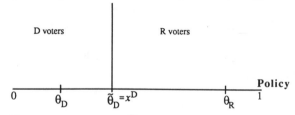

(c) In equilibrium, policy (x^D) equals the ideal point of the pivotal voter $(\tilde{\theta}_D)$.

Figure 3.2.   Legislative voting with D president in the second period

and can be visualized with the help of panel *a* of figure 3.2, which is drawn for the case of a D president. (The case of an R president is analogous.) Suppose that the bliss policy of the pivotal voter $\tilde{\theta}_D$ were on the left of the policy outcome x^D as shown in panel *a*, and consider the behavior of the voters with bliss points in between $\tilde{\theta}_D$ and x^D. These voters are voting R for the legislature, even though their bliss point is on the left of the policy outcome x^D. In other words, these voters vote R even though they would prefer a more left-wing policy than what they get; a policy to the left of x^D could be achieved by *reducing* the share of votes received by party R. Thus these voters are voting for the party they would like to see receive fewer votes: this behavior does not satisfy the *conditional sincerity condition* for equilibrium. A similar argument rules out $\tilde{\theta}_D$ to the right of x_D and, as well, any strategies which are not cutpoint.

It is also immediate to verify that a case such as $\tilde{\theta}_D < \theta_D$ (panel b of figure 3.2) cannot be an equilibrium. Voters with bliss points between $\tilde{\theta}_D$ and θ_D are voting R for the legislature, even though they would, because their bliss points are to the left of θ_D, prefer to see a legislature that is 100 percent D. The same argument rules out $\tilde{\theta}_R > \theta_R$. Thus the inequalities in equation (3.7) follow. Finally, given the specific functional forms adopted here, the specific expression for $\tilde{\theta}_D$ and $\tilde{\theta}_R$ given in equation (3.8) can be derived with simple algebra (see the appendix of this chapter).

In the legislative election, the voters are *conditionally sincere* since, *given the identity of the president*, they vote for the party they would like to see stronger. Nevertheless, not all the voters vote in the legislative election for the same party *regardless* of which party holds the presidency. Specifically, voters in between $\tilde{\theta}_D$ and $\tilde{\theta}_R$ vote differently, depending on which party holds the White House.

It is important to highlight the similarities and differences between our pivotal-voter theorem and the median-voter theorem. According to both theorems, the policy outcome equals the ideal policy of the pivotal voter, that is, of the voter who divides the two political camps. Our pivotal voter does not coincide (except by pure chance) with the overall median of the voting population, however, which, in our model, is at $\frac{1}{2}$. In fact, our pivotal voter is always in between θ_D and θ_R even when the two parties' ideal policies are on the same side of the median voter!

Summarizing, the pivotal-voter theorem establishes that the policy outcome equals the ideal point of the voter at the legislative cutpoint. (See panel c of figure 3.2.) Every voter to the left of the cutpoint would want a policy further to the left, thus a reduction in V_R. Similarly, voters to the right of the cutpoint want an increase in V_R. Voters use the legislative election to pull policy away from the incumbent president's most preferred policy: voters *moderate* the president with the legislature. Since $\tilde{\theta}_D < \tilde{\theta}_R$, *a party receives more votes in the legislative elections when it does not hold the presidency than when it does.*

3.6 SIMULTANEOUS ELECTION OF THE EXECUTIVE AND THE LEGISLATURE

In the first period both the executive and the legislature are elected simultaneously. Three important observations have to be highlighted immediately, before we proceed to examine this situation.

First, all the voters on the left of θ_D and on the right of θ_R will always vote D and R respectively, in *both contests*. The most desirable outcome for these voters is one in which one of the two parties holds the presidency and 100 percent of the votes in the legislature. Second, since both the distribution of voter preferences and party platforms are known, there cannot be any uncertainty about the electoral results: given the party platforms, each voter has all the necessary information to compute the electoral equilibrium. There is only one possible "knife edge" case of uncertainty: a tie in the presidential election. It turns out, however, that the ability of voters to simultaneously choose the president and the legislature implies that ties in presidential elections are never an equilibrium. This result is in sharp contrast with the median-voter theorem, in which every election ends up in a tie, since both parties adopt the same policy. Third, to characterize the equilibrium, we must recognize that now the voters have two choices: a presidential and a legislative vote. Thus, recalling our definition of equilibrium, we now must consider that given a certain electoral outcome, some voters may want to change either one of their votes, or both, to bring about a more desirable outcome.

The following proposition characterizes the voting equilibria:

Proposition 3.1
An equilibrium *always* exists, and it is given by either:

1) Party R wins the presidency with certainty; the legislative cutpoint in *both* periods is given by $\tilde{\theta}_R$; the policy outcome in both periods is $x^R = \tilde{\theta}_R = \theta_R/(1 + K)$.

2) Party D wins the presidency with certainty; the legislative cutpoint in *both* periods is given by $\tilde{\theta}_D$; the policy outcome in both periods is given by $x^D = \tilde{\theta}_D = (\theta_D + K)/(1 + K)$.

For some parameter values *both* of these outcomes are equilibria of the game; otherwise only one of the two outcomes is an equilibrium.

The most evident property of the equilibrium is that of *moderation*. Since $\theta_D < \tilde{\theta}_D < \tilde{\theta}_R < \theta_R$, policy is always interior to the bliss points of the two parties. When R is president, policy is pulled leftward by a factor of $1/(1 + K)$. Larger values of K lead to policies more to the left. Since $K = (1 - \alpha)(\theta_R - \theta_D)$, the leftward pull is increasing in the power of the legislature, captured by $1 - \alpha$, and increasing in the degree of polarization of the two parties, captured by $\theta_R - \theta_D$.

The formal proof of the proposition is in the appendix to this chapter. Here we develop the intuition behind it. In what follows, we assume that the utility function of the voters is symmetric around their bliss point. As emphasized in chapter 2 (figure 2.1) this implies that if a voter has to choose between two policies, he always prefers the one closer to his ideal point. Although it is easier to develop the intuition of our results for this case, this assumption is not necessary: Proposition 3.1 holds also for the case of asymmetric preferences.

First, assume that voting behavior is such that party R wins the presidency for sure; that is, more than half of the voters are voting R in the presidential election. By the same argument used to establish the pivotal-voter theorem, we must have $\tilde{\theta}_R$ as the unique cutpoint in the legislative election. In other words, given that the voters know for sure that party R is going to win the presidential election, they will vote in the first-period legislative election exactly as in the second period, when, since the presidency is not at contest, they know which party holds the presidency. Thus, if the voters are sure about the outcome of the presidential election, they have no reason to vote differently in the first and in the second-period legislative elections. In fact, the actual realization of the first-period elections does not reveal any new information to the voters, since they already knew who would have won and they knew which policies would have been implemented. A perfectly analogous argument holds for the case in which more than 50 percent of the voters are voting D for the presidency.

Next, we should clarify why ties in presidential elections cannot be equilibria. Even though a tie in a large election has an extremely low probability of occurring in practice, it is necessary and instructive for an understanding of the logic of our model to work out why ties can be ruled out as possible equilibria. With a tie, middle-of-the-road voters are unsure about which party will win the coin toss that resolves the presidential election. Since the voters are uncertain about the outcome of the coin toss, in the legislative elections they have to "hedge their bets", not knowing the outcome of the presidential election. Consider, for example, "moderately left" voters: voters close to but on the left of the median $\frac{1}{2}$. If these voters were sure that a relatively extreme left D president would win, they would vote R in the legislative election to balance. But under uncertainty about which party will win the coin toss they may not be willing to vote R for the legislature. This strategy would put "all their eggs in one basket". They would incur the risk of creating a strong R legislative contingent in the case in which R wins the presidency, an outcome that they greatly dislike if R is relatively extreme on the right. This argument, which will resurface in the next chapter, underlies why there is less moderation when presidential elections are uncertain.

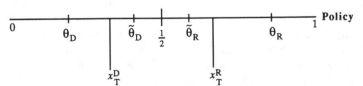

Figure 3.3. The median voter (1/2) prefers either certain outcome ($\tilde{\theta}_D$ or $\tilde{\theta}_R$) to either outcome if there is a tie (x_T^D or x_T^R).

With presidential ties and "incomplete" moderation, the two policy outcomes are, as shown in figure 3.3, x_T^R and x_T^D where T stands for ties. These policies are more extreme than $\tilde{\theta}_R$ and $\tilde{\theta}_D$. This is because, as emphasized above, there is less moderation with uncertainty about the presidential outcome than with certainty about it. For the reader inclined to work out an example, the case of parties symmetrically located around the median is particularly straightforward.[12]

The polarization induced by hedging leads middle-of-the-road voters to prefer an equilibrium in which the presidential outcome is certain and the legislative vote is tilted in favor of the party not holding the presidency, that is, $\tilde{\theta}_R$ or $\tilde{\theta}_D$ as in Proposition 3.1. Thus moderate voters would prefer to switch their votes in such a way that the presidential tie is broken but the victorious president is balanced by a legislative vote tilted in favor of her opponents. The switch results not just because voters can eliminate the risk connected with the lottery produced by a tie but for a more fundamental reason: the voters obtain an outcome they prefer to either outcome in the lottery.

This switching will occur, as figure 3.3 illustrates, even if the two parties locate symmetrically about the median voter, that is, with $\theta_R = 1 - \theta_D$. In the case of symmetric parties, in a pure presidential regime ($\alpha = 1$), there would be a tie. There would also be a tie in a pure parliamentary regime ($\alpha = 0$). It is the executive–legislative compromise that motivates voters to break the tie. It is now apparent in what sense this institutional structure creates a "coordination problem" for the voters: the need to coordinate in the aggregate arises because of the joint effect on policy formation of the two electoral contests. Moderation can be achieved with an R president and a strong D party in the legislature, or the other way around.

In contrast, if the voters were naïve and merely voted R in all contests if they prefer θ_R to θ_D and vice versa, depending on whether θ_R or θ_D is closer to the median, $\frac{1}{2}$, party R or D would win both the presidency and a majority of Congress. By coordinating to take advantage of the executive–legislative compromise, voters intermediate between θ_D and θ_R can achieve less extreme outcomes more to their liking. This coordination is consistent with sincerity in voting behavior. In fact, conditional on the presidential election, each voter votes with *conditional sincerity* in the legislative election by voting in favor of the party he wishes to see stronger. In the presidential election, given the result of the legislative election (i.e., given V_R), the voters face the choice between two policies, depending on which party wins the presidency. The equilibria of Proposition 3.1 are supported when each voter votes, again with *conditional sincerity*, for the policy (the party) he prefers between the

---

[12]In this case, $\theta_R = 1 - \theta_D$ and $\tilde{\theta}_R = 1 - \tilde{\theta}_D$. Furthermore, the legislative cutpoint if there were a tie would be $\tilde{\theta} = \frac{1}{2}$.

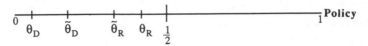

Figure 3.4. Both parties to the same side of the median (1/2). Party R is closer to the median and wins the presidency. There is a unique equilibrium policy outcome, equal to the legislative cutpoint, $\tilde{\theta}_R$.

two.[13] These two conditions of conditional sincerity identify the equilibria of Proposition 3.1.

3.7 DOES R OR D WIN THE PRESIDENCY IN EQUILIBRIUM?

Proposition 3.1 implies that there is a unique equilibrium or two equilibria, depending on parameter values. The punch line is that we have two equilibria when the parties are reasonably symmetrically located around the median; on the contrary, a unique equilibrium emerges when the party positions are asymmetric around the median, that is, when the median voter ideal policy is much closer to the ideal policy of one of the two parties than to the other one. Specifically, in the unique equilibrium the party closer to the median voter wins the presidency, and the other is relatively strong in the legislature. The reader less interested in formal modeling may skip the remainder of this section and proceed to the next one.

Consider a situation in which the two parties have ideal policies tilted toward the left end of the distribution of voters' ideal policies. For instance, as in figure 3.4, assume that both parties are on the left of the median voter: $\theta_D < \theta_R < \frac{1}{2}$. Then, by Proposition 3.1, $\tilde{\theta}_D < \tilde{\theta}_R < \frac{1}{2}$. Clearly, a majority of the voters prefers the outcome with an R president; furthermore, the voters on the right of θ_R, who *always* vote R in both elections, are part of this majority. Thus the outcome with a D presidential victory cannot be an equilibrium.

At the opposite extreme, consider a perfectly symmetric case, as in figure 3.5, where $\theta_D = 0.25$ and $\theta_R = 0.75$. In this case, $\tilde{\theta}_D$ and $\tilde{\theta}_R$ are also symmetric; for instance if $\alpha = \frac{1}{2}$, we have $\tilde{\theta}_D = 0.4$ and $\tilde{\theta}_R = 0.6$. The median voter (with a bliss point of 0.5) is indifferent between the policies $x^D = \tilde{\theta}_D = 0.4$ and $x^R = \tilde{\theta}_R = 0.75$. Intuitively, if the parties are perfectly symmetric, as in the example above, both outcomes ($\tilde{\theta}_D$ and $\tilde{\theta}_R$) are equilibria. The voters can

---

[13]In the language of game theory, each voter has a conditionally "weakly dominant strategy". Note that this strategy is only weakly dominant because of the effect of non-pivotal voters in this majority-rule election. Thus, as shown in the appendix, a majority that is voting sincerely must be supporting the winner, but voters who are not part of this majority are free to "spoil" their ballots.

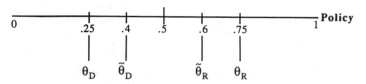

Figure 3.5. Parties symmetric about the median. There are two equilibria, $\tilde{\theta}_D$ and $\tilde{\theta}_R$. The numerical values shown represent the case where the president and the legislature have equal weight in policy formation ($\alpha = 1/2$).

achieve the same amount of moderation by favoring one party for the executive and the other one in the legislature. Given the perfect symmetry, there is no way of picking one outcome over the other.

The more general case is one in which the two parties are on opposite sides of the median but are not perfectly symmetric. Here we have one or two equilibria, depending on the degree of asymmetry: if the two parties are "almost" symmetric, two equilibria emerge; otherwise we have only one equilibrium. An illustration of this result sheds light on the nature of the equilibrium concept we use. The basic idea of the following example is that even if, say, θ_R is closer to the median than θ_D, the equilibrium with a D president may not be overturned for lack of a "credible" coalition of voters willing to switch the presidential outcome to the R party.

Consider a small change in the example of figure 3.5: in figure 3.6, we

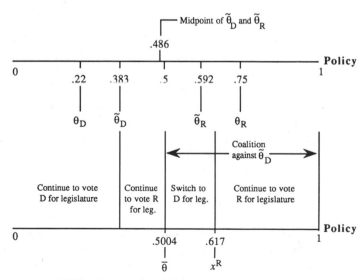

Figure 3.6. R slightly closer to the median than D. Two equilibria persist since the largest credible coalition against $\tilde{\theta}_D$ fails to be a majority. Numerical values shown are for $\alpha = 1/2$.

have $\theta_D = 0.22$; $\theta_R = 0.75$, $\alpha = \frac{1}{2}$. Now θ_D is further from the median than θ_R, and with these parameter values, $\tilde{\theta}_D = 0.383$, $\tilde{\theta}_R = 0.592$; $\tilde{\theta}_R$ is slightly closer to 0.5 than $\tilde{\theta}_D$, and, as a result, a majority of the voters strictly prefers the equilibrium in which $\tilde{\theta}_R$ is the policy outcome and R is president. In fact, the midpoint between $\tilde{\theta}_R$ and $\tilde{\theta}_D$ is on the left of 0.5, as shown in figure 3.6. It is intuitive that the $\tilde{\theta}_R$ outcome is an equilibrium, and the question is whether $\tilde{\theta}_D$ can also be one. Consider the outcome if D is president. Would any group of voters want to change either its presidential or its legislative vote or both? If the answer to this question is affirmative, the outcome is not an equilibrium.

Clearly, the voters most interested in changing their vote are the right-wing voters, who prefer the outcome $\tilde{\theta}_R$ to $\tilde{\theta}_D$: specifically, all the voters on the right of $(\tilde{\theta}_D + \tilde{\theta}_R)/2$ prefer $\tilde{\theta}_R$. In order to achieve $\tilde{\theta}_R$, all of these voters must be willing to vote R for president. If the voters on the right of $(\tilde{\theta}_D + \tilde{\theta}_R)/2$ elect an R president, however, they cannot switch the policy outcome from $\tilde{\theta}_D$ to $\tilde{\theta}_R$. To move from $\tilde{\theta}_D$ to $\tilde{\theta}_R$, voters in between $\tilde{\theta}_D$ and $(\tilde{\theta}_D + \tilde{\theta}_R)/2$ would have to switch their legislative vote from R to D. But these voters would not agree to do so, because they prefer $\tilde{\theta}_D$ to $\tilde{\theta}_R$.

Indeed, a credible right-wing coalition that would overturn $\tilde{\theta}_D$ must meet three requirements. First, it cannot include any voters to the left of $\bar{\theta}$, the voter type who is indifferent between $\tilde{\theta}_D$ and x^R, the new policy that results when R is president. Second, the only members of the coalition who can credibly shift their legislative votes to D are those voters to the left of x^R. Third, voters not in the coalition must be assumed to maintain the legislative votes given by the cutpoint $\tilde{\theta}_D$. These three requirements imply that the policy x^R is to the right of $\tilde{\theta}_R$, as there are fewer D legislative votes than with the cutpoint $\tilde{\theta}_R$ (see figure 3.6). But, since x^R is to the right of $\tilde{\theta}_R$, the median voter (bliss point of $\frac{1}{2}$) may prefer $\tilde{\theta}_D$ to x^R, even though he prefers $\tilde{\theta}_R$ to $\tilde{\theta}_D$. In the figure, we show that the largest possible right-wing coalition will have $\bar{\theta}$ to the right of the median. Consequently, there is no majority coalition that can overturn $\tilde{\theta}_D$ and elect R president. Thus the outcome with a D president and $\tilde{\theta}_D$ as the policy *is* an equilibrium, because it cannot be defeated by any group of voters making a credible change in its vote. More specifically, no group of voters can change its vote and achieve a policy outcome that every member of the group prefers to $\tilde{\theta}_D$.

As in figure 3.5, we have two equilibria in figure 3.6. The two equilibria reflected the fact that we had moved θ_D only to 0.22 from its original location of 0.25. As θ_D is moved further leftward and the degree of asymmetry thus increased, the equilibrium associated with a D president eventually disappears. For $\alpha = 0.5$ and $\theta_R = 0.75$, the critical value is 0.205. Once the D location is further left than 0.205, there is a unique equilibrium where R is president. Such a situation is illustrated by figure 3.7, where $\theta_D = 0.05$ with $\tilde{\theta}_D = 0.296$. In this case, a defecting coalition can be built with $\bar{\theta}$ to

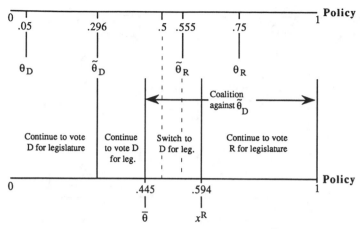

Figure 3.7. R much closer to the median than D. Only $\tilde{\theta}_R$ is an equilibrium. A majority coalition that is credible can form against $\tilde{\theta}_D$. Numerical values shown are for $\alpha = 1/2$.

the left of the median. The coalition is thus large enough to change the outcome of the presidential election from D to R, implying that $\tilde{\theta}_D$ is not an equilibrium.

Analogous arguments apply to the case in which θ_D is closer to the median than θ_R.

3.8 THE POSSIBILITY OF DIVIDED GOVERNMENT

Proposition 3.1 has two important substantive implications:

1. Divided government. For a range of parameter values government is divided; the party winning the presidency does not obtain a majority in Congress. For the range of parameter values for which two equilibria exist, divided government always occurs, but division emerges also for a large set of parameter values that admit only one equilibrium. In addition to θ_D and θ_R, the third parameter that influences the occurrence of divided government (and the number of equilibria) is α, the influence on policy of the president relative to the legislature.

Figure 3.8 highlights the range of parameter values for which the various outcomes occur. Note that these pictures are drawn for the more interesting case in which θ_D and θ_R are on opposite sides of the median. The case in which they are on the same side is trivial: for any value of α there is only one equilibrium and no divided government. Indeed, even if θ_D and θ_R are on opposite sides of the median, if $\tilde{\theta}_D$ and $\tilde{\theta}_R$ are on the same side of the median, there is only one equilibrium and no divided government.

63

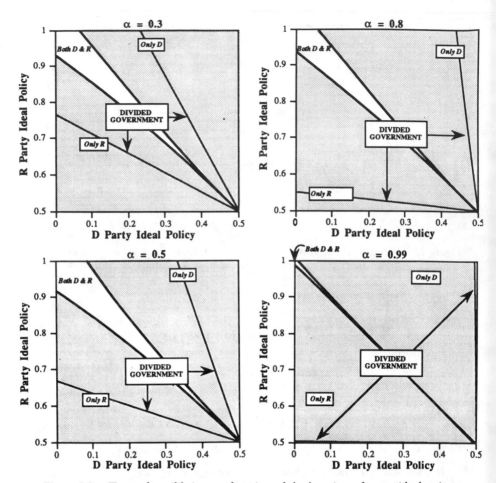

Figure 3.8. Type of equilibria as a function of the location of party ideal points. Each panel covers only ideal points on opposite sides of the median. (When parties are on the same side of the median, there is a unique equilibrium. See figure 3.4.) The value of the presidential power parameter (α) is indicated above each panel. In the panels, "Only R" indicates the region where there is a unique equilibrium with R president. In this case, R is much closer to the median than D. Conversely, "Only D" indicates the region where D is president. "Both D and R" indicates the region with two equilibria. "Divided Government" shows the region where the president's party does not have a majority in the legislature.

When α is high (when the executive is very powerful relative to the legislature), divided government generally occurs, unless the parties are very asymmetrically located around the median, indicating that a large majority of the electorate clearly prefers one party over the other. If the executive is very strong, in order to "moderate", the voters need to make the party not

64

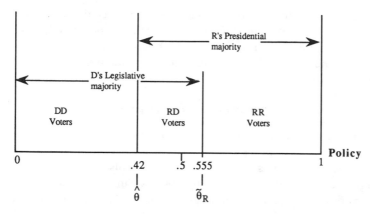

Figure 3.9. Split tickets and divided government. Voters between the legislative cutpoint $\tilde{\theta}_R$ and the presidential cutpoint $\hat{\theta}$ split their tickets, voting R for president and D for the legislature. The parameters are those of figure 3.7.

holding the presidency very strong in the legislature. In the face of an all-powerful president, the legislature is handed to the opposition. On the contrary, when the legislature is strong relative to the presidency, divided government is less likely to occur.

A typical configuration of a divided government outcome is shown in figure 3.9, where $\hat{\theta}$ represents the cutpoint for the presidential election (with an R victory). We have three types of voters: RR voters, on the right of $\tilde{\theta}_R$, who vote R in both elections; RD voters, in between $\hat{\theta}$ and $\tilde{\theta}_R$, who split their ticket by voting R for the presidency and D for the legislature; DD voters, on the left of $\hat{\theta}$, who vote D in both elections. Thus we have ticket splitting of only one type: nobody votes D for the presidency and R for the legislature.

The position of the cutpoint for the presidential election, $\hat{\theta}$, is, strictly speaking, indeterminate given the majority rule in this election. That is, if an R presidential victory (with $\tilde{\theta}_R$ as the legislative cutpoint) is the equilibrium, then all that is required to support the equilibrium is that $\hat{\theta}$ be on the left of $\frac{1}{2}$. Of course, the conditionally sincere cutpoint, $\hat{\theta}_R = [\tilde{\theta}_R + \theta_D + K(1 - \tilde{\theta}_R)]/2$, satisfies this requirement.[14] The indeterminacy in the cutpoint is eliminated when the presidential outcome is uncertain, as in the model developed in chapter 4.

2. *No midterm cycle.* Given that in both periods the legislative vote is identical, there is no midterm cycle: the party holding the presidency does

[14]When preferences are symmetric, the conditionally sincere presidential cutpoint is just the average of the outcome with R president and the outcome that corresponds to D being elected president with the R president equilibrium legislative vote.

not lose votes in the midterm legislative elections relative to the previous ones. This feature of the equilibrium highlights that, in our model, uncertainty is crucial for the midterm cycle. We obtain a midterm cycle only in chapter 4, where we make the model more realistic by adding uncertainty about voter preferences.

3.9 GENERALIZATIONS

The main qualitative conclusions of this chapter continue to hold even if we do not make some of the special assumptions we have made to facilitate the discussion. (See the appendix for formal proofs.)

First, the distribution of voter ideal points can be generalized to allow for densities that are continuous and always positive, as illustrated in figure 2.3.

Second, the functions that describe the nature of the "compromise" between the executive and legislature can be any functions that are continuous and strictly monotonic in the legislative voting. If party D is president, we could have:

$$x^D = \theta_D + g_D(V_R)$$

with g_D strictly increasing in V_R and $g_D(0) = 0$; if R is president, the policy function becomes

$$x^R = \theta_R - g_R(V_D)$$

with g_R strictly increasing in V_D and $g_R(0) = 0$. We do, as seems natural, need to constrain these functions in such a way that, for any level of the legislative vote, policy is always more to the left when D is president than when R is president:

$$\theta_D + g_D(V_R) < \theta_R + g_R(1 - V_R)$$

Third, our results continue to hold if we allow for alternative rules for breaking exact ties. We could allow for an unfair coin to be tossed or the election to be awarded by some arbitrary rule to one of the two candidates.

With these more general assumptions, the pivotal-voter theorem continues to hold. Actual policy must represent the ideal point of the pivotal voter in the legislative elections. Moreover, equilibria continue to be characterized by split-ticket voting, and the possibility of divided government persists.

3.10 "MAJORITARIAN" MODELS: CONDITIONALLY SINCERE AND UNCONDITIONALLY SINCERE VOTING COMPARED

The basic idea that divided government is the result of the voters' desire to achieve moderate, middle-of-the-road policies also underlies indepen-

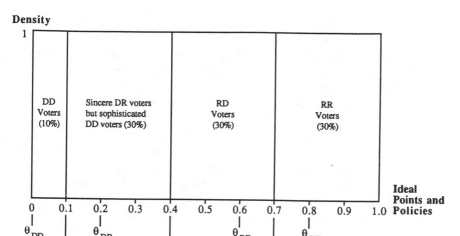

Figure 3.10.   Voting in the Fiorina model. There are only four possible policies, θ_{DD}, θ_{DR}, θ_{RD}, and θ_{RR}. The figure also indicates the midpoints (m) between adjacent policies.

dent work by Fiorina (1988). In this section we highlight similarities and differences between his model and the one just presented.

Fiorina considers a majoritarian model, so that only four policy outcomes are available (see figure 3.10): these are the outcomes corresponding to the four possible combinations of majorities in the two branches of government. Using our notation, we would have:

$$
\begin{aligned}
x^D &= \theta_{DD} && \text{if D president and } V_R \leqslant 0.5 \\
x^D &= \theta_{DR} && \text{if D president and } V_R > 0.5 \\
x^R &= \theta_{RD} && \text{if R president and } V_R < 0.5 \\
x^R &= \theta_{RR} && \text{if R president and } V_R \geqslant 0.5,
\end{aligned}
\tag{3.9}
$$

with $\theta_{DD} < \theta_{DR} < \theta_{RD} < \theta_{RR}$.

Our formulation of the policy formation process (i.e., the "share" model of equations (3.1) and (3.2)) and Fiorina's formulation (equation (3.9)) are clearly different, but not fundamentally so. Fiorina's model implies a discrete change in the policy outcome when the majority in the legislature switches hands. In our model, we have a continuum of possible policies (as opposed to four) and we do *not* have a discontinuity at $V_R = \frac{1}{2}$, when the majority in the legislature switches. Our model, however, can closely approximate such a discontinuity by choosing the functions $g(\cdot)$ (see section 3.9) so that they change value abruptly around $V_R = \frac{1}{2}$.

The more important difference is that Fiorina considers only *uncondi-*

tionally sincere voting. As shown in figure 3.10, an unconditionally sincere voter votes in the two contests by computing which of the four possible policy outcomes he most prefers and votes accordingly. There will be three cutpoints, as shown in figure 3.10: m_1 separates the voters who prefer a unified D government from those who prefer a divided government with D president; m_2 separates those who prefer a divided government with D president from one with R president; and, finally, m_3 separates those who prefer R president but with divided government to a unified R government.

What if, for example, voters were uniformly distributed, as we assumed earlier in the chapter, and $\theta_{DD} = 0$, $\theta_{DR} = 0.2$, $\theta_{RD} = 0.6$, and $\theta_{RR} = 0.8$? If voters have symmetric utility, such as the quadratic function shown in chapter 2, figure 2.1, which of these four outcomes a voter most prefers is simply the outcome closest to the voter ideal policies so that $m_1 = 0.1$, $m_2 = 0.4$, and $m_3 = 0.7$. The crucial difference between coordinating voters as in our framework and "globally" or "unconditionally" sincere voters as in Fiorina's model is the following. Each "globally sincere" voter chooses the party, or combination of parties, delivering the policy outcome closest to his bliss point. In our model, voters are only conditionally sincere: given the outcome of one election, they vote sincerely in the other election. That is, *some voters vote differently in legislative elections depending on the outcome of presidential elections.*

In the example of figure 3.10, the voters who most prefer a unified Democratic government are those to the left of 0.1, which is halfway between 0 and 0.2, the outcome with government divided between a D president and an R legislature. Since the distribution of voters is uniform, voters to the left of 0.1 are 10 percent of the electorate. Thus, unconditionally sincere voting would lead to a 10 percent DD vote. Similarly, as figure 3.10 illustrates, the vote would be 30 percent DR, 30 percent RD, and 30 percent RR. Consequently, although tickets would be split, the Republicans would get 60 percent of both the presidential and the congressional vote: there would be unified government. Now consider those voters between 0.1 and 0.4 who voted DR. They face their worst possible outcome, a unified R government. Suppose they vote DD instead of DR. In this case, R continues to win the presidency but D wins the legislature by a 70–30 margin. We thus have an equilibrium with divided government, and those voters between 0.1 and 0.4 are better off than before. Moreover, under conditionally sincere voting, there is just one type of ticket-splitting, RD.

Let us check, for each group of voters, whether our outcome makes sense. The 30 percent of the electorate between 0.4 and 0.7 get their first choice, so clearly they will want to continue to vote RD. The leftmost group of voters, those voting DD, want to see both institutions D, so they have no motivation to switch. Similarly, the RR voters have a dominant strategy of voting R in both contests. This leaves the 30 percent of the electorate between 0.1 and 0.4 who are now voting DD. Voting DR or RR would only make them worse off; voting RD would leave the outcome unchanged.[15]

In summary, voters between 0.1 and 0.4 are left-of-center "moderates". Their preferred outcome, therefore, is DR, and according to Fiorina's model they vote that way. But these voters know that, given party policies and voter preferences, D is a losing presidential candidate. Since they know that they will face an R president, according to our model they vote D in the legislature to moderate the president. These are the voters who adjust their legislative vote depending on which party holds the presidency.

As captured by the following proposition, we find that our coordinating, or conditionally sincere, voting model leads to more divided government than the unconditionally sincere voting model. More precisely, we can establish the following result.

Proposition 3.2
Whenever divided government occurs for sincere voting and the policy formation process is the one of equation (3.9), it also occurs in the equilibrium with "conditionally sincere" voting. Moreover, in some cases where unconditionally sincere voting produces unified government, conditionally sincere voting produces divided government.

We provide only an informal proof, which can be skipped by the reader not interested in formalization, who may proceed directly to the concluding section.

Under conditionally sincere voting, unified government will occur only if:

$$\text{A majority of the voters are to the right of } m_3 \qquad (3.10)$$

or

$$\text{A majority of the voters are to the left of } m_1 \qquad (3.11)$$

Otherwise, a majority prefers divided government to either form of unified government, and divided government will be the outcome to our game. In contrast, under unconditionally sincere voting, unified government will occur only if:

More than half the electorate are to the right of m_2 and more than half the electorate are in the two intervals $[m_1, m_2]$ and $[m_3, 1]$ $\qquad (3.12)$

or

More than half the electorate are to the left of m_2 and more than half the electorate are in the two intervals $[0, m_1]$ and $[m_2, m_3]$. $\qquad (3.13)$

---

[15]Exercise left to the reader. Show that divided government with a D president and an R legislature is not an equilibrium for this example.

Since the condition (3.10) implies (3.12) and the condition (3.11) implies (3.13), the proposition follows immediately. Our example in fact illustrated a situation where globally sincere voting led to unified government in a case where conditionally sincere voting implied divided government.

Proposition 3.2 is quite general in that it is valid for all continuous distributions of voter preferences and not just the uniform distribution. In addition, it does not require any symmetries in the positions of the four policies. *We conclude that divided government is fostered by voter sophistication.*[16]

Fiorina's model is the cleanest illustration of a majoritarian model. Note that in the example shown in figure 3.10, the *conditionally sincere* outcome corresponded to the policy of θ_{RD}, the policy most preferred by the median voter ($\frac{1}{2}$). This result holds more generally.

Proposition 3.3

In any majoritarian model, the voter equilibrium selects the policy most preferred by the median voter, unless the median voter is indifferent between two policies (one to her left, the other to her right). In this case, either of the two policies represents a voter equilibrium.

Proposition 3.3 is proved formally by Ingberman and Rosenthal (1994).[17] Here we give the basic intuition. If the outcome represents the median voter's preferred policy, to change the outcome will require the median voter's participation in the switch, given that all contests are majoritarian. Obviously, the median voter has no interest in switching the outcome. If the outcome were to the left of the median voter's preferred policy, the median voter and all the voters to her right could be better off by pivoting to the median voter's most preferred outcome. (Thus voters would not be voting with *conditional sincerity* if the outcomes were not the median voter's preferred

---

[16]Other work roots divided government in the preferences of the parties rather than those of the voters. More specifically, Ingberman and Villani (1993) have proposed a different rationalization for divided government based on the risk aversion of the two parties. They consider two parties that are purely electoralist, and not partisan. In a standard two-candidate election, the two parties would converge (see chapter 2), and the election would be defined by a fair coin toss. Consider now the executive–legislative interaction, and suppose, again, that the two parties adopt the same platform: once again, the voters vote either D or R in both elections, and both elections are decided by a coin toss. It follows that each party has a .25 probability of holding both the executive and the legislature, .5 probability of holding one of the two (.25 each), .25 probability of holding nothing. Suppose, instead, that the two parties adopt divergent policies on opposite sides of the median voter; this outcome leads to divided government with certainty. That is, each party wins a majority in one of the two institutions for sure. Thus in the case of non-convergence, each party is sure of winning one contest. In the case of full convergence, the parties face a lottery with four possible outcomes. Because of risk aversion, the two parties prefer the "sure" divided government to the lottery.

[17]These authors show that such outcomes are always Strong Nash equilibria.

policy.) A similar remark applies to outcomes to the right of the median voter's preferred policy.

Proposition 3.3 is a powerful result. It represents a generalization of the median voter theorem to a variety of institutional scenarios. Rather than Fiorina's model, which has four policies, consider the following illustration of an executive veto model. There is a status quo point between the two parties' ideal points. Then there are only three possible policies: party D's ideal point, party R's, and the status quo, the latter arising under both forms of divided government. Proposition 3.3 says that the equilibrium will be whichever of these policies is most preferred by the median voter. The executive veto model nicely illustrates the point we made about "gridlock" in chapter 1. If the status quo represents "gridlock", "gridlock" occurs because it is the available policy most preferred by the median voter.

3.11 CONCLUSIONS

When voters coordinate by using conditionally sincere strategies, they will always temper the preferences of the two polarized parties. When a Republican is president, policy is pulled to her left by Congress; conversely, policy is pulled to the right under a Democratic president. Nonetheless, the voters are unable to force full convergence in policy. It is impossible to push policy away from the president and past the ideal point of the pivotal voter in the legislative elections: these pivotal legislative voters, not the overall median voter, determine policy.[18]

Who is the pivotal voter depends, in midterm elections, on who is the president. In on-year elections, who is the pivotal voter depends on who the voters believe will win the presidency. With complete information concerning voter preferences, there is no uncertainty about the outcome of presidential elections, even *a priori*. Thus the voters know, before they ever go to the polls, who will be president. As a result, the legislative vote in on-year and midterm elections is identical. There is no midterm effect in a complete information setting.

The case of complete information is clearly a simplification of a more complex reality. Nevertheless, this simple case is consistent with two observations about American politics: first, the widely observed phenomenon of ticket splitting; second, the fact that divided government is a distinct possibility. Moreover, divided government is more likely when voters are sophisticated, conditionally sincere voters rather than naïve or unconditionally sincere.

We have provided a rational choice explanation for ticket splitting and

---

[18]Of course, there are knife-edge cases where the pivotal voter happens to be the median voter.

divided government that holds even when parties are homogeneous – so there is no candidate "personality" reason for ticket splitting – and when there is no favoritism to incumbents. We view this result as an important achievement, since divided government arose even before World War II, when the incumbency advantage (Fiorina (1989)) was much less, as were also, perhaps, the personal appeals of individual candidates. Nonetheless, complete information fails to grasp the uncertainty each voter has concerning the preferences of his fellow citizens and fails to account for the presence of a midterm cycle. Therefore, in the next chapter we study the situation in which uncertainty is explicitly taken into consideration.

Appendix to chapter 3

This appendix presents a technical treatment of the model discussed in chapter 3.

Description of the game

Political parties

There are two parties described by θ_D and θ_R, $\theta_D \leqslant \theta_R$. The parties are not players in the game; θ_D and θ_R are parameters.

Voters

There is a continuum of voters I indexed by i. I is described by the cumulative distribution function $H(i)$. We assume H is continuous and strictly increasing on (θ_D, θ_R).

Utility

Voter utility takes the form $U_i = u_i(x_1, i) + \beta u_i(x_2, i)$ where x_1, x_2, denote the policies in periods 1 and 2 and $0 \leqslant \beta \leqslant 1$. The function u_i is assumed to be single-peaked and differentiable in x.

More precisely, $u_i(,\cdot)$ is *single-peaked* if $u_i(w, i) < u_i(z, i)$ if $w < z \leqslant i$ or if $w > z \geqslant i$, with the index i denoting the *ideal point* of the voter. The notation u_i is used to indicate that voters may differ not only in their ideal points but in the "shape" of the utility function.

Voter preferences satisfy the *Single Crossing Property* (SCP) if for every pair of two-period policies $w = (w_1, w_2)$, $z = (z_1, z_2)$ such that $w, z \in [\theta_D, \theta_R] \times [\theta_D, \theta_R]$ and such that $i = \theta_D$ strictly prefers w to z, there is a unique indifferent voter type θ^* and if $i < \theta^*$, i prefers w to z and if $i > \theta^*$, i prefers z to w.

73

Note that single-peakedness does not imply SCP. However, if u_i is Euclidean (symmetric about i), then, since U_i is intertemporally additive, preferences satisfy SCP.

Voting

Each voter's action can be characterized by a vote triple $v_i = (v_i^{E1}, v_i^{L1}, v_i^{L2})$, where E indicates the election of the executive, L indicates the elections of the legislature, and "1" and "2" the two time periods, with $v_i \in \{D, R\} \times \{D, R\} \times \{D, R\}$. The measure of voters undertaking an action is denoted $\sigma(\cdot)$.

Let $V_R^{E1} = \sigma(i: v_R^{E1} = R)$. Define V_R^{L1}, V_R^{L2} similarly. Also, for each component, let $V_D = 1 - V_R$.

Electoral and policy outcomes

If $V_R^{E1} > \frac{1}{2}$, R is president at $t = 1$ and $t = 2$, if $V_R^{E1} < \frac{1}{2}$, D is president at $t = 1$ and $t = 2$, and if $V_R^{E1} = \frac{1}{2}$, the presidency at $t = 1$ and $t = 2$ is awarded on the basis of a fair coin toss at $t = 1$.

In period t, $t \in \{1, 2\}$, policy is given by:

$$x_t = \theta_R - g_R(V_D^{Lt}) \text{ if R is president at } t, \tag{3.A1}$$

$$x_t = \theta_D + g_D(V_R^{Lt}) \text{ if D is president at } t. \tag{3.A2}$$

The $g(\cdot)$ functions, which generalize the linear functions in the text, are strictly monotone increasing and differentiable, with

$$g(0) = 0 \tag{3.A3}$$

and

$$g(1) \leqslant \theta_R - \theta_D. \tag{3.A4}$$

Assumptions (3.A1)–(3.A4) guarantee that policies are always between the ideal points of the two parties: $\theta_D \leqslant x \leqslant \theta_R$.

Additional restrictions must be imposed on the g functions to ensure that policy with a D president is always to the left of policy with an R president. This is true when $g_D(\cdot) = g_R(\cdot)$. More, generally, we would require:

$$\theta_R - g_R(H(\theta)) \geqslant \theta_D + g_D(1 - H(\theta)) \quad \text{for all } \theta, \, \theta_D < \theta < \theta_R \tag{3.A5}$$

Our characterization of equilibrium depends critically on the assumption of (3.A5), SCP, and single-peakedness.

Randomization has no strategic purpose, so we simplify matters by considering only pure strategies. Voter strategies can be described as

$s_i = (s_i^{E1}, s_i^{L1}, s_i^{L2D}, s_i^{L2R}) \in \{D, R\} \times \{D, R\} \times \{D, R\} \times \{D, R\}$, with the third and fourth components expressing the conditioning of second-period votes on the outcome of the presidential election in the first period. In other words, our game has two possible sub-games, one induced by an R presidential victory, the other induced by a D victory. We use s to denote the set of strategies used by all voters in I. We denote the strategies implied by s in the two sub-games by s_R, s_D and denote the votes induced by s by $V_R^{E1}(s)$, $V_R^{L1}(s)$, $V_R^{L2D}(s)$, $V_R^{L2R}(s)$. The argument (s) is dropped when the meaning is clear.

Conditional sincerity

Let $EU_i(s)$ denote voter i's expected utility for strategy s. The expectations operator is needed because of the knife-edge possibility of a tied presidential contest. Let $\partial EU_i(s)/\partial V_R^{Lt}$ denote the partial derivative of i's expected utility with respect to a change in the legislative vote implied by s. This partial derivative exists as a consequence of the differentiability of u and g. At $t=1$, a voter votes with *conditional sincerity* in the legislative elections if

$$\partial EU_i(s)/\partial V_R^{L1} > 0 \Rightarrow s_i^{L1} = R$$
$$\partial EU_i(s)/\partial V_R^{L1} < 0 \Rightarrow s_i^{L1} = D$$
$$\partial EU_i(s)/\partial V_R^{L1} = 0 \Rightarrow s_i^{L1} = R \text{ or } D$$

The situation is similar for the second period, except that we must take into account, for example, that if s implies R president, the partial derivative with respect to V_R^{L2D} is 0 for all i. We, however, require conditional sincerity even "off the equilibrium path". For example, voters must be prepared to vote with conditional sincerity when D is president in the second period even though their strategies imply R elected president in period 1. At $t=2$, a voter votes with conditional sincerity in the legislative elections if:

$$\partial EU_i(s_j)/\partial V_R^{L2J} > 0 \Rightarrow s_i^{L2J} = R$$
$$\partial EU_i(s_j)/\partial V_R^{L2J} < 0 \Rightarrow s_i^{L2J} = D \qquad \text{for } J \in \{D, R\}$$
$$\partial EU_i(s_j)/\partial V_R^{L2J} = 0 \Rightarrow s_i^{L2J} = R \text{ or } D$$

Note that, if s implies that a sub-game can be reached at $t=2$, the partial derivative for the sub-game and the partial derivative for the entire game have identical signs.

Presidential elections are different: if strategies do not imply a tie, the partial derivatives are zero for all voters. If they do imply a tie, the partial derivatives do not exist. Therefore, we must state the definition of conditional sincerity in terms of discrete changes. The notation ΔV below denotes a discrete change in V and ΔEU the induced change in EU. A voter votes with conditional sincerity in the presidential election if:

(a) $V_R^{E1} = \frac{1}{2}$ and

$$\Delta EU_i(s) > 0 \text{ if } \Delta V_R^{E1} > 0 \Rightarrow s_i^{E1} = R$$
$$\Delta EU_i(s) < 0 \text{ if } \Delta V_R^{E1} > 0 \Rightarrow s_i^{E1} = D$$
$$\Delta EU_i(s) = 0 \text{ if } \Delta V_R^{E1} > 0 \Rightarrow s_i^{E1} = R \text{ or } D$$

(b) $V_R^{E1} < \frac{1}{2}$ and

$$\Delta EU_i(s) > 0 \text{ for some } \Delta V_R^{E1} > 0 \Rightarrow s_i^{E1} = R$$
$$\Delta EU_i(s) < 0 \text{ for some } \Delta V_R^{E1} > 0 \Rightarrow s_i^{E1} = D$$
$$\Delta EU_i(s) = 0 \text{ for all } \quad \Delta V_R^{E1} > 0 \Rightarrow s_i^{E1} = R \text{ or } D$$

(c) $V_R^{E1} > \frac{1}{2}$ Conditions symmetric to case (b).

Note that in case (a) any positive change in V makes R the presidential winner and any negative change makes D the winner; in case (b), majority rule implies that changes in utility can result only if ΔV is large enough to change the outcome.

With respect to the presidential contest, conditional sincerity is equivalent to using the weakly dominant strategy in the binary choice among presidential candidates, assuming the legislative components of strategies are fixed. Similar recourse to weak dominance leads to the assumption that a voter chooses the closer of the two candidates in standard spatial models of two candidate elections.

A strategy s_i is a *conditionally sincere voter strategy* if it is conditionally sincere in all components.

Equilibrium

A strategy profile **s** represents a *Conditionally Sincere Voter Equilibrium* if every s_i in **s** is conditionally sincere.

A strategy profile **s** represents a *Stable Conditionally Sincere Voter Equilibrium* if (a) **s** is conditionally sincere and (b) there does not exist $I_s \subset I$ and strategy **r** such that $r_i = s_i$ if $i \notin I_s$, and $EU_i(\mathbf{r}) > EU_i(\mathbf{s})$ and r_i is conditionally sincere if $i \in I_s$.

That is, stability requires that **s** be immune from a deviation by a "coalition" I_s that can improve the utility of all its members while maintaining conditional sincerity. (Note that, under **r**, the votes of I/I_s may no longer be conditionally sincere.)

The second period

In the second period, relevant only if $\beta > 0$, the president is fixed. Without loss of generality, take it to be R. Each voter's strategy set is $\{D, R\}$. The relevant utility in the sub-game is $u_i(x_2, i) = u_i(\theta_R - g_R(V_D^{L2}), i)$.

Appendix to chapter 3

Proposition 1: Pivotal-voter theorem

There exists a unique conditionally sincere voter equilibrium where voter strategies satisfy a cutpoint rule, denoted $\tilde{\theta}_R$, such that $x_2 = \tilde{\theta}_R$ and all voters with $\theta_i < \tilde{\theta}_R$ vote D and all voters with $\theta_i > \tilde{\theta}_R$ vote R.

Proof:

Assume not. Without loss of generality, assume $x_2 > i$ for some i with $s_i^{L2R} = R$. By the monotonicity of g_R, $s_i^{L2R} = R$ is not conditionally sincere if i's preferences are single-peaked. Thus, s that is not cutpoint with $x_2 = \tilde{\theta}_R$ cannot be conditionally sincere. Conversely, single-peakedness implies that a cutpoint s with $x_2 = \tilde{\theta}_R$ is conditionally sincere. That such s is unique follows directly from the fact that g_R is monotone increasing so x_2 is a monotone decreasing and continuous mapping of V_D into the interval $[\theta_D, \theta_R]$ and that for cutpoints θ, $V_D = H(\theta)$ is continuous and monotone increasing on $[\theta_D, \theta_R]$

Q.E.D.

Corollary 1.1

$\tilde{\theta}_R$ represents a stable conditionally sincere equilibrium.

Proof:

In the $t = 2$ sub-game, there is only one voting decision. At $x_2 = \tilde{\theta}_R$, voters voting R can increase their utility only through a decrease in V_D while the opposite is true for voters voting D. Hence, there is no I_s and associated strategy r that renders $\tilde{\theta}_R$ unstable.

Q.E.D.

Corollary 1.2

$\tilde{\theta}_R$ is found as the unique solution to:

$$\tilde{\theta}_R = \theta_R - g_R(V_R) \tag{3.A6}$$

$$V_D = H(\tilde{\theta}_R) \tag{3.A7}$$

Comments

1. If D is president, there is an analogous equilibrium denoted $\tilde{\theta}_D$.
2. In the text, we assumed:

$$x^R = \theta_R - K(1 - V_R) = \theta_R - KV_D \tag{3.4}$$

   We also assumed H uniform or $V_D = \tilde{\theta}_R$. Substituting $\tilde{\theta}_R$ for V_D and x^R in (3.4) and solving gives the expression for $\tilde{\theta}_R$ in (3.8).

3. With regard to the function g_R, neither continuity not differentiability nor strict monotonicity is critical. What is critical to our results is weak monotonicity. This point was in fact illustrated by voting for the legislature in the majoritarian function in the Fiorina example of section 3.10. In this case, the median voter, given the identity of the president, picks between two possible policies. In fact, voting for the legislature in

the majoritarian case is directly analogous to presidential voting. See Proposition 2, below.

4. Our results go through if a tied election is decided by the toss of an "unfair" coin where D wins the presidency with probability q, $0 < q < 1$.

5. In the case of a finite set of voters, two problems can arise. The first is that while voters on the left may vote D and those on the right vote R, the pivotal voter theorem may not hold in that policy may not equal the ideal point of the pivotal voter. The second is that stability may result even when the voters are not split by a cutpoint. While equilibria with finite voters are nonetheless qualitatively similar to those with a continuum of voters, the technical problems introduced by discreteness led us to work with a continuum.

The first period of the two-period model

We begin our analysis of the two-period model by imposing $\beta = 0$ to isolate the role of the first period.

Presidential voting

Assume that a strategy s implies a first-period legislative vote V_R^{L1}. Then (3.A1) and (3.A2) imply that there are only two possible first-period policies, $x_R(s)$ and $x_D(s)$.

Proposition 2 ($\beta = 0$)

Presidential voting for strategy s is conditionally sincere if and only if all v_i^{E1} follow a cutpoint rule with the cutpoint $\hat{\theta}$ given by:

$$u_i(\theta_R - g_R(1 - V_R^{L1}), i) = u_i(\theta_D + g_D(V_R^{L1}), i) \qquad \text{for } i = \hat{\theta}$$

Proof:
Follows directly from SCP and the observation that, conditional on the legislative vote, the voter has a binary choice. Q.E.D.

Proposition 3 (No ties, $\beta = 0$)

If s has $V_R^{E1} = \frac{1}{2}$, s is not a stable conditionally sincere equilibrium.
Proof:
By Proposition 2, if s is conditionally sincere in the presidential vote, s is characterized by $\hat{\theta}$ such that $H(\hat{\theta}) = \frac{1}{2}$. From single-peakedness, the indifference of the voter at $\hat{\theta}$, and (3.A.5), it must be the case that $x_D < \hat{\theta} < x_R$. By the continuity of H, and (3.A3) and (3.A4) there must exist a voter with ideal point x_R. For this voter, $\partial u/\partial x_R = 0$ and $\partial u/\partial x_D > 0$, implying $\partial u/\partial V_R^{L1} > 0$. This voter must vote R under s to

satisfy conditional sincerity. By the continuity of H and single-peakedness, there must exist other voters $i \in (\hat{\theta}, x_R)$ with $s_i^{L1} = R$. A measurable set, A, of these voters can adopt strategies $r_i^{L1} = D$, $r_i^{E1} = R$ such that, if no other strategies were altered, the R president policy would be x'_R satisfying $\sup_A i < x'_R < x_R$. Moreover, by the indifference of $\hat{\theta}$ under s and the continuity of H, there must be voters with $i \in (x_D, \hat{\theta})$ who prefer x'_R to both x_R and x_D. Designate these voters as B. There thus exists a set $I_s \subset (A \cup B)$ and strategy r with $r_i^{L1} = D$, $r_i^{E1} = R$ for $i \in I_s$, $r_i = s_i$ for $i \in I/I_s$ such that R wins the presidency and $x_1(r) < x_R$ is preferred to both x_R and x_D. It is direct to show that I_s satisfies conditional sincerity in the legislative vote. Let $x_D(r)$ be the implied outcome were D president with the r legislative vote. Then $x_D(r) < x_D$, $x_1(r)$ preferred to $x_D(s)$ and single-peakedness imply that I_s satisfies conditional sincerity in the presidential vote. The construction of I_s and r renders s unstable. $\hspace{2em}$ Q.E.D.

Proposition 4: Stable conditionally sincere equilibria $(\beta = 0)$
There are only two possible stable conditionally sincere equilibria both of which are cutpoint.

(i) *R president.* Legislative strategies described by cutpoint $\tilde{\theta}_R$ (given in Proposition 1) and presidential strategies described by $\hat{\theta}_R$ satisfying:

$$u_i(\tilde{\theta}_R, i) = u_i(\theta_D + g_D(1 - H(\tilde{\theta}_R), i) \qquad \text{for } i = \tilde{\theta}_R \qquad (3.A8)$$

(ii) *D president.* Legislative strategies described by cutpoint $\tilde{\theta}_D$ and presidential strategies described by $\hat{\theta}_D$ satisfying:

$$u_i(\theta_R - g_R(H(\tilde{\theta}_D), i) = u_i(\tilde{\theta}_D, i) \qquad \text{for } i = \tilde{\theta}_D \qquad (3.A9)$$

Proof:
1. By Proposition 3, we need only consider strategies that lead to a certain presidential winner.
2. If the presidential winner is certain, the proof of Proposition 1 applies directly to show that conditionally sincere legislative voting must satisfy the $\tilde{\theta}$ cutpoint.
3. If legislative voting satisfies the $\tilde{\theta}$ cutpoint, Proposition 2 implies that either (3.A8) or (3.A9), as appropriate, must hold.
$\hspace{2em}$ Q.E.D.

Proposition 5 (Existence, $\beta = 0$)
A stable conditionally sincere equilibrium exists.
Proof:
$\hspace{1em}$ Assume, without loss of generality, that the median voter weakly

prefers $\tilde{\theta}_R$ to $\tilde{\theta}_D$. We show that $\tilde{\theta}_R$ represents a stable conditionally sincere equilibrium.

1. Assume there exists I_s and associated strategy r that renders $\tilde{\theta}_R$ unstable. To satisfy conditional sincerity, the presidential outcome must change to either D president or a tie. Moreover, by SCP, if I_s is "better off" and the presidential outcome changes, the median voter is "better off". It suffices to show a contradiction; the median voter cannot be better off.

2. Assume there exists I_s which deviates to r such that D is president. Since I_s must satisfy conditional sincerity in the legislative vote, $x_1(\mathbf{r}) < \tilde{\theta}_D$. This fact, the assumption that the median voter prefers $\tilde{\theta}_R$ to $\tilde{\theta}_D$ and $\hat{\theta}_R$ cutpoint imply immediately that the median voter is worse off under r.

3. Assume there exists I_s which deviates to r such that there is a tie

   A. An argument parallel to "2" above shows that the median voter cannot be better off unless there is a change in the legislative vote under r.

   B. Assume, therefore, that $V_R^{L1}(\mathbf{r}) > V_R^{L1}(\mathbf{s})$. This shifts outcomes to the left. Consequently, SCP and single-peakedness imply that voters in I_s must follow a presidential cutpoint rule with the cutpoint to the left of $\hat{\theta}_R$. Since the median voter is to the right of $\hat{\theta}_R$, I_s cannot create a tie and satisfy conditional sincerity.

   C. Assume, finally, that $V_R^{L1}(\mathbf{r}) < V_R^{L1}(\mathbf{s})$. This implies that $x_R(\mathbf{r}) > \tilde{\theta}_R$. Moreover, conditional sincerity of the legislative vote for I_s implies that $x_D(\mathbf{r}) < \tilde{\theta}_D$. Again the assumption that the median voter prefers $\tilde{\theta}_R$ to $\tilde{\theta}_D$ implies the median voter cannot be better off under r. Q.E.D.

Corollary 5–1

If the median voter is indifferent between $\tilde{\theta}_R$ and $\tilde{\theta}_D$, both outcomes are conditionally stable.

Corollary 5–2

By continuity, two stable equilibria will continue to exist if the median voter does not have "too strong" a preference for one of the two potential equilibrium outcomes.

Proof:

Consider any I_s that could render the median voter's less preferred outcome, say $\tilde{\theta}_D$, unstable. Since voters in $I/I_s \neq \emptyset$ have $r_i = s_i$, $\tilde{\theta}_D$ may be stable because r produces not $\tilde{\theta}_R$ but only an outcome to the right of this preferred outcome.

Appendix to chapter 3

Corollary 5–3

In equilibrium, policy must equal the ideal point of the pivotal voter in the legislative election.

Thus, the pivotal-voter theorem continues to hold when the president and the legislature are elected simultaneously.

The two-period model: $\beta > 0$

We now consider equilibrium for the full model with two periods. Conditional sincerity immediately implies that the second-period strategy components must follow the cutpoint rules $\tilde{\theta}_R$ and $\tilde{\theta}_D$.

It also follows immediately that Proposition 2, restated for two periods, continues to hold.

Propositon 6

If preferences have SCP, and s is conditionally sincere in the second period, presidential voting for strategy s is conditionally sincere if and only if all v_i^{E1} follow a cutpoint rule with the cutpoint $\hat{\theta}$ given by:

$$u_i(\theta_R - g_R(1 - V_R^{L1}), i) + \beta u_i(\tilde{\theta}_R, i) = u_i(\theta_D + g_D(V_R^{L1}), i)$$
$$+ \beta u_i(\tilde{\theta}_D, i) \quad \text{for } i = \hat{\theta}$$

The proof is immediate.

Proposition 7 (No ties)

If s has $V_R^{E1} = \frac{1}{2}$, s is not a stable conditionally sincere equilibrium.

Proof:
Assume without loss of generality that the median voter weakly prefers $\tilde{\theta}_R$ to $\tilde{\theta}_D$. Then the construction used in the proof of Proposition 3 for $\beta = 0$ leaves I_s better off in both periods.   Q.E.D.

Proposition 8: Stable conditionally sincere equilibria

There are only two possible stable conditionally sincere equilibria both of which are cutpoint.

(i)   *R president.* Legislative strategies described by cutpoint $\tilde{\theta}_R$ in period 1 and $\tilde{\theta}_R$, $\tilde{\theta}_D$ in period 2, and presidential strategies described by $\tilde{\theta}_R$ satisfying:

$$(1 + \beta) u_i(\tilde{\theta}_R, i) = u_i(\theta_D + g_D(1 - H(\tilde{\theta}_R), i) + \beta u_i(\tilde{\theta}_D, i) \quad \text{for } i = \hat{\theta}_R$$
$$(3.A10)$$

(ii) *D president.* Similar to R president.
      The proof is directly parallel to that of proposition 4 for $\beta = 0$.

Proposition 9 (Existence)

A stable conditionally sincere equilibrium exists.

Proof:

1. Second period conditional sincerity implies that for any I_s and associated strategy **r**, the second-period strategy components must maintain the **s** components.
2. The fixity of second-period outcomes and the assumption that the median voter weakly prefers $\tilde{\theta}_R$ to $\tilde{\theta}_D$ immediately implies that the $\beta = 0$ proof applies, *a fortiori*.   Q.E.D.

Corollary

In a stable conditionally sincere equilibrium, policy is identical in both periods.

There is no midterm cycle with complete information.

Comment

The concept of conditional sincerity is a straightforward application of individual rationality to voter behavior. With a finite number of voters, the idea is that, in legislative elections, each voter's vote should have the correct marginal impact on the outcome. In presidential elections, even if a voter is not pivotal, the voter wants to vote the "correct" way in case other voters make mistakes. That is, being conditionally sincere is closely related to the notion of "trembling hand" equilibrium (Selten (1975)). The notion of stability is closely related to the concept of Coalition Proof Nash equilibrium (Bernheim, Peleg, and Whinston (1987)). Greenberg (1989) showed that, for the dominance relation implicit in Coalition Proof, an isomorphism between Coalition Proof Nash and Von Neumann–Morgenstern abstract stable sets. These sets can also be characterized for a continuum of players. In Alesina and Rosenthal (1991) we show that the Coalition Proof/ Von Neumann–Morgenstern Abstract Stable equilibrium outcomes are identical to the outcomes supported by stable conditionally sincere equilibria. The legislative components of stable conditionally sincere strategies are identical to those of abstract stable strategies. Conditional sincerity in the presidential vote "refines" the abstract stable presidential components.

4

The midterm cycle

4.1 INTRODUCTION

One of the strongest regularities in American elections is the midterm cycle: the party holding the White House loses votes and seats in each midterm congressional election, relative to the previous, on-year, election. Figure 4.1 displays this remarkable regularity for the period since 1918. The president's party lost vote share in all of the 18 midterm elections shown in the figure. Very few phenomena in politics appear so regularly and consistently: the midterm cycle calls for an explanation that goes beyond specific personalities, or specific events such as, for example, Watergate or the Vietnam war.[1]

In this chapter we argue that the midterm effect is part of the balancing effort of the electorate, who face two polarized parties. We study an important element of uncertainty concerning the distribution of voters' preferences: the model of chapter 3 is extended by the assumption that the ideological position of the median voter is not known with certainty, by anybody. Even though the parties' ideal policies continue to be known by everybody, this uncertainty concerning voter preferences makes the electoral results, and, in particular, the results of presidential elections uncertain. The voters do not know for sure which party is going to win the presidency; they can only evaluate the probability of the two possible outcomes, as in chapter 2. In midterm elections, instead, they know which party holds the presidency.

The difference between the on-years, in which legislative elections are held *under uncertainty* about the identity of the president, and midterms, in which the uncertainty is removed, is the key to the midterm cycle. In on-years, middle-of-the-road voters have to hedge their bets in legislative elections, since they do not know which president they will face. Consider,

---

[1] It goes without saying that specific events also influence the size of midterm effect. For instance, the very poor performance of the Republican party in 1974 (see figure 4.1) reflects Watergate as well as the typical midterm loss.

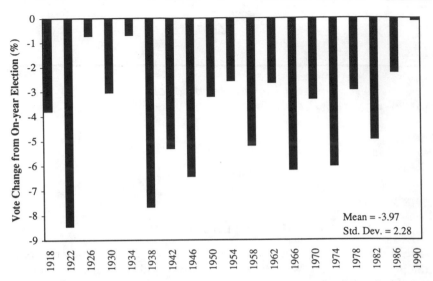

Figure 4.1. The midterm cycle, 1918–1990. The graph shows the change in the vote share of the president's party. The change is always negative.

for instance, right-of-center voters. They would like to have a Republican president balanced by a relatively strong Democratic delegation in Congress. Suppose these voters think that there is a fifty–fifty chance that a Republican president will, in fact, be elected. If they vote D for the legislature, they take a chance of making the Democratic party stronger in Congress *and* ending up with a Democratic president. This is an outcome that these voters greatly dislike. Therefore they vote R for the legislature. If the Republican party wins the presidency, however, the same types of voters can now safely achieve the desired balancing by reinforcing the Democratic party in the midterm election. In fact, in midterm there is no uncertainty about the presidency, and center-right voters know, for sure, that by voting D for Congress, they are balancing a Republican president. Thus in our model the voters who generate the midterm effect are those who are not willing to split their ticket under uncertainty about the outcome of presidential elections, but are willing to vote against the party holding the White House in midterm, when there is *no* uncertainty about the presidency.[2]

More generally, we will show below that the midterm cycle is *always expected* to occur, as long as the presidential elections are not completely certain, as in the case developed in chapter 3. The size of the midterm cycle, however, depends in our model on the degree of surprise associated with

[2]The reader may recall that this is a generalization of the argument given above in chapter 3, when we discussed ties in presidential elections.

the outcome of presidential elections: the more unexpected the outcome of the presidential election, the larger the expected midterm loss of the president's party. The intuition is simple. Suppose that the Democratic candidate unexpectedly wins the presidency. Many middle-of-the-road voters have voted D in the on-year legislative election, thinking that they were going to balance a Republican president. Many of these voters in midterm will want to switch to balance the unexpected Democratic president.

It is important to emphasize that, in our model, only one piece of information is relevant to voter decision-making at midterm: which party has won the presidency. We do not imply that, in reality, this is the *only* thing the voters learn in the first two years of a new administration. The point is, instead, that the midterm cycle occurs *even* in such a stylized model. In reality, in the first two years of a presidential term, voters learn much more about the president than her party affiliation, but this information could be favorable or unfavorable to the president's party. Thus, it is not clear why additional information concerning the new president's competency, personality, character, or ideology should always imply a negative midterm effect. Shouldn't the voters, at least occasionally, be happy with the president's party at midterm? The strength of the regularity displayed in figure 4.1 suggests the existence of something very systematic about the midterm cycle, which our model captures, within the context of our balancing approach. Later in the book (chapter 8) we will discuss other realistic forms of uncertainty, especially lack of information concerning the administrative competence of different administrations. The midterm effect does not disappear in this richer setup.

Alternative explanations for the midterm cycle were analyzed by Erikson (1990). These include "regression to the mean"; for example, an unusually strong Republican showing in an on-year is likely to be followed by a less strong performance two years later. In other words, when the vote is a purely random process, a strong showing is likely to be followed by a more average result two years later. But occasionally, the luck of the draw in the random process should lead to an even stronger showing at midterm. Erikson ruled out regression to the mean because the midterm cycle is so pervasive. Another potential explanation is a "surge" in on-year elections engendered by presidential coattails (Calvert and Ferejohn (1983)) followed by a "decline", with no coattails. Here the problem is that some presidential winners, such as Kennedy and Carter, have had *negative* coattails, running behind their party's House vote. Even in such cases, however, the midterm cycle appears. In the last section of this chapter we show that, although our model incorporates both "regression to the mean" and "coattail" effects, the midterm effect is driven by the balancing behavior of middle-of-the-road voters. Erikson points out that, empirically, only balancing, which he describes as "presidential penalty", survives, among competing models, as an explanation for the midterm cycle.

This chapter is organized as follows. Section 4.2 discusses how uncertainty about the preferences of the electorate changes the basic framework developed in chapter 3. Section 4.3 begins to analyze the midterm elections and presents a generalization of the pivotal-voter theorem for the case of uncertainty. Section 4.4 considers the voting equilibrium in the complete two-period model, building on the results of the previous section. Section 4.5 discusses the substantive and testable implications of our model concerning the interaction between "divided government" and the midterm cycle. We also discuss how our explanation of the latter compares to alternatives. Section 4.6 treats "reversals". Even though a midterm cycle is always *expected*, a midterm "shock" to preferences especially favorable to the president's party could, on occasion, reverse the cycle. The section shows that, for a range of parameter values, reversals will not occur. The last section summarizes and concludes.

4.2 VOTING UNDER UNCERTAINTY

In this chapter we introduce an important and realistic change to the model of chapter 3: we now assume that the distribution of voters' bliss points is not known with certainty by anybody. This uncertainty will imply that electoral results cannot be perfectly predicted in advance.

A simple way of formalizing this uncertainty is the following. Assume that the distribution of the voter bliss points, θ_i, is uniform on the segment (of length one), $[a, 1 + a]$ where a is a random variable that is itself distributed uniformly, with a mean of zero and minimum and maximum realizations equal to $-w$ and $+w$ respectively. Figure 4.2 helps to visualize this construction. Figure 4.2a shows the case in which the random variable a is at its mean value of zero, so that the θ_i are distributed uniformly between zero and one. Figure 4.2b shows the case in which a is at its minimum value of $-w$, so that the θ_i are distributed in the interval $[-w, 1 - w]$. Figure 4.2c shows the situation in which a is at its maximum value of w, so that the θ_i are distributed between w and $1 + w$. All the intermediate cases are possible, depending on the actual realization of a between the two extremes, $-w$ and $+w$. If a is below zero (its average value), this means that the distribution of voters' preferences is tilted to the left, and vice versa. The bliss point of the median voter is $\frac{1}{2} + a$; thus the expected bliss point of the median voter is still at $\frac{1}{2}$, but its actual value depends on the realization of the variable a. Although voters know the *distribution of the random variable a, they do not observe its realization* before voting.

The easiest way to think about the voters' lack of complete information about preferences is to focus upon turnout. Suppose that the voting

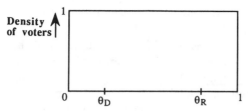

(a) The random variable **a** = 0.

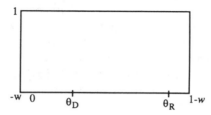

(b) The random variable **a** = -w.

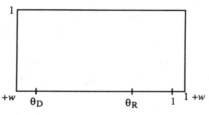

(c) The random variable **a** = +w.

Figure 4.2.   In the uncertainty model, the distribution of voter ideal points depends on the realization of the random preference shock, **a**. In the top panel, **a** is at its average value, 0. In the middle panel, **a** is at its minimum value, $-w$. In the bottom panel, **a** is at its maximum value, $+w$.

population is distributed on the interval $[-w, 1 + w]$ but in each election only those individuals between **a** and $1 + \textbf{a}$ actually vote. Thus, in each election we have the same number of voters, but the distribution of voter preferences changes as a function of **a**.[3]

As in chapter 3, we continue to assume that the voters cannot communicate their preferences to each other directly. Thus, the only way for anyone to

---

[3]An alternative interpretation would be to assume full turnout in each election but that each individual's ideal point is subject to a common preference shock, **a**. This alternative interpretation is technically more complicated because each voter in this case is uncertain before the first period election about his own preferences in the second period. We conjecture, however, that the qualitative nature of our results would not change using this alternative interpretation.

infer the actual distribution of the electorate preferences is to observe the electoral results.

An interesting issue is whether the realizations of the random variable **a** are independent in on-year and midterm. If in each period an independent realization of the random variable occurs, any information derived from the on-year electoral results does not help in predicting midterm policy outcomes. This assumption facilitates exposition of the analytical results. It has, however, two drawbacks. First, it posits no persistence in the random shocks, an assumption of dubious validity. Second, it implies differences in turnout in the two elections: not all the voters who voted in on-year vote in midterm. Furthermore, as figure 4.2 makes clear, while moderates always vote, the extreme voters who are close to 0 or 1 may or may not go to the polls depending on the realization of **a**. Empirical evidence suggests that extremists tend to vote more often than moderates, in contrast to this formalization.

The opposite assumption holds that the shock **a** is completely permanent, with the realization drawn in the first period persisting through the midterm election. This formalization does not have the two problems mentioned above, but it is slightly more cumbersome analytically. All our results not only go through in this opposite case but also generalize to include any hypothesis about the correlation of the draws of **a** in the two periods. Some of the analytical expressions would change, but none of the results would change qualitatively.

In the text of this and later chapters, we adopt the assumption of independent realizations of **a**. In the appendix to this chapter, we also analyze the model in the case of a single realization of **a**. The intermediate case of correlated shocks is left to the technically oriented reader. A related exercise would be to show that the results are unaffected if the amount of uncertainty, represented by the parameter w, differs from the on-year to the midterm election.

At this point, an important caveat needs to be addressed. Consider again figure 4.2b and, in particular, the voters with ideal policies, θ_i, below zero. These voters, by the very knowledge of their own preferences, know something about the realization of **a**. In this example, voters with bliss points below zero know that the realization of **a** is below its mean, and they can use this information when voting. We assume that all the voters who have some information about the realization of **a** are the extreme voters who will always want to vote for the same party in every election. Recall, from chapter 3, that by "extreme voters" we mean those to the left of θ_D, the ideal point of party D, and those to the right of θ_R, the ideal point of party R. Formally, we impose that

$$w < \theta_D < \theta_R < 1 - w \tag{4.1}$$

These inequalities (see figures 4.2b and 4.2c) imply that for any realization of **a**, there are always voters both to the right of the Republican party and to the left of the Democratic party. Furthermore, the conditions (4.1) imply that all the voters interested in balancing – that is, the voters between θ_D and θ_R – act with no information on the realization of **a**.[4] This assumption not only greatly simplifies the formal analysis, but is also realistic. In fact, if condition (4.1) were not satisfied, it would be possible that for some realizations of voter preferences, one of the two parties would be more extreme than the *most extreme* voter. Such a possibility appears quite unrealistic.

All the other features of the model remain unchanged from chapter 3. It should be pointed out, however, that the results presented in this chapter can be formally derived only for the case of quadratic utility functions; that is, for the case in which voter i's utility function[5] is given by:

$$u(x, \theta_i) = -\tfrac{1}{2}(x - \theta_i)^2 - \beta\tfrac{1}{2}(x - \theta_i)^2 \tag{4.2}$$

where x_1 and x_2 are the policies in periods 1 and 2 and β is a discount factor which can take any value between 0 and 1, including the extremes. The discount factor allows the voters to place less weight on the second-period outcomes.

In summary, we have augmented the model of chapter 3 with a simple form of uncertainty. The key consequence of our uncertainty model is that the location of the median voter's ideal policy is not known with certainty: it can vary from $[\tfrac{1}{2} - w]$ to $[\tfrac{1}{2} + w]$, depending on whether the electorate is relatively left-leaning or right-leaning in any particular electoral year.

The fact that the median voter's ideal point is not known with certainty can render the outcome of presidential elections uncertain. Given the legislative strategies that are to be used in periods 1 and 2, electing a Republican president would give the voter a bundle consisting of the Republican president's ideal policy moderated by the congressional vote in period 1 and again by the congressional vote in period 2. Electing the Democratic president would produce a different bundle. Because **a** is random, the actual policies in each bundle are not known with certainty. As a result, the expected utility of each bundle must be computed. Thus each voter is confronted with a binary choice between expected two-period policy utilities – one utility corresponds to electing a Republican president,

---

[4]This observation suggests an interesting argument concerning voters' communication of their preferences. The voters who have something to communicate, i.e., who know something about the realization of **a**, are the "extremists," those on the right of θ_R and on the left of θ_D. These voters always have an incentive to lie. They would like to make the other voters believe that there are fewer extremists than there really are, to influence the behavior of the moderate voters.

[5]The $\tfrac{1}{2}$ in front of the utility function obviously has no effect on results. It is convenient to have it because the multiplicative term of 2 disappears when derivatives are taken.

the other to electing a Democratic president. The probability that a majority of the electorate prefers the R bundle to the D bundle is simply the probability that the actual median voter $[\frac{1}{2} + a]$ prefers bundle R to bundle D. If the voter at $\frac{1}{2}$ (the expected median) is indifferent between the two bundles, the probability of electing R is $\frac{1}{2}$. If the voter at the expected median prefers the R bundle to the D bundle, the probability that R will be president is greater than $\frac{1}{2}$. If the voter at $[\frac{1}{2} - w]$ (that is, the leftmost type that could be actual median voter) prefers the R bundle, the probability is 1. Obviously, the two policies (in the first and second period) associated with the two different presidents depend upon the legislative vote, which has to be determined endogenously.

We now analyze voter equilibrium under uncertainty.

4.3 MIDTERM ELECTIONS

As in chapter 3, we begin by considering the legislative election in the second period. The results under uncertainty are entirely parallel to those for certainty presented in chapter 3. In fact, we can establish a generalized pivotal-voter theorem.[6] We indicate with the subscript 2 the second-period cutpoints and policies, so, for instance, x^{R2} represents the policy in the second period with a Republican president, and so forth.

The generalized pivotal-voter theorem

If the president in office is R, the unique cutpoint in the legislative election in the second period is $\tilde{\theta}_{R2} = \tilde{\theta}_R = \dfrac{\theta_R}{1 + K}$.

If the president in office is D, the unique cutpoint in the legislative election of the second period is $\tilde{\theta}_{D2} = \tilde{\theta}_D = \dfrac{\theta_D + K}{1 + K}$.

The legislative cutpoints are equal to the expected policies:

$$\tilde{\theta}_{R2} = E(x^{R2}) \quad \text{if R is president, and}$$

$$\tilde{\theta}_{D2} = E(x^{D2}) \quad \text{if D is president.}$$

The actual policies are as follows:

$$x^{R2} = \frac{\theta_R}{1 + K} + Ka \quad \text{if R is president, and}$$

$$x^{D2} = \frac{\theta_D + K}{1 + K} + Ka \quad \text{if D is president.}$$

The analogy with the pivotal-voter theorem presented in chapter 3 should

[6]For a formal proof of this theorem, see Alesina and Rosenthal (1991).

be clear. That theorem implies that actual policies equal the bliss points of the pivotal voters. Note that the two cutpoints $\tilde{\theta}_{R2}$ and $\tilde{\theta}_{D2}$ are identical to the cutpoints of the certainty model. The only differences here are that: (1) voters have to compute expectations about electoral and policy outcomes, and (2) expected outcomes differ from actual outcomes. Here the *expected* policies equal the bliss points of the pivotal voters.

The argument given in the "proof" of the pivotal-voter theorem in chapter 3 applies here, as well, in expectations. Consider a case in which the cutpoint in the legislative election is *not* equal to the expected policy outcome. Then, exactly the same argument given in figure 3.2 applies here: some voters are voting for the party that they would prefer to see less strong (in expectations).

We now derive formally the policies (x^{R2} and x^{D2}) given in the theorem; the reader not interested in this derivation may move directly to the next section.

Consider the policy function (see chapter 3) for the case of the R president:

$$x^{R2} = \theta_R - KV_{D2} = \theta_R - K(1 - V_{R2}) \tag{4.3}$$

where

$$V_{R2} = 1 + a - \tilde{\theta}_{R2} \tag{4.4}$$

That is, voters on the right of $\tilde{\theta}_{R2}$ vote R; voters on the left vote D. Remember that the voters' bliss points are distributed uniformly on the interval $[a, 1 + a]$. Thus, substituting (4.4) into (4.3), we obtain:

$$x^{R2} = \theta_R - K\tilde{\theta}_{R2} + Ka \tag{4.5}$$

By the generalized pivotal-voter theorem the following obtains:

$$\tilde{\theta}_{R2} = \frac{\theta_R}{1 + K} \tag{4.6}$$

Thus, substituting (4.6) into (4.5), we have:

$$x^{R2} = \frac{\theta_R}{1 + K} + Ka \tag{4.7}$$

Note that if $a = 0$, then the actual policy, x^{R2}, is equal to the expected policy, which is just the policy of the certainty model, developed in chapter 3, where $a = 0$ by assumption. If a is positive, we have an electorate that has shifted in a conservative direction, and the policy outcome is to the right of its expected value. The opposite is true if a is negative. Analogous arguments apply with a D president:

$$x^{D2} = \theta_D + KV_{R2} \tag{4.8}$$

$$V_{R2} = 1 + a - \tilde{\theta}_{D2} \tag{4.9}$$

$$x^{D2} = \theta_D + K - K\tilde{\theta}_{D2} + Ka \qquad (4.10)$$

Thus, using $\tilde{\theta}_{D2} = (\theta_D + K)/(1 + K)$ in (4.10), we obtain:

$$x^{D2} = \frac{\theta_D + K}{1 + K} + Ka \qquad (4.11)$$

In summary, the legislative elections in the second period in this model with uncertainty are very similar to those of the certainty case.[7] The only difference pertains to the realization of the preference shock a, which implies that actual outcomes are not equal to expected outcomes. More important differences from the certainty model appear in the first-period elections, to which we now turn.

4.4 EQUILIBRIUM UNDER UNCERTAINTY

The crucial difference from the certainty model is that presidential election results remain uncertain. For any given legislative vote, the choice between the two possible presidents implies a binary choice over policy outcomes. Given the uncertainty about voter preferences, the outcome of majority voting over a binary choice is uncertain. The voters can compute the probability that one outcome will prevail over the other, but they cannot predict the outcome with certainty. For some values of the parameters θ_D, θ_R, and w, there is no uncertainty – that is, for *any* possible realization of a one outcome always gets a majority – but, for the moment, we focus on cases in which the uncertainty does not disappear.

If there is uncertainty about presidential elections, the voters can compute the probability, represented by P, of an R presidential victory. *All* voters must vote with conditional sincerity in the presidential elections. The intuition behind this observation is simple. Any shift in voter behavior will produce a small shift in probability. So changes by any small group of voters make a difference. Therefore, all voters must, *conditional on the legislative vote*, vote for the party they would like to see win the presidency. As a consequence of conditional sincerity, under uncertainty the presidential vote must follow a cutpoint rule; there must exist a cutpoint, which we indicate with $\hat{\theta}$, such that voters on the left of $\hat{\theta}$ vote D and voters on the right of $\hat{\theta}$ vote R in the presidential election. The probability of an R victory will depend on the position of this cutpoint of the presidential contest. Thus,

---

[7]This similarity is driven by our simplifying assumptions. For quadratic utility, it is well known that the expected utility of a lottery of policies can be written as additive functions of the mean policy and the variance of policies. In turn, condition (4.1) guarantees that a constant fraction of voters always remains in the interval $[\theta_D, \theta_R]$. Since the legislative cutpoint must be on this interval, (4.1) implies that the variance of policies is constant. Hence utilities can be reduced to functions of means, and the equilibrium cutpoints are identical to those of chapter 3.

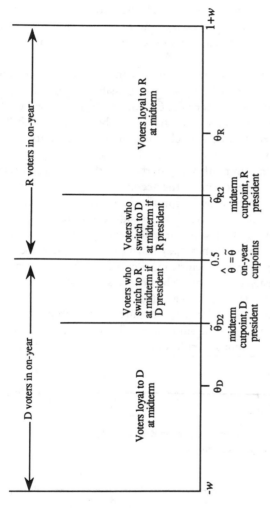

Figure 4.3. The midterm cycle in a dead heat for the presidency. In the uncertainty model, the median voter is equally likely to be located anywhere from $1/2 - w$ to $1/2 + w$. The parties are symmetric about the center $(1/2)$ of the distribution of the median voter's ideal point. Some voters to the right of $1/2$ switch their legislative votes at midterm if D is president; some voters to the left switch if R is president.

the complete characterization of the first-period electoral equilibrium involves the determination of two cutpoints, one for the presidential election, $\hat{\theta}$, and another for the legislative election, which we indicate with $\tilde{\theta}$.

The key to the midterm effect is that the first-period legislative cutpoint, $\tilde{\theta}$, has to be in between the two second-period cutpoints: $\tilde{\theta}_{D2} < \tilde{\theta} < \tilde{\theta}_{R2}$. Figure 4.3 helps visualize the mechanics of the midterm cycle in our model. This picture is drawn for the case in which the two parties are symmetric around the expected median, $\frac{1}{2}$. This symmetry immediately suggests (and we show below) that if the presidential outcome is uncertain, the cutpoints are $\hat{\theta} = \tilde{\theta} = \frac{1}{2}$.

The central question is why the cutpoint $\tilde{\theta}$ cannot lie outside the interval between $\tilde{\theta}_{D2}$ and $\tilde{\theta}_{R2}$. Figure 4.4 displays two possible configurations of the legislative cutpoints in the two periods, $\tilde{\theta}$, $\tilde{\theta}_{D2}$, and $\tilde{\theta}_{R2}$. In case (a), $\tilde{\theta}$ is on the right of $\tilde{\theta}_{R2}$. Consider voters with bliss points between $\tilde{\theta}_{R2}$ and $\tilde{\theta}$. They vote D in the first-period legislative election, under uncertainty about the presidential result. That is, they vote D for the legislature even though they know that they may end up reinforcing party D in the legislature when the same party holds the presidency. In the second period with a Republican president, the same voters vote R for the legislature. This behavior is inconsistent: under uncertainty about the presidential outcome, thus under uncertainty concerning a right-wing or a left-wing policy outcome, these voters make the left stronger. When they learn that the right-wing outcome has prevailed in the presidential election, they turn around and make the right stronger in the legislature. This behavior runs opposite to the incentive that the voters have to balance. In case (b), $\tilde{\theta}_{R2} = \tilde{\theta}$. This implies that in both legislative elections, with or without uncertainty about presidential results, the voters always vote the same way. This is also inconsistent with balancing. Analogous arguments rule out the case of $\tilde{\theta}$ on the left of or

(a) The second period cutpoint ($\tilde{\theta}_{R2}$) when R wins the presidency is to the left of the first period cutpoint ($\tilde{\theta}$).

(b) The second period cutpoint ($\tilde{\theta}_{R2}$) when R wins the presidency equals the first period cutpoint ($\tilde{\theta}$).

Figure 4.4.   Two examples of inconsistent legislative cutpoints

equal to $\tilde{\theta}_{D2}$. Thus the only possibility remaining is the one described in figure 4.3:

$$\tilde{\theta}_{D2} < \tilde{\theta} < \tilde{\theta}_{R2} \qquad (4.12)$$

This is the basic argument underlying the midterm effect in this model. Consider the voters between $\tilde{\theta}$ and $\tilde{\theta}_{R2}$ in figure 4.3. In the first period they vote R for the legislature, under uncertainty about the presidential outcome. If R is elected president, in midterm they turn to voting D for the legislature. Thus party R *loses* votes in midterm relative to on-year legislative elections. Once again, the key is that in on-years the legislative vote is cast under uncertainty about the outcome of the presidential elections. An analogous argument applies if party D wins the presidency. The voters who create the midterm effect are those in between $\tilde{\theta}_{D2}$ and $\tilde{\theta}$.

In order to characterize the equilibrium fully, we now have to determine jointly $\hat{\theta}$ and $\tilde{\theta}$, that is, the two cutpoints of the two elections. Since policy outcomes depend on the results of *both* elections, *voter behavior in one contest is not independent of the expected result in the other*. This is the vital point of our entire model.

First, for a given presidential election cutpoint, $\hat{\theta}$, we can derive a probability $P(\hat{\theta})$ of a Republican presidential victory. Note that if $\hat{\theta} < \frac{1}{2} - w$, then $P(\hat{\theta}) = 1$: the Republican wins the presidency for sure. In fact, $\frac{1}{2} - w$ is the most left-wing position possible for the median ideal point. Thus if $\hat{\theta}$ is to the left of such a realization, for sure the R party obtains more than 50 percent of the votes. Analogous arguments imply that if $\hat{\theta} > \frac{1}{2} + w$, $P(\hat{\theta}) = 0$. Thus, if $\hat{\theta}$ is in between $(\frac{1}{2} - w)$ and $(\frac{1}{2} + w)$, $P(\hat{\theta})$ is between zero and one. Furthermore, $P(\hat{\theta})$ is decreasing in $\hat{\theta}$ within this range; in fact the further to the right the presidential cutpoint, the less likely it is that the realization of a will imply a Republican victory.

Formally, given the uniform distribution of a in the interval $[-w, +w]$ we have:

$$P(\hat{\theta}) = 1 \qquad \text{if } \hat{\theta} \leqslant \frac{1}{2} - w$$

$$P(\hat{\theta}) = \frac{\frac{1}{2} + w - \hat{\theta}}{2w} \quad \text{if } \frac{1}{2} - w < \hat{\theta} < \frac{1}{2} + w \qquad (4.13)$$

$$P(\hat{\theta}) = 0 \qquad \text{if } \hat{\theta} \geqslant \frac{1}{2} + w$$

A simple extension of the argument given in chapter 3 implies the following:

$$\tilde{\theta} = P(\hat{\theta})\tilde{\theta}_{R} + (1 - P(\hat{\theta}))\tilde{\theta}_{D} \qquad (4.14)$$

Equation (4.14) states that the first-period legislative cutpoint, $\tilde{\theta}$, is equal to a linear combination of the certainty cutpoint derived in chapter 3, with weights given by the probabilities of the two possible presidential outcomes.

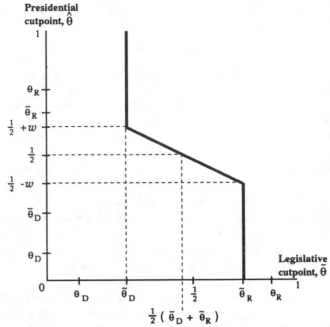

Figure 4.5. The legislative cutpoint in on-years. When the presidential outcome is sure to be R, the legislative cutpoint is $\tilde{\theta}_R$. If a D president is certain, the cutpoint is $\tilde{\theta}_D$. The cutpoint is a weighted average of $\tilde{\theta}_R$ and $\tilde{\theta}_D$ when the outcome is uncertain.

Thus, using the expressions for $\tilde{\theta}_D$ and $\tilde{\theta}_R$, we have:

$$\tilde{\theta} = P(\hat{\theta})\frac{\theta_R}{1+K} + (1 - P(\hat{\theta}))\frac{\theta_D + K}{1+K} \tag{4.15}$$

The intuition is clear: if $P(\hat{\theta}) = 0$, party D wins the presidency for sure. Thus, as in the certainty model, $\tilde{\theta} = \tilde{\theta}_D = \tilde{\theta}_{D2} = (\theta_D + K)/(1 + K)$, and the on-year legislative election voting decisions are identical to those at midterm. Similarly, if $P(\hat{\theta}) = 1$, $\tilde{\theta} = \tilde{\theta}_R = \tilde{\theta}_{R2} = \theta_R/(1 + K)$. In the intermediate range, the higher is $P(\hat{\theta})$, the more likely it is that party R wins the presidency, the more the legislative vote resembles the case of a sure Republican presidential victory. Equation (4.15) implies a downward-sloping relationship between $\tilde{\theta}$ and $\hat{\theta}$, as displayed in figure 4.5. This relationship can be read as follows: given $\hat{\theta}$, the corresponding $\tilde{\theta}$ can be read on the horizontal axis of figure 4.5.

We now need a second relationship between the two cutpoints to find a voting equilibrium. Given $\tilde{\theta}$, how will the voters choose in presidential elections? For fixed $\tilde{\theta}$, we can compute an expected legislative vote. In fact,

$$V_{R1} = 1 + a - \tilde{\theta} \tag{4.16}$$

It follows that

$$E(V_{R1}) = 1 - \tilde{\theta} \qquad (4.17)$$

Given $E(V_{R1})$, the expected period 1 policy outcomes are:

$$E(x^{D1}) = \theta_D + KE(V_{R1}) = \theta_D + K(1 - \tilde{\theta}) \qquad (4.18)$$

$$E(x^{R1}) = \theta_R - (1 - K)E(V_{R1}) = \theta_R - K\tilde{\theta} \qquad (4.19)$$

where equation (4.18) represents the policy with a D president and equation (4.19) with an R president.

We are now ready to analyze voting in the presidential election. Given the legislative cutpoints $\tilde{\theta}$, $\tilde{\theta}_{R2}$, and $\tilde{\theta}_{D2}$, the presidential votes must be conditionally sincere. Voters will choose between two policy bundles, voting for the party that, in expectation, delivers the higher utility. Note that in taking this decision, each voter will account for the second-period policy outcome, since the president remains in office for two periods. Moreover, in considering the second period, the voter will take into account that in midterm the legislative vote is adjusted to balance the president. Thus each voter knows that if D wins the presidency, the two policies in the D bundle are:

$$x^{D1} = \theta_D + K(1 + a - \tilde{\theta}) \qquad \text{in period 1}$$

$$x^{D2} = \frac{\theta_D + K}{1 + K} + Ka \qquad \text{in period 2}$$

If R wins the presidency, the two policies are:

$$x^{R1} = \theta_R - K(\tilde{\theta} - a) \qquad \text{in period 1}$$

$$x^{R2} = \frac{\theta_R}{1 + K} + Ka \qquad \text{in period 2}$$

(While we have not time-subscripted a, recall that independent values of a are drawn in the two periods.)

Using the four policy outcomes given above the possible realizations of a, one can compute a voter's expected utility given D president and the expected utility given R president. Conditional on the legislative voting decisions, voters will vote sincerely for the presidential candidate expected to deliver the highest utility. The voter at the cutpoint, $\hat{\theta}$, gets equal utility from both candidates and is therefore indifferent. Equivalently, as shown in the appendix, the voter at $\hat{\theta}$ is indifferent to an increase in the expected presidential vote of either one of the two parties or, in other words, is indifferent to a change in $P(\hat{\theta})$ which would be generated by changes in the expected presidential voters. The appendix derives this indifference relation-

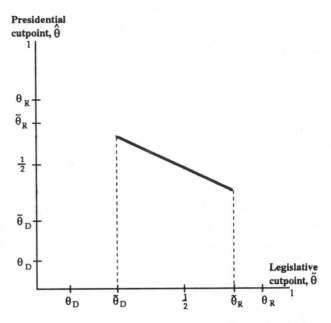

Figure 4.6. The presidential cutpoint as a function of the legislative cutpoint. The downward slope indicates that voters are less likely to vote D for president as the expected D legislative share increases.

ship as:

$$\hat{\theta} = \frac{\frac{1}{2}\{[\theta_R + \theta_D][(1+K)^2 + \beta] + \beta K\} - K(1+K)^2\tilde{\theta}}{(1+\beta - K^2)(1+K)} \qquad (4.20)$$

The large number of terms in (4.20) masks the simplicity of the equation, which gives the presidential cutpoint, $\hat{\theta}$, as just a linear function of the legislative cutpoint, $\tilde{\theta}$. That is, given $\tilde{\theta}$, which determines the expected legislative vote, the voter who is indifferent between the presidential candidates is $\hat{\theta}$ as given by (4.20).

Since $\tilde{\theta}$ ranges from a minimum value of $\tilde{\theta}_D$ to a maximum value of $\tilde{\theta}_R$, the downward-sloping relationship in (4.20) is defined only for the interval $[\tilde{\theta}_D, \tilde{\theta}_R]$. A graph of this relationship is given in figure 4.6.

Equations (4.15) and (4.20) must be satisfied simultaneously in equilibrium. Expected policy in the first period must equal the ideal point of the pivotal voter. Given the legislative votes, as long as the presidential outcome is uncertain, all voters who prefer a Democratic president to a Republican president must vote Democratic and vice versa. Since the presidential cutpoint (4.20) is given as a function of $\tilde{\theta}$ as $\tilde{\theta}$ ranges from $\tilde{\theta}_D$ to $\tilde{\theta}_R$, and since the legislative cutpoint curve becomes vertical at $\tilde{\theta}_D$ and $\tilde{\theta}_R$, there

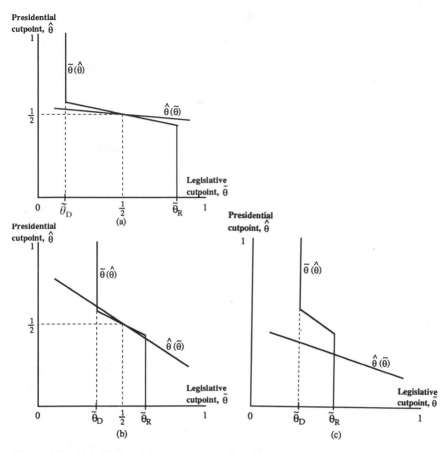

Figure 4.7. Equilibria with incomplete information. (a) The intersection shows a unique equilibrium where the outcome of the presidential election is uncertain. (b) the outer two intersections represent the stable equilibria, one with D president for sure and the other with R president for sure. (c) The intersection shows a unique equilibrium with R president for sure.

must be at least one pair $(\hat{\theta}, \tilde{\theta})$ that simultaneously solves (4.15) and (4.20). The two downward-sloping relationships can in fact cross in a variety of ways. The nature of these crossings determines the type of equilibrium.

With the help of figure 4.7 we can investigate the possible equilibria.

(*a*) *One equilibrium with uncertain presidential outcome.* This is the case of figure 4.7a. The two curves cross only once, and the intersection is in a region where the cutpoint of the presidential election makes the outcome

99

of this contest uncertain. Formally, as argued above, this occurs when

$$\frac{1}{2} - w < \hat{\theta} < \frac{1}{2} + w \tag{4.21}$$

In fact, if $\hat{\theta}$ is outside that range, for any realization of **a**, one party wins the presidential election for sure. Thus, if equation (4.21) holds, we have a unique equilibrium characterized by first-period cutpoints $\tilde{\theta}$ and $\hat{\theta}$ and second-period cutpoints $\tilde{\theta}_{D2}$ and $\tilde{\theta}_{R2}$.

(b) *Equilibria with a certain presidential victory.* Even with an uncertain distribution of voter preferences, it is possible that in equilibrium there is no uncertainty in presidential elections. Figure 4.7c represents another case in which the two curves cross only once, but this time the R party wins the presidency for sure, and $\tilde{\theta} = \tilde{\theta}_{R2}$, that is, the first-period legislative cutpoint is the same as the second-period one. An analogous situation could occur if the two curves crossed in the region for which $\tilde{\theta} = \tilde{\theta}_{D2}$ and D wins the presidency for sure.

Figure 4.7b represents a case in which we have two equilibria with certainty: a sure D presidential victory and an R presidential victory are both equilibria. The curves cross three times, but the interior crossing does not represent an equilibrium. Even though equations (4.15) and (4.20) are simultaneously satisfied with an intersection in the range with uncertainty, the electorate would bring about one of the two certain outcomes in the presidential election. The intuition for this result is very similar to the explanation, provided in chapter 3, of why tied presidential elections are not equilibria.

The equilibria represented by the two intersections with sure presidential outcomes are essentially identical to those derived in the certainty model of chapter 3. The only difference here is that some uncertainty about the legislative shares remains. Why we may have two "certain" equilibria has been explained in chapter 3.

An important question, then, is what determines whether the type (a) unique equilibrium with uncertainty occurs or type (b) equilibria with no uncertainty occur. The crucial discriminating factor is the amount of uncertainty, captured by the range of values the random variable **a** can assume.

The following example clarifies this point. Consider a case of no preference shocks (**a** is always zero, as in chapter 3), and assume that θ_R and θ_D are such that party R has a solid majority for the presidency, whereas party D is relatively strong in the legislature. This situation occurs if θ_R is much closer to the median than θ_D; see chapter 3. Now introduce a "small" amount of uncertainty; that is, **a** can now assume any value between $-w$ and $+w$ but w is very small. The most left-wing realization of the median voter is $\frac{1}{2} - w$. For w very small, even this left-most possible median voter type will prefer to see R president. Since all possible median voters prefer to hand the presidency to the Republican party, there is no uncertainty about who will win.[8]

Therefore one needs more than an infinitesimal amount of uncertainty about voters' preferences to change the nature of the equilibria obtained in the certainty model. Specifically, there exists a minimum w that is necessary to have equilibria of type (a) with uncertainty. Analytically, the condition on w that ensures that the two curves cross as in figure 4.7a, thus generating an equilibrium of type (a), is the following:[9]

$$w > \frac{(\theta_R - \theta_D - K)K}{2(1 + \beta - K^2)} \tag{4.22}$$

There are two important observations concerning (4.22). First, the higher the value of β, the lower the critical value of w needed to obtain an equilibrium with an uncertain presidential election. Voters know that it will be possible to moderate the president fully in the second period; their incentive to coordinate on a president in the first period falls as they care more about the second period. Second, for θ_R, θ_D, and β fixed, the largest w needed to satisfy (4.22) occurs for some value of α *intermediate* between 0 and 1. In fact, note that after substituting $(1 - \alpha)(\theta_R - \theta_D)$ for K in (4.22), one finds that the critical value of w is 0 both for $\alpha = 1$ and $\alpha = 0$. For $\alpha = 1$, one has a pure presidential regime with no opportunity for balancing. Consequently, voters vote sincerely for president. Unless one party is much closer to the expected median than the other, the outcome remains uncertain. For $\alpha = 0$, the legislature determines the expected policy outcome and there is no incentive to eliminate the uncertainty in the presidential election. In contrast, when there is a balance $(0 < \alpha < 1)$ between the executive and legislative institutions, an uncertain presidential outcome may not correspond to a stable conditionally sincere voting equilibrium since voters have incentives to produce a certain presidential winner who is balanced by the legislature.

[8]A slightly more subtle argument applies to the case of symmetric parties. Suppose that we have no uncertainty, i.e., $a = 0$, and the two parties are symmetric around the median, i.e., $\theta_D + \theta_R = 1$. In this case, as shown in chapter 3, the presidential election *does not* end in a tie. On the contrary, two equilibria with a *certain* presidential outcome are possible. Introduce now a small amount of uncertainty. Now the median voter is in the "small" range between $(\frac{1}{2} - w)$ and $(\frac{1}{2} + w)$. If w is small, then the argument used in chapter 3 to break the ties in presidential elections applies here as well. For instance, the voters slightly on the left of $\frac{1}{2}$ (up to $\frac{1}{2} - w$) find it in their best interest to vote R for the presidency; in doing so they eliminate the uncertainty about this election and can achieve the "optimal" moderation with a sure president. On the contrary, if w is large, the group of voters on the left of $\frac{1}{2}$ needed to eliminate any uncertainty and throw the presidential election to the Republican becomes too large. That is, voters close to the left of this range, i.e., close to $\frac{1}{2} - w$, prefer the uncertainty to a sure Republican victory.

[9]See Alesina and Rosenthal (1991) for more details on the derivation.

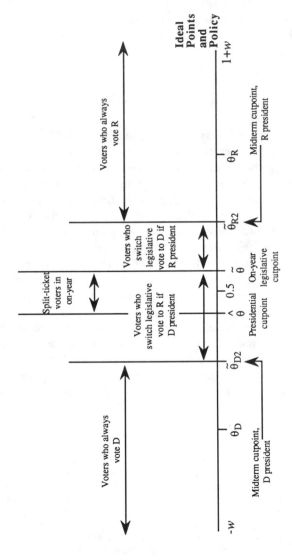

Figure 4.8.   The midterm cycle in a tight race that favors R for the presidency

4.5 DIVIDED GOVERNMENT WITH A MIDTERM CYCLE

We now examine more closely the case in which condition (4.22) holds, so that we obtain equilibria of type (i), characterized by the four cutpoints $\hat{\theta}$, $\tilde{\theta}$, $\tilde{\theta}_{R2}$, $\tilde{\theta}_{D2}$.

(a) *The midterm cycle.* Since $\tilde{\theta}_{D2} < \tilde{\theta} < \tilde{\theta}_{R2}$, we should always expect a loss of votes in midterm for the party holding the White House. The size of the midterm effect depends on how unexpected the presidential election result was. For instance, suppose that in equilibrium, $\hat{\theta}$ is such that the probability of an R victory in the presidential election is high – that is, $P(\hat{\theta})$ is above $\frac{1}{2}$. This case is shown in figure 4.8. It follows that $\tilde{\theta}$ is close to $\tilde{\theta}_{R2}$, because in the first period the voters are fairly sure that party R will win the presidency. (Recall equation (4.15).) If party R actually wins, the midterm effect is small: it involves voters between $\tilde{\theta}$ and $\tilde{\theta}_{R2}$ switching their votes from D to R in the midterm elections. If, instead, contrary to the odds, party D wins the presidency, then the midterm effect is much larger: it involves all the voters between $\tilde{\theta}_{D2}$ and $\tilde{\theta}$ switching their vote from D to R in midterm.

(b) *Split-ticket voting.* In on-year elections, split-ticket voting occurs. For instance, if $\hat{\theta} < \tilde{\theta}$, voters on the left of $\hat{\theta}$ vote DD, voters in between $\hat{\theta}$ and $\tilde{\theta}$ vote R for the presidency and D for the legislature, voters on the right of $\tilde{\theta}$ vote RR. The only case with no split-ticket voting occurs when the two-party ideal policies are perfectly symmetric around the median, when $\theta_D + \theta_R = 1$. In this case, simple algebra shows that $\hat{\theta} = \tilde{\theta} = 0.5$, and $P(\hat{\theta}) = \frac{1}{2}$. That is, both parties have a 50–50 chance of winning the presidency and the legislature. For every value of θ_D and θ_R other than the perfectly symmetric case, the model predicts some split-ticket voting.

(c) *Divided government and the midterm cycle.* Depending on the parameter values, divided government can occur as a result of the on-year or the midterm elections. For example, consider again figure 4.8. Since $\hat{\theta} < 0.5$, party R is expected to win the presidency with probability greater than $\frac{1}{2}$; $\tilde{\theta}$ is on the right of 0.5, implying that party D is expected to obtain a majority in the legislature. Thus divided government is expected as a result of the on-year elections. If party R wins the presidential elections, party D is reinforced in midterm. If, unexpectedly, party D wins the presidential elections, it is expected to suffer a large loss in midterm: in the face of an unexpected D presidential victory, the legislature is handed to the Republicans at midterm. For other parameter values, whichever party wins the presidential election also obtains a legislative majority in the on-year. Even so, the losing party in the presidential election is expected to gain a legislative majority at midterm: divided government occurs as a result of the midterm cycle. For yet other parameter values, divided government is not expected after either on-year or midterm elections.

(d)   *Coattails and regression to the mean.*   The preference shock **a**, which affects voting in both presidential and legislative elections, incorporates a mechanism analogous, observationally, to coattails. When one party receives an unusually high presidential vote, that party also does relatively well in the legislative elections. In fact, an unexpectedly large vote for one party in the presidential elections implies that the electorate's preferences are unexpectedly tilted in one direction. Thus one of the two parties "makes it big" (unexpectedly) in both elections.

Furthermore, because the random variable **a** is drawn independently for each election year, our model also incorporates a mechanism of "regression to the mean". Consider, for instance, a case in which $\hat{\theta}$ is close to 0.5, but on the left of it. This location implies that party R is a slight favorite in the presidential race. Suppose that the realization of the random variable **a** is very high, say close to its maximum value of $+w$. This case implies that the voters are much more right-leaning than "normal". As a result, party R wins the presidency with a landslide (i.e., with a much larger margin than expected) *and* party R receives more votes than expected in the legislative elections. (Recall that $V_R = 1 + \mathbf{a} - \tilde{\theta}$.) In midterm, if the realization of the random variable **a** is back to normal (i.e., close to its expected value of zero), we have a midterm effect for two reasons: first, the balancing argument emphasized in the previous section; second, the return to the mean of the distribution of voter preferences, that is, the return to the mean of the random variable **a**.

In the next section we address a related question. Elections in our model are uncertain because of the random variable **a**. It is striking, therefore, that the midterm cycle is so pervasive (remember figure 4.1). Shouldn't we observe, at least occasionally, that the pattern of realizations of the random variable **a** reverses the midterm effect? We show below that we can find parameter values for which the probability of a reversal is zero, even though the outcomes of elections are stochastic.

The reader not interested in formalization may proceed directly to section 4.7.

4.6 WHEN THE MIDTERM CYCLE IS CERTAIN

Assume, without loss of generality, that a Republican has been elected president in the first period. Then the probability that there will be a reversal of the midterm cycle is just the probability that the Republican congressional vote in the second period is greater than the same vote in the first period. That is, noting that $V_{R2} = \tilde{\theta}_{R2} + \mathbf{a}_2$ and $V_{R1} = \tilde{\theta} + \mathbf{a}_1$, we find:

$$\text{Prob(no midterm cycle)} = \text{Prob } (V_{R1} < V_{R2})$$
$$= \text{Prob}(\mathbf{a}_2 - \mathbf{a}_1 > \tilde{\theta}_{R2} - \tilde{\theta}) \qquad (4.23)$$

Consider now the special case where the parties are symmetric about the median so that $\theta_R = 1 - \theta_D$. Using the generalized pivotal-voter theorem and symmetry, we obtain:

$$\tilde{\theta}_{R2} = \frac{\theta_R}{1 + K}, \quad \tilde{\theta}_{D2} = 1 - \tilde{\theta}_{R2}, \quad \tilde{\theta} = \hat{\theta} = \frac{1}{2} \tag{4.24}$$

In order to observe a reversal, we need a combination of a relatively low on-year R vote and a relatively high midterm R vote. But since the Republican party holds the presidency and the same realization of a applies to both presidential and congressional elections, we know that the on-year vote actually had to be relatively high. In fact, when the parties are symmetric about the median, a Republican presidential victory requires $a_1 > 0$. Therefore the lowest possible value of a_2 that could lead to a reversal of the cycle is given by $(\tilde{\theta}_{R2} - \tilde{\theta})$. For $w < \tilde{\theta}_{R2} - \tilde{\theta}$, the cycle cannot be reversed.

Consider the parameter values $\theta_R = 0.75$, $\beta = 0.5$, and $\alpha = 0.5$. Then, the minimum w that satisfies the necessary condition for an equilibrium given in (4.22) is $\frac{1}{50}$. The maximum value allowed by equation (4.1) is $\frac{1}{4}$. But for these parameters, we have $\tilde{\theta} = 0.5$ and $\tilde{\theta}_{R2} = 0.6$. That is, $\tilde{\theta}_{R2} - \tilde{\theta} = 0.1$. Therefore, for any w between $\frac{1}{50}$ and $\frac{1}{10}$, a reversal of the cycle cannot occur, even though there is uncertainty in the election results. Similarly, there would not be a cycle reversal were the Democratic party to win the presidential election.

The intuition for this result is the following. The difference in the on-year and midterm cutpoints can be sufficiently large that even the worst case draws (which are $a_1 = -w$, $a_2 = +w$) of the a variable will not be enough to inhibit a midterm cycle. Of course, for the other parameters fixed, w can be increased to the point where a cycle reversal is possible: cycles are more likely to be reversed as the uncertainty increases.

The values we have used in the example are fairly realistic. The parties locate at the first and third quartiles of the voters. With a w of 0.075, near the center of the $[\frac{1}{50}, \frac{1}{10}]$ range where the cycle always occurs, the fraction of the electorate with a dominant strategy of always voting R can range from 20 to 30 percent.

In the appendix to this chapter, we develop, for uniformly distributed preferences, a general expression for the probability of reversing the midterm cycle. The important observation remains that a reversal is ruled out altogether for a reasonable range of parameter values.

4.7 CONCLUSIONS

The midterm cycle is an extremely regular occurrence in American politics. We have argued that this phenomenon is part of the institutional balancing pursued by the electorate.

In on-year elections, the congressional vote is cast under uncertainty about the identity of the next president. Right-of-center voters, for instance, vote for the Republican presidential candidate *and* vote for the same party in congressional elections. They fear that if they vote Democratic for Congress, they take the risk of facing, with some probability, a Democratic president and a Democratic congressional delegation made stronger by their vote. If the Republican presidential candidate wins, at midterm the same right-of-center voters can now safely turn to the Democratic party, to balance the president. Uncertainty about presidential elections is, therefore, the key to our explanation of the midterm cycle.

Divided government can occur either as a result of on-year elections or at midterm, or it may never occur, depending on parameter values. Specifically, the critical parameters are the party positions relative to the median voter and the relative influence in policy formation of the president and Congress.

Finally, the observation of positive "coattails" is encompassed by our model. For instance, a particularly right-wing realization of voter preferences leads to an unexpected landslide for the Republican presidential candidate and a large congressional vote for the same party. After such a landslide, at midterm one should observe a particularly big loss for the Republican party as a result of two combined forces: the balancing effect and the return to the mean of the electorate's preferences. In chapter 9 we will attempt to disentangle these two effects empirically.

Appendix to chapter 4

4.A1 THE UNCERTAINTY MODEL WITH SHOCKS IN BOTH PERIODS

This section parallels the appendix to chapter 3. In contrast to chapter 3, the analysis here relies on specific functional forms for utilities, the distribution of voter preferences, and policy outcomes. The setup of the appendix to chapter 3 is assumed to hold where no explicit change is made.

Description of the game

Political parties

Identical to chapter 3.

Voters

At time t, $t = 1, 2$, there is a continuum of voters I_t indexed by i_t. I_t is described by the uniform cumulative distribution function $H_t(i_t)$ with support a_t, $1 + a_t$. The support itself is uniformly distributed on the interval $[-w, +w]$. Thus a_t has, over its support, density $\frac{1}{2}w$. The time subscript is dropped when the meaning is clear. The random variables a_1 and a_2 are assumed independent. We further assume:

$$w \leqslant \theta_D < \theta_R \leqslant 1 - w \qquad (4.A1)$$

Voters in the interval (θ_D, θ_R) do not have weakly dominant strategies. Assumption (4.A1) guarantees us that this type of voter not only plays the game in both periods but also learns nothing about the value of a from observing his own ideal point. Players outside the interval are possibly informed about a, but, since they have weakly dominant strategies, this information has no strategic value.

107

Interpretation of the model

The intervals I_1 and I_2 are different. One interpretation of these two intervals is that the set of voters differs in the two time periods. For example, if $a_2 > a_1$, there are voters in the interval $[a_1, a_2)$ in the first period but not in the second and voters in the interval $(1 + a_1, 1 + a_2]$ in the second period but not the first. Since all period 1 voters who risk not participating in period 2 have weakly dominant strategies, the analysis below is unaffected by having some players participate for only one period.

The varying-players interpretation of the models would have to be motivated by the assumption that electoral participation is predominantly driven by non-voting from alienation (Hinich and Ordeshook (1969), Rosenthal and Sen (1973)) where non-voters are disproportionately extremists. But it would fail to take into account non-voting by indifferent middle-of-the-road voters.

A model where the set of voters does not change can be developed by allowing **a** to be drawn only once, in the first period. The first-period vote reveals **a** to the electorate, which then plays the second period with complete information. This variant of the model is sketched in section 4.A2.

Utility

Voter utility is assumed to take the form:

$$U_i = -\tfrac{1}{2}(x_1 - i)^2 - \beta\tfrac{1}{2}(x_2 - i)^2 \tag{4.A2}$$

where x_1, x_2, denote the policies in periods 1 and 2 and $0 \leqslant \beta \leqslant 1$.

Voting

Each voter's action can be characterized by a vote triple v_i with specification identical to chapter 3. Let $V_R^{E1}, V_R^{L1}, V_R^{L2}$ be defined as in chapter 3.

Electoral and policy outcomes

If $V_R^{E1} > \tfrac{1}{2}$, R is president at $t = 1$ and $t = 2$, if $V_R^{E1} < \tfrac{1}{2}$, D is president at $t = 1$ and $t = 2$, and if $V_R^{E1} = \tfrac{1}{2}$, the presidency for both $t = 1$ and $t = 2$ is awarded on the basis of a fair coin toss at $t = 1$. The coin toss rule is provided only for completeness. For $w > 0$, an exact tie is a zero measure event; thus the tie-breaking rule is irrelevant.

In period t, $t \in \{1, 2\}$, policy is given by:

$$x_t = \theta_R - KV_D^{Lt} \text{ if R is president at } t \tag{4.A3}$$

$$x_t = \theta_D + KV_R^{Lt} \text{ if D is president at } t \tag{4.A4}$$

Assumptions (4.A3) and (4.A4) guarantee that policies are always between the ideal points of the two parties:

$$\theta_D \leqslant x \leqslant \theta_R \tag{4.A5}$$

Randomization and the specification of voter strategies is unchanged from chapter 3.

Conditional sincerity

The specification of conditional sincerity is more complicated than in chapter 3 since the vote outcomes V_R are stochastic. A "purist" approach to specifying conditional sincerity would be to relate changes in expected utility to small changes in strategy components. This would just introduce more notation and make the development more cumbersome. We can simplify matters considerably by recognizing that the concept of conditional sincerity implies that voters outside (θ_D, θ_R) always use their weakly dominant strategies. Note that for any strategy **s** thus characterized by voters at or to the left of θ_D always voting D and at or to the right of θ_R always voting R, we can express the vote for a contest as:

$$V_R = EV_R + \mathbf{a} \tag{4.A6}$$

where EV_R denotes the expected vote.

Consider, then, the expected utility for voter i:

$$\text{if } \tfrac{1}{2} - w < EV_R^{E1} < \tfrac{1}{2} + w$$

$$
EU_i = -\frac{1}{2}\Bigg\{ \int_{1/2-EV_R^{E1}}^{+w} \bigg[(\theta_R - K + KEV_R^{L1} + Ka_1 - i)^2
$$

$$
+ \beta \int_{-w}^{+w} (\theta_R - K + KEV_R^{L2R} + Ka_2 - i)^2 \frac{1}{2w} da_2 \bigg] \frac{1}{2w} da_1
$$

$$
+ \int_{-w}^{1/2-EV_R^{E1}} \bigg[(\theta_D + KEV_R^{L1} + Ka_1 - i)^2
$$

$$
+ \beta \int_{-w}^{+w} (\theta_D + KEV_R^{L2D} + Ka_2 - i)^2 \frac{1}{2w} da_2 \bigg] \frac{1}{2w} da_1 \Bigg\}
$$

$$
= -\frac{1}{2}\Bigg\{ \frac{w - \dfrac{1}{2} + EV_R^{E1}}{2w} \bigg[(\theta_R - K + KEV_R^{L1} - i)^2
$$

$$
+ \beta(\theta_R - K + KEV_R^{L2R} - i)^2 \bigg]
$$

$$+ \frac{w + \frac{1}{2} - EV_R^{E1}}{2w} \left[(\theta_D + KEV_R^{L1} - i)^2 + \beta(\theta_D + KEV_R^{L2D} - i)^2 \right]$$

$$+ \frac{1}{2w} K(w^2 - (\tfrac{1}{2} - EV_R^{E1})^2)(\theta_R - \theta_D - K) + \frac{K^2 w^2 (1 + \beta)}{3} \Bigg\} \qquad (4.\text{A7})$$

where the notation "L2R" and "L2D" denotes that the expected second-period vote will depend on the outcome of the presidential election.

It can be seen that (4.A7) is a function solely of the parameters of the model, the voter's ideal point, and the expected votes for the various contests. Moreover, as (4.A7) is differentiable in the *EV*s, the chapter 3 definitions of conditional sincerity based on derivatives apply not only to the legislative votes but also to the presidential vote (for $\frac{1}{2} - w < EV_R^{E1} < \frac{1}{2} + w$), with *EV* substituted for *V*.

If $\frac{1}{2} + w < EV_R^{E1}$, R is elected president with probability 1 and $\partial EU_i / \partial EV_R^{E1}$ equals zero. Increasing R votes will never change utility. Decreasing R votes may change utility if a large enough set of voters switches from R to D. The smallest set required occurs when **a** is least favorable to R, that is when $\mathbf{a} = -w$. Parallel to chapter 3, we therefore specify:

$$\text{If } \tfrac{1}{2} + w \leqslant EV_R^{E1},$$

voter *i* votes with conditional sincerity in the presidential election if:

$$EU_i(s)|\mathbf{a} = -w, \text{ R president } >$$
$$EU_i(s)|\mathbf{a} = -w, \text{ D president } \Rightarrow s_i^{E1} = R$$
$$EU_i(s)|\mathbf{a} = -w, \text{ R president } <$$
$$EU_i(s)|\mathbf{a} = -w, \text{ D president} \Rightarrow s_i^{E1} = D$$
$$EU_i(s)|\mathbf{a} = -w, \text{ R president } =$$
$$EU_i(s)|\mathbf{a} = -w, \text{ D president} \Rightarrow s_i^{E1} = R \text{ or } D$$

Conditional sincerity for legislative components continues to be defined as in chapter 3.

Finally, if $\frac{1}{2} - w \geqslant EV_R^{E1}$, analogous remarks apply.

As in chapter 3, strategy s_i is a *conditionally sincere voter strategy* if it is conditionally sincere in all components.

Equilibrium

The discussion in the appendix to chapter 3 applies.

Note that in (4.A7), utility is, holding other components constant, quadratic, thus single-peaked, in each of the *EV*s. Consequently, the heart of the ensuing analysis is simply repeated application of the proof of the pivotal-voter theorem, Proposition 1, in the appendix to chapter 3.

The second period

In the second period, the president is fixed. Without loss of generality, take it to be R. Each voter's strategy set is $\{D, R\}$. From (4.A7), the portion of utility that is relevant is given by:

$$U_{i2R} = -(\theta_R - K + KEV_R^{L2} - i)^2 \qquad (4.A8)$$

Proposition 1: Generalized pivotal-voter theorem

See main text of the chapter for the statement of the proposition.
Proof:

The proof of Proposition 1 in the appendix to chapter 3 applies directly to (4.A8). The solution for $\tilde{\theta}_{R2}$ is found by substituting $1 - \tilde{\theta}_{R2}$ for EV_R^{L2}, differentiating (4.A8), substituting $\tilde{\theta}_{R2}$ for i, setting equal to zero, and solving.

Q.E.D.

The first period of the two-period model

Let $P(s)$ denote the probability R wins the presidential election.

$$P(s) = \begin{cases} = 1 & \text{if } EV_R^{E1} \geq w + \frac{1}{2} \\ \dfrac{w - \frac{1}{2} + EV_R^{E1}}{2w} & \text{if } w - \frac{1}{2} < EV_R^{E1} < w + \frac{1}{2} \\ = 0 & \text{if } EV_R^{E1} \leq w - \frac{1}{2} \end{cases}$$

(Note that when presidential voting has cutpoint $\hat{\theta}$, $EV_R^{E1} = 1 - \hat{\theta}$.)

Legislative voting

Proposition 2: First-period pivotal-voter theorem

If s is conditionally sincere with respect to the first-period legislative vote, s must be cutpoint in the first-period legislative component, with cutpoint $\tilde{\theta}$ satisfying:

(a)   If $P(s) = 1$, $\tilde{\theta} = \tilde{\theta}_{R2}$.
(b)   If $P(s) = 0$, $\tilde{\theta} = \tilde{\theta}_{D2}$.
(c)   If $0 < P(s) < 1$,

$$\tilde{\theta} = P(s)\tilde{\theta}_{R2} + (1 - P(s))\tilde{\theta}_{D2} \qquad (4.A9)$$

111

Proof:

1. Since second-period utility is independent of the first-period legislative components, second-period terms in (4.A7) can be ignored in the derivation of the first-period cutpoint.

2. If $P(s) = 1$ or $P(s) = 0$, there is a certain presidential winner. This and (1) imply that Proposition 1 of this appendix can be applied directly to the first period. Thus cases (a) and (b) are proven:

3. If $0 < P(s) < 1$, it can be shown that the relevant portion of utility from (4.A7) is:

$$U_{i1} = - \left\{ \frac{w - \frac{1}{2} + EV_R^{E1}}{2w} (\theta_R - K + KEV_R^{L1} - i)^2 \right.$$

$$\left. + \frac{w + \frac{1}{2} - EV_R^{E1}}{2w} (\theta_D - KEV_R^{L1} - i)^2 \right\} \qquad (4.A10)$$

4. Since (4.A10) is quadratic in EV_R^{L1}, the pivotal-voter theorem from chapter 1 and routine algebra and differentiation then establish the result for case (c).

Q.E.D.

Presidential voting

Proposition 3

Let the legislative components of **s** be cutpoint with second-period cutpoints $\tilde{\theta}_{R2}$, $\tilde{\theta}_{D2}$, and first-period cutpoint $\tilde{\theta}$. If **s** is conditionally sincere in the presidential component, **s** must be cutpoint with cutpoint $\hat{\theta}$ given by:

if $P(s) = 0$,

$$\hat{\theta} = \frac{\frac{1}{2}\{[\theta_R + \theta_D + K][(1 + K)^2 + \beta]\} + K(1 + K)^2 w - K(1 + K)^2 \tilde{\theta}}{[1 + \beta + K][1 + K]}$$

if $0 < P(s) < 1$,

$$\hat{\theta} = \frac{\frac{1}{2}\{[\theta_R + \theta_D + K][(1 + K)^2 + \beta] - K(1 + K)^2\} - K(1 + K)^2 \tilde{\theta}}{[1 + \beta - K^2][1 + K]}$$

$$= \frac{\frac{1}{2}\{[\theta_R + \theta_D][(1 + K)^2 + \beta] + \beta K\} - K(1 + K)^2 \tilde{\theta}}{[1 + \beta - K^2][1 + K]} \qquad (4.A11)$$

if $P(s) = 1$,

$$\hat{\theta} = \frac{\frac{1}{2}\{[\theta_R + \theta_D + K][(1 + K)^2 + \beta]\} - K(1 + K)^2 w - K(1 + K)^2 \tilde{\theta}}{[1 + \beta + K][1 + K]}$$

Proof:

By (4.A7) quadratic, the pivotal-voter theorem indicates that the presidential component must be cutpoint for $0 < P(s) < 1$. The solution (4.A11) is found by substituting $1 - \hat{\theta}$ for EV_R^{E1} in (4.A7) and substituting the legislative cutpoints, differentiating, substituting $\hat{\theta}$ for i, and solving.

The solution for $P(s) = 0$ is found by equating expected utilities over the two periods when $a = + w$ in the first period, substituting $\hat{\theta}$ for i and solving. Quadratic utility implies that all voters to the left of $\hat{\theta}$ prefer D to R and all to the right prefer R to D. Thus the strategy represented by $\hat{\theta}$ satisfies conditional sincerity. By arguments similar to those used to prove the pivotal-voter theorem, it is direct to show that no other strategy is conditionally sincere for $\tilde{\theta}$ that imply a solution with $P(s) = 0$.

The $P(s) = 1$ case is similar to $P(s) = 0$.   Q.E.D.

Proposition 4: Conditionally sincere voting equilibria

The strategy s is a conditionally sincere voting equilibrium if and only if it is cutpoint with second-period cutpoints $\tilde{\theta}_{R2}$, $\tilde{\theta}_{D2}$ and first-period cutpoints that simultaneously solve (4.A9) and (4.A11).

The proof is obvious.

Proposition 5: Existence

A conditionally sincere voting equilibrium exists for all $w > 0$ satisfying (4.A1).

Proof:

The second-period cutpoints $\tilde{\theta}_{R2}$ and $\tilde{\theta}_{D2}$ obviously exist. Equation (4.A9) maps $\hat{\theta}$ into $[\tilde{\theta}_{D2}, \tilde{\theta}_{R2}]$. As equation (4.A11) is monotonic and continuous (albeit with two kinks) in $\hat{\theta}$ over this interval, it must intersect (4.A9) at least once, so (4.A9) and (4.A11) have at least one solution.

     Q.E.D.

Intuition of the solution with an uncertain presidential outcome

Consider the following parameters, $\theta_D = 0.2$, $\theta_R = 0.7$, $\alpha = 0.5$, $w = 0.1$, $\beta = 0$. We immediately obtain $K = 0.25$. Solving (4.A9) and (4.A11) (with $\beta = 0$), one finds $\tilde{\theta} = 0.54$, $\hat{\theta} = 0.42$, $P(\text{R president}) = 0.9$.

Note that D wins the presidency for draws of a between -0.1 and -0.08 and R wins for a between -0.08 and $+0.1$. (See figure 4.A1.) If there were no uncertainty, the two first-period outcomes would be $x_D = 0.315$ and $x_R = 0.565$. The indifferent voter would have ideal point $0.44 = (0.315 + 0.565)/2$. Why is the actual cutpoint of 0.42 less than 0.44? Because there is a D president only for very low draws of a, the average value of the policy

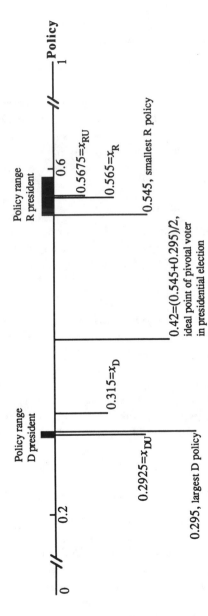

Figure 4.A1. Finding the ideal point of the pivotal presidential voter. The pivotal voter is indifferent between the most rightward possible policy were D president and the most leftward possible policy were R president. The parameters used in the figure are $\alpha = 1/2$, $\beta = 0$, $\theta_D = 0.2$, and $\theta_R = 0.7$.

with a D president under uncertainty is $x_{DU} = 0.2925 < 0.315 = x_D$ while the average with R president is $x_{RU} = 0.5675 > x_R$. The voter who would be indifferent between these two average policies has a lower ideal point $0.425 = (0.2925 + 0.5676)/2$. But the actual cutpoint is still lower. Note that the highest possible value of the policy under a D president is 0.295 while the lowest possible value under an R president is 0.545. The voter at the actual cutpoint of 0.42 is indifferent between these two policies. Why? *At the margin, increasing the expected R vote for president trades the highest policies under D for the lowest policies under R. The pivotal voter must be indifferent between the highest D policy and the lowest R policy.* Because there is more variability in policy for the likely winner R, the voter at 0.425, who is indifferent between the expected policies, will be closer to the lowest R policy than to the highest D policy. Therefore, this voter will definitely vote for R.

Note further that this indifferent voter does *not* derive equal expected utility from the two presidents. The voter who is indifferent between the two expected policies derives less utility when R is elected because there is more variance over the R policies. Therefore, the voter who derives equal expected utility is to the right of 0.425 whereas the pivotal voter at 0.42 is to the left of 0.425.

To rephrase the discussion, for $0 < P(s) < 1$, there is, in equilibrium, a critical value of **a**. For realizations above the critical value, R wins the presidency while D wins for lower values. *Conditional sincerity implies that every voter votes as if she were pivotal for this critical value of* **a**. When there is a certain presidential outcome, *every voter votes as if she were pivotal at an extreme realization of* **a** ($+w$ or $-w$).

The solution for $\hat{\theta}$ in (4.A11) is independent of the measure of uncertainty, w. This is a peculiar consequence of our technical assumptions. As w changes, for fixed $\tilde{\theta}$, the lowest R policy and the highest D policy remain invariant (as long as $w > 0.08$ in the example), so the indifferent voter does not change. Of course, w does affect the equilibrium value of $\hat{\theta}$ since w enters (4.A9).

Proposition 6: Stable conditionally sincere equilibria
For all $w > 0$ that satisfy (4.A1), there exists at least one and at most two stable conditionally sincere equilibria.
Proof:
Case A. Equations (4.A9) and (4.A11) do not have an interior solution with $0 < P < 1$. In this case, there is a unique conditionally sincere equilibrium. Its stability can be proved by arguments similar to the certainty case in chapter 3.
Case B. There exists a unique interior solution and no solutions with

$P = 0$ or $P = 1$. This occurs if there is an interior solution and

$$w > w_C = \frac{K(\theta_R - \theta_D - K)}{2(1 + \beta - K^2)}$$

It is obvious that in any strategy **r** that would render the interior solution **s** unstable, second-period components must remain fixed. Assume that there is an I_S which shifts to strategy **r** where either EV_R^{E1} or EV_R^{L1} is increased and the other is not decreased over the corresponding values in **s**. This produces outcomes equivalent to those produced by a shift in the cutpoints to $\hat{\theta}' \leqslant \hat{\theta}$ and $\tilde{\theta}' \leqslant \tilde{\theta}$. But conditional sincerity and (4.A9) and (4.A11) imply that at the ' cutpoints, both *EV*s should be decreased. (See figure 4.A2.) Hence increasing both *EV*s is inconsistent with conditional sincerity in I_s. Next consider shifts equivalent to cutpoints $\hat{\theta}'' > \hat{\theta}$ and $\tilde{\theta}'' < \tilde{\theta}$. But at these cutpoints, either EV_R^{E1} should be increased or EV_R^{L1} decreased since $w > w_c$. (Again see the figure.) Hence changing *EV*s is again inconsistent with conditional sincerity. The remaining possibilities have a similar analysis. Consequently, the unique interior solution is stable.

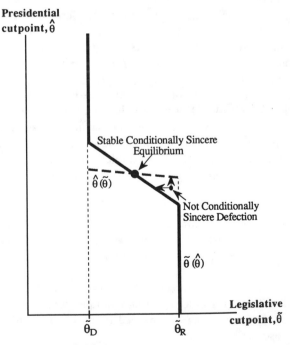

Figure 4.A2. A stable equilibrium where the presidential outcome remains uncertain. The uncertainty (w) about voter preferences is high.

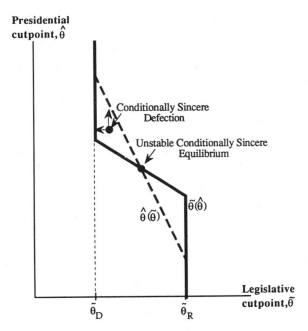

Figure 4.A3. The equilibrium where the presidential outcome remains uncertain is unstable. The uncertainty (w) about voter preferences is low.

Case C. There exists an interior solution and two exterior solutions ($w < w_c$).

In this case the interior solution is unstable. If EV_R^{E1} is decreased and EV_R^{L1} is increased to produce outcomes equivalent to those produced by the defection point in figure 4.A3, (4.A9) implies a further increase in EV_R^{L1} and (4.A11) a further decrease in EV_R^{E1}. Consequently, it is possible to find an I_s, r that satisfy conditional sincerity. It is direct to show that the members of I_s have higher utility under r. The interior solution is thus unstable.

In this case, either one or both of the exterior solutions are stable, by arguments similar to those used in the certainty case.

Case D. An infinity of interior solutions ($w = w_c$). Pick any interior solution. There exists I_s, r that can generate any other interior solution. It can be shown that a move in one direction always improves expected utility. Consequently, no interior solution is stable. Again, at least one of the two end points is stable. Q.E.D.

The reader can readily choose parameter values that illustrate cases A, B, C, and D.

4.A2 THE MODEL WITH a DRAWN ONLY IN THE FIRST PERIOD

When only a single a is drawn, its value is revealed at the end of the first period. The second period thus returns us to the analysis of the certainty model with cutpoints:

$$\tilde{\theta}_{R2}(a) = (\theta_R + Ka)/(1 + K) \qquad \text{and}$$

$$\tilde{\theta}_{D2}(a) = (\theta_D + K + Ka)/(1 + K) \qquad (4.A12)$$

In this case, the expected utility condition becomes, instead of (4.A7):

$$
\begin{aligned}
EU_i = -\frac{1}{2}\Bigg\{ &\int_{1/2 - EV_R^{E1}}^{+w} \Bigg[(\theta_R - K + KEV_R^{L1} + Ka_1 - i)^2 \\
&+ \beta\left(\frac{\theta_R + Ka_1}{1+K} - i\right)^2 \Bigg]\frac{1}{2w}\,da_1 \\
&+ \int_{-w}^{1/2 - EV_R^{E1}} \Bigg[(\theta_D + KEV_R^{L1} + Ka_1 - i)^2 \\
&+ \beta\left(\frac{\theta_D + K + Ka_1}{1+K} - i\right)^2 \Bigg]\frac{1}{2w}\,da_1 \Bigg\} \\
= -\frac{1}{2}\Bigg\{ &\frac{w - \frac{1}{2} + EV_R^{E1}}{2w}\Bigg[(\theta_R - K + KEV_R^{L1} - i)^2 + \beta\left(\frac{\theta_R}{1+K} - i\right)^2 \Bigg] \\
&+ \frac{w + \frac{1}{2} - EV_R^{E1}}{2w}\Bigg[(\theta_D + KEV_R^{L1} - i)^2 + \beta\left(\frac{\theta_D + K}{1+K} - i\right)^2 \Bigg] \\
&+ \frac{1}{2w}(w^2 - (\tfrac{1}{2} - EV_R^{E1})^2)(\theta_R - \theta_D - K)\left(1 + \frac{\beta}{(1+K)^2}\right) \\
&+ \frac{K^2 w^2(1 + \beta/(1+K^2))}{3} \Bigg\} \qquad (4.A13)
\end{aligned}
$$

Equation (4.A9) continues to hold with $\tilde{\theta}_{R2} = \tilde{\theta}_{R2}(0)$ and $\tilde{\theta}_{D2} = \tilde{\theta}_{D2}(0)$. An analysis parallel to that of the draws of independent values of a shows that the presidential cutpoint for an interior solution is given by:

$$
\hat{\theta} = \frac{[\theta_R + \theta_D]\left[1 + \dfrac{\beta}{(1+K)^2}\right] - 2K\tilde{\theta}}{2\left[1 + \dfrac{\beta}{(1+K)}\right] - K\left[1 + \dfrac{\beta}{(1+K)^2}\right]} \qquad (4.A14)
$$

Parallels to Propositions 5 and 6 hold.

4.A3 THE PROBABILITY OF A REVERSAL OF THE MIDTERM CYCLE

The probability of a reversal of the cycle can be written as:

$$\text{Prob(Reversal)} \equiv Q = \text{Prob(R president)} \times \text{Prob(Reversal}|\text{R president)}$$
$$+ \text{Prob(D president)} \times \text{Prob(Reversal}|\text{D president)}.$$

We have immediately:

$$\text{Prob(R president)} = \frac{1}{2w}\left[w - \hat{\theta} + \frac{1}{2}\right]$$

$$\text{Prob(D president)} = \frac{1}{2w}\left[w + \hat{\theta} - \frac{1}{2}\right]$$

$$\text{Prob(Reversal}|\text{R president)} = \text{Prob}(a_2 - a_1 > \tilde{\theta}_{R2} - \tilde{\theta})$$

The joint distribution of a_1, a_2 conditional on R president is uniform on the rectangle shown in figure 4.A4. The figure also shows the triangular region that corresponds to draws of the a's that produce a reversal. Routine geometric calculations then provide the following result.

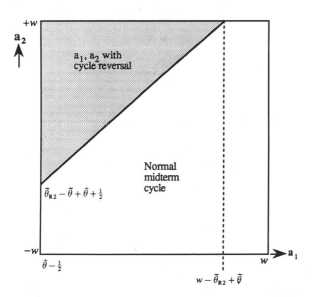

Figure 4.A4. Midterm cycle reversal with R president. The shaded area shows the combinations of low first-period shocks (a_1) and high second-period shocks (a_2) that lead to a reversal where the R legislative vote increases in the second period. The overall probability of a reversal is given by the ratio of the area of the shaded points to the area of the rectangle.

119

$$\text{Prob(Reversal}|\text{R president)} = 0 \qquad \text{if } w \leqslant w_R \equiv \tilde{\theta}_{R2} - \tilde{\theta} + \hat{\theta} - \tfrac{1}{2}$$

$$= \frac{(w - \tilde{\theta}_{R2} + \tilde{\theta} - \hat{\theta} + \tfrac{1}{2})^2}{4w(w - \hat{\theta} + \tfrac{1}{2})} \qquad \text{otherwise}$$

Similarly,

$$\text{Prob(Reversal}|\text{D president)} = 0 \qquad \text{if } w \leqslant w_D \equiv \tilde{\theta} - \tilde{\theta}_{D2} - \hat{\theta} + \tfrac{1}{2}$$

$$= \frac{(w + \tilde{\theta}_{D2} - \tilde{\theta} + \hat{\theta} - \tfrac{1}{2})^2}{4w(w + \hat{\theta} - \tfrac{1}{2})} \qquad \text{otherwise}$$

Combining these results, we obtain, if $w > \max\{w_D, w_R\}$:

$$Q = \frac{1}{8w^2}[\,(w - \tilde{\theta}_{R2} + \tilde{\theta} - \hat{\theta} + \tfrac{1}{2})^2 + (w + \tilde{\theta}_{D2} - \tilde{\theta} + \hat{\theta} - \tfrac{1}{2})^2]$$

In the case of parties symmetric about the median, this simplifies to:

$$Q = \frac{1}{4w^2}[w - \tilde{\theta}_{R2} + \tfrac{1}{2}]^2$$

Routine differentiation and algebra establishes in this case that

$$\frac{\partial Q}{\partial \tilde{\theta}_{R2}} < 0$$

Differentiation and use of the fact that $\tilde{\theta}_{R2} > \tfrac{1}{2}$ shows

$$\frac{\partial Q}{\partial w} > 0$$

5

Diversity, persistence, and mobility

5.1 INTRODUCTION

This chapter explores three extensions of the basic model presented in chapters 3 and 4. These developments show how our framework is useful for analyzing a variety of issues in voting theory in a rich and realistic institutional setup.

We begin, in section 5.2, by exploring the case of heterogeneous parties. While in chapters 3 and 4 we assumed that *both* the president and the congressional delegation of a party have the same ideal policy, here we generalize our analysis by considering cases in which the president and the congressional delegation of the same party have *different* preferences. In chapter 3, we showed that, with homogeneous parties, the policy outcome was always in between the ideal policies of the two presidents: it was always the legislature which moderated the president. With heterogeneous parties, once again the voters use the "checks and balances" provided by the Constitution to achieve moderation; however, the president may now play a moderating role. Specifically, if the congressional delegation of a party is more extreme than the president of the same party, the final policy outcome may be in between the two ideal policies of the president and the legislators of the same party. In this case, *the president moderates Congress*.

In section 5.3 we address another institutional aspect of the American electoral system, namely the staggered terms of office for senators. This feature has important implications for voter behavior, but does not change the nature of our results concerning moderation.

Finally, in section 5.4 we allow the two parties to choose their platforms: we assume that the two parties can adopt binding platforms as in the Wittman–Calvert model reviewed in chapter 2. Therefore, the parties are not constrained to adopt their ideal policies, but can assume more moderate platforms to increase their chances of victory. The basic point which we emphasize is that if presidential candidates know that, when in office, they will be balanced by Congress, they have *less* incentive to "converge" and be moderate than otherwise. The voters know that by splitting control they can achieve moderation; thus an "extreme" presidential candidate may find it both not as rewarding to be moderate *and* more costly because an adverse legislature will pull her even further away from her ideal policy. Thus, congressional balancing leads to moderation of *policies* but polarization of party *platforms*.

5.2 HETEROGENEOUS PARTIES

We capture intra-party heterogeneity by allowing the president and the legislative delegation of the same party to have different ideal policies. For simplicity, we continue to assume homogeneity within legislative delegations. In the United States, heterogeneous legislative delegations reflect plurality elections of representatives and senators in districts and states. Here we retain our assumption of proportional representation in a single national district.[1]

We denote the four ideal policies with two subscripts: the first identifies the party, D or R, the second identifies the "executive", E, or the "legislature", L. So for instance, θ_{DL} is the ideal policy of the legislative delegation of party D.

We impose only the following conditions:

$$\theta_{DE} < \theta_{RE}; \qquad \theta_{DE} < \theta_{RL}$$
$$\theta_{DL} < \theta_{RE}; \qquad \theta_{DL} < \theta_{RL} \qquad (5.1)$$

These four inequalities indicate that while both ideal policies of party D are on the left of both ideal policies of party R, there are no restrictions on the relative positions of the two ideal points *within party*. Thus, for instance, the Republican congressional delegation can be either on the right or on the left of the Republican president, but it is certainly on the right of both the Democratic president and the Democratic congressional delegation.

The policy outcomes are now obtained by generalizing expressions presented in chapter 3 in a manner that accounts for the difference between the ideal policies of the congressional delegations and those of the presidential candidates. Specifically, when D is president, policy is given by:

$$x^D = \alpha\theta_{DE} + (1 - \alpha)[V_R\theta_{RL} + (1 - V_R)\theta_{DL}] \qquad (5.2)$$

and when R is president policy is given by:

$$x^R = \alpha\theta_{RE} + (1 - \alpha)[V_R\theta_{RL} + (1 - V_R)\theta_{DL}] \qquad (5.3)$$

---

[1]For a model of balancing within Senate delegations of each state see Alesina, Fiorina, and Rosenthal (1991).

Equations (5.2) and (5.3) are the direct generalization of equations (3.1) and (3.2), which characterize policy outcomes for the case of homogeneous parties. As in chapters 3 and 4, the policy outcome is a compromise between the ideal policy of the president and that of the legislature. The president's weight in this compromise continues to be captured by α.

For brevity and simplicity, we analyze only the case of complete information, as in chapter 3. We do not develop explicitly the case of incomplete information, but it will be clear how our basic arguments of chapter 4 generalize to the case of heterogeneous parties.

Even with heterogeneous parties the pivotal-voter theorem holds. Policy outcomes continue to equal legislative cutpoints. In fact, the reader can easily verify that the policy outcomes with a D and an R president are as follows:

$$x^D = \tilde{\theta}_D = \frac{\alpha\theta_{DE} + (1-\alpha)\theta_{DL} + K'}{1+K'} \tag{5.4}$$

$$x^R = \tilde{\theta}_R = \frac{\alpha\theta_{RE} + (1-\alpha)\theta_{RL}}{1+K'} \tag{5.5}$$

where

$$K' \equiv (1-\alpha)(\theta_{RL} - \theta_{DL}) \tag{5.6}$$

These expressions are the appropriate generalizations of the corresponding ones, given in chapter 3. Note that if $\theta_{DE} = \theta_{DL}$ and $\theta_{RE} = \theta_{RL}$, as in the case of homogeneous parties, expressions (5.4) and (5.5) reduce to the expressions in Proposition 3.1 and (5.6) reduces to (3.5). The basic features of the two-period equilibrium described in chapter 3 still hold. First, the legislative vote for a party is always higher when the party does not control the presidency, i.e., $\tilde{\theta}_R > \tilde{\theta}_D$. Second, divided government is possible. Third, the midterm legislative vote is identical to the on-year one; thus, we have no midterm cycle.

With homogeneous parties, the policy outcomes are always in between the ideal policies of the two presidents: the latter are moderated by the legislature. With heterogeneous parties, the policy outcomes are always in between the two most extreme ideal points. Formally, this amounts to the following inequalities:

$$\min\{\theta_{DE}, \theta_{DL}\} < x^D < x^R < \max\{\theta_{RE}, \theta_{RL}\} \tag{5.7}$$

An interesting question is the following: when, with heterogeneous parties, are presidents moderated by the legislature, namely $\theta_{DE} < x^D < x^R < \theta_{RE}$, as with homogeneous parties?

To address this question we focus, without loss of generality, on the case of R president; the case of D president is symmetric. Also, we treat only the most interesting case, in which the two parties are on opposite sides of the median, that is:

$$\max\{\theta_{DE}, \theta_{DL}\} < \tfrac{1}{2} < \min\{\theta_{RE}, \theta_{RL}\} \tag{5.8}$$

Straightforward algebraic manipulations establish that $x^R < \theta_{RE}$ if equation (5.8) holds and *any* of the following three conditions holds:

(1) $\theta_{RE} \geqslant \tfrac{2}{3}$ Executives are always moderated if they are further than $\tfrac{1}{6}$ from the median.

(2) $\theta_{DL} + \theta_{RL} = 1$ Executives are always moderated if the legislative parties are symmetric around the median.

(3) $\theta_{RE} \geqslant \theta_{RL}$ A president who is more extreme than his legislative party is always moderated.

A parametric example in which none of the conditions holds and equilibrium policies are exterior to the president's ideal policy is given by $\theta_{DE} = 0$, $\theta_{DL} = \tfrac{1}{4}$, $\theta_{RE} = \tfrac{15}{28}$, $\theta_{RL} = 1$, $\alpha = \tfrac{1}{2}$. In this example, the executives are sharply to the left of their legislative parties with the R executive just to the right of the median (which equals $\tfrac{1}{2}$). Using (5.4) and (5.5), we have:

$$\theta_{DE} < x^D = \tfrac{4}{11} < \theta_{RE} < x^R = \tfrac{43}{77}$$

While with a D president the outcome would be between the two presidential ideal points, it would *not* with an R president: with a Republican president, the policy outcome is on the right of the president's ideal policy. The outcome with an R president, however, is the more moderate of the two; this outcome is closer to the median than the outcome with a D president, and it implies divided government. In fact, for these parameter values x^R is the only equilibrium; a middle-of-the-road president moderates a conservative legislature. Thus, the idea of balancing readily generalizes to the case of heterogeneous parties.

In chapter 4 we showed that the crucial element that generates the midterm cycle is uncertainty about the presidential election. The assumption of heterogeneous parties does not change this basic mechanism of the midterm cycle, which, therefore, persists in this more general framework.

5.3 STAGGERED TERMS OF OFFICE FOR THE LEGISLATURE

We have up to now assumed that the entire legislature was re-elected each period by proportional representation. While this simplified the analysis considerably, it of course does not capture two key aspects of the American system. One is that plurality rule is used to elect members to individual seats with a geographic basis. Ingberman and Rosenthal (1994) have recently shown that our basic qualitative results hold when the legislature is elected from individual member districts rather than by proportional representation.

Policy will be close to the ideal point of the median voter in the pivotal legislative district. The second is that senators are elected to staggered terms of office, with roughly one-third of the Senate elected every two years. When the entire legislature is elected every two years and the executive every four, theoretical analysis can be simplified to the study of a two-period model representing on-year and midterm elections. Since all political offices are up for grabs in on-years, there is no incentive for rational voters to plan beyond two periods, namely one presidential term. With staggered terms, longer term dynamics become relevant, since not all the legislature is re-elected every two years. Nevertheless, staggered terms of office do not change the basic implications of our theory, as can be seen, most easily, in the complete information version of our model.

Assume that only a fraction Γ of the legislature is elected in each period; thus a fraction $(1 - \Gamma)$ is carried over from previous elections. We then have:

$$W_{Rt} = (1 - \Gamma)W_{Rt-1} + \Gamma V_{Rt} \qquad (5.9)$$

where W_{Rt} is R's share of the legislature in period t and V_{Rt} the fraction of R votes for the legislature in period t. Equation (5.9) implies that we can no longer study a two-period model.

Assume, however, that there was an initial period in which the entire legislature was selected. Continue to assume that the electorate is identical in all periods. Assume the legislative voting equilibrium for the basic model was represented by the cutpoint $\tilde{\theta}_R$ with $V_R = 1 - \tilde{\theta}_R$. If in some initial period, the entire legislature was elected, this cutpoint could simply be repeated in future periods with $V_{Rt} = W_{Rt-1} = W_{Rt} = 1 - \tilde{\theta}_R$. In other words, in a world of stable preferences, staggered terms are of no consequence.

The Founders, in contrast, implemented staggered terms because they were concerned about preference instability. An extreme case of preference instability would be represented by a complete turnover of the electorate in every election with the new electorate having a discount factor of 0. Alternatively, one might consider an electorate that voted myopically, without taking into consideration the dynamic implications of their current actions. In this case, the pivotal-voter theorem continues to hold, except that the expressions for the policy must be adjusted to reflect the inherited level of W_{Rt-1}. In place of the expression for $\tilde{\theta}_D$ in (3.8) we would have:

$$\tilde{\theta}_D = \frac{\theta_D + K[(1 - \Gamma)W_{Rt-1} + \Gamma]}{1 + K\Gamma} \qquad (5.10)$$

Analysis of this expression shows that the policy will be intermediate between that which prevailed in the previous period and that which would obtain in our model without staggered terms. The basic logic of an intermediate policy carries over if voters have a finite horizon that begins at time zero and ends at T (with the last midterm election). In the T period setting, it is instructive to consider the situation of an initial period with the legislative vote not at its equilibrium value, namely $W_{R0} \neq 1 - \tilde{\theta}_R$. Given the staggered structure, how does the system move from W_{R0} to the equilibrium value of W_R, namely $(1 - \tilde{\theta}_R)$?

In order to solve these dynamic problems, one needs to start from the last period and solve backward. In the midterm election of period T the voters inherit W_{RT-1}. The equilibrium in period T would correspond to the unstaggered case except that the strategies would be adjusted for the stock represented by W_{RT-1} as in (5.10). That is, in voting for Congress in period T, the voters would take into account that the composition of the Tth Congress will depend not only on the election in period T, but on the inherited part of Congress which is not at contest in period T, summarized by W_{RT-1}. The vote in period T, thus the legislative cutpoints, $\tilde{\theta}_{RT}$ and $\tilde{\theta}_{DT}$, would depend upon W_{RT-1}, since the voters care about the composition of the entire Congress. Period T then has two "conditional" cutpoints: $\tilde{\theta}_{RT}(W_{RT-1})$ and $\tilde{\theta}_{DT}(W_{RT-1})$. At time $(T-1)$, voter decisions in both the presidential and legislative elections will be taken, in light of the conditional cutpoints $\tilde{\theta}_{RT}$ and $\tilde{\theta}_{DT}$. In particular, the pivotal voter in the legislative election at $T-1$ must, in terms of his utility over both periods $T-1$ and T, want to see V_{RT} neither increased nor decreased, given the stock represented by W_{RT-2}. The solution for $T-1$ can then be used to solve for $T-2$ and so on until the first period is reached.

The basic feature of balancing continues to prevail with staggered terms. The initial composition of Congress, represented by W_{R0}, influences the dynamic path of congressional vote shares. For instance, if party R always wins the presidency in the T periods, the composition of Congress converges from the initial W_{R0} to the unstaggered "equilibrium" value, given by $1 - \tilde{\theta}_R$. That is, election by election, renewing one fraction Γ of Congress, the voters aim at the "steady-state" composition of Congress. The values of T, Γ, and W_{R0} determine the "speed of convergence", and whether full convergence is achieved within T periods. For instance, the higher is Γ the faster is convergence because a larger fraction of Congress can be adjusted every period.[2] The complexity of solving this dynamic problem convinced us to restrict the main part of this book to the simpler case of unstaggered terms. Our basic results generalize to the more complex case of staggered terms.

There is, however, one important insight that emerges specifically in the staggered case: the idea that *history matters*. With staggered terms, the

---

[2] An additional technical problem is raised by the possibility of multiple equilibria (see chapter 3). If in the path between time zero and T both a D and an R presidential victory are equilibria, then it is, in principle, impossible to identify which equilibrium would be chosen.

adjustment path of congressional vote in the uncertainty case (chapter 4) would depend upon the history of realizations of the variable a, which characterizes the distribution of voter preferences. This dependence on history occurs even when there are independent realizations of a. In fact, if, say, there is a low realization of a at time t, that is, the electorate is left-leaning, then V_{Rt}, the fraction of the electorate voting R in period t, is low. It follows that W_{Rt} is low and W_{Rt}, as emphasized above, influences the composition of the legislature from time t onward.

Finally, we note a connection between the staggered term case and the widely observed phenomenon of incumbency advantage in Congress. Suppose, for instance, that in period $(T-2)$ party D were relatively strong in Congress. In both the certainty and uncertainty models the election of an R president would be more likely than it would be if there were no staggered terms. The reason is that if the voters cannot make a large enough adjustment to W_{RT-1} and W_{RT}, they will want to turn to an R president to moderate a D legislature. Indeed, incumbency effects should produce results with much the flavor of staggered terms. If, independent of national policy concerns, voters engage in a "personal vote" (Cain, Ferejohn, and Fiorina (1987)), then incumbents who provide constituency services are favored. If the incumbents are overwhelmingly Democrats, national policy balance is achieved by electing a Republican president. In chapter 6, we provide a more extensive theoretical and empirical treatment of the connection between incumbency and balancing in congressional elections.

5.4 "MOBILE" PARTIES[3]

Thus far we have studied situations in which the two parties adopt their ideal policies as their platforms. That is, in the model of the previous two chapters a president unconstrained by Congress would follow her party's ideal policy (θ_D or θ_R). In chapter 2 we have grounded this assumption with an argument concerning the credibility of electoral platforms. If a presidential candidate cannot make a credible commitment to implement her platform if elected, the only two credible platforms are the parties' ideal policies (see section 2.4).

This section explores the case in which the two parties can make binding commitments to their platforms. Chapter 2 also showed that, in this case, the platforms are not necessarily identical to ideal policies. Remember, however, that polarization of party platforms occurs only with uncertainty about the distribution of voter preferences. Without this uncertainty, even policy-oriented parties fully converge. In this section, which is concerned with the degree of platform convergence with executive–legislature interac-

[3]The material covered in this section draws heavily upon Alesina and Rosenthal (1992).

tion, we proceed under the realistic assumption of incomplete information about the distribution of voter preferences.

In summary, we extend the model developed in chapter 4 by allowing the two political parties to choose their platforms. We show that our results concerning policy moderation, divided government, and the midterm cycle do not rely on the fixity of parties' platforms. The polarization of party platforms does not disappear; on the contrary, the presidential–congressional interaction *increases* the tendency of parties to polarize. In fact, each party knows that, if it wins the presidency, Congress will have an influence on policy. Therefore, the presidential candidate adopts a platform which is more extreme than the one that would be chosen without congressional moderation. It is even possible that the two parties adopt platforms which are more distant from each other than their ideal policies. For instance, the Republican party, knowing that if it wins the presidency, it is likely to face a Democratic-controlled Congress, may choose a platform which is to the right of its true ideal policy![4]

We now proceed to a formal development of this argument. The structure of the game is exactly as in chapter 4 except that now the two parties are allowed to simultaneously choose platforms (denoted ψ_D and ψ_R) before the on-year elections. The electoral platforms cannot be changed either before or after the presidential election for the entire presidential term.[5] After platforms are chosen, the on-year presidential and congressional elections take place. In midterm, new congressional elections occur, exactly as in chapters 3 and 4.

The policy functions are as in chapters 3 and 4. Namely, if party D wins the presidency, policy is given by:

$$x^D = \alpha\psi_D + (1-\alpha)[V_R\psi_R + (1-V_R)\psi_D] \qquad (5.11)$$

If R wins the presidency, policy is given by:

$$x^R = \alpha\psi_R + (1-\alpha)[V_R\psi_R + (1-V_R)\psi_D] \qquad (5.12)$$

These expressions are the exact analog of (3.1) and (3.2). The only difference is that now we have the policy platforms (ψ_D and ψ_R) in (5.11) and (5.12), rather than the parties' ideal policies (θ_D and θ_R), as in (3.1) and (3.2).

The two utility-maximizing parties choose the platforms ψ_D and ψ_R. As in chapter 2, each party's objective function depends upon both the policy outcomes and a positive premium for winning the White House. Thus, the

---

[4]The recent 1992 campaign is rather suggestive on this point. The Republican party adopted a very conservative platform (for instance on abortion) and the Bush–Quayle campaign often emphasized the need to balance the Democrats, expected to be strong in Congress.

[5]Thus, in this section there is no "incumbency advantage" in either presidential or legislative elections.

policy objective function of party D is given by:

$$u_D = u(x_1, \theta_D) + \beta u(x_2, \theta_D) \tag{5.13}$$

This expression is the analog of (2.1). The only difference is that we now explicitly account for the two-period presidential term. In addition to the policy utility, a party receives an additional benefit of $(1 + \beta)\hat{u}$. As discussed in chapter 2, $\hat{u}$ captures the benefits of holding the White House *per se*. The corresponding expression for party R is:

$$u_R = u(x_1, \theta_R) + \beta u(x_2, \theta_R) \tag{5.14}$$

As before, θ_R and θ_D are the ideal policies of the two parties, and x_1 and x_2 are the policies in periods 1 and 2 respectively. We do not include any electoralist premium for winning congressional elections; this would only introduce a complication that would not bring additional insights.

The electoral game has two stages. In the first stage the two parties choose the platforms ψ_D and ψ_R. In the second stage, given ψ_D and ψ_R, the voters cast their ballots in the presidential and congressional elections.

We begin with the second stage, when the two platforms are given and fixed. The analysis of voting behavior in the second stage parallels our treatment of chapter 4. Specifically, assume that ψ_D and ψ_R are fixed. (In equilibrium, as in chapter 2, $\psi_D < \psi_R$.) We can derive the presidential cutpoint $\hat{\theta}$, and the three legislative cutpoints $\tilde{\theta}$ (on-year elections) and $\tilde{\theta}_D$ and $\tilde{\theta}_R$ (midterm elections cutpoints with a D or an R president respectively). These cutpoints are exactly as in chapter 4. The expressions derived in chapter 4 for $\hat{\theta}$, $\tilde{\theta}$, $\tilde{\theta}_D$, and $\tilde{\theta}_R$ are identical here except that we need to substitute ψ_D instead of θ_D and ψ_R instead of θ_R.

The four cutpoints, $\hat{\theta}$, $\tilde{\theta}$, $\tilde{\theta}_D$, and $\tilde{\theta}_R$, identify the four policies as a function of ψ_D and ψ_R, and the realization of the preference shock $\mathbf{a}$, namely:

$$x_1^D = x_1^D(\psi_D, \psi_R, \mathbf{a}); \qquad x_2^D = x_2^D(\psi_D, \psi_R, \mathbf{a}) \tag{5.15}$$

$$x_1^R = x_1^R(\psi_D, \psi_R, \mathbf{a}); \qquad x_2^R = x_2^R(\psi_D, \psi_R, \mathbf{a}) \tag{5.16}$$

In addition, one can also derive the probability of a D victory in the presidential election, as a function of the two platforms:[6]

$$P = P(\psi_D, \psi_R) \tag{5.17}$$

In the first stage ψ_D and ψ_R are simultaneously chosen by the two parties, which know that $x_1^D, x_2^D, x_1^R, x_2^R$, and P, will be determined via expressions (5.15), (5.16), and (5.17). In words, for any given pair ψ_D and ψ_R, the

---

[6]The reader will remember that P is strictly between 0 and 1, i.e., we do not have a "sure" winner when the amount of uncertainty concerning voter preferences is above a certain minimum level. Analogous conditions on the amount of uncertainty, captured by · the parameter w (see chapter 4), hold here. See Alesina and Rosenthal (1992) for further details.

two parties can compute how these platforms will be translated into policies by the executive–legislative interaction and can calculate the odds of the presidential race.

Given that each party has no control over its opponent's choice, the appropriate way to analyze this game is to find the Nash equilibrium. As in chapter 2, party R finds the platform, ψ_R, which maximizes its welfare, taking the platform of party D as given. Recalling that the four policy outcomes and P depend on both ψ_D and ψ_R, the problem faced by party R can be written as follows:

$$\max_{\psi_R} \delta P[E(u(x_1^R, \theta_R) + \beta[u(x_2^R, \theta_R)])] + \delta(1 - P)[E(u(x_1^D, \theta_R)$$

$$+ \beta u(x_2^D, \theta_R))] + (1 - \delta)(1 + \beta)P\hat{u} \tag{5.18}$$

where δ is, as in chapter 2, the value placed on policy relative to officeholding; the expectations operator E is with reference to the distribution of the congressional vote conditional on the presidential outcome.

The analogous problem for party D is to maximize its utility, taking ψ_R as given:

$$\max_{\psi_D} \delta P[E(u(x_1^R, \theta_D) + \beta u(x_2^R, \theta_D))] + \delta(1 - P)[E(u(x_1^D, \theta_D)$$

$$+ \beta u(x_2^D, \theta_D))] + (1 - \delta)(1 + \beta)(1 - P)\hat{u} \tag{5.19}$$

These expressions are the exact analog of (2.9) and (2.10). The only difference is that we now explicitly acknowledge that presidential terms last two periods and the platforms, ψ_D and ψ_R, are different from actual policies because of the executive–legislative interaction.

An explicit solution to problems (5.17) and (5.18) is not easy to derive. However, we have evaluated the solutions (ψ_D and ψ_R) numerically for given parameter values. For details, the reader can consult Alesina and Rosenthal (1992). We have chosen values for the exogenous parameters in our model, namely θ_D, θ_R, w, α, and $\hat{u}$. Given these parameter values we have computed the solutions ψ_D and ψ_R. By varying the values of the exogenous parameters we can explore how they influence the platforms chosen by the parties.

The most important results of this exercise can be summarized as follows:

(1) Whenever an equilibrium exists, the solution is unique with $\psi_D \leqslant \psi_R$. Complete convergence, i.e., $\psi_D = \psi_R$, occurs when $\hat{u}$ is sufficiently high or w is sufficiently low. That is, exactly as in chapter 2, polarization of party platforms requires both that parties are sufficiently policy-motivated (i.e., $\hat{u}$ is low) and that there is a sufficient amount of uncertainty about the preferences of the electorate (i.e., w has to be high). Indeed, a basic result

is that the parties converge with $0 < \alpha < 1$ if and only if they converge for $\alpha = 1$.

(2) When the two parties do *not* converge, the executive–legislative interaction *increases* the polarization of party platforms. In fact, consider a pure presidential regime; Congress is uninfluential in the policy process, and thus $\alpha = 1$ in equations (5.11) and (5.12). This is the Calvert–Wittman model studied in chapter 2. Consider specific values for θ_D, θ_R, $\hat{u}$, and w and derive the platforms, denoted ψ_D^1 and ψ_R^1. Remember that these presidential platforms equal policy outcomes, since there is no Congress. Consider now the solution for ψ_D and ψ_R with the same parameter values for θ_D, θ_R, $\hat{u}$, and w, but with $\alpha < 1$, that is for the case in which Congress has an influence in policy formation. We find that in this case policy platforms are *more polarized*: ψ_D is on the left of ψ_D^1 and ψ_R is on the right of ψ_R^1.

The intuition of this result is clear. Both parties know that, if they win the presidency, they will be balanced by Congress. Thus, they counteract by choosing relatively extreme platforms: the latter are more extreme than if the president has her way without having to deal with Congress. Furthermore, the electorate knows that a president elected with an extreme platform can be moderated by reinforcing the opposition in Congress. Thus, when a party chooses an extreme platform, it knows that its candidates will not lose as much in the eye of the electorate as they would without the balancing role of Congress. These strategic considerations lead to the adoption of platforms which are more polarized when the role of Congress is taken into account, than when it is not.

(3) For a range of parameter values, the two parties choose platforms which are *more extreme than their ideal policies*. Namely ψ_D is on the left of θ_D and ψ_R is on the right of θ_R. The actual policies implemented as a result of executing legislative interaction, however, are always within the interval delimited by the two ideal points, θ_D and θ_R. In our model, the parties care about policy outcomes and about winning, not about platforms *per se*. Given the institutional balancing, in order to bring about the desired policy outcome, the two parties may have to choose platforms even more extreme than their true ideals. This outcome cannot occur if Congress has no influence in policymaking.

These results are quite suggestive. They contribute to explaining the polarization of the positions of representatives of the two American parties documented in section 2.6. Far from enforcing party moderation, the executive–legislative interaction in policy formation leads to divergence of party platforms. Party platforms are, however, more extreme than the actual policies, which are implemented as a result of executive–legislative bargaining: Bush's reneging on "read my lips".

(4) When α is too small, relative to the other parameter values, there

is no equilibrium. In particular, there is never an equilibrium when $\alpha = 0$, namely when there is no president and the legislature is elected with pure proportional representation. The logic is that, for a fixed position of its opponent, a party has an incentive to take a relatively exteme position in order to "pull" the average that makes policy (5.11) or (5.12) in the direction of its ideal point. But this causes the opponent to "respond" by going to an even more extreme position in the opposite direction. The sequence of "best responses" continues in an explosive fashion.

(5) When the parties have ideal points symmetric about the median, platforms and policies are relatively insensitive to the degree of polarization of ideal points. That is, it is hard to infer the parties' true preferences from their platforms.

(6) In spite of the divergence of platforms, policies are quite insensitive to the value of α. Policies are only slightly more extreme, when equilibrium exists, for $\alpha < 1$ than for $\alpha = 1$. The intuition is that the voters, in the second-stage game, moderate the relatively extreme platforms. As emphasized over and over in this volume, the executive–legislative interaction achieves policy moderation even in the presence of extreme party platforms. However, policy divergence increases as w increases. This is directly parallel to the results of chapter 4, where high values of w inhibited the voters' ability to coordinate on moderate outcomes.

The divergence in party platforms is always sufficiently strong that it outweighs the influence of moderating institutions. In the scenario of chapter 4, where parties were "immobile", committed to their ideal points as their platforms, increasing the power of the legislature increased policy moderation, in the sense that the difference between the policies when D is president and R is president is decreased. In contrast, in the scenario of this chapter, increasing the power of the legislature (slightly) increases the divergence in policies.

The intuition for divergence in policies is clear. In the case of a purely presidential regime, $\alpha = 1$, a party's platform influences policy only when the party succeeds in winning the election. Since parties care about policy and not platforms, in any institution, even a moderating one, where platforms do not influence the policy when the opponent wins the presidency, the platforms would maintain the policy equilibrium that exists when $\alpha = 1$. There would be invariance in policy with respect to the institutional design. But in the moderating institution used throughout the book, a party, by moving its platform, also influences policy (see (5.11) and (5.12)) when its opponent wins the presidency. This gives an added incentive to polarize. This additional polarization is only partially counterbalanced by voter moderation, leading to divergence in policies as legislative power increases.

In order to illustrate our conclusions, we consider an example in which the party ideal points are symmetric around the location of the expected median. As in chapter 4, voters are uniformly distributed but the location of the distribution is subject to a random shock that is uniformly distributed on $[-w, +w]$. We let $\beta = 0$, so voters consider only the first period. We also include no electoralist premium; the parties are purely policy oriented. Because of the symmetry, we know that the voter equilibrium has both the legislative and executive cutpoints at $\frac{1}{2}$. Moreover, the equilibrium platforms of the parties must be symmetric about the median as must the expected first-period policies, $E(x_1^D)$ and $E(x_1^R)$.

We computed the equilibrium platforms and expected policies for the two-stage game with mobile parties. The results are shown in Figures 5.1 and 5.2. The first figure is based upon wide separation in party ideal points, with D located at 0, the expected lower end of the distribution of voter ideal points. The second figure shows less polarized parties, with D located at 0.25. In each figure, we vary the amount of presidential power, α, for three levels of uncertainty. Recall that the case of $\alpha = 1$ corresponds to the models of Wittman and Calvert. The figures illustrate the following points.

- Platform polarization is highly sensitive to presidential power. Polarization increases sharply as α falls.
- For sufficiently weak presidents (low α), parties "posture" and adopt platforms more extreme than their ideal points.
- For even lower α, equilibrium fails to exist – the curves do not extend to $\alpha = 0$. When one party moves to a more extreme position, the other party, because of the proportional representation in the legislature, has an incentive to go even farther out in the opposite direction. The process explodes.
- Policy is much less sensitive to presidential power, since voters moderate in stage 2. The policy curves are virtually flat.
- Polarization is increasing in uncertainty (w).
- Polarization is only modestly affected by the degree of polarization of ideal points. The curves in figure 5.1 are very similar to those in 5.2.

Putting these results together, we find that platform polarization is increasing in uncertainty, echoing chapter 2, and the power of the legislature. In contrast, policy polarization depends mainly on uncertainty. Neither platform polarization nor policy polarization is affected by the degree of polarization of ideal points. Competitive pressures force very extreme parties to move to more centrist positions.

Actual politics probably lies somewhere intermediate to the extreme scenarios of fully immobile and fully mobile parties. With fully mobile parties, the actual ideal point of the party is irrelevant to the decisions of voters. The voter equilibrium is determined solely by the platforms of the parties. But if voters know the ideal policies and associate movement away

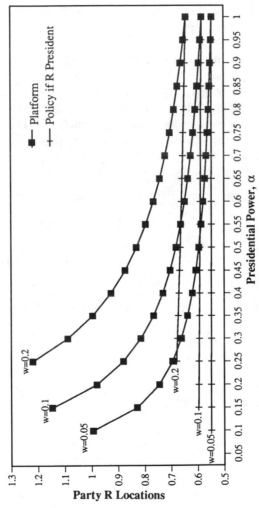

Figure 5.1. Moderating election equilibrium platforms and policies. The parties have ideal points $\theta_D = 0$ and $\theta_R = 1$. The equilibrium platform of party R and the expected policy if R is president are graphed, for three values of the uncertainty parameter, w, as functions of the presidential power parameter α. The case of $\alpha = 1$ is the traditional two-candidate model. Decreasing presidential power polarizes party platforms but leads to little change in policies. (The locations for party D are symmetric to those for party R.)

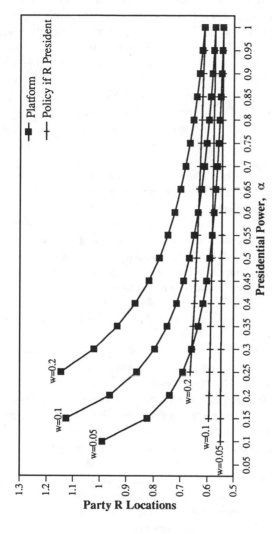

Figure 5.2. Moderating election equilibrium platforms and policies. The parties have ideal points $\theta_D = 0.25$ and $\theta_R = 0.75$. Comparison with figure 5.1 shows that moving the party ideal points closer together has little effect on the equilibrium.

from them with a loss of credibility (Bernhardt and Ingberman, (1985)), movement away from the ideal policies will be costly to the parties. In different words, the reality of American political institutions lies somewhere in between the completely immobile parties of chapters 3 and 4 and the completely mobile parties of this section. The more "costly" it is to change party platforms the more closely the model of chapters 3 and 4 approximates reality; the less costly, the better is the approximation of this chapter. Furthermore, observation (4) above concerning the nonexistence of equilibria for low values of α heavily relies on the assumption of costless mobility. With costs of moving, the "explosive" divergence described above is prevented by the associated explosive costs. Thus, these costs of mobility would create well-defined equilibria even for the case of low values of α.

5.5 CONCLUSIONS

The balancing consequences of the executive–legislative interaction are quite robust to important relaxations of our initial assumptions.

In our analysis of staggered terms of office, we showed that the qualitative nature of our results does not change when we allow for institutions like the United States Senate in which only one-third of the seats are chosen every two years. Voter behavior and, in particular, the cutpoint in legislative elections takes into account the effects of staggered terms, but the nature of the institutional balancing does not change.

Institutional moderation also occurs with heterogeneous parties, namely when the president and the legislative delegation of the same party have different policy positions.

Finally, and this is probably the most important result of this chapter, we showed that the immobility of party platforms at their ideal points is not crucial for our results. The final policies, influenced by the legislature, change very little if the parties are free to move and. choose variable platforms. In particular, the midterm cycle remains intact, since voters care about policy outcomes not platforms *per se*.

In conjunction with our discussion of staggered terms of office, we briefly mentioned the issue of incumbency advantage. We showed that incumbency advantage had effects analogous to staggered terms. Institutional balancing would persist, with an adjustment for incumbency advantage. The logic, developed for complete information, carries over to the incomplete information case where there is a midterm cycle. Even though voters have a predilection for incumbents, including those of the president's party, a midterm cycle can still be present. That the cycle and incumbency advantage do coexist is demonstrated in the empirical analysis in the next chapter.

6

Incumbency and moderation

6.1 INTRODUCTION

The primary focus of this book is on partisan politics where voters are concerned with policies that can be positioned on a liberal–conservative dimension. An alternative view of American politics is that voters are concerned with how a larger share of the federal pie can be garnered for their state, their congressional district, and, ultimately, themselves. These distributive concerns, coupled with the seniority system in Congress, provide voters with strong incentives to re-elect incumbents. In addition, incumbents, in part through use of the perquisites of office, have strong informational advantages over challengers. As a consequence, "incumbency advantage" is a major determinant of congressional elections.[1] The "incumbency advantage" is particularly evident in the House in the postwar period where, until the wave of retirements in 1992, over 90 percent of incumbents stood for re-election and, of those standing, over 90 percent were re-appointed.[2] These high rates of re-election have led recent elections to produce, especially relative to earlier periods of American history, small changes in seat shares.[3]

Thus far this book has ignored incumbency advantage. Instead, we have emphasized the balancing behavior of voters, which generates split-ticket voting and the midterm cycle. In this chapter we discuss how incumbency advantage and balancing behavior coexist.

The model of chapter 4 predicts substantial changes in *vote* shares as a result of the midterm cycle. While the theoretical prediction of a shift in votes receives overwhelming empirical support (figure 4.1), the shift in the

---

[1]King and Gelman (1991) contains an excellent and up-to-date summary of the literature. See also Fiorina (1989).

[2]Fiorina (1989), p. 7.

[3]Note that in the 1992 election, despite a tide of anti-incumbency feeling, marked by widespread popular approval of term limitations, and despite a reapportionment to their benefit, the Republicans managed to gain only eight seats.

vote has not had much impact on seats. Finding a midterm cycle that is far stronger in votes than in seats raises an important question. How can moderation of policies take place, given that so many incumbents are reappointed in midterm? This chapter offers an answer, based upon the interplay of incumbency advantage and moderating behavior. Our claim is that the voters send a signal of moderation both by reducing the margin of victory of the incumbents and by favoring the party not holding the presidency in open-seat House races. Specifically, we advance the following *Signaling Hypothesis*:

American voters use the midterm election to signal that they do not want extreme policies. However, this signaling is costly for voters if they prefer to re-elect the incumbent for various reasons (lower risk than challengers, demonstrated competence in constituency service, increased seniority, etc.) and by voting against the president's party they do not reappoint incumbent legislators. Consequently, while the midterm cycle will affect vote shares in all districts, the president's party is likely to lose a seat only in districts with open seats. In districts with incumbents of the president's party, incumbency bias will be sufficient to offset the midterm signal, but margins of victory will be smaller than those of incumbents of the opposite party. These reduced margins send a signal of moderation to the president's party.

The idea is simple. Middle-of-the-road voters face two incentives in midterm elections: for constituency level issues they would like to favor incumbents and for national level issues they would like to balance the president. Our Signaling Hypothesis summarizes the aggregate implications of voter behavior influenced by these two motivations. Some voters in marginal[4] districts will opt to moderate but they will be offset by voters who place more value on retaining incumbents. The net result is that incumbents of the president's party remain favored to retain their seats. Of course, incumbents from the party out of the White House will be very likely to be reelected with relatively large margins since both moderation and incumbency work in their favor. In open-seat races, since only the moderating incentive is at work, candidates of the party out of the White House are favored.

In the remainder of this chapter we successfully test the Signaling Hypothesis. We conclude that incumbency advantage and moderating behavior coexist and jointly explain voting behavior in midterm House elections.

We adopt a methodology for measuring incumbency advantage developed by Gelman and King (1990) and King and Gelman (1991). These authors realistically assume that the parameters that determine incumbency advantage vary from election to election. That is, they allow for intertemporal variation in how incumbency advantage influences the fortunes of the two parties.

---

[4]"Marginal" is political science jargon for seats that were close to a 50–50 split in the previous election.

One may observe intertemporal variation in the House vote for several reasons including temporary shifts in voter preferences arising from changes in economic conditions, scandals, wars, and other events close to the election date; midterm balancing; and structural changes in the effects of these and other influences on congressional voting. An example of structural change would be increased incumbency advantage in the postwar period. By allowing for all the parameters to vary from election to election, Gelman and King capture, in addition to structural change in incumbency advantage, many other sources of intertemporal variation. The midterm cycle is one important source of intertemporal variation. Gelman and King can explain a much larger fraction of the variance of congressional voting by allowing parameters to change over time, relative to a more parsimonious model in which the parameters are fixed.

How much of this gain in explanatory power is due to the effect of the midterm cycle? The answer is two-thirds. Moreover, the midterm cycle does not exhibit structural change. Its impact is similar for all Republican presidents and similar for all Democratic presidents.

The "two-thirds" is produced solely as the result of periodic shifts in control of the White House. Despite a sizable midterm effect, we show that the incumbency advantage is strong: *incumbents are always expected to retain their seats.* In contrast, open seats in marginal districts are generally expected to be lost by the president's party. (An important exception is discussed later.) The midterm effect does not translate into more substantial seat swings because there are very few marginal, open seats.

In summary, this chapter shows that preferences for incumbents and for moderation are both major determinants of voter behavior in congressional elections.

The remainder of the chapter is organized as follows. We begin by describing our sample in section 6.2. Section 6.3 provides a more precise statement of how to measure the midterm cycle and presents results for some simple "pure" midterm cycle models. Section 6.4 introduces the Gelman and King incumbency advantage model and then shows results for a specification which incorporates both incumbency advantage and a midterm cycle. Sources of intertemporal variation other than the midterm cycle are investigated in section 6.5. Section 6.6 presents a refinement of the basic model that recognizes that open seats are less predictable than races with incumbents. We employ a model which incorporates this observation in section 6.7 to test for the midterm cycle and to test the Signaling Hypothesis. Section 6.8 concludes.

6.2 DESCRIPTION OF THE SAMPLE

Our sample includes congressional races in 1950, 1954, 1958, 1966, 1970, 1974, 1978, and 1986. We exclude the midterm elections of 1962 and 1982 because of redistricting. We also excluded any race in which the two-party split was more extreme than 85–15, in either the midterm year or the preceding year, to avoid problems inherent to uncontested elections.[5] This selection choice eliminated observations mainly in the South.[6] We were left with 2,538 observations. Three of the years, 1950, 1966, and 1978, had a Democratic president. Relative to the on-year, the Democratic vote should have declined in these years. The other five midterm elections in the sample had Republican presidents; in these elections the Democrats would be expected to make gains.

Following Gelman and King (1990), we choose the percentage Democratic of the two-party vote as our dependent variable. Whereas Gelman and King were concerned with all postwar elections, we focus solely on the vote in midterm races, which we denote as V_{Dt}^m, $t = 1950, 1954$, etc.[7] The vote in the previous on-year elections is denoted V_{Dt-2}^p. (In this chapter, t denotes calendar years, unlike the previous chapters, where t denoted two-year periods.)

6.3 THE MIDTERM CYCLE IN CONGRESSIONAL DISTRICTS

The midterm effect at the district level can be specified in two ways:

(1) Conditional on the presidential year House vote in the district, the midterm year Democratic vote is higher when a Republican is president than when a Democrat is president. Formally.

$$V_{Dt}^m \mid V_{Dt-2}^p, \text{R president} \quad > \quad V_{Dt}^m \mid V_{Dt-2}^p, \text{D president}$$

(2) When a Republican is president, the Democratic midterm vote is higher than the vote in the previous House election and vice versa when a Democrat is president:

$$V_{Dt}^m > V_{Dt-2}^p \text{ if R president}, \qquad V_{Dt}^m < V_{Dt-2}^p \text{ if D president}$$

---

[5]Truncating the sample at 85–15 splits obviously introduces econometric problems of selection bias. We accept this problem in exchange for two benefits. First, we do not have to address modeling the decisions that lead candidates and parties to contest elections, an issue not of primary interest to us here. Second, we do have to address whether there is a regime shift in voter behavior in elections that are clearly lopsided.

[6]Most California districts were excluded immediately after World War II. At that time, California permitted candidates to run in both primaries. As often happened, one candidate won both primaries. This obviously led to a greater than 85–15 split in the general election.

[7]We also investigated using In $(V_{Dt}/(100 - V_{Dt}))$. Results were similar. Moreover, our estimates show stable dynamics in that the predicted vote for an incumbent who is repeatedly re-elected converges to a steady-state value well below 100 percent. Consequently, we use the more readily interpretable linear model.

As the second form of the cycle implies the first, we make the second, stronger specification our main focus. Furthermore, this specification directly follows from the theoretical model of chapter 4, which implies the cutpoint in midterm races with a Democratic president is to the left of the cutpoint when there is a Republican president.

In chapter 4, however, we did not consider the heterogeneity arising from the division of a nation into geographically based constituencies. While we continue to maintain the theoretical proposition that there is a single national cutpoint for congressional elections, we must recognize that the national distribution of voter preferences is the aggregation of the distributions in individual districts. We continue to assume, parallel to chapter 4, that, in each district, voter ideal points are uniformly distributed over an interval of length one. On average, this interval will extend from 0 to 1. But in a specific district i and a specific year t, the interval will be shifted by three influences:[8]

- d_i A fixed, temporally invariant effect that tells us how, to use political science jargon, to find the "normal" vote of the district.
- $\mathbf{a}_t$ A national preference shock described in chapter 4.
- $\mathbf{d}_{it}$ A district-year specific preference shock that tells us how a particular election "plays in Peoria".

The total shift in the destribution is given by the sum of these three influences:

$$\mathbf{a}_{it} \equiv d_i + \mathbf{a}_t + \mathbf{d}_{it}$$

The actual preference distribution for district i in year t is then uniform on $[\mathbf{a}_{it}, 1 + \mathbf{a}_{it}]$.[9]

Since each district has its own preference distribution, *the House vote will vary across districts even if all voters use a common, national cutpoint.* Of course, in keeping with the random shock to preferences in chapter 4, the midterm cycle should hold with respect to the expected vote. Since the legislative cutpoint shifts between presidential and midterm elections, we predict, other things equal, a midterm cycle in each district. Finding "reversals" at the district level does not invalidate the model.[10] Since each district has an independent shock to preferences, reversals could occur in individual districts, even when the data, aggregated to the national level, manifests a midterm cycle.

---

[8]The national distribution of preferences, aggregated from the individual districts, will now no longer be uniform. However, the qualitative properties of the model of chapter 4 persist.

[9]The shocks **a** and **d** are assumed to be uncorrelated. In addition, the shocks are independently and identically distributed.

[10]See section 4.6 for a discussion of reversals.

Table 6.1. *Democratic gains and losses in individual districts*

Year	Total	Districts with Dem. Vote Gain	Districts with Dem. Vote Loss	Net Gain	Districts with Dem. Seat Gain	Districts with Dem. Seat Loss	Net Gain
Democratic President							
1950	300	69	231	-162	1	30	-29
1966	334	47	287	-240	6	48	-42
1978	314	120	194	-74	10	20	-10
Republican President							
1954	310	258	52	+206	20	4	+16
1958	312	284	28	+256	47	1	+46
1970	332	239	93	+146	18	7	+11
1974	325	254	71	+183	54	12	+42
1986	311	213	98	+115	15	8	+7

Note: "Total" refers to number of districts with less than 85-15 splits in two-party vote shares in the midterm election and previous presidential year House election. Vote gains and losses refer to share of two-party vote.

Having specified the midterm cycle and discussed how district level analysis relates to the theoretical model of chapter 4, we now turn to empirical evaluation of the theory.

Table 6.1 shows the extent of the midterm cycle in our sample. In contested districts, the president's party generally performs less well than the opposition: the number of districts in which the president's party loses is much higher than the number in which this party gains. With the slight exception of 1978, districts where the president's party loses votes outnumber those where it gains by at least a two-to-one margin. We find the same pattern for seats: we always observed a net loss in seats for the president's party. Yet, the net shift in seats is never as much as one-fourth of the net number of districts where the opposition gains votes.

We now turn to a regression analysis which develops the basic insights of table 6.1. A suitable benchmark prediction is that the current election simply reproduces the past:

$$V_{Dt}^m = V_{Dt-2}^p \qquad (6.1)$$

This benchmark holds that, while there can be cross-sectional variation in voting, since the distribution of preferences may vary, any intertemporal variation is purely random. Although (6.1) is a totally uninteresting model, there are two reasons to expect it will work quite well as a predictor. First, the economic and demographic factors that underlie political preferences vary sharply across congressional districts but are relatively stable in time. Second, incumbency persists in time. Any bias that favors a two-term Democratic member of the House seeking a third term is likely to persist when, two years later, the member goes for the fourth term.

How can we measure the success of this prediction? The standard measure of total prediction error is the average, across all districts, of squared prediction errors. Formally, this is written as:

$$\sum (V_{Dt}^m - V_{Dt-2}^p)^2 / N$$

where $\sum$ denotes summation *across all districts and elections* and $N = 2{,}538$ denotes the total number of observations in the sample.

A standard procedure is to compare the average squared prediction error of the theoretical model to the average squared error that results from using the mean of the dependent variable as the predictor. These average squared errors represent the sample variance. Formally, we have:

$$\sum (V_{Dt}^m - \text{Mean}(V_{Dt}^m))^2 / N = \text{Var}(V_{Dt}^m)$$

where

$$\text{Mean}\,(V_{Dt}^m) = \sum V_{Dt}^m / N$$

To compare the average squared error from the theoretical prediction with the average squared error from predicting the mean, one uses a proportionate-reduction-in-error measure that is 1.0 if the theoretical predictions are perfect and 0.0 if they are no better than the mean predictions. The measure is:

$$R^2 = 1 - \frac{\sum (V_{Dt}^m - V_{Dt-2}^p)^2}{N \,\text{Var}(V_{Dt}^m)}$$

The value of R^2 for our data, 0.622, indicates that a very substantial fraction of the cross-sectional variation is explained by continuity with the past. This benchmark R^2 appears in the first column of table 6.2.

However, the theoretical model of chapter 4 points to a systematic midterm effect. Recall that the on-year congressional vote was determined by a cutpoint $\tilde{\theta}$ and the midterm vote by $\tilde{\theta}_{D2}$, if there is a D president, and $\tilde{\theta}_{R2}$, if there is an R president, with $\tilde{\theta}_{D2} < \tilde{\theta} < \tilde{\theta}_{R2}$. Therefore, the midterm

Table 6.2. *Midterm cycle and incumbency models*

Variable	(1)	(2)	(3)	(4)	(5)	(6)
			Estimated Coefficients			
V^p_{Dt-2}	1.0	1.0	.574	.901	.635	.639
	n.a.	n.a.	(28.5)	(79.3)	(32.6)	(35.4)
DEM		-3.79		1.54		
		(-14.3)		(2.31)		
REP		4.71		9.50		
		(23.0)		(16.3)		
DWIN×DEM					19.6	12.2
					(15.4)	(9.91)
DWIN×REP					27.3	20.2
					(22.6)	(16.9)
RWIN×DEM					10.6	17.4
					(11.9)	(19.7)
RWIN×REP					18.3	24.9
					(23.6)	(31.8)
DWIN			20.9			
			(15.6)			
RWIN			24.9			
			(28.3)			
INC			7.84			7.95
			(18.1)			(20.8)
R^2	.622	.707	.720	.715	.743	.780

Note: t-statistics in parentheses. See text for definition of variables.

$N=2,538$ in all regressions.

cycle is generated by voters in between $\tilde{\theta}_{D2}$ and $\tilde{\theta}$ when D is president and between $\tilde{\theta}$ and $\tilde{\theta}_{R2}$ when R is president. Specifically, the structure of our two-period model at the district level can be represented as:

$$V^p_{Di,t-2} = \tilde{\theta} - a_{it-2}$$
$$V^m_{Dit} = \tilde{\theta}_{D2} - a_{it} \quad \text{if president is Democrat}$$
$$V^m_{Dit} = \tilde{\theta}_{R2} - a_{it} \quad \text{if president is Republican}$$

(6.2)

(The equations above follow directly from the uniform distribution of preferences.)

We can obtain a very simple and instructive regression model by starting out assuming that the national shocks, a_t, are zero. Combining the equations in (6.2) and omitting the district subscript leads to:

$$V_{Dt}^{m} = V_{Dt-2}^{p} + \beta_1 \, DEM + \beta_2 \, REP + \phi_t \qquad (6.3)$$

where

$$\beta_1 = \tilde{\theta}_{D2} - \tilde{\theta},$$
$$\beta_2 = \tilde{\theta}_{R2} - \tilde{\theta},$$
$$\phi_t = \mathbf{a}_{i,t-2} - \mathbf{a}_{it}$$

and

$$DEM = 1 \quad \text{if} \quad t = 1950, \, 1966, \, 1978$$
$$= 0 \quad \text{if} \quad t = 1954, \, 1958, \, 1970, \, 1974, \, 1986$$
$$REP = 0 \quad \text{if} \quad t = 1950, \, 1966, \, 1978$$
$$= 1 \quad \text{if} \quad t = 1954, \, 1958, \, 1970, \, 1974, \, 1986$$
$$\text{Thus}, \, REP = 1 - DEM$$

That is, DEM is an indicator variable which "picks" the midterm elections with a Democratic president; REP picks those with a Republican president.

The theory *constrains the coefficient on the lagged vote* V_{Dt-2}^{p} *to 1.0* and predicts that β_1 should be negative and β_2 positive.[11]

Our least squares estimates of β_1 and β_2 and the overall R^2 for the equation are reported in the second column of table 6.2. We find an increase in explanatory power to 0.707. The statistical likelihood that either of the coefficients is truly zero is infinitesimal as is the likelihood that their difference is zero. A sizable segment of the electorate, estimated at 8.5 percent, is represented by "moderators" who potentially vote differently at midterm than in presidential election years. This figure represents the sum of the 3.8 percent swing, with respect to the presidential year, to the Republicans when there is a Democratic president and the 4.7 percent swing to the Democrats when there is a Republican president. The midterm cycle is strongly supported.

6.4 INCUMBENCY ADVANTAGE AND THE MIDTERM CYCLE

To address how the midterm cycle and incumbency advantage interact, we utilize an incumbency advantage model developed by Gelman and King (1990). To motivate their model, we again begin with the benchmark provided by equation (6.1). Even in the absence of a midterm cycle, the benchmark needs to be modified to take into account regression to the mean produced by such factors as reduced campaign effort by the previous winners and reduced turnout by supporters of the winning party. If all seats tended to

---

[11]The theory of chapter 4 would in fact be contradicted by $\mathbf{a} = 0$ for all elections. We allow for variation in $\mathbf{a}$ later in this chapter.

145

swing back toward a "competitive" vote of 50 percent Democratic, the appropriate model would be:

$$V^m_{Dt} = 50 + \beta_1(V^p_{Dt-2} - 50) + \phi_t \qquad (6.4)$$

Thus, if the Democrats had previously received about 50 percent, they would be expected to lose an amount proportional to the excess over 50. The fraction lost would be given by β_1, which should satisfy $0 < \beta_1 < 1$. Regression toward a level of 50 in all districts is not sufficiently realistic. Gelman and King see winning the previous election as conferring an extra advantage to the winning party, regardless of incumbency status. This advantage can be expressed formally as:

$$
\begin{aligned}
V^m_{Dt} &= 50 + \beta_1(V^p_{Dt-2} - 50) + DADV + \phi_t \text{ in districts won by D at } t-2 \\
V^m_{Dt} &= 50 + \beta_1(V^p_{Dt-2} - 50) + RADV + \phi_t \text{ in districts won by R at } t-2
\end{aligned}
\qquad (6.5)
$$

The expectation of advantage to the previous winner translated into $DADV > 0 > RADV$.

After thus taking into account advantage to the previous winner and regression to the mean, one can introduce a variable to measure the effect of incumbency. Assume incumbency adds, over the expected vote for an open seat, an amount β_4 to the Democratic vote in every district with a Democratic incumbent and subtracts the same amount if the incumbent is a Republican.

If we add an incumbency variable and combine the two equations of (6.5) into a single equation, we obtain:

$$V^m_{Dt} = \beta_1 V^p_{Dt-2} + \beta_2 DWIN + \beta_3 RWIN + \beta_4 INC + \phi_t \qquad (6.6)$$

where

DWIN $= 1$ if $V^p_{Dt-2} \geqslant 0.5$, that is if the Democratic party had the majority in the previous election.

$= 0$ otherwise.

RWIN $= 1 - DWIN$.

INC $= +1$ if there a Democratic incumbent seeking re-election

$=\quad 0$ if there is an open seat

$= -1$ if there is a Republican incumbent seeking re-election.[12]

The regression to the mean parameter β_1 and the incumbency advantage parameters β_4 appear directly in equation (6.6). The "winner advantage"

---

[12]The interpretation of the error term differs from that of equation (6.3) but we continue to use ϕ_t to minimize notational changes.

parameters can be found as $DADV = \beta_2 - 50(1 - \beta_1)$, $RADV = \beta_3 - 50(1 - \beta_1)$. Note that $DADV > RADV$ implies $\beta_2 > \beta_3$.[13]

Note that, if the β coefficients in equation (6.6) are not reestimated for each election, equation (6.6) represents a model where all the variation in the data is ascribed to *district level* variables: incumbency, the winner of the past election, and the level of the past vote. "Pooling" the data across elections to estimate equation (6.6) leads to a pure model of incumbency advantage that does not allow for a midterm effect.[14] That is, the pooled model does not permit differentiating years with Republican presidents from those with Democratic ones. In contrast, equation (6.3) estimates coefficients only for *national level* variables that reflect the midterm cycle.

The comparison of the pure incumbency advantage model (6.6) with the pure midterm cycle model (6.3) is instructive. The pooled Gelman–King estimates, shown in column 3 of table 6.2, are, in terms of fit, only slightly better than those of the more parsimonious midterm model given in column 2. The R^2 value increases only by .013, from .707 to .720. This comparison suggests that incumbency advantage and the midterm cycle are effects of roughly equal importance. Like the midterm cycle, incumbency voting involves a significant fraction of the electorate. The estimated coefficient of the INC variable shows that an additional 7.8 percent of the electorate supports a party's candidate when the candidate is an incumbent than when the candidate is running for an open seat.

We now study the joint effects of the midterm cycle and of incumbency advantage by extending our midterm cycle model.

The first extension takes into account that there may be regression to the mean rather than simple continuity with the past vote. Statistical regression of the mean represented by, say, a high value of $a_{i,t-2}$ followed by a lower value of a_{it} has been explicitly accounted for via the ϕ_t error in equation (6.3). But there may also be systematic regression to the mean as in equation (6.4). The regression equation is:

$$V_{Dt}^m = \beta_1 V_{Dt-2}^p + \beta_2 DEM + \beta_3 REP + \phi_t \qquad (6.7)$$

The estimated V_{Dt-2}^p coefficient of 0.901, shown in column 4 of table 6.2, is very significantly less than 1.0 in terms of a statistical test, given our large sample size. Substantively, however, we note that the R^2 value increases only from 0.707 in column 2 to 0.715 in column 4. Moreover, the estimated difference between the midterm vote with a Republican president and a Democratic president is 8.0 (9.50 − 1.54) percent[15] very close to the previous

---

[13]Actually, Gelman and King (1990) use a constant and DWIN whereas we use DWIN and RWIN. The two parameterizations are equivalent.

[14]Nor does the pooled model with linear trend in incumbency advantage used in King and Gelman (1991).

[15]The *t*-statistic for the difference is 23.69.

8.5 percent calculated from column 2. In other words, the simple balancing process assumed in our theoretical model is surprisingly good.

This regression supports both versions of the midterm cycle. First, the expected Democratic vote is always greater when the Republicans control the White House than when the Democrats control the White House. Second, the predicted midterm vote for the president's party is always less than the preceding on-year vote.[16]

The second extension allows for advantage inherent to the party winning the past election. We estimated the following regression:

$$V_{Dt}^m = \beta_1 V_{Dt-2}^p + \beta_2(\text{DWIN} \times \text{DEM}) + \beta_3(\text{DWIN} \times \text{REP})$$
$$+ \beta_4(\text{RWIN} \times \text{DEM}) + \beta_5(\text{RWIN} \times \text{REP}) + \phi_t \qquad (6.8)$$

In contrast to the results in the fourth column of table 6.2, this regression, shown in the fifth column, allows for different midterm effects in districts that were won by Democrats and in districts won by Republicans. While there is an improvement in fit, with the R^2 increasing to 0.743 from 0.715, the two midterm effects are essentially identical! In districts previously won by Democrats, the midterm effects is 7.72 percent ($27.34 - 19.62$, $t = 17.66$) while in districts won by Republicans, the effect is 7.75 percent ($t = 14.49$). The difference between the two is statistically insignificant ($t = 0.04$).

Thus, the increase in fit from column 4 to column 5 reflects not differential midterm cycles but the ability of the DWIN and RWIN variables to capture advantage to previous winners and, indirectly, incumbency. In districts won by the Democrats, the intercept for the Democratic vote is substantially higher than in districts won by the Republicans (compare 19.6 to 10.6 and 27.3 to 18.3). This last result suggests that, even though the simple midterm models provide strong support for the uncertainty model of chapter 4, it is important to control directly for incumbency.

Therefore, we extend the model to include the INC variable. The results for equation (6.8) augmented by the INC variable are shown in column 6 of table 6.2. With this additional variable, the R^2 increases to 0.780. Once again the midterm cycle is independent of the identity of the previous winner: the effect is 8.04 percent when the Democrats won the on-year House race ($t = 19.87$) and 7.51 percent when the Republicans won ($t = 17.42$). The difference in the two estimated effects is, again, statistically insignificant ($t = 0.91$). These effects have a very similar magnitude to that found in the regressions without incumbency while the incumbency effect, now estimated at 7.95 percent, is close to its value in the pooled model without a midterm

---

[16]There is a very slight exception. When the Democrats control the White House, they are predicted to do better at midterm when their on-year vote is below 15.47 percent. For this extremely low vote level, regression to the mean outweighs the midterm cycle.

cycle. In other words, the midterm cycle and incumbency are two virtually independent effects!

The regression model reported in column 6 exhibits a key difference with respect to that of column 3 of table 6.2. In column 3, the coefficients of the variables are constrained to be identical for all election years in the sample. In column 6, we introduce the midterm cycle by allowing the coefficients on DWIN and RWIN to be different for years with a Republican president than for years with a Democrat in the White House. Adding the intertemporal variation predicted by the midterm cycle leads to a significant increase in fit, from 0.72 to 0.78.

The increase from 0.72 to 0.78 may look to be fairly small but remember that the benchmark, column 1, accounts for 62 percent of the total variation. Adding regression-to-the-mean and incumbency bias effects, two obviously important influences on voting behavior, adds another 10 percent in column 3. Allowing for intertemporal variation only in the form of a midterm cycle, in column 6, adds another 6 percent. Thus, when one looks at explanatory power beyond the benchmark, the midterm cycle is important, even after controlling for regression-to-the-mean and incumbency bias.

6.5 PREFERENCE SHOCKS

Up to this point, we have investigated the systematic portion of intertemporal variation induced by the midterm cycle. We have not considered the non-systematic national shocks to preferences that are a vital part of the model of chapter 4. We can do so by returning to equations (6.2) and (6.3). Allowing for non-zero values of the shock a and combining, we now obtain:

$$V_{Dt}^m = V_{Dt-2}^p + \beta_t + \phi_t \tag{6.9}$$

where

$$\beta_t = \tilde{\theta}_D - \tilde{\theta} + a_t - a_{t-2}, \quad \text{if president is Democrat}$$
$$= \tilde{\theta}_R - \tilde{\theta} + a_t - a_{t-2}, \quad \text{if president is Republican}$$

Therefore we need to estimate eight different β values for this model, one for each of the midterm elections in our sample.[17] The results are shown in table 6.3.

One prediction of the theoretical model is that the national shocks are important and we should thus reject the restriction on (6.9) implicit in (6.3) where only two β values were estimated. While the R^2 increases only modestly from 0.707 to 0.719, we easily reject the restriction.[18] Furthermore, one can use the estimated values to derive an estimate of the standard

[17]Readers familiar with econometrics will note that we are running a simple dummy variable regression.
[18]$F(6,2530) = 18.97$.

Table 6.3. *The theoretical model with preference shocks*

Year	Estimated Coefficients
Democratic President	
1950	-2.85
	(-6.18)
1966	-6.49
	(-14.8)
1978	-1.82
	(-4.03)
Republican President	
1954	4.01
	(8.83)
1958	6.57
	(14.5)
1970	3.33
	(7.55)
1974	6.36
	(14.3)
1986	3.32
	(7.32)
R^2	.719

Note: t-statistics in parentheses. Each year corresponds to a β cofficient in equation (6.9). R^2 calculated with reference to variance of midterm vote. See text. $N = 2,538$.

error of **a**. The calculated value, 1.3 percent, appears in the range acquired by the theoretical model of chapter 4; there is enough uncertainty about preferences to induce the cycle, but not so much to render our equilibrium model inappropriate.[19]

Another prediction of the theoretical model is that the βs for Democratic president years should all be negative and those for Republican years should

[19]Assume $\alpha = \frac{1}{2}$, $\beta = 0.5$, $\theta_D = 0.25$, $\theta_R = 0.75$. Then the inequalities (4.1) and (4.22) imply that our uncertainty equilibrium requires $0.25 > w > 0.02$. The standard error of the uniform distribution is $w\sqrt{(1/12)}$. This implies that for the chosen parameters, $0.0721 > $ std. error of **a** > 0.0058. The empirical value of 0.013 is within this range.

all be positive. This is because we expect the systematic effects in the midterm cycle to exceed the magnitudes of preference shocks; reversals should be rare. Table 6.3 confirms this prediction. Every β both has the correct sign and is very significantly different from zero.

Although they do not discuss the midterm cycle, King and Gelman (1991) were also concerned with intertemporal variation. Specifically, their goal was to show that the incumbency advantage coefficient had increased in the postwar period. Consequently, they ran separate regressions for each election. This disaggregation of the pooled model is equivalent to running a "giant" regression within which the four variables of equation (6.6) each get a distinct coefficient for each election in the sample, leading to $4 \times 8 = 32$ coefficients.

The "giant" regression leads to only a fairly small rise in R^2. In moving from column 3 to column 6 of table 6.2, we estimated only two additional coefficients and increased R^2 from 0.720 to 0.780. Between column 6 and the "giant" regression, an additional 26 coefficients are estimated but R^2 increases only to 0.813.[20] (The coefficient estimates are not reported). That is, once the systematic effect of the midterm cycle and the systematic effect of incumbency is accounted for, there is relatively little additional variance explained by allowing not only for intertemporal changes in incumbency advantage, but also for Watergate, Vietnam, and other special circumstances associated with particular elections.

Put differently, the R^2 of 0.780 achieved by adding a midterm cycle effect to the pooled Gelman–King regression captures two-thirds of the jump from 0.720 to 0.813 that one obtains by moving from the pooled regression to the "giant" regression.

Beyond examining, via the "giant" regression, for intertemporal variation in the midterm cycle, we tested for other variable interactions. In particular, we explored whether the midterm cycle varied as a function of the level of the past vote and whether open seats and incumbent running seats had different regimes. We found no important additional effects, a result that provides further support for the notion of common national cutpoints, adjusted for incumbency.

---

[20]The various models nest. For example, the model of column 6 of table 6.2 restricts the 8 coefficients in the "giant" model on the lagged vote to be equal. Similarly, the 8 coefficients on incumbency are restricted to be equal. The coefficients on the DWIN variable are restricted to one value in years with a Democratic president and another in years with a Republican president. The same is true for RWIN. Given our sample size, the null hypothesis represented by this restriction is easily rejected; we find $F_{26,2506} = 17.313$, which has an infinitesimal p-value. While there are thus statistically significant sources of intertemporal variation not captured by the midterm cycle, these sources are nonetheless relatively small in magnitude compared to the cycle effect.

Table 6.4. *The pooled incumbency bias model with a midterm cycle*

Variable	Estimated Coefficients	
	Ordinary Least Squares	Weighted Least Squares
V^p_{Dt-2}	.639 (35.4)	.663 (37.8)
DWIN×DEM	12.2 (9.91)	9.92 (8.11)
DWIN×REP	20.2 (16.9)	18.2 (15.3)
RWIN×DEM	17.4 (19.7)	16.9 (18.7)
RWIN×REP	24.9 (31.8)	24.7 (30.7)
INC	7.95 (20.7)	8.58 (19.0)
Overall Std. Error	7.07	
Incumbent Std. Error		6.62
Open Seat Std. Error		9.98

Note: t-statistics in parentheses. See text for definition of variables. $N=2{,}538$.

6.6 OPEN SEATS

We now study how the incumbency effect and the midterm cycle interact. Incorporating either the preference shock specification of (6.9) or the wider set of sources of intertemporal variation represented by the "giant" regression would considerably complicate our discussion without yielding extra substantive insights. Consequently, we focus on the model of column 6 of table 6.2.

We need to take account of the fact that open seats are less predictable than seats with incumbents running. In fact, the sample standard errors, calculated from the regression residuals, are 9.98 for open seats and only

6.62 for seats with incumbents running. [21] In other words, open seats are "noisier"; since they have a larger standard error, they are less predictable. We have employed a standard econometric technique, weighted least squares, to take into account the lesser predictability of open seats. The basic idea is that, in estimating the regression coefficients, one gives less emphasis to open seats and more emphasis to districts with incumbents running. The weights are given by the reciprocals of the standard errors for the two types of districts.

The weighted least squares estimates are reported in the second column of table 6.4; for convenience, the first column reproduces column 6 of table 6.2. We find that the estimates of persistence and incumbency effects and the differences between DEM years and REP years all increase by about 10 percent as a result of weighting the incumbency districts more heavily. Our main interest in the two-stage estimates, however, is in the calculations, below, of the probability that a party will retain a seat. These calculations are sensitive to the estimates of the standard errors. Wishing to recognize the difference in "noise" levels, we base our remaining discussion on the weighted least squares estimates.

6.7 THE SIGNALING THEORY OF THE MIDTERM CYCLE

Our signaling theory of the midterm cycle is broadly confirmed by our empirical analysis based on the weighted least squares method.

The first specification of the midterm cycle is easier to test, and we find strong confirmation of the theory. Recall that this first specification was simply that, after controlling for the previous on-year vote, the Democratic vote should be higher with a Republican in the White House than with a Democrat. The results show that the estimated vote in districts previously won by Democrats is 8.3 percent higher with a Republican president than with a Democrat president ($t = 21.2$) and 7.8 percent higher ($t = 18.7$) when the district was previously won by a Republican. The difference in the magnitude of the cycle between Democratic and Republican districts is, once again, not significant ($t = 0.74$). This observation further confirms that the midterm cycle is a relatively constant, national phenomenon.

The second specification holds that the Democratic vote rises, relative to the on-year, with a Republican president and falls with a Democratic president. In order to test this formulation, we must condition on the values of the right-hand side variables in the weighted least squares regression equation. Because of this, matters are a bit more complicated. We have

---

[21]An F-test leads to overwhelming rejection of the null hypothesis of equality of the standard errors.

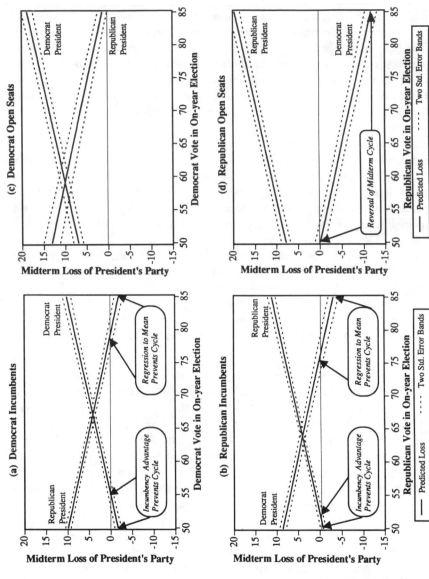

Figure 6.1. The midterm cycle in congressional districts. Panels (a) and (c) are both only for districts in which the Democrats won the preceding on-year election. Panels (b) and (d) are similarly for Republican on-year wins only.

summarized the results in figure 6.1. Panel (a) of the figure considers races with Democrat incumbents where the Democrats won the on-year elections. Panel (b) is the similar picture for Republican incumbents. Panels (c) and (d) pertain to open seats, the first to seats where the Democrats won in the on-year, the second to seats with on-year Republican victories.[22]

All four panels plot the predicted midterm loss for the president's party against the vote for the party winning the seat in the on-year. There are two solid lines in each panel, one corresponding to the case with a Democratic president, the other to the case of a Republican president. That the lines are not horizontal is a consequence of regression to the mean; namely, as pointed out above, the coefficient on V_{Dt-2}^{P} in the regression is less than 1.0. The second specification of the midterm cycle is confirmed whenever the loss is positive; that is, whenever the lines in the figure are above zero. Each solid line is enclosed in broken lines that indicate two standard errors of the forecast. The broken lines show that the forecast votes are very precisely estimated, with somewhat less precision for open seats than for incumbents.

The panels for Democratic incumbents and Republican incumbents are quite similar. With incumbents running, we confirm the second specification, except for two special cases.

The first case is important for the Signaling Hypothesis. The midterm effect is reversed in races where a marginal incumbent of the same party as the president is running. These marginal incumbents actually gain votes at midterm; in the jargon of political scientists, they "surge". As the on-year vote for the incumbent increases, however, the surge becomes smaller and eventually turns into a loss, as a result of regression to the mean. If the net result is taken as the "signal", the signal is provided in districts with safe incumbents, while the signal is turned off for marginal incumbents.

The second case arises when the party of the incumbent representative does not control the White House. A very large midterm "surge" occurs, in line with the theory, for marginal incumbents in this case. The surge persists in non-marginal districts, even though it is attenuated by regression to the mean as the previous vote for the incumbent becomes more lopsided. The attenuation blocks the midterm signal only when the incumbent has a very high (over 75 percent) on-year vote.

When we turn to open seats, we always find the predicted midterm effect in districts previously won by Democrats. The story for seats previously won by Republicans is more complicated. When there is both an open seat and a Republican president, Republican candidates take a drubbing at the

---

[22]Cases with incumbents where the party lost the on-year election are omitted. These arise only in the event of death and other unusual circumstances. Only 26 cases in the sample are not covered by the four scenarios displayed in the panels.

polls; there is always a midterm cycle. But they also do poorly when the Democrats hold the White House. In a district they had previously won with just 50 percent (plus one vote), the Republicans almost stand to break even, but they are predicted losers by a gnat's eyelash. As their previous vote increases, their midterm loss also increases, as a result of regression to the mean. The overall poor performance of the Republicans responds to the observation of Fiorina (1989) that Republicans do not do better with open seats than they do in the House as a whole; on average, Republicans, as the minority party, lose open seats. Note, however, that because the total vote is increasing in the previous vote, when the Democrats hold White House, the Republicans are, except for very marginal seats, always predicted to retain an open seat they previously held.

In summary, the second form of the midterm cycle hypothesis is strongly supported for incumbents, except for the special cases represented by marginal incumbents of the president's party and a systematic regression to the mean in some very lopsided districts. For open seats, the hypothesis is supported except for previously Republican districts in years when a Democrat is president. In this last case, the disinclination of the voters to support Republicans for Congress has more impact, with incumbency removed, than the effect of moderating behavior at midterm.

This failure of the midterm model reflects the fact that the Democratic vote is expected to be higher in very marginal open-seat districts previously won by Republicans than won by Democrats. This unexpected reversal is not just a consequence of our midterm cycle model. It also arises, as can be seen by inspection of the coefficients in column 3 of table 6.2, in the pure incumbency bias model and for four of the eight elections in the disaggregated estimates of the "giant" regression.[23] In other words, the RWIN coefficients are greater than the DWIN coefficients, contradicting the theoretical developments of section 6.4. The result suggests some need for improved specification; perhaps Republican seats tend to become open because incumbents know they are in difficulty and are less willing than Democrats to face a tough race.[24]

While most districts have an expected midterm cycle in *votes*, the situation for *seats* is quite different. We make the point by considering the most precarious case, one in which the winner had received only 50 percent (plus 1 vote) of the on-year vote. The on-year winner becomes a predicted midterm loser when the predicted vote falls below 50 percent. We therefore computed,

---

[23]The paradox persists when the incumbency coefficient in column 6 of table 6.2 is allowed to depend linearly on calendar year, as in King and Gelman (1991). Although we do, like King and Gelman, find that incumbency bias increases significantly in time, the increase in R^2, from .780 to .784, does not warrant our complicating the discussion to account for the trend in incumbency bias.

[24]On the Republicans' difficulty in finding candidates, see Jacobson (1991).

Table 6.5. *Predicted midterm vote when the on-year vote was split 50–50*

Condition	Predicted Vote for On-Year Winner	t-statistic for Null Hypothesis that Midterm Vote=50
Incumbent Runs		
D wins on-year, D president, D incumbent	51.6	4.45
D wins on-year, R president, D incumbent	59.9	29.79
R wins on-year, D president, R incumbent	58.6	22.76
R wins on-year, R president, R incumbent	50.8	2.32
Open Seats		
D wins on-year, D president	43.1	-12.19
D wins on-year, R president	51.3	2.46
R wins on-year, D president	49.997	0.00
R wins on-year, R president	42.2	-15.07

for various scenarios, the *t*-statistic for the null-hypothesis that the expected vote was 50 percent. The results are shown in table 6.5.

With regard to open seats, note that the *president's party is always expected to lose a marginal open seat*, except in the case of a Republican on-year winner with a Democratic president. In this case, the race essentially ends in a tie. For the other cases, the expected percentage is always, in a statistical sense, significantly different from 50. Thus, for open seats, the

Table 6.6. *Probability winning party in on-year House elections wins at midterm*

Condition	On-year Vote for Winning Party		
	50%	55%	60%
Incumbent Runs			
D wins on-year, D president, D incumbent	.60	.77	.89
D wins on-year, R president, D incumbent	.93	.98	.99
R wins on-year, D president, R incumbent	.90	.96	.99
R wins on-year, R president, R incumbent	.55	.73	.87
Open Seats			
D wins on-year, D president	.24	.36	.49
D wins on-year, R president	.55	.68	.79
R wins on-year, D president	.50	.65	.75
R wins on-year, R president	.22	.32	.45

midterm cycle in vote shares will often make a difference in seats. In contrast, incumbents are sufficiently protected that they are always predicted to retain their seats. Their expected vote is always, in a statistical sense, significantly greater than 50. Since there have been typically few open seats in the postwar period, the very substantial midterm vote against the president's party can only serve a moderating role in the guise of a signal.

Finally, we present an alternative summary of our results in table 6.6. We calculate the probability the on-year winner retains the seat at midterm. Incumbents always have a good shot at re-election. The worst off are Republicans running with a Republican president, but they still have a 55 percent chance of winning even when they barely eked out a victory two years previously. If they had won 60–40 in the on-year, their re-election chances are greatly enhanced since the chance of winning goes to 87 percent. Incumbents running against the president always have a better than 90 percent chance of winning, even when their previous share was as low as 50 percent.

In contrast to the case for incumbents, a party that holds the presidency is very unlikely to retain a marginal open seat at midterm. The retention probability is only .24 for Democrats and .22 for Republicans. Even with 55 percent of the on-year vote, the odds are about 2 to 1 that the seat will be lost. There is an even chance of retention only with an on-year vote above the 60 percent level.

In contrast, when a party is running against the president, it is likely, except for very marginal open seats, to retain a seat it had won previously.

6.8 CONCLUSIONS

The incumbency advantage and the moderating midterm cycle are two very important determinants of House elections. Our analysis suggests that, at midterm, the American voter seeks both to reappoint incumbents and to moderate the president by favoring the party not holding the White House.

Moderation is accomplished in the following way. First, the margins of victory of non-marginal incumbents of the president's party are reduced. Second, incumbents from the party not in the White House "surge" as they benefit both from the moderating vote and the incumbency advantage. Third, in open-seat races, the voters favor the candidates of the party not holding the presidency.

The above three effects combine to send a "signal" of moderation to the president's party. At the same time, the objective of retaining incumbents is accomplished since, in marginal seats held by members of the president's party, the midterm penalty is more than offset by the incumbency advantage. Thus the incumbency advantage results in swings in seats at midterm that are relatively modest compared to vote swings. With more open seats, the midterm cycle would produce larger swings in seats: the midterm cycle would be accentuated by term limits that produced more open seats. As such, Republicans would have improved chances of gaining control of the House at midterm, but only at times when they could balance a Democratic president and not when they could assist a Republican in implementing conservative policies.

Without term limits, incumbency based voting renders policy change accomplished via changing seats in Congress somewhat difficult. On the other hand, if the vote share is an important signal that is used in the bargaining between the president and Congress, midterm elections will be relevant politically. If this is the case, our theoretical model, which emphasizes shares rather than majority control, is all the more relevant.

With this chapter we conclude our discussion of the theory of voter behavior with moderating institutions and polarized parties. In the next chapter we analyze the implications of political polarization for macroeconomic policies and outcomes. Then, in chapters 8 and 9, we integrate voting theory and macroeconomic theory to develop and test a unified model of national elections and the macroeconomy.

7

Partisan business cycles

7.1 INTRODUCTION

One of the most important public policy issues is the definition of an economic policy that controls the level of inflation, GNP growth, and unemployment by means of monetary and fiscal stimuli. In order to analyze the effects of partisan politics on the economic cycle, one needs a view of how the economy works, a model linking economic policies to economic outcomes. Our economic model, although very simple, blends two important elements that are widely emphasized in modern macroeconomic theory: the "rational expectations" and the "wage–price rigidity" hypotheses.

The mechanism of expectation formation and the extent of price and wage flexibility have been at the core of the macroeconomic debate in the last thirty years. In the fifties and sixties, mainstream Keynesians held that policymakers could easily control real macroeconomic variables, such as GNP growth and unemployment. The crucial relationship in this Keynesian approach is the "Phillips curve", which relates inflation to unemployment (or GNP growth). A relatively stable inverse relationship between inflation and unemployment was thought to be exploitable for policy purposes: by means of appropriate combinations of monetary and fiscal policies, the policymakers were supposed to be able to choose a point along this macroeconomic trade-off; for instance, by expanding aggregate demand and accepting the costs of some inflation, policymakers could expand economic activity, at least up to a point. Thus, the effects of macroeconomic policies, both fiscal and monetary, were thought to be predictable and stable.

Accepting this conventional wisdom about how the economy works, Hibbs (1977) pointed out that, in industrial democracies, the parties of the left choose inflation/unemployment combinations systematically different from those chosen by parties of the right. The left is more willing than the right to bear the costs of inflation in order to reduce unemployment and increase GNP growth.

The stable Phillips trade-off came under attack as early as 1967 in Milton Friedman's famous presidential address to the American Economic Association (Friedman (1968)). Friedman argued that the trade-off between inflation and unemployment is hardly stable and cannot be easily exploited by interventionist macroeconomic policies. The decade that followed, marked by long periods of both high inflation *and* high unemployment, seemed to support Friedman's hypothesis that the Phillips curve was dead, at least as a stable, medium-long run relationship between inflation and unemployment.[1]

The "rational expectation" approach to macroeconomic analysis pioneered by Lucas (1972) and Sargent and Wallace (1975) pushed Friedman's arguments even further by establishing the famous "neutrality result". The idea is that, if economic agents use all available information (including how the economy works and the policymakers' goals and instruments) in forming expectations and if prices and wages adjust freely, aggregate demand policy in general, and monetary policy in particular, have no real effects. Specifically, the economy has a tendency to self-adjust and converge to the "natural" rate of unemployment. Any attempt to increase the level of economic activity with an expansionary monetary policy simply increases inflation without affecting any real variable: money is neutral, both in the short and in the long run.

The keys to this result are, first, that economic agents can anticipate the effects of monetary policy, and second, that prices and wages can adjust immediately, so that real wages and relative prices remain unaffected by monetary policy. In fact, according to the rational expectation school, not only is an interventionist policy ineffective, but it may also be counterproductive, by increasing uncertainty in expectations formation. For these reasons, Friedman and the rational expectation theorists recommended a non-interventionist macroeconomic policy. Simple rules, such as a constant rate of growth of the money supply, are better than discretionary, active, and less predictable policies.

The intellectual challenge posed by these revolutionary (at least for the post-Keynes era) ideas was enormous, and the policy implications drastic. The idea that expectation formation has to be modelled as a rational process soon became a broadly accepted point of view amongst economists. After all, if "homo economicus" is supposed to act rationally when investing, saving, shopping, and working, why shouldn't he be rational when forming expectations about the policymakers' behavior? Neo-Keynesian economists, for the most part, concentrated their criticisms of the rational expectation school on the ground that the wage–price mechanism is not as flexible as

[1] Several economists (most notably Bruno and Sachs (1985)), however, pointed out that the stagflation of the seventies was the result of supply shocks and institutional rigidities in labor markets.

needed to obtain the neutrality result. The recent collection of articles edited by Mankiw and Romer (1991) brings together the main efforts of this line of research in the past fifteen years.

As early as 1977, Fischer (1977) and Taylor (1979) pointed out that the neutrality result disappears if wage contracts are signed in nominal terms and remain unchanged for a substantial period of time, say one to three years. If a policy change occurs *after* wage contracts have been signed and they cannot be renegotiated immediately, the wage setters cannot react to the new policy by changing the wages. Thus, an expansionary monetary policy creates some inflation, reduces real wages in the short run (until all the contracts expire and can be adjusted), and therefore increases short-run growth, since employment is expanded in response to temporarily lower real wages. In other words, if monetary policy can be adjusted more frequently than wages, the policymakers can use interventionist methods for stabilization. This wage contract model was widely used as the simplest example of the kind of models with wage–price rigidities in which monetary policy is non-neutral in the short run.

Today, about twenty years after the rational expectation revolution, no new consensus has emerged, although most macroeconomists would disagree with both the most extreme models of policy neutrality and the Keynesian models in vogue in the sixties, in which economic policy on the aggregate demand side was predictable, powerful, and effective in the medium-long run.

The economic model which we use in this book is squarely in this eclectic spirit; it incorporates rational expectation formation, but allows for wage rigidities. We adopt this model for analyzing the choice of macroeconomic policies within the partisan model of executive–legislative interaction developed in the first part of the book. For expositional purposes, this chapter ignores the role of the legislature in policy formation: the legislature reappears in the next chapter.

We consider two polarized executives; as in the work by Hibbs (1987) we posit that Democratic presidents are more concerned with GNP growth and unemployment than with inflation, relative to Republican presidents. Because of these different preferences, the two parties target two different inflation rates when in office. Economic agents have to take account of the two possibilities in forming expectations and signing wage contracts *before* elections. Uncertainty about election results will generate uncertainty about inflation, since *ex ante* it is not known with certainty whether the low-inflation or the high-inflation party will win the election. After the election, the low-inflation or the high-inflation policy will materialize, depending on which party has won. If the high-inflation Democratic party wins, an "unexpected" inflation shock occurs, since the wage setters had accounted for the possibility of a Republican victory. This shock generates a short-run economic expansion, which lasts until new contracts have been signed incorporating the high-inflation policy pursued by the Democratic administration in office. At that point, output returns to its "natural" rate of growth, that is, the rate of growth the economy can sustain without policy interventions. The opposite occurs if the Republican party wins; a "below natural" rate of growth occurs because of the less than expected inflation rate. When all the contracts are readjusted, the economy returns to its natural rate of growth with low inflation. Thus, because of wage rigidity, the model predicts a difference in the rate of GNP growth at the beginning of new administrations, whereas the two types of administrations will have similar growth performance in the second part of their terms.

It is important to emphasize that, in our model, the low growth that follows Republican presidential victories does not occur because the Republicans like and pursue low growth. Recessions occur during Republican administrations because this party targets lower inflation than the Democratic party and economic agents have to hedge against these two possibilities. Were it certain there would always be a Republican president, growth would always be at its natural rate. In short, in our model the business cycle results because of the uncertainty generated by competitive partisan politics.

These implications are different from Hibbs's (1977, 1987) partisan model. In Hibbs's model, partisan influence on real economic activity is expected to lead to permanent effects rather than to transitory ones as in our model. The reason is that Hibbs relies on macroeconomic models without rational expectations that allow changes of policies, associated with changes in administrations, to have relatively permanent effects.

Our empirical predictions also sharply contrast with those of the traditional "political business cycle" model pioneered by Nordhaus (1975). That model, in fact, predicts that every administration, both Republican and Democratic, should begin with growth *below* average and end with growth *above* average. The empirical evidence on the United States business cycle, which we begin to analyze in this chapter, suggests that the partisan model with rational expectations adopted in this book performs much better, empirically, than both Nordhaus's traditional political business cycle model and Hibbs's version of the partisan model.

This chapter is organized as follows. Section 7.2 presents our model of the economy and discusses its assumptions. The policy preferences of the two parties are discussed in section 7.3. After section 7.4 derives the economic cycle associated with the electoral cycle, section 7.5 compares the results with the traditional political business cycle literature. Section 7.6 suggests that even a cursory look at the evidence on GNP growth and inflation in the United States provides strong support for our partisan model with wage contracts and rational expectations. Section 7.7 concludes by discussing some issues that have been raised concerning our model of the economy.

7.2 A SIMPLE MODEL OF THE ECONOMY

The model of the economy which we adopt has had a relatively long tradition in economics; it is a version of the wage contract model of Fischer (1977).[2] The economy is characterized by a supply function in which the rate of output growth depends on the rate of growth of real wages. Low growth in real wages implies that firms will be willing to hire more workers to increase production. Capital accumulation and the cost of capital are completely ignored. Thus the rate of output growth in this economy is:

$$y_t = \gamma(\pi_t - w_t) + \bar{y} \qquad (7.1)$$

where y_t is the rate of growth of GNP at time t; γ is a positive parameter; π_t is the inflation rate; w_t is the rate of growth of nominal wages; $\bar{y}$ is the "natural" rate of growth. That is, if the real wage is constant, thus $w_t = \pi_t$, output grows at rate $y_t = \bar{y}$. Unemployment and GNP growth are inversely related (by virtue of "Okun's Law"); thus we could have written (7.1) in terms of unemployment rather than GNP growth. Since our empirical work focuses on GNP growth, we use this variable in the theoretical development of the model.

Nominal wages are set in labor contracts that last one "period". (A period may be thought of as representing two calendar years.) These contracts specify a nominal wage and are not indexed to the inflation rate. We can think of the labor market as competitive, or as controlled by one or several monopolistic labor unions. In the case of a competitive market, a rate of growth of nominal wages equal to the inflation rate ensures a constant real wage at the level that clears the labor market. (We ignore labor productivity growth.) In the second case, the union(s) set the desired real wage given union members' preferences and attempt to keep it at that level, by compensating for the effects of inflation with nominal wage increases.

Under either of these assumptions about the labor market, it follows that nominal wage growth is set equal to the expected inflation rate:

$$w_t = \pi_t^e \qquad (7.2)$$

where π_t^e denotes the inflation rate expected at the *beginning* of period t, when the labor contracts have to be signed. As always in this book, we assume that expectations are rational, that is, the wage setters use all the available information to form expectations of inflation. Formally, this

---

[2]For an introductory general treatment of this kind of model, the reader is directed to any textbook of macroeconomics, for instance Mankiw (1992). For a more advanced treatment, see Blanchard and Fischer (1989), chapter 8.

implies that:

$$\pi_t^e = E(\pi_t | I_{t-1}) \tag{7.3}$$

Equation (7.3) highlights that π_t^e is the expected value (E) of π_t given all the available information accumulated up to the end of period $(t-1)$, that is, I_{t-1}. By (7.1) and (7.2), equation (7.4) immediately follows:

$$y_t = \gamma(\pi_t - \pi_t^e) + \bar{y} \tag{7.4}$$

This equation shows the basic feature of this model: output growth differs from its natural rate ($\bar{y}$) only as a result of unexpected inflation (or deflation). If inflation is correctly anticipated, it does not affect any "real" variable such as output growth.

Equation (7.4), which summarizes our simple model of the economy, can be derived from a richer economic structure. For instance, a model of an economy with price setters and monopolistic competition delivers the same equation. See Blanchard and Fischer (1989, chapter 8) for an in-depth discussion of a variety of neo-Keynesian models which can be summarized by equation (7.4). Our interpretation based on the wage-contract model keeps complications at a minimum. This equation has been widely used in the recent literature on economic policy, surveyed by Persson and Tabellini (1990) and Cukierman (1992).

The rational expectation assumption embodied in equation (7.3) distinguishes our work from that of Hibbs (1977, 1987), who assumes that expectations are adjusted with a backward-looking mechanism that implies that expected inflation depends only on past values of inflation. A more extensive comparison of our approach with Hibbs's model is presented in section 7.5.

Equation (7.4) represents the "supply" side of our economy. The demand side is not explicitly modelled. Rather, we assume that the inflation rate, π_t, is directly controlled by the policymaker. In reality, inflation is not under direct policy control: policy instruments such as the rate of money growth, the discount rate, tax rates, and spending programs affect the level of aggregate demand, which, indirectly, affects the rate of inflation. By assuming that the latter is under the policymakers' direct control, we simplify the exposition by not explicitly linking the inflation rate to the policy instruments. For instance, if the policy instrument considered is the rate of money growth, we could write a money demand function, solve for the rate of inflation as a function of money growth, and substitute away inflation in equation (7.4). This process would lead to an equation for output growth in which the latter depends on unexpected money growth rather than unexpected inflation. Since the focus of this book is not a study of the links between money creation and inflation, we disregard this issue by simply assuming that the policymaker sets π_t directly, as is commonly done in the macroeconomic policy literature.[3] We can now turn to the policymakers' preferences.

7.3 THE PARTY PREFERENCES

As in the first part of this book, we consider two parties with different preferences. Party D is more concerned with growth and unemployment, favors expansionary policies and government intervention, and is less concerned with inflation. Party R is more concerned with inflation than party D, and more averse to government intervention. Although each party faces a trade-off between inflation and growth, they have different preferences about it. Formally, party D's objective function in each period is summarized as follows:

$$u^D = - (\pi_t - \bar{\pi}_D)^2 + b_D y_t$$
$$\bar{\pi}_D > 0; \qquad b_D > 0 \tag{7.5}$$

The first part of this objective function is, as in chapter 2, a quadratic function in which the "bliss point" on the inflation rate is $\bar{\pi}_D > 0$. Economic theory suggests that the optimal inflation rate is not zero, for several reasons. First, inflation is a tax on nominally denominated assets. If a certain amount of government spending has to be financed, it is optimal to distribute the burden of taxation by using, in addition to other forms of taxes, the inflation tax.[4] Second, the empirical evidence suggests a negative correlation between *real* interest rates and the inflation rate. Thus, some inflation may bring about, at least temporarily, lower real interest rates. Third, Tobin (1972) argues that some moderate inflation facilitates the "smooth" adjustment of relative prices and wages across sections. If, as appears to be the case empirically, certain prices or, especially, wages, are rigid downward, some inflation permits movements in relative prices with few or no nominal wage or price cuts.[5]

The second term in equation (7.5) represents the benefit of higher growth: since b_D is positive, the higher growth is, the higher the utility for party

---

[3]For more discussion of this point see Rogoff (1985), Persson and Tabellini (1990), and Cukierman (1992). Alesina and Sachs (1988) and Alesina (1988b) focus on models similar to the one of this book, in which the emphasis is on unexpected money growth rather than on unexpected inflation.

[4]The original argument is by Phelps (1973). See Atkinson and Stiglitz (1980) for a more general treatment of optimal taxation theory. Mankiw (1990) argues, by looking at two hundred years of U.S. data, that inflation was in fact used as a form of optimal taxation.

[5]Note that downward rigidity of wages or prices is not inconsistent with rational behavior, as pointed out in the recent neo-Keynesian line of research. See Mankiw and Romer (1991) and, especially, Ball and Mankiw (1992).

D. By substituting (7.4) into (7.5) one obtains:

$$u^D = -(\pi_t - \bar{\pi}_D)^2 + b_D\gamma(\pi_t - \pi_t^e) + b_D\bar{y} \tag{7.6}$$

This expression highlights a key feature of this model: the policymaker benefits by an *unexpected* burst of inflation.[6]

The incentive to increase growth above the "market" or "natural" level can be due to one of three reasons. First, the labor unions may keep the real wage too high, since they maximize the welfare of union members without properly taking into account their effect on the unemployed. Since the policymaker cares not only about union members, but also about the unemployed, she would like to achieve a higher rate of growth than the one compatible with the real wage imposed by the unions. The second argument, which applies also to a competitive labor market, emphasizes the effects of distortions in this market. For instance, income taxes, by reducing the labor supply, keep the natural rate of unemployment high, and the natural rate of growth low; such low growth generates an incentive for the policymaker to compensate by creating inflation shocks.[7] The third argument emphasizes deviations from perfect competition in the goods market. Monopolists on monopolistically competitive producers would undersupply relative to perfectly competitive suppliers.

The objective function for party R is analogous to that of party D, but with different bliss points:

$$u^R = -(\pi_t - \bar{\pi}_R)^2 + b_R y_t \tag{7.7}$$

The partisan differences between the two parties are captured by the following conditions:

$$\bar{\pi}_D > \bar{\pi}_R > 0; \qquad b_D > b_R > 0 \tag{7.8}$$

The first inequality in (7.8) states party D is more willing to use the inflation tax to support larger spending programs or to reduce real interest rates. The second inequality states that party D, compared to party R, cares *relatively* more about growth than inflation. It should be stressed that the parameters b_D and b_R capture *relative* evaluation of the two targets, namely

---

[6]Since growth enters linearly in equation (7.5), unexpected inflation enters linearly in (7.6). But the same results are obtained in a different specification in which the objective function is quadratic on *both* inflation and growth, with a target on growth *above* the natural rate, $\bar{y}$. The linear specification simplifies the algebra without affecting the nature of the results; see Alesina (1988b) and Alesina and Sachs (1988) for more discussion. The substantive point is that in either a linear specification or a quadratic specification with a growth target above the natural rate, the policymaker has an incentive to increase growth above $\bar{y}$. As a result, the policymaker benefits from a burst of unexpected inflation, because the natural level of growth is not considered sufficient.

[7]See Cukierman (1992) for both a discussion of this point and a survey of the economic literature on this policy model.

inflation and growth. For instance, the fact that b_R is smaller than b_D does not mean that party R dislikes growth, but that this party cares less than party D about growth *relative* to inflation. As a matter of fact, in *absolute* terms party R may care about growth and unemployment as much as party D (or even more!); in this case b_R could still be lower than b_D if, in absolute terms, party R dislikes inflation more than party D. Republican party claims of aversion to unemployment, even if perfectly sincere, do not constitute evidence against our formulation of party preferences.

Hibbs (1987) has examined the official party platforms in several recent presidential elections. Even though both parties declare that they are strenuous fighters of both evils, inflation and unemployment, the Republican party platforms place relatively much more emphasis on controlling inflation. On the contrary, the Democratic platforms emphasize unemployment. These differences in party preferences may arise because of the distributional consequences of different macroeconomic policies. The lower middle class, which mostly supports the left, tends to suffer during recessions relatively more than the upper middle class. For the United States, the evidence assembled and reviewed by Hibbs (1987) is unambiguous concerning the effect of unemployment: when unemployment rises, the income shares of the two poorest quintiles of the population decrease and the shares of the two richest quintiles increase, while the middle quintile is essentially unaffected. Hibbs (1987) calculates that a one-year increase in the rate of unemployment from 6 to 10 percent would shift 0.95 percentage points of income from the bottom two-fifths to the upper two-fifths of the income distribution.[8]

The redistributive effects of inflation are less clear-cut. In principle, several channels are open. First, there may be redistribution of after-tax income if income tax brackets are not adjusted for inflation, which was the case until the mid-seventies. Second, the interaction between the tax structure and a firm's financial structure can have redistributive effects. Third, inflation alters the real value of nominally denominated assets such as savings accounts. Finally, there are distributional consequences from changes in the relative prices of the baskets of goods purchased by different income groups. Hibbs's (1987) reasonable conclusion is that if inflation has had any overall effect on income distribution in the United States, it has been from the rich to the poor. Along the same lines, Minford (1985) argues that the political right is more concerned with defending the real value of nominally denominated assets, which are held in greater quantity by the upper middle class relative to the lower class. Furthermore, higher inflation may also be the consequence

---

[8]Of course, the real income of the upper quintiles could decrease with aggregate unemployment even if their share of income were increasing. Nonetheless, the evidence presented by Hibbs supports the claim that, relative to the poor, the well-to-do care more about inflation than about unemployment.

of higher government spending programs that disproportionately favor the poor.

In summary, the evidence concerning the distributional effects of macro-economic policies is consistent with the hypothesis that the left, supported by the lower middle class, should favor relatively high government spending, high inflation, high growth, and low unemployment policies. Examining American party platforms, Hibbs (1987) provides direct evidence that, indeed, the two American parties had different macroeconomic programs. Kiewiet (1983) studies poll responses and shows that the Amercian voters understand these differences in economic policy and vote accordingly.

Before we proceed toward analyzing our model, we should underline an important point concerning a difference in notation between chapters 7–9 and the first part of the book. Because of the policy problem considered here, the party of the left (party D) has "higher" bliss points than party **R**. That is, $\bar{\pi}_D > \bar{\pi}_R$ and $b_D > b_R$. *In the context of economic policy, the political left prefers higher policies than the political right.* On the contrary, in the first part of the book we had adopted the general convention of having the left associated with "lower" policies, for obvious geometric reasons.

The voters, as in the first six chapters, have preferences analogous to those of the parties; the utility function of the generic voter i is given by:

$$u^i = -(\pi_t - \bar{\pi}_i)^2 + b_i y_t \qquad (7.9)$$

Thus each voter has an optimal inflation rate, $\bar{\pi}_i$, and, as long as $b_i > 0$, prefers higher to lower growth. Note that, using (7.3), equation (7.9) becomes:

$$u^i = -(\pi_t - \bar{\pi}_i)^2 + b_i \gamma (\pi_t - \pi_t^e) + b_i \bar{y} \qquad (7.10)$$

At first sight this expression may appear peculiar: voter i benefits from an inflation surprise, although, as a wage setter, his utility is maximized if he correctly predicts the inflation rate. (Recall equation (7.2).) Nevertheless, there is no contradiction. As a wage setter, individual i benefits if he correctly predicts inflation, *and, in the aggregate,* his fellow wage setters are surprised by an inflation shock. In this case, wage setter i achieves the best of both worlds: his real wage is intact, but aggregate employment is expanded, an outcome that he, as a citizen, favors. In equilibrium, since each wage setter has the same information, expectations are the same for everybody, but this is an equilibrium condition, not a feature of individual preferences.[9]

This subtle interaction between the aggregate benefits of an inflation shock and the incentive to predict the inflation rate correctly give rise to a

---

[9]The preferences summarized in equation (7.10) are even easier to justify using the interpretation of our labor market with unions. Non-union members, perhaps unemployed, may be perfectly happy to observe a positive inflation shock that cuts real wages of the employed and increases employment.

"time inconsistency" problem that was pointed out originally by Kydland and Prescott (1977) and then further explored by Barro and Gordon (1983). The nature of this problem, which has become a dominant theme in economic policy discussions, will become apparent in the next section.[10]

7.4 A "RATIONAL PARTISAN THEORY" OF THE BUSINESS CYCLE[11]

Let us begin by considering the policy choice of, say, party D, leaving aside for a moment the issue of elections and electoral uncertainty. If in office, party D chooses π_t to maximize its utility, given in equation (7.6). (Remember that, as in chapter 2, party D may also be "office motivated", but once in office such motivation does not affect its policy choices.)

The timing of events is as follows. At *the beginning* of the period, wages are set equal to expected inflation, π_t^e. *After* expectations are formed, the policymaker chooses π_t. Therefore, in choosing π_t, the policymaker has to take expectations as given, since they are not under his control and are already set when policy is chosen.

A simple exercise in optimization readily establishes that the utility of party D is maximized by an inflation rate π^{D*} such that:

$$\pi_t = \pi^{D*} = \bar{\pi}_D + \frac{b_D \gamma}{2} \tag{7.11}$$

Since the public is rational and knows the objective function of party D, it is aware that party D will choose this policy. Thus, recalling that for the moment we have no electoral uncertainty:

$$\pi_t^e = \pi^{D*} = \bar{\pi}_D + \frac{b_D \gamma}{2} \tag{7.12}$$

It follows that there is no unexpected inflation, and output growth is at its natural level:

$$y_t = \bar{y} \tag{7.13}$$

This simple problem highlights the issue of time inconsistency. Suppose that party D could commit to a policy π' such that

$$\pi_t^e = \pi' = \bar{\pi}_D \tag{7.14}$$

In this case, growth is at its natural rate, $y_t = \bar{y}$, and inflation is at the most

---

[10]The most recent surveys of the literature on time consistency are in Persson and Tabellini (1990) and Cukierman (1992).

[11]The original formulation of this model is in Alesina (1987). The term "rational partisan theory" was used first by Alesina (1989) to distinguish this model from Hibbs's "partisan theory".

desired level for party D, namely $\bar{\pi}_D$. The policy π' is clearly superior to π^{D*}, since output is at $\bar{y}$ in both cases and π^{D*} *is above its most desired level*, $\bar{\pi}_D$.

So why can't D adopt the policy π'? Suppose $\pi^e = \pi'$, because the public believes in the policy. Then, after π_t^e is formed and set at π', suppose that the policymaker chooses π^{D*} instead of π'. From equation (7.4) it follows:

$$y_t = \gamma(\pi^{D*} - \bar{\pi}_D) + \bar{y} = \frac{b_D\gamma^2}{2} + \bar{y} \tag{7.15}$$

By creating an inflation surprise, the policymaker achieves a level of growth greater than $\bar{y}$ and, as is easily verified, a level of utility higher than would be obtained following the expected policy π'. The public, aware of this incentive, will never believe in any policy announcements other than π^{D*} and will set their expectations accordingly. Thus in equilibrium we must have $\pi_t^e = \pi^{D*}$, since once expectations are set at that level, the best the policymaker can do is to follow the policy π^{D*}.

The time inconsistency problem can then be summarized as follows. if the policymakers could irrevocably commit in *advance* to follow the policy rule π', they would achieve a level of utility, $\bar{u}_D$, such that:

$$\bar{u}_D = b_D\bar{y} \tag{7.16}$$

Equation (7.16) is obtained by substituting $\pi_t = \pi' = \bar{\pi}_D = \pi_t^e$, in party D's objective function (7.6). In practice, however the policymaker can always change his mind and break a promise. If the public expects π' and the policymakers choose π^{D*}, the utility of this "cheating" strategy u_D^{ch} is given by substituting $\pi_t^e = \pi'$ and $\pi_t = \pi^{D*}$ in party D's objective function, leading to:

$$u_D^{ch} = \left(\frac{b_D\gamma}{2}\right)^2 + b_D\bar{y} \tag{7.17}$$

Since $u_D^{ch} > \bar{u}_D$, π' cannot be a credible equilibrium: the policy π' would not be followed. Furthermore, in equilibrium, expectations cannot be systematically incorrect, by the rationality assumption. Thus the only possible equilibrium is one in which $\pi^{D*} = \pi_t$, leading to the following level of utility:

$$u_D^* = -\left(\frac{b_D\gamma}{2}\right)^2 + b_D\bar{y} \tag{7.18}$$

The equilibrium with π^{D*} yields a lower utility for party D than the hypothetical case of $\pi' = \pi_t^e = \bar{\pi}_D$, because π^{D*} is higher than $\bar{\pi}_D$, without leading to any increase of the growth rate. The "inflation bias" is given by the term $b_D\gamma/2$ in equation (7.11): this term guarantees that the inflation rate is high enough that the policymaker does not have any further incentive to surprise the public by creating even higher inflation to speed up growth.[12]

If party R is in office, analogous arguments imply that the policy choice (π^{R*}) of this party is given by:

$$\pi^{R*} = \bar{\pi}_R + \frac{b_R \gamma}{2} \qquad (7.19)$$

Thus:

$$\pi_t^e = \pi^{R*} = \bar{\pi}_R + \frac{b_R \gamma}{2} \qquad (7.20)$$

and

$$y = \bar{y}. \qquad (7.21)$$

The inflation rate with party D in office is higher than with R in office for two reasons. The optimal inflation rate, $\bar{\pi}_D$, is higher for party D, *and* this party cares more about growth relative to inflation; thus b_D is greater than b_R. The more a party cares about growth, the stronger is its incentive to create unexpected inflation, and the higher is the equilibrium inflation rate. Thus, in summary, we have:

$$\pi^{D*} > \pi^{R*} \qquad (7.22)$$

Inflation is higher with the D party holding the executive branch

We are now ready to analyze the effects of elections. As before, the president remains in office two periods. Since in this model a period also corresponds to the length of a labor contract, we are implicitly assuming that the length of a contract is two years. This assumption is not unreasonable for the American economy, where the majority of labor contracts last between one and three years.

The timing is as follows (see box 7.1). First, contracts are signed. Then elections take place; then policy is chosen. At the end of the first period, contracts are adjusted. Afterward, policy is chosen for the second period. The first and second periods of each term are designated by subscripts 1 and 2. Since in this chapter we ignore Congress, there are no midterm elections.

---

[12]The inflation bias argument has been used as a positive theory of inflation, namely as an explanation for why many countries find it difficult to maintain low inflation rates. Several institutional and policy reforms have been discussed to mitigate this problem. For a discussion of the role of reputation in enforcing low inflation equilibria, see Barro and Gordon (1983) and Rogoff (1987). For a discussion of institutional arrangements such as Central Bank independence, see Rogoff (1985), Alesina (1988b), Alesina and Summers (1993), Lohmann (1992), and Cukierman (1992). For a discussion of international aspects of the time inconsistency problem, see Giavazzi and Giovannini (1989) and Alesina and Grilli (1992, 1993).

Box 7.1

THE TIMING OF THE ECONOMIC MODEL FOR ONE PRESIDENTIAL TERM

Contracts signed for period 1

Elections for period 1

Winner chooses π_i for period 1

Growth occurs in period 1

Contracts signed for period 2

Period 1 winner chooses π_i for period 2 (no new elections)

Growth occurs in period 2

Electoral results are uncertain. Party D (now the "high" policy party) wins the presidency with probability P; party R with probability $(1 - P)$. In this chapter, P is simply the probability that more than 50 percent of the voters prefer policy π^{R*} to policy π^{D*}. Let us take P as given for the moment; its derivation will be discussed below.

We now show, for given P, the cyclical behavior, termed the "rational partisan business cycle", induced in the economy by the electoral uncertainty. In the first period we have:

$$\pi_1^e = P\pi^{R*} + (1 - P)\pi^{D*} \tag{7.23}$$

If D wins we obtain:

$$y_1^D = \gamma(P)(\pi^{D*} - \pi^{R*}) + \bar{y} \tag{7.24}$$

Equation (7.24) is obtained by substituting (7.23) into (7.4), noting that if D wins, $\pi_1 = \pi^{D*}$.

If R wins we have:

$$y_1^R = -\gamma(1 - P)(\pi^{D*} - \pi^{R*}) + \bar{y} \tag{7.25}$$

Equation (7.25) is obtained by substituting (7.23) into (7.4) and noting that if R wins, $\pi_1 = \pi^{R*}$.

In the second period expectations adjust, so that:

$$\pi_2^e = \pi^{D*} \qquad \text{if D is in office} \tag{7.26}$$

$$\pi_2^e = \pi^{R*} \qquad \text{if R is in office} \tag{7.27}$$

$$y_t = \bar{y} \qquad \text{with either R or D in office} \tag{7.28}$$

Equation (7.28) is determined by substituting (7.26) or (7.27) into (7.4).

The key for this electoral cycle is equation (7.23), which underscores that electoral uncertainty forces the public to take account of both possible

174

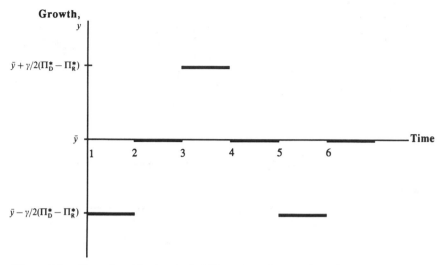

Figure 7.1. Growth with the probability of an R presidential victory, $P = 1/2$, assuming that R wins the presidency at $t = 1$ and $t = 5$, and D wins at $t = 3$

outcomes in forming first-period expectations. In the second period, instead, there is no electoral uncertainty; thus expectations are always correct, as equations (7.26) and (7.27) imply.[13]

The following cycle is generated by this electoral uncertainty. In the first period of a D administration, inflation is higher than expected and output growth is above the natural rate. In the first period of an R administration, on the contrary, inflation is lower than expected and growth is below its natural rate. In the second period of both administrations, growth is at its natural rate. The cyclical pattern of growth is illustrated in figure 7.1. The time path of inflation is illustrated in figure 7.2.

The amplitude of these deviations of output growth from the natural

[13]Note that the expected rate of growth before the election is equal to $\bar{y}$. In fact, expected growth, $E(y)$, is equal to:

$$E(y) = Py_1^D + (1 - P)y_1^R$$
$$= P[\bar{y} + \gamma(\pi_1^{D*} - \pi_1^e)] + (1 - P)[\bar{y} + \gamma(\pi_1^{R*} - \pi_1^e)]$$
$$= \bar{y} + \gamma([P\pi_1^{D*} + (1 - P)\pi_1^{R*}] - \pi_1^e)$$

But since:

$$\pi_1^e = P\pi_1^{D*} + (1 - P)\pi_1^{R*},$$

it follows that:

$$E(y) = \bar{y}$$

The intuition is that even though an increase in P raises the likelihood of observing π^{D*} instead of π^{R*}, the effect is compensated by a change in inflationary expectations, π^e.

175

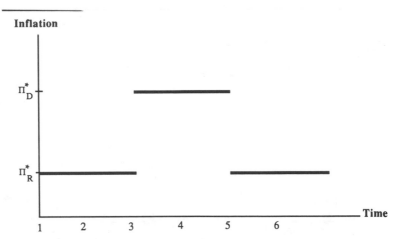

Figure 7.2.   Inflation when R wins the presidency at $t = 1$ and $t = 5$, and D wins at $t = 3$.

rate is positively correlated with the distance between the "points of view" of the two parties. In fact, the more different are the optimal rates of inflation for the two parties ($\bar{\pi}_D$ and $\bar{\pi}_R$) and the more different their incentives to increase growth (b_D and b_R), the bigger are the deviations of output growth from $\bar{y}$. Thus *more political polarization produces wider economic fluctuations.* In addition, the degree of surprise of the policy outcome influences the amplitude of output fluctuations. For instance, the higher is P, the probability of a D victory, the larger is the recession generated by an R victory, because the less expected is the inflation shock.

It is worth re-emphasizing that party R causes growth downturns or even recessions not because this party likes recessions; in fact, since $b_R > 0$, party R prefers *higher* to *lower* growth. The problem is that, as shown in equation (7.23), expectations of inflation are kept high by the possibility of a D victory; the first-period downturn during an R administration is the "necessary" price to pay to eradicate inflationary expectations from the public. In some sense, the model supports President Reagan's claim that his 1981–82 sharp recession was the necessary "medicine" to eliminate inflation (and inflationary expectations) introduced in the system by President Carter's expansionary and inflationary policies in the late seventies.

Although output fluctuates only in the first period, inflation is *always* higher during a D administration than during an R administration.[14] Thus

---

[14]The rate of inflation for both parties is constant for the entire term of office, because output enters linearly in the objective function of the two parties. Had we assumed a quadratic objective function in output, the inflation in the first period of a D administration would be lower than the inflation in the second period. More details on this case can be found in Alesina and Sachs (1988) and Alesina (1988b).

in the second period of a D administration, output growth falls toward its natural rate and inflation remains high. On the contrary, in the second half of an R administration, output growth is increasing toward its natural rate and inflation remains low.

We can now turn to the determination of P. Each individual has preferences captured by the parameters $\bar{\pi}_i$ and b_i. The joint distribution of these parameters, like the distribution of ideal points in chapter 4, is subject to a random shock. For the purposes of this chapter, the only important assumption about the distribution and this shock is that there is enough variability to leave the outcome of the presidential election uncertain.

The generic voter i votes R if his utility with an R president, u_R^i, is higher than with a D president, u_D^i. Thus, recalling that β is the discount factor, assumed equal for everybody, and that in the second period growth is equal to $\bar{y}$ with either party, it follows that:

$$u_R^i = -(\pi^{R*} - \bar{\pi}_i)^2 + b_i y_1^R + \beta[-(\pi^{R*} - \bar{\pi}_i)^2 + b_i \bar{y}] \qquad (7.29)$$

and

$$u_D^i = -(\pi^{D*} - \bar{\pi}_i)^2 + b_i y_1^D + \beta[-(\pi^{D*} - \bar{\pi}_i)^2 + b_i \bar{y}] \qquad (7.30)$$

where y_1^D and y_1^R are given above in equations (7.24) and (7.25), respectively. Thus P is the probability that for more than 50 percent of the voters the following inequality holds:

$$u_R^i > u_D^i \qquad (7.31)$$

Recalling that $y_1^D > \bar{y} > y_1^R$, it follows that "high b" voters prefer party D to party R. Similarly, "high $\bar{\pi}$" voters prefer party D. Note that, even though we have a single policy variable, π, voting occurs on two dimensions, since the voters and the parties differ on two parameters, $\bar{\pi}$ and b. But since the two parties have fixed positions, π^{D*} and π^{R*}, voters have only a binary choice and P is determined by the distribution of the shock to voter preferences. Furthermore, although not required for the formal analysis, it is natural to assume that "high b" voters are also "high $\bar{\pi}$" voters: given two voters, i and j, if $\bar{\pi}_i > \bar{\pi}_j$, then $b_i > b_j$. Voter i is on the "left" of voter j. Under this natural assumption, the "high $\bar{\pi}$ and b" people (i.e., the "left-wing" types) are the D voters and the "low $\bar{\pi}$ and b" (i.e., the "right-wing" types) people are the R voters.

Finally, this model implies that the voters should pay *no attention* to the state of the economy in the election or pre-election years: the voters have no reason to be retrospective. They know the two parties' preferences; they know which policy to expect from them; and they know the effects of these policies on the economy. Voters can obtain no useful information by observing the economy since everything is known in advance, except for the electoral outcome. A role for retrospective voting will appear in chapter 8 when we extend the model to incorporate differences in the

competence of different administrations and incomplete information about
such competence.

7.5 COMPARISONS WITH OTHER MODELS OF
ELECTORAL CYCLES

The two most important alternative models to the rational partisan theory
discussed in this chapter are the partisan model by Hibbs (1977, 1987) and
the political business cycle model by Nordhaus (1975).

Hibbs's partisan theory

Hibbs's assumptions about the preferences of the two parties are, for
all practical purposes, identical to ours. The main difference between our
model and his concerns expectations. Instead of the rational expectation
assumption, embodied in equation (7.3), Hibbs assumes a backward-looking
expectation-formation mechanism of the following type:

$$\pi_t^e = \lambda_1 \pi_{t-1} + \lambda_2 \pi_{t-2} + \lambda_3 \pi_{t-3} \ldots \tag{7.32}$$

where the λs are non-negative parameters smaller than 1. In addition, the
sum of the λs does not exceed 1. Substituting (7.32) into the growth equation
given in (7.4), one obtains

$$y_t = \gamma \pi_t - \hat{\gamma}_1 \pi_{t-1} - \hat{\gamma}_2 \pi_{t-2} - \hat{\gamma}_3 \pi_{t-3} \ldots + \bar{y} \tag{7.33}$$

where $\hat{\gamma}_1 = \gamma \lambda_1$, and so on. Equation (7.33), which is essentially a traditional
Phillips curve, highlights two important differences from our model. First,
for given π_{t-1}, π_{t-2}, and so on, the policymaker can always increase output
growth by creating higher inflation. Thus, as long as inflation is increasing,
growth can be sustained at a level chosen by the policymaker for any period
of time. Second, following a "once and for all" increase in inflation,
expectations take several periods to adjust. Thus, after an expansionary
policy shock, growth remains above the natural level for several periods.
The intuition is that, since expectation formation is backward looking, it
takes several periods for expected inflation to catch up.

A crucial distinction from our model is that in Hibbs's model expectations
do not adjust immediately and discretely following a change in administration. Regardless of the electoral results, the public always looks at past
inflation to predict future inflation. For example, the election of a self-
proclaimed very expansionary Democratic administration does not imply
an upward revision in expectation of inflation. Even in this case, expected
inflation rises slowly, as actual inflation accumulates.

The implication is that differences in real economic variables, such as
GNP growth and unemployment, between the two types of administration,

should be long-lived rather than transitory, as in our model. For instance, in Hibbs's model a Democratic administration should be able to maintain unemployment permanently lower than a Republican administration. Once again, the main difference is the speed of expectation adjustment. In our model, expectations are forward looking and adjust as soon as wage contracts can be renewed. In Hibbs's model expectations are backward looking and the economy takes longer to adjust.

A second important difference is that our model makes a prediction concerning the degree of electoral uncertainty and the amount of "surprise" and the effects of policy changes on the real economy. Hibbs's formulation is agnostic on this point, because the process of expectation adjustment is imposed exogenously.

Nordhaus's political business cycle

The traditional political business cycle model assumes that the parties are only opportunistic: they maximize only the probability of re-election, and, as in Hibbs's work, an exploitable Phillips curve is available to the policymakers. Both parties adopt the same policy: they create an outburst of growth immediately before an election. The (lagged) effects of the pre-electoral expansionary policies on inflation are eliminated by a post-electoral recession. The voters, who are backward looking, have short memories, and never learn from past mistakes, reward the incumbent because of the pre-electoral expansion, without remembering from past experience that they will have to pay for it with a post-electoral downturn.

Two elements of non-rational behavior are crucial for Nordhaus's model. The first, as in Hibbs's work, is the backward-looking formation in expectations. The second is naïve retrospective voting, which implies that the public rewards opportunistic incumbents who manage to create pre-electoral economic expansions.

Whether or not a political business cycle of the Nordhaus type can survive in a model with rational expectations and rational voter behavior is an open question. Recent research by Cukierman and Meltzer (1986), Rogoff and Sibert (1988), Rogoff (1990), and Persson and Tabellini (1990) suggests that some of Nordhaus's results can be obtained in a model in which the voters, although fully rational, are imperfectly informed about either the policymakers' objectives or their competence. The rationality of voters' behavior, however, despite their less than full information, severely limits the latitude of the policymakers' ability to behave opportunistically. These "rational" models are consistent with occasional, short-lived pre-electoral policy manipulations. They cannot be consistent with a regular four-year cycle of unemployment and growth as predicted by Nordhaus's political business cycle model. Alesina (1988b), Persson and Tabellini (1990), and

Alesina, Cohen, and Roubini (1992, 1993) provide a more extensive theoretical and empirical discussion of these models.

7.6 EVIDENCE ON THE ''RATIONAL PARTISAN THEORY''

The implications of the rational partisan theory for macroeconomic fluctuations can be summarized as follows. GNP growth should be higher than average in the first half of a Democratic administration and lower than average in the first half of a Republican administration. In the second half of either type of administration, growth should be at its average ("natural") level. Inflation should be permanently higher during Democratic administrations.

Table 7.1 reports the yearly rate of real GNP growth for the period 1949–1991.[15] The rate of growth in the first halves of Republican administrations has been well below the sample average, which, in turn, is below the average growth rate in the first half of Democratic administrations. The growth rate in the second halves of the two types of administration is very similar. Every Republican administration since the Second World War, until the second Reagan administration, had a recession that began within the first year of the term.[16] On the contrary, none of the Democratic administrations had a recession .or even a downturn in their first halves. Table 7.1 also highlights a remarkable difference in GNP growth between administrations in the *second year*, rather than in the first. This timing is consistent with the well-known fact that the effect on the economy of a change in aggregate macroeconomic policy has a lag of three to five quarters (see, for instance, Romer and Romer (1989)).

These observations contrast sharply with Nordhaus's political business cycle model, which predicts that *every* administration, both Democratic and Republican, should begin with a recession and end with above-average growth. The only recession that occurred during a Democratic presidency is the short recession of 1980, at the time of the second oil shock. The timing of this recession is not consistent with either the partisan theory or the political business cycle model.

These observations are also not consistent with Hibbs's partisan model, which implies "permanent" differences across administrations. Although growth was high at the end of the Truman administration, it was not unusually high at the end of the Kennedy/Johnson or Carter administrations.

---

[15]This table updates Alesina and Sachs (1988).

[16]The recession of the Bush administration probably started a few months into the second year, although it has been particularly difficult to establish the beginning of this recession with the usual precision.

Table 7.1. *Rate of growth of GNP in real terms*

Democratic Administrations			
	Year		
	First	Second	Third	Fourth
Truman	0.0	8.5	10.3	3.9
Kennedy/Johnson	2.6	5.3	4.1	5.3
Johnson	5.8	5.8	2.9	4.1
Carter	4.7	5.3	2.5	-0.2*
Average	3.3	6.2	5.0	3.3
Average First/Second Halves	4.8		4.1	
Republican Administrations			
	Year		
	First	Second	Third	Fourth
Eisenhower I	4.0	-1.3	5.6	2.1
Eisenhower II	1.7	-0.8	5.8	2.2
Nixon	2.4	-0.3	2.8	5.0
Nixon/Ford	5.2	-0.5	-1.3*	4.9
Reagan I	1.9	-2.5	3.6	6.8
Reagan II	3.4	2.7	3.4	4.5
Bush	2.5	0.9	-0.7	
Average	3.0	-0.3	2.7	4.3
Average First/Second Halves	1.4		3.5	

Source: *Economic Report of the President 1992*

*Oil shocks

Similarly, growth was not low in the second halves of the Eisenhower, Nixon/Ford, and Reagan administrations.

The following regression equation captures the basic message of table 7.1. The dependent variable is the yearly rate of growth, y_t, from table 7.1, and the independent variable is a dummy (PDUM) assuming the value of $+1$ in the second year of a Democratic administration, -1 in the second year of a Republican administration, and zero otherwise; thus the theory predicts a positive sign for the coefficient of this dummy variable.

$$y_t = 3.39 + 3.29\, \text{PDUM}_t + \varepsilon_t$$
$$(11.01) \quad (5.41)$$

sample: 1949–1991; $R^2 = 0.42$; D.W. $= 1.85$

181

Table 7.2. *Partisan dummies*

Quarters[*]	1	2	3	4	5	6	7	8	9	10	11	12	13	14	15	16
DD1	1	2	3	4	4	3	2	1	0	0	0	0	0	0	0	0
D2	0	0	0	0	0	0	0	0	1	1	1	1	1	1	1	1

[*] The dummy RR1 is identical to DD1 for Republican administrations.

The *t*-statistic, in parentheses, shows that the coefficient on the political variable is significant at a very high level of confidence. The value of this coefficient implies that the difference in the rate of growth in the second year of the two types of administrations is almost 7! What is truly remarkable about this really "minimalist" regression is that a constant and one dummy variable capture almost half of the variation in the annual GNP growth series![17]

A second regression, which makes use of quarterly observations of GNP growth, highlights even more explicitly the implications of the rational partisan theory. Table 7.2 defines three dummy variables, DD1, RR1, and D2. The dependent variable, $\hat{y}_t$, is the rate of GNP growth, *quarterly* observations of annual rates:[18]

$$\hat{y}_t = 1.19 + 1.04\hat{y}_{t-1} - 0.165\hat{y}_{t-2} - 0.225\hat{y}_{t-3}$$
$$(5.78) \quad (13.61) \quad (-1.48) \quad (-3.05)$$

$$+ 0.219DD1_{t-1} - 0.303RR1_{t-1} + 0.163D2_{t-1}$$
$$(2.26) \qquad (-3.46) \qquad (0.58)$$

$$R^2 = 0.83 \qquad \text{sample: 1949.1–1991.4}$$

The dummies DD1 and RR1 capture the first-half fluctuations in growth. The "spiked" shape which they assume is meant to capture the cumulative

[17]The Durbin–Watson statistic indicates that there is very little autocorrelation of the residuals. In fact, adding a lagged dependent variable leaves the results virtually unchanged:

$$y_t = 3.000 + 0.120y_{t-1} + 3.271\,PDUM_t$$
$$(5.94) \quad (0.98) \qquad (5.30)$$

$$R^2 = .43$$

[18]The dependent variable is defined as follows:

$$\hat{y}_t = (\lg Y_t - \lg Y_{t-4}) \times 100,$$

where Y_t is the *level* of GNP in quarter t. This regression is an updated version of similar results presented by Alesina (1988b).

effect of policy changes and the gradual return to the natural rate of growth. Analogous results are obtained, however, when the two dummies assume the value of 1 in every quarter of the first halves of the two administrations. Three lagged values of the dependent variable are necessary to correct for autocorrelation of the residuals, common in quarterly macroeconomic time series.[19]

The coefficients on RR1 and DD1 have the sign predicted by the theory and are significant at the 5 percent confidence level or better; t-statistics are in parentheses. On the contrary, the dummy D2, which assumes the value of one in the second half of Democratic administrations, has a coefficient that is insignificantly different from zero, indicating that on average there is no difference in the growth performance in the second halves of the two administrations. This result contrasts with Hibbs's partisan model, which implies permanent differences in the "real" effect of different macroeconomic policies of different administrations.[20]

Let us now turn to inflation. In addition to the partisan effect, two major events in the postwar period have influenced the rate of inflation: the abandonment of the Bretton Woods system of fixed exchange rates in favor of a flexible-rate regime in 1971, and the movements of the price of oil.

The following regression on quarterly observations of the inflation rate, defined as the rate of change of the CPI, includes as independent variables: (a) a partisan dummy (R) that assumes the value of 1 during Republican administrations and zero otherwise; (b) a "Bretton Woods" variable (BW) that assumes the value of 1 from the beginning of the sample (1949.1) throughout 1971.4 and zero otherwise; (c) a price of oil dummy (OIL) that assumes the value of 1 from 1973.3 to 1974.4 and from 1979.4 to 1980.4. Finally, four lags of the dependent variable are needed to correct for autocorrelation.

$$\pi_t = 1.084 + 1.250\pi_{t-1} - 0.346\pi_{t-2} + 0.120\pi_{t-3}$$
$$\quad (5.67) \quad (17.16) \qquad (-2.95) \qquad (+1.02)$$

$$\quad - 0.195\pi_{t-4} - 0.167R_{t-3} - 0.683BW_t + 0.797OIL_t$$
$$\quad (-2.78) \qquad (-2.55) \qquad (-4.14) \qquad (2.78)$$

$$R^2 = 0.93 \qquad\qquad \text{sample: } 1949.1-1991.4$$

The partisan dummy R is lagged three quarters to capture the delays between changes in policies and changes in the inflation rate. Macroeconomic

---

[19]The lag structure was chosen on the basis of Lagrange multiplier tests. The Durbin–Watson statistic is not reported, because it is not appropriate for this type of specification.

[20]Our results are quite robust. They remain unchanged if a variable capturing the effect of oil price changes is added, or if other measures of real economic activity are used; for instance, unemployment exhibits analogous patterns consistent with the theory; see Alesina (1988b).

analysis suggests that the effect of changes in aggregate demand policy have first an effect on output, then after a few quarters on inflation (see Romer and Romer (1989) and the references cited therein). For this reason it is appropriate to have a longer lag on the political dummy in the inflation regression than in the growth regression.[21] All the coefficients on both the partisan dummy and the BW and OIL variables have the expected sign and are significant at the 5 percent confidence level or better.[22] In particular, the negative coefficient on the variable R implies that inflation has been lower with Republican administrations than with Democratic administrations.

7.7 DISCUSSION

The rational partisan theory incorporates partisan politics in a model of the economy consistent with contemporary macroeconomic theory, a model characterized by rational behavior and by frictions in the wage–price adjustment mechanism. We have argued that the rational partisan theory captures the evidence of the U.S. electoral macroeconomic cycle much better than both of its major alternatives, Hibbs's partisan theory and Nordhaus's political business cycle. More general results on elections and the economic cycle are presented in chapter 9.

Before we proceed, however, we should tackle several comments, most cogently and recently raised by Hibbs (1992), concerning the macroeconomic model used in this chapter.

The first issue is why optimizing agents would lock themselves into nominal wage contracts of one or two years' duration. Such criticism can be (and has been) raised against this entire "neo-Keynesian" research strategy, which assumes wage–price rigidities. It has found several rebuttals in the macroeconomic literature; see, for instance, Mankiw and Romer (1991). Two types of answers to this criticism can be given. The first one has to do with the complexity of writing state-contingent wage contracts. In our model, the only shock on which the contracts should be made contingent is the election result: nominal wages should be "high" if party D wins, "low" if party R wins. Even a simple indexation clause would work; in fact, actual, rather than expected, inflation is automatically added to indexed wages.

In reality, one rarely observes very complicated wage contracts. Even

---

[21]In any case, the same inflation regression was run using the dummy variable R lagged one period, as in the growth regression. The sign of the coefficient of this dummy variable is unchanged, although its statistical significance is reduced.

[22]Alesina (1988b) finds analogous results by looking at the rate of growth of M1. This finding is in accordance with Hibbs (1987), who shows that monetary policy has been looser with Democratic presidents than with Republican presidents.

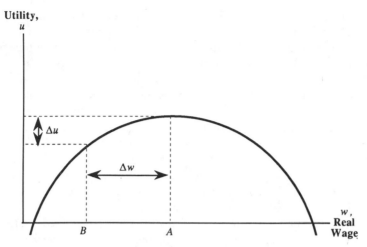

Figure 7.3. Effect on union members' utility of a small change from the optimal real wage (*A*) to a lower wage (*B*). The utility change is small relative to the wage change.

full indexation is not optimal in a world with several "demand" and "supply" shocks. Gray (1978) shows that optimal indexation schemes should imply salary increases when certain types of shocks occur, but not others.[23] If the nature of the economic shocks cannot be identified with certainty, full indexation may be worse than no indexation, and it is certainly worse than partial indexation. Milesi-Ferretti (1991) extends the study of optimal indexation schemes to the case of electoral uncertainty, modelled along the lines of the present chapter. He shows that in the presence of both monetary and real disturbances and of electoral uncertainty, *partial* rather than full indexation is optimal. Our results apply also to a model with partial indexation, one in which a certain *fraction* of actual inflation is automatically added to wage contracts.

In summary, the complexity of real-world inflation shocks makes it very difficult to write wage contracts that correctly adjust for what they should and do *not* adjust for what they should *not*.

Another response, originally suggested by Mankiw (1985) in a different context, has to do with the effects in an imperfectly competitive market of "small" costs of changing prices, or in our context, nominal wages. Suppose that a monopolistic union sets the real wage, given union members' preferences, market conditions, union "power", and so forth. We can think of a union having an objective function that reaches a maximum at the real

[23]Specifically, Gray (1978) shows that the optimal degree of indexation is between zero and 1 and increases with the variance of "demand" shocks relative to the variance of "supply" shocks.

wage chosen, as in figure 7.3. Suppose that because of an unexpected inflation shock the real wage falls from A to B in figure 7.3. Because of the concavity of the objective function, the loss in utility (Δu) for union members is relatively small, in technical terms "second order", relative to the size of the fall in real wages (Δw). Thus even a small cost of recontracting the wage to account for a shock would be enough to not make it worthwhile for the union to change the wage. Such small costs could be the time and effort spent in organizing meetings and bargaining with the employers. Nevertheless, even though the effect on union members' utility of the inflation shock may be small, the aggregate effects on employment may be large. For example, a 3 percent unexpected inflation may imply a loss for the employed workers with fixed wages that is small, relative to the aggregate employment effects of the same inflation shock.

A second, related criticism is that contracts should be signed *after*, rather than before elections, thus eliminating the electoral uncertainty. This criticism takes the model too literally. The assumption that all the contracts are signed just an instant before the election is an obvious simplification to facilitate exposition. If wage contracts were signed all at the same time, then it would be relatively easy to coordinate the timing of contracts so that they are all signed after the election. In reality, contract terms are staggered and overlapping, as in Taylor (1979). Different industries or firms may have different cycles, and it might be relatively costly to coordinate all of these different cycles. With staggered contracts, at least a fraction of them will "go over" the election date. Thus the basic message of our model survives in a more realistic staggered contract world.

A third criticism is that since several presidential elections were not uncertain, given the pre-electoral opinion polls, no important real effects on the economy should be observed after such elections. First, as the 1948 election proves, polls can be wrong; even "sure bets" may lose. Second, the relevant uncertainty is not the one remaining in the early morning of election day, but the uncertainty present at the time when the relevant price and wage decisions were taken. For instance, with, say, staggered contracts with an average length of two years, the relevant electoral uncertainty has to be evaluated roughly six months to a year before the election date. At that time, very few, if any, elections have no uncertainty left, including the 1980 one used by Hibbs (1992) as an example of this critical remark. Given these considerations, and despite the efforts by Chappell and Keech (1988), an empirical testing of the relationship between electoral uncertainty and policy effects remains a difficult though worthwhile enterprise.[24]

[24]Cohen (1993) has used poll data to construct an index of pre-electoral uncertainty. He tested the hypothesis that this uncertainty about elections affects expected inflation as measured by the term structure of interest rates. He finds that financial markets do expect Democratic administrations to be more inflationary than Republican ones.

More generally, a different argument that can be used in support of the neo-Keynesian modelling strategy embodied in the rational partisan theory is its empirical success, as exemplified in the preceding section. As a matter of fact, such sticky-price models implying short-run non-neutralities are criticized on both sides: by the rational expectation purists, who do not believe in such price rigidities, and by hard-core Keynesians, who believe in traditional, exploitable Phillips curves, such as those employed in Hibbs's work. But the empirical implications of a "rational-expectation–flexible-price" model with complete neutrality of policy *and* those of an exploitable Phillips curve in the medium-long run are both inconsistent with the empirical evidence. The middle-ground model of rational expectations and price-wage stickiness employed in this chapter, which combines elements of both schools of thought, does a better job of capturing critical features of the macroeconomic data.

Finally, it is worth emphasizing that partisan and opportunistic political business cycle models are not necessarily incompatible; a more elaborate model could encompass both motivations in a unified framework. As early as 1978, Frey and Schneider (1978) suggested that partisan politicians become opportunistic when the election time approaches and they are in danger of losing, whereas they go for their partisan goals when they are electorally confident. This insightful idea was, however, not explicitly derived in a rational choice framework.[25]

An additional interesting point is that the opportunistic behavior of different partisan politicians might be different. A "run toward the middle" might be the most effective opportunistic policy for a partisan politician. For example, a high-inflation Democratic administration (such as President Carter's) would find it not electorally rewarding to expand the economy even more, creating even more inflation before an election. If it wants to appeal to the middle-of-the-road voters, it may need to turn to a more anti-inflationary policy. A low-inflation administration (say the first Reagan one) faces the opposite problem. Thus, a run toward the middle may imply different pre-electoral macroeconomic policies for different administrations.[26]

The incorporation of both partisan and opportunistic incentives in a fully specified rational choice model of the political business cycle is an important topic of research. The next chapter moves a step in this direction.

[25]The empirical results of Frey and Schneider (1978) were criticized by Alt and Chrystal (1983).

[26]See Hibbs (1987), Alesina (1989), and Alesina, Cohen, and Roubini (1992, 1993) for discussion of the empirical evidence on this point.

8

The president, Congress, and the economy

8.1 INTRODUCTION

The previous chapter did not address three important questions about the American political economy. How do economic conditions affect voting behavior? Does the electorate care about administrative competence in addition to ideology? How does economic policy depend upon the interaction between the administration and Congress?

We address these issues by enriching the model of the economy developed in the previous chapter. First, we allow different administrations to exhibit different levels of competence in handling the economy. Competence-based voting provides a basis for explaining, in a rational choice perspective, the observation that voting in presidential elections is influenced by the state of the economy just prior to the elections. Second, as in the first part of this book, we allow Congress to have a moderating influence on economic policy. Thus, a Republican president's macroeconomic policies are less extreme if Congress is controlled by the Democratic party.[1] We apply the voting model developed in chapter 4 to this specific macroeconomic policy question. The general model of the American political economy which we build in this chapter will be tested with data for the period 1915–1988 in chapter 9.[2]

Let us begin by outlining our rational choice model of voting based on the state of the economy, which is the novel element introduced in this chapter. We posit that administrations differ in competence as well as in policies; more competent administrations achieve higher rates of growth,

---

[1]Several essays in Alesina and Carliner (1991) argue that the so-called "Reagan revolution" lasted only two years. Beginning in 1983 the reinforced Democratic contingent in both the House and the Senate managed to swing the barometer of American politics back toward the middle of the road.

[2]Sections 8.1–8.3 are largely based on Alesina, Londregan, and Rosenthal (1993).

without increasing inflation. In the previous chapter, since competence played no role, growth was determined solely by inflation policies. But once competence comes into play, voters will face a trade-off between their partisan preferences and efficiency. If one party is likely to be far more competent than its opponent, it may attract voters whose preferences would usually lead them to support the other party. Since the electorate prefers more to less competent administrations, both partisan preferences *and* efficiency arguments affect voters' decisions. However, competence is not directly observable; the voters detect only its impact on the economy: the voters observe growth and inflation, not competence. Since these economic variables can be affected by a variety of exogenous shocks, such as oil price changes, wars, technological innovations, etc., the voters cannot distinguish with absolute certainty the effects of luck from administrative competence.

How would rational voters proceed when competence and luck cannot be easily distinguished? This question has been addressed by Persson and Tabellini (1990), who adapted a model developed by Rogoff and Sibert (1988). We substantially modify Persson and Tabellini's model and integrate it in our framework. We argue in this chapter (and test in the next one) that rational voters observe the state of the economy and use optimally all the available information to infer administrative competence: high growth is a good signal of competence for the incumbent administration. Moreover, competence does not vanish immediately; an incumbent who is competent today is also expected to be competent tomorrow. Because growth signals competence that is likely to persist in the future, voters have an incentive to be "rationally retrospective". They are *retrospective* because the state of the economy before an election influences their vote: they favor the incumbent if growth is high. They are *rationally* retrospective because they efficiently use all the available information to disentangle the effects of administrative competence from the effects of luck. This assumption of rationality (and auxiliary assumptions) implies testable restrictions on "how" and "how much" rational voters should care about the economy when voting.

When, in chapter 9, we conduct empirical tests of this model, we ask two questions concerning retrospective voting. First, is there evidence that variations in the competence of different administrations are an important determinant of economic growth in the United States? Second, is there evidence that the electoral response of voters to the state of the economy is more complex than the simple response that would be implied by naïve retrospection?

In addition to these tests related to rational retrospective voting, the empirical analysis will demonstrate that the model developed in this chapter is consistent with five important regularities found in the literature on elections and the economy in the United States:

189

(i)   Presidential elections are strongly influenced by the business cycle. The vote share of the incumbent president's party's presidential candidate increases with the rate of GNP growth in the election year; other economic variables such as unemployment or inflation are less significant in explaining presidential results.

(ii) Congressional elections are less sensitive to economic conditions than are presidential elections.

(iii) The party holding the White House loses plurality in midterm congressional elections. This is the midterm cycle.

(iv) Since World War II, in the first half of Republican administrations, economic growth generally decelerates, reaching its minimum during the second year of each term, while the economy grows more rapidly during the first half of Democratic administrations. In the last two years of each term, one cannot detect significant differences between growth rates for Democratic and Republican administrations.

(v)   The rate of GNP growth in the election year is not systematically higher than average.

Earlier research had studied those five regularities in isolation, one or two at a time. For instance, Kramer (1971) and Fair (1978, 1982, 1988) focus upon (i). Kramer (1971) and Erikson (1989, 1990) study (ii). Erikson (1988) and Alesina and Rosenthal (1989) study (iii). Alesina and Sachs (1988), Chappell and Keech (1988), Alesina (1988b), and Beck (1992) highlight (iv). McCallum (1978), Golden and Poterba (1980), Hibbs (1987), Alesina (1988b), and Beck (1992) document (v).[3] The model of this chapter incorporates all five observations in a unified, "general equilibrium" framework.

Before we analyze the model, it is useful to highlight an example of how it works. Suppose that a Democratic president is elected, and the Republican delegation is relatively weak in Congress. As shown in chapter 7, the positive inflation shock increases growth above its natural rate. At midterm, as shown in chapter 4, the Democratic party loses votes in the congressional elections: the voters want a more moderate macroeconomic policy. In the second half of the term, the voters look at the state of the economy to evaluate the competence of the incumbent administration. Suppose that growth is relatively low. Then, the voters infer that the Democratic incumbent is not particularly competent and turn to the Republican challenger. Perhaps the incumbent is also unlucky; unexpected oil shocks have negative effects on the economy. Aware of these adverse shocks, but unable to perfectly distinguish incompetence from bad luck, the voters heavily penalize the incumbent. As a result, the Republican challenger wins

---

[3]That is, these authors reject the political business cycle model by Nordhaus (1975).

the presidential race. Following the election, inflation is reduced by contractionary macroeconomic policies, which cause a recession. At the following midterm elections, the Democratic party gains, since the voters want to moderate the Republican administration.

This "hypothetical" example may be taken as a realistic characterization of the events of 1976–1984 during the Carter and first Reagan administrations.

The example also highlights a non-obvious implication of our model. The first half of a Democratic administration is characterized by high growth; a standard "retrospective voting" model such as the one developed by Kramer (1971) would imply that the Democratic party does *well* in midterm elections. Our model, instead, predicts that this party will *lose* plurality in midterm because of the "moderation" effect: this non-obvious implication will be supported by the empirical evidence. More generally, the combination of the "rational partisan cycle" and the balancing Congress implies correlations between economic conditions and voting in congressional elections that are consistent with observation (ii) above.

This chapter is organized as follows. Section 8.2 introduces our notion of competence, and discusses rational retrospective voting in presidential elections. Section 8.3 analyzes the role of Congress, along the lines of the first part of this volume, and discusses its implications, which will be tested in chapter 9. Section 8.4 addresses some general issues concerning the relationship between information, rationality, and voter memory. The last section concludes.

8.2 A MODEL OF COMPETENCE[4]

The model of GNP growth introduced in chapter 7 is extended by adding a role for competence and one for exogenous shocks.[5] The structure of wage setting behavior is as in chapter 7; the growth equation is now as follows:

$$y_t = \gamma(\pi_t - \pi_t^e) + \bar{y} + \varepsilon_t \qquad (8.1)$$

The shock ε_t consists of two components which cannot be observed separately by the electorate. One component is competence: more competent

---

[4]A model of administrative competency was originally introduced by Rogoff and Sibert (1988) and Rogoff (1990). These papers studied a budget problem in which competence is defined as a low level of waste in tax collection. Cukierman and Meltzer (1986) in related work define administrative competence as the ability to make accurate forecasts of exogenous shocks, in order to promptly react to them. Persson and Tabellini (1990) adapt Rogoff and Sibert's model of competence to an inflation–unemployment problem; the following section substantially modifies their formalization.

[5]In fact, exogenous shocks were included in the regression model of section 7.6 even though, to facilitate the presentation, they had been excluded from the theoretical discussion.

administrations achieve higher growth. A second element reflects various exogenous shocks which affect the rate of growth independently of government's policy and competence. Thus, we can decompose ε_t as follows:

$$\varepsilon_t = \eta_t + \xi_t \qquad (8.2)$$

The term ξ_t represents economic shocks beyond government control, such as oil shocks and technological innovations. The term η_t captures the idea of government competence, that is the government's ability to increase the rate of growth without inflationary surprises. In fact, even if $\pi_t = \pi_t^e$, the higher is η_t the higher is growth, for given ξ_t. We can think of this competence as the government's ability to avoid large scale inefficiencies, to promote productivity growth, to avoid waste in the budget process so that lower distortionary taxes are needed to finance a given amount of government spending, etc.[6] Both η_t and ξ_t have zero mean and fixed variances, respectively σ_η^2 and σ_ξ^2.

Competence does not come and go; on the contrary, it is persistent. If a certain administration is competent today, it is expected to remain as such for some time in the future. Indeed, we model competence as inherent to a party's management team rather than the persona of specific presidents. This choice reflects the observation that important figures, such as Robert Kennedy and James Baker, have served under two successive presidents of the same party. Moreover, beginning in 1932 and interrupted only by 1952, either the incumbent president or vice-president has run in each election. To capture competence as inherent to the party, we assume that if the same administration is in office in two periods (either because there are no presidential elections or because the incumbent *party* is re-elected in presidential elections) the following relationship holds:

$$\eta_t = \mu_t + \rho \mu_{t-1} \qquad (8.3)$$

where $0 < \rho \leqslant 1$.

Equation (8.3) is a so-called Moving Average process of the first order (MA(1)). This specification implies that competence at time t, η_t contains both a component, μ_t, realized at time t and a fraction of the realization of the preceding period, μ_{t-1}. The fraction, ρ, could be the entire thing; that is, ρ could be 1. Without loss of generality we normalize at zero the *ex-ante* expected value of μ_t in every period. The variance of μ_t is fixed at σ_μ^2. This

---

[6]There might also be a systematic difference in competence between the two parties. Thus, the natural rate of growth $\bar{y}$ in equation (8.11) might be replaced by two distinct rates $\bar{y}^D$ and $\bar{y}^R$. Petrocik (1990) presents evidence that voters perceive the Republican party as having higher competence than the Democrats with regard to economic policies. Any systematic difference, however, would only induce a shift in the cutpoint for presidential elections. This generalization is conceptually easy but adds notation and algebra. Therefore we abstract from it.

MA(1) specification is adopted for reasons of tractability that will become apparent in the succeeding paragraphs. However, we point out that the econometric study of the economy by Nelson and Plosser (1982) suggests that the annual growth series follow a low order ARMA (auto regressive moving average) process and that MA(1) is about as good as any more complex specification of the growth rate for the United States.

Nobody has information concerning the competence of a challenger, since the competence process is MA(1) and an administration lasts two periods. Thus, any information about a challenging party's performance the last time it was in power is irrelevant since the challenging party would have been out of power for at least two periods before the current election. In other words, the best forecast of the competence of the challenger is zero, the expected value of μ_t. Once again, this assumption is just a normalization. The level of the challenger's competence could be fixed at any exogenously given value different from zero without any change in the nature of our results.

Note that we incorporate variations in the competence of the presidency but not of Congress. Congress is a body whose composition changes slowly. Its decisions reflect 535 members whose competence levels are very likely to be uncorrelated. Consequently, as there is likely to be little variation between the competence of successive Congresses, we can safely exclude congressional competence from the model.

The role for retrospective voting in this model already appears from equations (8.1) to (8.3). Suppose that presidential elections are held at the end of period t. Recall that in the second period of any administration, *expected* growth is always equal to the natural rate $\bar{y}$ since there is no unexpected inflation or deflation. The voters observe *actual* growth in period t, y_t. This observation allows them to compute (using (8.1)) the total shock to the economy ε_t,

$$\varepsilon_t = \eta_t + \xi_t = y_t - \bar{y} \tag{8.4}$$

Suppose growth is high, namely y_t is greater than $\bar{y}$, so that $\eta_t + \xi_t > 0$. The voters cannot observe the two components, η_t and ξ_t, separately. Thus, they do not know whether the high growth is achieved because of high competency (η_t) or "luck" (ξ_t). It is reasonable to infer that if growth is high, then there is a good chance that η_t is high, namely, the administration is competent. In other words, if growth is high, the voters learn something about whether the incumbent merits re-election. Specifically, voters gain information about how competent the incumbent will be in the next period. In fact, the incumbent's competence in the next period is given by:

$$\eta_{t+1} = \mu_{t+1} + \rho \mu_t \tag{8.5}$$

Since μ_t is part of η_t (see equation (8.3)), if η_t is high, then η_{t+1} is expected to be high. More specifically, the crucial question is: at the end of period t, what is the best estimate of η_{t+1}, knowing y_t? The expected value of η_{t+1} at time t is:

$$E(\eta_{t+1}) = E(\mu_{t+1}) + \rho E(\mu_t|y_t) = \rho E(\mu_t|y_t) \tag{8.6}$$

Recall, in fact, that $E(\mu_{t+1}) = 0$. If voters knew μ_t at time t, their best forecast of future competency, η_t, would simply be $\rho\mu_t$. The voters' lack of knowledge about μ_t means, however, that they need to base their forecast on y_t.

A critical assumption in the model is that the voters do learn the competency shock, but with a one-period delay, namely in period t the value of μ_{t-1} becomes known. This implies that they base their forecasts not just on y_t but, as rational voters using all available information, on μ_{t-1} as well. That is, they can compute:

$$\mu_t + \varepsilon_t = y_t - \bar{y} - \rho\mu_{t-1} \tag{8.7}$$

The voters incorporate this knowledge in their optimal forecast for η_{t+1}. This forecast, rather than $\rho\mu_t$, is given by:[7]

$$E(\eta_{t+1}) = \rho \frac{\sigma_\mu^2}{\sigma_\mu^2 + \sigma_\xi^2} (y_t - \bar{y} - \rho\mu_{t-1}) \tag{8.8}$$

where the terms σ_μ^2 and σ_ξ^2 are the noise levels, or variances, of the competency shocks and exogenous shocks, respectively. The electorate is assumed to know (or observe) every component of the right-hand side of equation (8.8), which shows that the higher is y_t the higher is $E(\eta_{t+1})$. It follows that if y_t is high, the voters assign some probability that this outcome is the result of high competence and lean in favor of the incumbent: *they are retrospective, since good pre-electoral economic conditions increase the likelihood of an incumbent victory.*

The voters, however, are "rationally" restrospective. They use their knowledge of the model described in equations (8.1) to (8.3) and all their available information to compute their optimal forecast of the incumbent competence, namely η_{t+1}; technically, this implies solving a "signal extraction problem". One interesting implication of this optimal forecast of competence is that it depends in a very intuitive way on the relative variability between the competency component, μ, and the exogenous shock component of growth, ξ. If μ has a high variance (σ_μ^2) relative to that of ξ, (σ_ξ^2), the voters are more prone to believe that high growth results from high competence, which varies much more than the other possible shocks. Conversely, if the economy is likely to be hit by large exogenous shocks, namely, the variance of ξ is high, then the voters discount high values of y_t as the likely result of good shocks, and *not* of government competence.

[7]The forecast is derived more fully in Alesina, Londregan, and Rosenthal (1993).

It may appear that this model of rational retrospective voting makes some fairly heavy requirements on the voter's knowledge of variances and ability to compute conditional probabilities in order to arrive at the forecast represented by (8.7). However, this construction has to be interpreted *cum granum salis*. The important point that this formalization captures is that intelligent, rational voters will try, as best they can, not to hold the government responsible for bad luck.

The difference between this kind of rational retrospective voting and naïve retrospection should now be apparent. Naïve voters do *not* try to disentangle luck from competence. They simply favor the incumbent when growth is high without paying any attention to the variance of different shocks. In other words, a naïve retrospective voter would punish the incumbent for a pre-electoral recession even if it is quite clear that such a bad economic outcome is the result of, say, an oil shock. A rational retrospective voter would not. The restrictions imposed on retrospective voting by the assumption of rationality, which implies "optimal" forecasting, will be tested in the next chapter. Before doing so, however, we introduce Congress in this model of the economy.

8.3 THE PRESIDENT, CONGRESS, AND THE ECONOMY

The impact of Congress on policy formation is modeled as in chapters 3 and 4: the legislature moderates the president. The policy variable is inflation. Thus, with a D president the inflation rate is given by:

$$\pi^D = \alpha\pi^{D*} + (1 - \alpha)[V_R\pi^{R*} + (1 - V_R)\pi^{D*}] \qquad (8.9)$$

$0 < \alpha < 1$. With an R president the inflation rate is:

$$\pi^R = \alpha\pi^{R*} + (1 - \alpha)[V_R\pi^{R*} + (1 - V_R)\pi^{D*}] \qquad (8.10)$$

As before, V_R is the share of the vote received by party R in the legislature, and π^{D*} and π^{R*} are the policies derived in chapter 7: these are the policies which would be followed by the two presidents if unconstrained by Congress. Equations (8.9) and (8.10) are the analogs of equations (3.1) and (3.2) of chapter 3. Namely, they imply that the policy outcome, π^D or π^R, is the linear conbination of the policy which would be pursued by an all-powerful president (π^{D*} or π^{R*}) and the policy ($V_R\pi^{R*} + (1 - V_R)\pi^{D*}$) preferred by Congress. The parameter which captures the weight of the administration in policy formation is α, as in previous chapters.

The assumptions concerning the distribution of voters' preferences remain unchanged from chapter 4. Specifically, the bliss points of the voters, $\bar{\pi}^i$, are distributed on the interval $[a, 1 + a]$ where a is a random variable which is also distributed uniformly with mean zero and minimum and maximum values equal to $-w$ and $+w$, respectively. In this chapter, we assume that w has a value that leads to an equilibrium where the presidential outcome is uncertain, as discussed in chapter 4. For expositional purposes, we adopt the simplifying assumption that the second parameter identifying the voters' preferences, b^i, is the same for every voter. Thus, the utility function for voter i in period t is given by:

$$u_t^i = -\tfrac{1}{2}(\pi_t - \bar{\pi}^i)^2 + by_t \qquad (8.11)$$

By a development directly parallel to that of equation (7.12), the bliss point of voter i is given by:

$$\pi^{i*} = \bar{\pi}^i + \frac{b\gamma}{2} \qquad (8.12)$$

Alesina, Londregan, and Rosenthal (1993) discuss the more general case in which the parameter b is not the same for all voters. They give the conditions under which our results generalize. In particular, our results hold both when b^i *and* $\bar{\pi}^i$ are statistically independent and when b^i is a strictly increasing function of $\bar{\pi}^i$. This second case is quite realistic: it implies that the left-leaning voters have both a high $\bar{\pi}^i$ and a high b^i, i.e. they are more tolerant of inflation and care relatively more about growth than about inflation. The opposite holds for right-wing voters.

The electoral equilibrium in this model is identical to the one developed in chapter 4, with inflation policy playing the role of the ideological dimension. There is one important caveat. In chapter 4, the probability of electing the Republican president, $P(\cdot)$, was a function only of the bliss points of the two parties relative to the uncertain bliss point of the median voter. In this chapter, voting is determined not only by these ideological bliss points but also by the competence effect which implies rational retrospection.

We begin by studying the midterm elections, which, as in chapter 4, are characterized by two cutpoints, one for the case of a Republican president in office, $\tilde{\pi}^R$, and one for the case of a Democratic president, $\tilde{\pi}^D$. Because competence pertains only to the president and not to Congress, the cutpoints for congressional elections reflect only inflation preferences. Moreover, the generalized pivotal-voter theorem of chapter 4 implies, for this specific policy problem, that the cutpoints equal the expected inflation policy outcome:

$$\tilde{\pi}^R = E(\pi^R) = \frac{\pi^{R*} + K}{1 + K} \qquad (8.13)$$

$$\tilde{\pi}^D = E(\pi^D) = \frac{\pi^{D*}}{1 + K} \qquad (8.14)$$

Needless to say, we have $\tilde{\pi}^D > \tilde{\pi}^R$. As in chapter 7, since the Democrats represent high inflation policies, they are the party at the "right" end of the policy continuum. To maintain symmetry with chapter 4, remember that we now *define* P as the probability of a Democratic victory.

Consider now the first-period elections. As in chapter 4, we need to find cutpoints for both elections, with the presidential cutpoint denoted $\hat{\pi}$ and the legislative cutpoint denoted $\tilde{\pi}$. Also as in chapter 4, the probability of a democratic presidential victory is a simple function, $P(\hat{\pi})$, of the presidential cutpoint.

The legislative cutpoint satisfies the following condition:

$$\tilde{\pi} = P\tilde{\pi}^D + (1 - P)\tilde{\pi}^R \qquad (8.15)$$

Since, by equation (8.15), $\tilde{\pi}$ is in between $\tilde{\pi}^R$ and $\tilde{\pi}^D$, we obtain the midterm cycle. For example, when the Republicans win the Presidency, voters with ideal points in between $\tilde{\pi}^R$ and $\tilde{\pi}$ vote R in the first-period legislative elections, and then switch to D in midterm elections. Condition (8.15) highlights that the lower is P, i.e., the less expected is the Democratic presidential victory, the larger the size of the midterm effect. The intuition and the formalization of this effect are completely identical to those in chapter 4.

The difference between this chapter and chapter 4 lies in the determination of the cutpoint for the presidential election. In casting their presidential votes with conditional sincerity, voters will be seeking to maximize their expected utilities conditional on the legislative cutpoints. Note that (8.11) implies:

Expected Utility = Expected Inflation Policy Utility + b × (Expected Growth)

The part of expected utility that results directly from inflation policy is directly analogous to the ideological model of chapter 4. Therefore, we focus attention on the growth term.

Expected growth influences the cutpoint in a very straightforward manner. Developments directly parallel to the appendix of chapter 4 show that:

$$\hat{\pi} = \frac{\frac{1}{2}\{(\pi^{D*} + \pi^{R*})((1 + K)^2 + \beta) + \beta K\} - K(1 + K)^2\tilde{\pi} - E(\eta_1)}{(1 + \beta - K^2)(1 + K)} \qquad (8.16)$$

where $K = (1 - \alpha)(\pi^{D*} - \pi^{R*})$ and $E(\eta_1)$ is given by (8.8) and represents expected competency in period 1 if D remains in control of the White House.

Except for the $E(\eta_1)$ term, (8.16) is directly analogous to (4.20). Let us motivate why competence enters (8.16) in such a simple fashion. Note that:

$$E(y_2^R) = E(y_2^D) = \bar{y} \qquad (8.17)$$

That is, *at the time when presidential elections are held*, the voters expected the same level of growth in the second half of both types of administrations.

Specifically, in the second halves of either Republican or Democratic administrations, growth is expected to be at its natural level $\bar{y}$. These results follow from two observations. First, as shown in chapter 7, in the second half of any administration there cannot be any inflation surprise due to uncertainty about presidential election results. Second, *before* the first-period elections, the voters expect the same level of competence for the second halves of the two administrations, regardless of which of the two is the incumbent. This observation follows from the model of competence of section 8.2. If the incumbent is perceived as very competent, the voters know that for the *next period*, i.e., the first period of a new term of office, the incumbent's competence will remain high. However, *because competence persists for only one period*, current economic conditions provide no information about competence in the second period (last two years) of the new term of office. Therefore, rationally retrospective voters can only predict that the incumbent's competence will return to its average value in the second period. Since, by assumption, the competence of the challenger, on whom there is no information, is at its mean value in *both* periods, there is no difference in the expected competence level and in expected growth for the second halves of the two administrations.[8]

In summary, when the voters go to the polls for the first-period elections, $E(y_2^D) = E(y_2^R) = \bar{y}$. Since expected second-period growth is equal for both parties, the second period has no influence on the determination of either the cutpoint $\hat{\pi}$ or, equivalently, P.

On the contrary, the first-period growth rates represented by y_1^D and y_1^R are not expected to be equal: this feature captures the critical difference between the model of this chapter and that of chapter 4. Suppose a Democratic president is the incumbent. Then we have:[9]

$$E(y_1) = \bar{y} + P(\hat{\pi})E(\eta_1) \qquad (8.18)$$

That is, before the election, growth is expected to be just average growth plus expected D competence weighted by the probability of a D victory. Although *actual* post-election growth is determined by the inflation surprise discussed in chapter 7, expected growth differs from the long-run average $\bar{y}$ only as a result of competence. Why? As P increases, it is more likely that one will obtain the higher growth rate associated with Democratic presidents. However, the magnitude of the D growth surprise falls as P increases. This is because expected inflation adjusts to the increase in P. Thus, any change in P is offset by a change in the magnitude of the surprises such that expected growth is constant, except for the effect of competence.

---

[8] The model can be extended to the case of competence lasting more than one period.
[9] See note 13 in chapter 7 for a technical discussion.

Moreover, the expected competence of the R challenger is zero. Any change in the cutpoint $\hat{\pi}$ therefore influences expected utility only via $E(\eta_1)$.

Even with the addition of expected competence, (8.16) discloses that the presidential cutpoint, $\hat{\pi}$, can be written as a linear function of $\tilde{\pi}$. Similarly, equation (8.15) gives the legislative cutpoint as a linear function of the presidential cutpoint. Once again echoing chapter 4, these two equations have a unique solution for $\hat{\pi}$ and $\tilde{\pi}$.[10]

The implications of this model of competence and ideology should now be clear. Presidential elections depend upon both the distribution of voters' preferences characterized by b and $\bar{\pi}^i$, and on the perceived ability of the incumbent to sustain growth. Left-wing voters, namely those with high $\bar{\pi}^i$, vote D in presidential elections.[11] They need a substantial pre-electoral recession to be convinced that the incumbent Democratic president is so incompetent that they should turn to the Republican challenger. Middle-of-the-road voters, whose preferences are somewhere in between those of the two parties, are more sensitive to pre-electoral economic conditions, since they vote mostly on the basis of competence. In fact, their preferred policy is close to being equidistant to the two party policies. These voters are, therefore, those who fluctuate more substantially depending upon the state of the economy before elections. (The reader may recognize in this description the 1980 "Reagan Democrats".) Right-wing voters, those with low $\bar{\pi}^i$, instead favor the Republican challenger even if the economy does relatively well before the election. Analogous, symmetric arguments hold for the case of a Republican incumbent. Finally, as in chapter 4, the legislative vote balances the president, and divided government may follow the on-year or midterm elections as a moderating device.

This model generates an interesting connection between competence and legislative moderation. Suppose a Republican incumbent president is perceived as very competent because the economy is doing well in the election year; then $1 - P$, the probability of reappointing the incumbent Republican, is high. An increase in the likelihood of a Republican presidential victory increases the expected congressional vote for the Democratic party. Thus, with a Republican president, Republican members of Congress may worry if the economy does too well before elections!

This result, which, in a sense, resembles a reverse coattail effect, depends crucially on the assumption that different administrations, but not Congress, exhibit different degress of competence. Note, however, that this effect does not imply that our model is inconsistent with the observation of, say, a

---

[10]As in chapter 4, we need to impose a condition on w to ensure that there is enough uncertainty in the preference shock to produce uncertainty in the presidential election.

[11]In the generalized model where voters vary in both $\bar{\pi}$ and b, "left" votes are characterized by high values of both $\bar{\pi}$ and b. See the appendix to Alesina, Londregan, and Rosenthal (1993).

landslide Republican presidential victory and a strong congressional result for the same party. A landslide Republican presidential victory can be the result of a particularly right-wing realization of voters' preferences. In other words, an *expected* landslide presidential victory of the incumbent Republican president (because growth is high in the election year) should be accompanied by a relatively strong result for the Democratic party in Congress. An *unexpected* landslide for the Republican incumbent should be accompanied by a relatively poor performance of the Democratic party in Congress. In the next chapter we will test this empirical implication.

Before we proceed it is useful to emphasize a comparison between our model and the traditional opportunistic political business cycle model of Nordhaus (1975), discussed in chapter 7. The political business cycle model makes two basic predictions: voters are retrospective, in the sense that they reward the incumbent if growth is high in the election year; politicians take advantage of this behavior by artificially increasing the rate of economic growth in election years.

The empirical evidence strongly confirms the presence of retrospective voting.[12] On the contrary, the evidence fails to support the second half of the story, that there is an artificially high rate of growth in election years.[13] Our model based on competence is consistent with this evidence, at first sight puzzling. On the one hand, this model predicts that high growth in election years increases the likelihood of reappointment for the incumbent. Because voters are incompletely informed, an incumbent suffers whether he misjudges the ball or inadvertently suffers misfortune. On the other, however, the incumbent *cannot systematically increase the rate of growth in the election year*. Given a certain level of competence, the incumbent cannot fool the voters by systematically increasing the rate of growth when necessary.[14] The competence model predicts that the rate of growth of the economy should *not* be higher than average in election years.

8.4 RATIONALITY, MEMORY, KNOWLEDGE, AND RETROSPECTION

The purpose of this section is to illustrate the difficulties inherent to any attempt at evaluating rationality in voting behavior. It is important to

[12]See, for instance, Kramer (1971) and Fair (1978, 1982, 1988).
[13]For data drawn from other OECD democracies see Paldam (1979), Lewis-Beck (1988), Alesina and Roubini (1992), and Alesina, Cohen, and Roubini (1992, 1993).
[14]This is contrasted with the model by Persson and Tabellini (1990, chapter 5). Using certain somewhat artificial assumptions concerning the distribution of information, they show that the incumbent can appear more competent than she actually is by pursuing expansionary policies before elections.

keep these difficulties in mind when evaluating the empirical results of chapter 9.

The model of rational and restrospective voting of section 8.2 made some specific assumptions about what the voters know and do not know: (a) voters know that the economy follows an MA(1) process that is linked to changes in administration; (b) they know the parameters of that model, namely, ρ, σ_μ^2, and σ_ξ^2; (c) they learn the election year growth rate in the election year; and (d) they learn the competence component of growth μ only with a one-period delay. These very specific assumptions underlie our analysis of voter behavior. Different assumptions concerning knowledge and memory, the flow and storage of information, will lead to different behavior of rational retrospective voters. In this section, we develop some alternatives to our model of rational retrospection.

Throughout this section, we maintain assumptions (a) and (b) above. That is, as is standard in rational expectations approaches, voters calculate on the basis of an underlying model of the economy. Different models lead to a different calculus. An advantage of the MA(1) approach is that it facilitates closed-form solutions that lead to testable predictions. We also maintain assumption (c), that voters know the election year growth rate, since this is standard in even naïve retrospective voting models. Our investigation focuses on modifying assumption (d), how voters learn about competence.

In imposing a one-period delay, we were trying to capture the idea that voters have difficulty in distinguishing between administrative and non-administrative contributions to growth. While growth is perceived instantaneously, it takes longer to grasp what causes growth. We now consider two polar alternatives to the one-period delay hypothesis.

The first alternative is that the competence component is also learned instantaneously. As indicated in section 8.2, if voters knew μ_t at time t their best forecast of future competency η_{t+1} would simply be $\rho\mu_t$. As with equation (8.7), voters would focus on a component of current growth, so increases in the current growth rate would continue to be correlated with voting for the incumbent, but the component would be different. That is, with current knowledge of competence, a lucky break would not increase the chances of reappointing the incumbent, since voters can perfectly disentangle competence from luck. This is in contrast with both the naïve model in which the voters do not even try to disentangle competence from luck, and from the one-period delay model in which the voters can separate the two only imperfectly. Needless to say, with current learning of competence, past observations of growth rates do not reveal any additional information to the voters, and voter memory is irrelevant.

The second alternative, opposite to no delay learning, is that competency is never learned. In this case, memory of past growth rates is an important component of the calculus of rational retrospective voting. With a one-period delay in learning, the voters need to know only current growth in order to make an intelligent forecast. When the delay is infinite since competence is never learned, the more past growth rates the voters remember, the better their forecast of future growth. In fact, current growth contains the current innovation to competence and lagged competence. Without knowledge of lagged competence, voters cannot distinguish among these two components of competence. But lagged competence is also part of the lagged growth rate, so if voters not only know current growth but can also remember previous growth, they can gain information about what part of the current growth rate is due to lagged competence.

We can see how memory is valuable, when competence cannot be learned directly, by looking at two forecasts of future competence. The first is when only the current growth rate is remembered:

$$E(\eta_{t+1}| \text{ knowledge of } y_t \text{ only}) = \rho \frac{\sigma_\mu^2}{(1 + \rho^2)\sigma_\mu^2 + \sigma_\xi^2}(y_t - \bar{y}) \quad (8.19)$$

When only the current growth rate is known, equation (8.19) implies that competence based retrospective voting is identical to naïve retrospective voting. The voters focus on the difference between current growth and average growth. Average growth, multiplied by ρ and the term with the variances, will be embedded in the constant of any empirical regression. The same multiplication of current growth will be embedded in the regression coefficient of current growth. Consequently, naïve voting cannot be distinguished from rational voting under limited information and limited memory.

Let us now look at the forecast for η_{t+1} when both y_t and y_{t-1} are observed and remembered by the voters. Some algebra establishes the following result:

$$E(\eta_{t+1}|y_t \quad \text{and} \quad y_{t-1}) = \rho \frac{\sigma_\mu^2}{(1 + \rho^4)\sigma_\mu^2 + (1 + \rho^2)\sigma_\xi^2}(y_t - \rho y_{t-1} - (1 - \rho)\bar{y})$$

$$(8.20)$$

When both the current and the immediately past period are remembered, both appear in the competency forecast when the competency innovations are not learned by the voters. Since ρ is the persistence parameter of the MA(1) process, it is intuitive that lagged growth is weighted less than current growth, by a factor equal to ρ, in equation (8.19). If voters remember even more past periods, they incorporate all of the past growth rates in their forecast up to the previous change in party control of the White House, but always weighing the remote past less heavily than the recent past. These forecasts resemble the distributed lag empirical specifications of Hibbs (1987).

In summary, this section has made clear that different assumptions about information and memory lead to different specifications of rational retrospective voting. In any competence based model, voting for the incumbent should be correlated with past growth rates. However, the nature of this correlation depends upon informational assumptions. Therefore, in testing a particular model, one tests the assumption of rationality *and* specific informational assumptions. In the next chapter, we address the empirical evidence on rational retrospection.

8.5 CONCLUSIONS

This chapter has studied an important problem of public policy in the context of our executive–legislative balancing framework. The result is a model of the American political economy in which both economic and electoral outcomes are endogenous. The only exogenous variables are the party preferences, the relative weight of the executive and legislature in policy formation, the variances of the competence and technological shocks, and the preferences of the electorate.

The polarized preferences of the two parties concerning inflation and growth combine with the uncertainty about the electorate's preferences to create electoral uncertainty. This uncertainty in turn creates a partisan business cycle in an economy with wage rigidities. The electorate's desire for moderation of the partisan inflation policies, their concern about administrative competence, and their opportunity to engage in institutional balancing determine the outcomes of both presidential and congressional elections.

Our model of the American political economy has several specific and testable empirical implications for both the economic cycle and national elections. The next chapter is entirely devoted to an empirical test of our model.

9

Economic growth and national elections in the United States: 1915–1988

9.1 INTRODUCTION[1]

The model of the American political economy described in chapter 8 has several empirical implications. These are tested in this chapter using United States data for the period 1915 to 1988. We examine the behavior of the annual growth rate of the gross national product and of vote shares in presidential elections and in elections for the House of Representatives.

Throughout this volume we have stressed the interdependence of politics and economics. A basic theme is that partisan politics introduces uncertainty in both the polity and the economy; both the voters and the economic agents need to hedge. Specifically, uncertainty in presidential elections leads economic agents to hedge by expecting an inflation rate equal to an average of the inflation policies that would be followed by the two parties. Similarly, voters adjust their on-year congressional votes so that there is not a decisive tilt towards either party. At midterm, the identity of the party of the president for the next two years is known; thus the voters can complete their balancing of the president.

In other words, expectations about future policies tie the political and economic systems together. Therefore we undertake a simultaneous estimation of four equations: one for GNP growth; one for the vote share in presidential elections; one for House vote shares in on-years; and another for House vote shares in midterms.

Our most general formulation of the GNP growth equation incorporates the two basic determinants of growth highlighted in the previous two chapters: the partisan macroeconomic policies of the two parties and the competence of different administrations. Similarly, the most general formulation of the presidential voting equation is linked to the growth equation via our notion of rational retrospective voting described in chapter 8. The

[1]Much of the material in this chapter is based on collaborative research with John Londregan. See Alesina, Londregan, and Rosenthal (1993). We thank the American Political Science Review for permission to reproduce material from that article.

fact that there are two equations for House elections reflects our incorporation of the theory of the midterm cycle and the desire to test for presidential coattails in on-years.

A single exogenous variable which is not explicitly considered in our theoretical model is entered in our regressions.[2] This variable is "military mobilization", defined as the change in the percentage of the population in the armed forces. Why just this one variable? Should we not include more "controls" for important behavioral influences that are outside the formal model? Doing so would create a problem in the econometric estimation of the model. With small samples, as one adds variables one typically quickly loses precision in the estimates of all parameters, including the parameters that relate to the formal model. In other words, adding potentially relevant variables comes at the cost of using up degrees of freedom in estimation. In studies of the aggregate political economy, degrees of freedom are indeed precious because presidential elections occur only once every four years. Even starting as far back as 1915, we have only 19 presidential elections (through 1988). Wars, however, are of evident importance, particularly for the economy, and it would not be reasonable to ignore their influence.

An additional important aspect of reality which is not directly addressed in our theoretical model (see, however, chapter 6) is incumbency advantage. In congressional elections, incumbency advantage (Fiorina (1989)) can arise through at least four mechanisms. First, at the constituency level, individual incumbents are advantaged because the seniority system in Congress generates a strong incentive to re-elect the same individual. Second, shocks to voter preferences may be correlated over time, rather than independent as in our theoretical model. If so, a party that is strong today is likely to remain strong tomorrow. Third, at the national level, a strong party attracts resources, such as campaign contributions, that help it to remain strong. Thus, corporate PACs who would prefer a Republican Congress find it useful to purchase access from incumbent Democrats.[3] Fourth, in the case of the presidency as well as Congress, the electorate has a less precise estimate of the challenger's position than of the incumbent's. For risk-averse voters, this informational asymmetry implies that, *ceteris paribus*, incumbents are advantaged (Bernhardt and Ingberman (1985)).

Even though incumbency advantage was assumed away, for simplicity, in our theoretical model, it clearly cannot be ignored in our empirical

[2]We do not need exogenous variables to identify each equation because of the recursive structure of the shocks. In presidential election years, shocks to the economy affect both the economy and the election outcomes, but shocks to voting behavior do not feed back into the economy immediately. The electoral surprise to the economy affects growth only in succeeding years.

[3]See Snyder (1990) and McCarty and Poole (1992).

analysis. In order to capture the effect of incumbency we have entered the House vote from the previous election (lagged vote) in all three voting equations.[4] We also test, in the presidential equation, for the existence of a bias in favor of presidential incumbents.[5]

The estimation provides strong support for our model on several grounds.

First, we confirm the empirical success of the rational partisan theory of chapter 7 as to its prediction of post-election effects on GNP growth. The theory survives both the extension of the sample back to 1915 (from the post–World War II sample used in chapter 7 and in the literature on this subject) and the explicit consideration of the effects of military mobilizations and demobilizations on growth. Second, in accordance with the model, we find that the only significant effects on the midterm House vote are the balancing vote against the president's party and the incumbency advantage. There is no effect of the economy at midterm. Third, in on-years we find evidence of moderating behavior in the form of split tickets with a bias in favor of the Republicans in presidential elections. Fourth, consistent with the prediction of the model, voting based on the state of the economy is important in presidential elections but not in House elections.

In summary, most of the basic implications of the model are consistent with the empirical evidence. A notable exception is that the economy does not appear to influence presidential elections via "rationally retrospective" voting on competence. In fact, we reject our specification of administrative competence and the associated rational retrospective voting behavior. In section 9.9, we discuss this rejection in detail and suggest several reasons why one should not shut the door on rational choice analysis of voting on the economy. Nonetheless, the assumption of voter rationality is put in question by our results in the sense that *the American electorate seems to place "too much" weight on the state of the economy in the election year when choosing a president.*

Another aspect of our theory which may not capture the complexity of the American political economy pertains to the magnitude of the effects of uncertainty in presidential elections. We predict that inflation surprises, thus growth fluctuations and midterm voting cycles, should occur only following presidential elections which were substantively uncertain, *ex ante*. If, instead, everyone expected a presidential landslide, which, in fact, materializes, the economy should not deviate from its natural rate of growth and one should not expect a midterm loss for the president's party. In

---

[4]See also Erikson (1990) for discussion of why lagged variables should be included. Note, however, that Alesina and Rosenthal (1989) present estimation of Senate as well as House elections in a direct test of our formal model of the midterm cycle. This chapter and that paper together show that results are robust to the inclusion of lags.

[5]Bias for presidential incumbents plays an important role in the model of Fair (1978, 1982, 1988).

reality, both growth fluctuations following presidential elections and the midterm cycle have been pervasive. They appear to have followed both presidential landslides and close presidential races.

The landslide problem does not appear to be critical with respect to the predictions of economic growth. If we think of the wage contracts being signed throughout the twelve months leading up to the election, uncertainty clearly is always an important factor. In some cases, the relevant economic plans must be made before it is even clear who will be the presidential nominees. In contrast, voters can pick their strategies on election day, when there is much less uncertainty about the outcome of presidential elections.

We do not attempt to measure uncertainty in our empirical work. There are difficulties in translating *ex post* vote margins into *ex ante* expectations. Reliable pre-electoral polls did not exist for much of our sample period. The photograph of a jubilant Harry Truman holding up a Chicago paper headlined "Dewey Wins" suggests, in any event, that polls may not entirely remove voter uncertainty. Furthermore, accommodating an uncertainty variable would place an additional tax on degrees of freedom. Nonetheless, *the American electorate seems to produce the midterm cycle too often to be fully consistent with our theoretical model.*

These anomalies in empirical results are expected as a normal interplay between theory and empirical testing in science. As Karl Popper (1959) puts it, a "good" model is one that can be rejected. Our model is easily rejectable since it is based on well-specified assumptions which lead to specific and stringent predictions on observable variables. While we can take comfort from the substantial amount of empirical success we obtained, the rejections point the way to two lines of investigation. First, why do voters seem to care so much about the state of the economy immediately before a presidential election? Second, what is the measurable effect of the degree of uncertainty of presidential elections?[6]

The chapter is organized as follows. Section 9.2 reviews various approaches used in the related literature and emphasizes the value of a simultaneous, multi-equation approach. Section 9.3 discusses our choice of sample period

[6]With respect to closeness, there is an interesting parallel to the theory of turnout. In reality one observes less voting when races are not close, in line with the qualitative predictions of the theory of turnout (Riker and Ordeshook, 1968), but the magnitude of the response is weak relative to theoretical expectations under the assumption of costly voting. If voting is costly, turnout is too high. To some extent the turnout data can be reconciled by assuming that voters have biased assessments of closeness. Voters who turn out because they believe, rightly or wrongly, they make a difference, would act consistently with their beliefs if they hedged in the on-year. Such biased assessments would thus be consistent with a pervasive midterm cycle. On closeness and voting, see Riker and Ordeshook (1968), Ferejohn and Fiorina (1974), Rosenthal and Sen (1973), Palfrey and Rosenthal (1985), and Hansen, Palfrey, and Rosenthal (1987), and many references cited in these papers.

and data. In sections 9.4 and 9.5 we develop our empirical specification and link it to the model of chapter 8. Section 9.4 focusses on the growth equation. Section 9.5 presents the voting equations and a means of testing for naïve retrospective voting. Section 9.6 presents the results for our preferred specification of the four equation model. Section 9.7 simulates the model in the absence of shocks and shows that it converges to a steady-state cycle where the Republicans usually hold the White House and government is usually divided. Section 9.8 compares our results with the previous literature and, in particular, with Fair's (1978, 1982, 1988) work on presidential elections. Section 9.9 discusses the issue of "rationality" in retrospective voting. The last section concludes.

9.2 MODELLING THE POLITICAL ECONOMY OF THE UNITED STATES

In contrast to our four equation model, previous empirical research has largely focussed on single equation models of each time series. For example, Hibbs (1987), Alesina (1988b), Alesina and Sachs (1988), Chappell and Keech (1988), and Beck (1992) have studied the growth rate. Related single equation work on the economy includes studies of unemployment by McCallum (1978), Hibbs (1987), and Alesina (1988b). Single equation studies of voting include the work of Fair (1978, 1982, 1988) and Erikson (1989) on presidential elections, and of Alesina and Rosenthal (1989) and Erikson (1990) on elections for the House of Representatives.

In part, these single equation approaches arose because the authors had more specific purposes. McCallum's goal was to show that politics, at least in the form envisaged in the electoralist political business cycle model of Nordhaus (see section 7.5), had no effect on the economy. Both Hibbs and Alesina sought to show, on the contrary, that partisan politics mattered.

With respect to voting, the single equation approaches reflect, in a sense, a reversal of course. In fact, in a seminal paper in empirical political economy, Kramer (1971) carried out a simultaneous, maximum-likelihood estimation of presidential and House elections. Kramer basically was testing for naïve retrospective voting. He assumed that the structure of the model was the same for both presidential and House elections. But after Lepper (1974) showed that presidential and House elections were structurally different,[7] single equation work became prevalent. Our theoretical model not only points to a structural difference but also allows us to combine the estimation in the spirit of Kramer's work.[8]

---

[7] In econometric jargon, the presidential and House elections didn't "pool".

[8] Independent of our work, Chappell and Suzuki (1990) have developed a simultaneous model of presidential and congressional elections. See below.

Tying the political and economic equations together has important benefits.

Consider the presidential vote equation. Since we are using annual GNP data and current GNP growth has an impact on the presidential vote, there is a need to correct for simultaneity bias. In addition, we can use information about the growth shocks from the growth equation to test whether voters react to economic performance in the form of traditional, naïve retrospective voting or, alternatively, differentiate among various components of economic growth.

Second, consider the on-year House vote equation. Here we are interested in the linkage between the House vote and the presidential vote. If the economy has an effect on the House vote, is it simply an effect that is transmitted by "coattails" through the economy's effect on the presidential vote? More generally, we want to test whether presidential coattails arise either through measurable influences on the presidential vote or, as in Kramer (1971), through unmeasurable influences, such as candidate personality, that are treated as "shocks". We need an econometric model that ties the equations together, in order to properly study both the economic and other coattails effects on House voting.

Third, the estimation will gain in efficiency (make better use of the data) if we account for the lagged effects in all equations.

Fourth, our integrated theoretical model imposes several non-obvious restrictions on the specification. For example, our model of rational retrospective voting in a rational expectations model of the macroeconomy (see chapter 8) implies that rational retrospective voters do not have to look back more than one year in evaluating the performance of the incumbent president. By making such stringent and specific assumptions on the theoretical structure of the economy we can derive tests of the rationality of voter behavior. The problem is, however, that these tests are *joint tests* of rationality *and* of all the other assumptions underlying the model. If these tests reject the theory, it is not clear which is the rejected assumption within the several which are jointly tested. This problem, which we clarify below, is common in the vast economic literature testing for "rationality", for instance in financial markets.

9.3 SAMPLE PERIOD AND DATA SOURCES

Our sample covers the period 1915 to 1988. Choosing a beginning date involves several trade-offs. A longer period confers the benefit of a larger sample size and more degrees of freedom. This consideration is particularly important in our model where presidential elections, which occur only once every four years, play a critical role. But the longer the period, the less likely it is that the structure that underlies the model will remain constant.

With respect to the political process, it is easy to point to important structural changes during our sample period. One is the "realignment" of the Great Depression (Sundquist (1983)). A second is the extension of the suffrage to women in 1920. Another is the period of the civil rights conflict from, roughly, the late 1930s to the mid 1960s, when Southern Democrats had positions very distinct from those of Northern Democrats. Still another is the great increase in the size of the federal government and government spending (Cameron (1978)) accompanied by a great rise in constituency service (Cain, Ferejohn, and Fiorina (1987)) that appears to have been translated into increased incumbency advantage (Fiorina (1989), King and Gelman (1991)).

The work of Poole and Rosenthal (1991a, 1993b) on congressional roll call voting (see also chapter 2) provides some justification for neglecting this problem of structural shifts. They claim that congressional roll call voting over our sample period can largely be accounted for by a one-dimensional model with some improvement from introducing a second dimension to handle the civil rights "perturbation" that lasted roughly from 1940 to 1970. For example, they claim that the Depression was not a dimensional realignment but, in line with the unidimensional perspective of this book, a "shock" that produced large Democratic majorities within pre-existing lines of policy conflict. Moreover, for our sample period, Poole and Rosenthal (1986) show that the mean liberal–conservative position in the Senate depends, fully in line with our specification in chapters 3 to 5, nearly entirely on the seat shares of the two parties. They view this enduring liberal–conservative dimension of conflict as one of economic redistribution, a theme closely related to our model of conflict over the rate of inflation and the trade-off between inflation and growth. In any event, we are forced to ignore these structural changes. In order to consider some of them we would indeed have had to split an already small sample.

On the economic side, there are indeed several arguments for beginning only after World War II, as is common in the related literature. One is that, in a formal sense, government assumed responsibility for growth only with the Full Employment Act of 1946. A second is that the accuracy of economic data improved after World War II. A third is that the two world wars were obviously major structural disruptions. Each of these arguments has a rebuttal. First, economic policy has been at the center of political debate at least since the end of the Civil War. On this point, see Friedman and Schwartz (1971), Poole and Rosenthal (1993b), and Frieden (1991). Second, recent historical research by Romer (1989) and Balke and Gordon (1989) has provided more reliable and similar estimates of the annual time series for real GNP. (We use the Balke and Gordon series.) Third, we can account for wars with the military mobilization variable. In addition, since the previous research on political and partisan business cycles have all used

Table 9.1. *Descriptive statistics*

Variable	Mean	Std. Deviation	N
Growth Rate of Real GNP	3.061	5.940	74
Nonelection Year Growth Rate (Year 1 and 3 of each term)	3.610	4.899	37
Midterm Year Growth Rate (Year 2 of each term)	1.527	7.960	18
Presidential Year Growth Rate (Year 4 of each term)	3.446	5.260	19
Presidential Vote for Incumbent's Party (two party share)	53.053	7.597	19
Midterm Year House Vote for Incumbent's Party (two party share)	49.220	4.783	18
Midterm Partisan Effect ($= +1$ if R in year 2, -1 if D)	0.000	1.000	18
Presidential Year House Vote for Incumbent's Party (two party share)	49.906	5.460	19
Party of President (D=0, R=1)	0.486	0.499	74
Lagged Midterm Year House Vote	53.320	4.423	18
Lagged Presidential Year House Vote	49.279	4.662	19
Military Mobilization (% Change Population in Armed Forces)	0.009	1.000	74

Sources: U.S. Bureau of the Census, *Historical Census of the United States, Colonial Times to 1970*; *Statistical Abstract of the United States 1990*, Erikson (1989,1990), Balke and Gordon (1989), and *Citibase*.

post–World War II data, it is important to check whether the results are robust to the sample period.

From both economic and political perspectives, there is much to be said for including the Great Depression. (Quite in character with the results of chapter 7, the Depression also began in the first half of a Republican administration!) By any model of retrospective voting, the Depression should have produced an immense Democratic victory. And given incumbency bias and the impetus to the economy from World War II, this advantage should have persisted for many years. Indeed (see table 9.1), the Democrats have occupied the White House for just about half our sample period. But the long period of Republican dominance before the Depression and again from 1972 onward suggests that there is a steady-state equilibrium where Republican presidents are moderated by Democratic strength in Congress. It is thus important to see if this steady state indeed falls out of the estimation, with the Democratic victories from 1932 onwards being recognized as responses to major economic shocks and wars.

But why go back only to 1915? On the political side, the Bull Moose campaign of Theodore Roosevelt in 1912 generated the largest third-party vote for president since the Civil War. Excluding this one observation in the middle of the time series would have considerably complicated the estimation since our equations contain lagged values of variables and shocks. On the economic side, there are two important considerations. The first is that 1914 marks the beginning of a new financial and macroeconomic regime with the creation of the Federal Reserve System; Mankiw, Miron, and Weil (1990) provide convincing evidence that 1914 demarcates an important policy regime shift. The second argument is that the reliability of economic data before this date becomes much more questionable (see Romer (1989) and Balke and Gordon (1989)).

Picking the end date for the estimation was much easier. We began the work reported here in the spring of 1990.

Our choice of real GNP growth as our measure for the economy was an easy one. Not only is it widely recognized as the best summary measure of economic activity, but it also is, according to Fair (1978), the best predictor of presidential elections. Furthermore, Alesina and Rosenthal (1989) show that, with respect to congressional elections, results do not change in important ways when income is used rather than GNP. The choice of presidential vote share was also direct. We focussed on the House rather than the Senate because the Senate is not fully elected every two years and because there may have been regime shifts associated with direct election of the Senate beginning only in 1912. In any event, for post–World War II data, Senate election data gives similar results to those from the House (Alesina and Rosenthal (1989)).

Table 9.1 shows summary statistics for our data. The notes to the table contain the sources. A listing of the observations appears in table 9.A1 (see the appendix to this chapter). Several preliminary observations are in order.

On the surface, there is little support for a Nordhaus type political business cycle. Growth is not particularly high in election years; it is in fact slightly lower in election years than in the first and third years (non-election years) of terms. Also, to find a partisan business cycle we need to rely on controlling for other effects. While the growth rate is most variable in the second (midterm) years of terms, as predicted, the overall low average growth rate is not consistent, at first blush, with high growth under Democrats and low growth under Republicans.

With regard to the voting variables, there does seem to be some support for incumbency bias in presidential elections, since the incumbent party has averaged 53 percent of the two-party vote. The 3 point slippage between the presidential vote and the presidential year House vote is suggestive of balancing effects in on-years. On the other hand, a midterm effect is hardly apparent from the marginal distribution since the incumbent party's midterm House vote of 49 percent only slightly favors the opposition. Finally, the parties have shared the presidency about evenly over the sample period. As stated previously, we will investigate whether this reflects even competition or whether, after correcting for "shocks" such as the Great Depression, the Republican party displays an advantage in the presidential race.

Econometric estimation of the structural model is, of course, greatly preferable to inspecting the rough data. To the estimation we now proceed.

9.4 ECONOMIC GROWTH AND PARTY COMPETENCE

Let us recall from chapter 8 that our theoretical specification for economic growth is given by:

$$y_t = \bar{y} + \gamma(\pi_t - \pi_t^e) + \varepsilon_t \qquad (9.1)$$

The first term on the right-hand side corresponded to the "natural rate" of growth, the second term to the partisan inflation surprise, and the third to exogenous shocks which were decomposed into competency shocks and exogenous shocks as shown in equation (9.2):

$$\varepsilon_t = \eta_t + \xi_t \qquad (9.2)$$

where ξ is an exogenous shock unrelated to government behavior and η is the result of administrative competence.

Our empirical specification is:

$$y_t = \gamma_0 + \gamma_1 pe_t + \gamma_2 mm_t + \varepsilon_t$$

$$t = 1915, 1916, 1917, 1918, \ldots, 1988 \qquad (9.3)$$

We now relate this specification to the theory.

The natural rate of growth

The intercept term, γ_0, measures the natural rate of growth ($\bar{y}$).

The partisan inflation surprise

The coefficient γ_1 captures the effect of the partisan inflationary surprise. In fact, the variable pe_t takes the value of "+1" during the second year of a Republican administration, "−1" during the second year of a Democratic administration, and "0", otherwise. The theory implies that the estimate of γ_1 should be *negative*.

Note that we posit that there should be a partisan surprise to the economy only in the *second* year of each presidential term. As already noted in chapter 7, economists agree that monetary and fiscal policy changes do not affect output in less than two to four quarters. In a study using quarterly data, Alesina (1988b) shows that the post-electoral effects on the economy appear no sooner than two quarters after a presidential election and reach maximum strength in about five to six quarters, and disappear by ten quarters. This timing is perfectly consistent with independent evidence on the lags between changes in monetary policy and growth effects (Friedman and Schwartz (1971), Romer and Romer (1989)). Alesina and Roubini (1992) report analogous results for several other countries.

When an inflation surprise occurs, our empirical specification holds that the magnitude of the effect is equal for Republicans and Democrats. In contrast, equations (7.24) and (7.25) showed that the magnitude of the surprise depends on P, the probability of a Democratic victory. Thus, our empirical specification of the growth equation implicitly assumes $P = \frac{1}{2}$. Theoretically, however, there is no reason to expect $P = \frac{1}{2}$ or even to expect that P is constant over time. As discussed in the introduction to this chapter, we are unable to measure or estimate a P_t for each election. We did experiment with estimating separate unexpected inflation impacts for Democrats and Republicans; this corresponds to estimating a fixed P valid for the entire 1915–88 period. We were unable to reject the null hypothesis of $P = \frac{1}{2}$, a not surprising result given our small sample size.

While our empirical specification incorporates inflationary surprise only via the presidential outcome captured in the *pe* variable, the theoretical model also allows for surprise inflation from the outcome of congressional elections. We have chosen to exclude congressional elections because the surprise is clearly a second order effect.[9]

Military mobilization

A rapid change in economic activity from producing "guns" to producing "butter" or vice versa is an obvious source of transitory effects that can be

---

[9]In the first period, we can write expected inflation, for $P = \frac{1}{2}$ as:

$$E(\pi_1) = \tfrac{1}{2}(\pi^{R*} + K - K\bar{V}_R) + \tfrac{1}{2}(\pi^{D*} + K\bar{V}_R)$$
$$= \tfrac{1}{2}(\pi^{R*} + \pi^{D*} + K) - K\bar{V}_R$$

where $\bar{V}_R$ is the expected legislative vote in period 1 whereas the possible realizations are: if R president, $\pi_1^R = \pi^{R*} + K - KV_R$; if D president, $\pi_1^D = \pi^{D*} - KV_R$. Note that V_R is the actual realization of the Republican House vote while $\bar{V}_R$ is the expected value.

With $P = \frac{1}{2}$, an R victory and a D victory generate surprises of equal magnitude, so we need only cover the case of an R presidential victory. Particularly if presidential influence on policy is likely to exceed that of Congress (see Hibbs (1987) and Fiorina (1988)), so that K is small, $\tfrac{1}{2}(\pi^{R*} + \pi^{D*} - K) - \pi^{R*}$ will be large relative to $|KV_R - K\bar{V}_R|$ if there is little variation in V_R. That there is indeed little unexpected variation in the congressional vote is indicated by the small forecast errors in the House equations, below. Consequently, we simplify the empirical model by excluding congressional surprises.

included in the analysis.[10] The coefficient γ_2 captures the effects on the economy of switching between wartime and peacetime. We have chosen to measure military activities, especially wars, by the rate of military mobilization. Define m_t to be the number of individuals in military service as of June 30 of year t and POP_t to be the population of the United States for the same year. Then the rate of military mobilization is given by:

$$mm_t = (m_t - m_{t-1})/POP_t \qquad (9.4)$$

Since mm_t enters linearly in equation (9.3), implicitly we treat mobilizations and demobilizations symmetrically. We expect γ_2 to be positive. Essentially we assume that in going to war a government is able to commandeer unused capacity and labor in the economy and increase output dramatically, while the return to peace incurs delays in redirection of capacity and labor that depress output in the short run. Because the effects on output are from changes in the level of military activities, the model assumes that wars, hot or cold, have no long-run effect on economic growth.

With reference to the formal model, the military mobilization shock is part of the transitory component ξ. Thus, the term ε in the empirical model represents competence and transitory shocks net of military mobilization. Whether the military mobilization shock is known to the voters is not critical. Knowledge of the military shock changes the inference calculations (see section 8.2) of rationally retrospective voters, but leaves the qualitative results unchanged, as long as voters cannot differentiate competence from the non-military transitory shocks.

Competence: are the growth shocks supportive of the model?

The last term in both the theoretical equation (9.1) and the empirical equation (9.3) contains an error term ε which combines an exogenous shock and a competence shock. The stochastic behavior of this error term can be characterized in terms of its mean and its variance–covariance structure. By assumption, the mean is zero. Consider the following form for the variance–covariance structure:

$v_0 =$ Variance in any year in which there is no change in

the party holding the presidency.

$v_1 =$ Variance in years in which the presidency changes parties,

specifically, 1921, 1933, 1953, 1961, 1969, 1977, and 1981.

$c_0 =$ Covariance between current year and preceding year $\qquad (9.5)$

in any year in which there is no change.

[10] Oil shocks might also merit attention. As adding a measure of oil prices to our growth equation leaves results unchanged and uses degrees of freedom, we have chosen not to include this variable. (See also Alesina (1988b).)

c_1 = Covariance between current year and preceding year

in years in which the presidency changes parties.

0 = Covariance between current year and all other years.

The competency model of chapter 8 implies, as simple algebra will verify, that $v_0 = v_1$ and that $c_0 > c_1 = 0$. In words, there should be no covariance when the presidency changes hands, because a new team comes in and, by assumption, there is no correlation in competence across parties. But since competence evolves by a Moving Average process of the first order (MA(1)), there should be covariance as long as the same party retains the executive. The model has strictly zero covariance in the case of turnover because it does not allow for covariance in the exogenous shocks. However, the qualitative prediction that covariance is greater in the absence of party change than in the presence of turnover should hold in any model of competence.

In contrast to our reformulation of the Persson and Tabellini (1990) model, which ascribes all the serial dependency in "errors" to partisan competence, the standard MA(1) model has $v_0 = v_1$ and $c_0 = c_1 > 0$. Nelson and Plosser (1982) present evidence that this model is not rejected in favor of more complicated Autoregressive Moving Average (ARMA) models, that is, dynamic models of GNP growth with longer lags.

In table 9.2, the last column presents estimates for the standard model. In the next-to-last column, the restriction $c_0 = c_1$ is relaxed. The improvement in the log-likelihood is very small: a statistical test fails to reject the null hypothesis of this restriction. Indeed, counter to the central hypothesis of competency shocks, the estimated covariance is higher when there is turnover than when there is not. When both the variance and the covariance restrictions are relaxed (column 1 of table 9.2), we find that the two covariances are essentially equal. Again a statistical test fails to reject the null hypothesis of the restriction. There is no evidence that a change in party control of the White House makes a difference in aggregate economic growth in the year following the election.

Thus, we conclude that our model of administrative competence effects on growth is rejected by the evidence. Since this model provides the basis for the specification of "rational retrospective voting", we reject also the latter. In other words, the only reason why rational voters in our model should be retrospective, i.e., pay attention to the economy when voting, is to figure out administrative competence. *Since we find no evidence that administrative competence matters for growth, rational voters should not be retrospective in our model.*

The lack of evidence of effects of administrative competence on growth leads to a simplification of the growth equation, which we will adopt in the estimation of the system of four equations. Our specification is just

Table 9.2. *Nested growth models: single-equation estimates*

Variable	Coefficient	Model, with Variance-Covariance Restrictions			
		Unrestricted	$c_0 = c_1$	$v_0 = v_1$	$c_0 = c_1$ and $v_0 = v_1$
Constant	γ_0	3.100 (4.42)	3.101 (4.71)	3.081 (4.37)	3.047 (4.29)
Partisan Effect	γ_1	-1.806 (-2.12)	-1.805 (-2.13)	-1.862 (-2.12)	-1.900 (-2.23)
Military Mobilization	γ_2	3.147 (6.21)	3.148 (6.29)	3.136 (6.24)	3.090 (6.31)
Same Party Variance	v_0	20.046 (4.80)	22.027 (5.46)	20.825 (5.44)	20.981 (5.42)
Different Party Variance	v_1	11.761 (3.06)	11.769 (3.08)	—	—
Same Party Covariance	c_0	8.356 (3.40)	8.333 (3.90)	7.853 (3.52)	8.260 (3.63)
Different Party Covariance	c_1	8.301 (2.97)	—	10.512 (2.64)	—
	log-likelihood	-208.139	-208.139	-209.673	-209.874

Note: t-statistics in parentheses.

the standard MA(1) model with a *single* disturbance, $\varepsilon_t = \mu_t + \rho\mu_{t-1}$.[11] To reiterate: this shock is not due to competence but to exogenous factors influencing the economy. Our growth equation in the four equations system does differ from the last column of table 9.2 in one respect. We allow for hetcroskcdasticity; wc do *not* impose cquality of variance in non-election years, midterm election years, and years with a presidential election. These three different variances are denoted as $\sigma_{\mu n}^2$, $\sigma_{\mu m}^2$ and $\sigma_{\mu p}^2$, repectively. Allowing for heteroskedasticity simplifies the computation in the estimation; the estimated variances do not, in fact, exhibit significant differences.

Results on partisan surprise and mobilization

While we fail to find that party competence is important to growth, the single equation estimates in table 9.2 confirm, for a different sample period, chapter 7's basic message concerning the rational partisan business cycle. The estimates of the structural parameters shown in the table are quite robust to the covariance specifications in the three columns. In particular, the -1.9 estimate for γ_1 is well over twice, in magnitude, the estimated standard error,

[11]The variance of the shock is $\sigma_\varepsilon^2 = (1 + \rho^2)\sigma_\mu^2$ and the covariance is $\text{cov}(\varepsilon_t, \varepsilon_{t-1}) = \rho\sigma_\mu^2$.

implying a t-statistic above 2. It indicates that growth in the second year of Democratic administrations is nearly 4 percent higher than in the second year of Republican administration. The size of this coefficient demonstrates the robustness of the results of chapter 7, which used a different sample period, data frequency, and econometric methodology.

A dramatic effect is also apparent for military mobilizations. The estimated coefficient shows that moving 1 percent of the population into the armed services increases growth by 3 percent but, when they are eventually demobilized, growth falls by the same amount. The demobilization effect is particularly important relative to the recession of 1946, which occurred in the second year of a Democratic administration. Finally, as shown by the estimate of γ_0, the natural rate of growth is estimated to be about 3 percent per year.

9.5 VOTING

In the absence of competence based voting, the theoretical model becomes simpler. Specifically, given the evidence presented in the previous section we can strip away the theoretical dependence of voting on growth. Without growth, voting, as in chapter 4, takes the form of simple cutpoint rules that do not change over time. That is, as in equation (8.16), the presidential cutpoint is $\hat{\pi}$, but without the expected competence term. We have:

$$\text{Republican vote (in \%)} = 100\hat{\pi} - 100\mathbf{a} \tag{9.6}$$

where $\mathbf{a}$ is the random disturbance on voter preferences from section 4.2. Of course, the cutpoint is a function of the parameters $(\alpha, w, \bar{\pi}_R, \bar{\pi}_D, \text{ and } \beta)$ which we cannot identify from equation (9.6).

For convenience in estimation, for both presidential and congressional elections, we specify the dependent variables as *shares of the two party vote for the party of the incumbent president* in year t, denoted by v_t.

This involves rewriting equation (9.6) as:

$$v_t = 100\hat{\pi} - 100\mathbf{a} \qquad \text{if incumbent is Republican} \tag{9.7}$$

$$v_t = 100 - 100\hat{\pi} + 100\mathbf{a} \qquad \text{if incumbent is Democrat}$$

We can rewrite (9.7) as a standard linear regression equation which takes the form:

$$v_t = \psi_0 + \psi_1 r_t + \varphi_t \tag{9.8}$$

where $r_t = 1$ if incumbent is R, $r_t = 0$ if incumbent is D.

(Comparison of (9.7) and (9.8) shows that $\psi_0 = 100 - 100\hat{\pi}$, $\psi_1 = 200\hat{\pi} - 100$, $\varphi_t = -100\mathbf{a}$ if R incumbent, $= +100\mathbf{a}$ if D incumbent.)

If we were to adopt this simple model, we could easily test for incumbency bias. In the absence of incumbency bias, the predicted share when R is incumbent and the predicted share when D is incumbent should sum to 100. Thus, the null hypothesis would be $2\psi_0 + \psi_1 = 100$. Positive incumbency bias would show $2\psi_0 + \psi_1 > 100$. We could also use ψ_1 to test for a bias toward one of the parties, with $\psi_1 = 0$ representing the null hypothesis of no bias. If $\psi_1 > 0$, the Republicans are more likely to win the contest than the Democrats.

Note finally that the error term, φ_t, can exhibit a sign difference with respect to the theoretical model. This is not a problem since a is independently distributed. Our estimation procedure does not make a distributional assumption about the voting errors, such as normality. We would obtain consistent estimates even if the errors were uniformly distributed, as in the theoretical model.[12]

Rather than use this direct test of the theoretical model (but see Alesina and Rosenthal (1989)), we augment the equations in ways that take into account previous research on voting behavior. We first develop our equation for presidential voting and then turn to voting for the House of Respresentatives.

Presidential elections

Our presidential voting equation includes the lagged House vote, that is the previous midterm vote (v_{t-2}^{hm}), for reasons covered in the introduction. We also include economic growth, to allow for retrospective voting, and military mobilization, to test for "rally 'round the flag" support for the incumbent party. When these variables are added to the specification of equation (9.8), the full equation for the presidential vote v_t^p is:

$$v_t^p = \psi_0 + \psi_1 r_t + \psi_2 v_{t-2}^{hm} + \psi_3 mm_t + \psi_4 \hat{y}_t + \psi_5 \mu_t + \varphi_t^p \qquad (9.9)$$

$$t = 1916, 1920, 1924, \ldots, 1988$$

In equation (9.9) the growth term has been broken into two components, $\hat{y}_t$ and μ_t. The first term is forecast (or instrumented) growth which results from the growth equation:

$$\hat{y}_t = \gamma_0 + \gamma_2 mm_t + \rho \mu_{t-1}$$

The forecast does not include the variable *pe* because there is no surprise inflation in a presidential election year, but does include military mobiliza-

---

[12]Note that our voting specifications, such as (9.8), are all in the form of linear probability models. Since the range of the observed shares is between 30 percent and 70 percent, there is no advantage in "heteroskedasticity corrections" such as logistic transforms. Making the left-hand side variable a percentage, on the other hand, facilitates interpretation of the results.

tion and the lagged growth shock. It does not include the contemporaneous shock, μ_t, which is entered separately.[13]

The reason for introducing $\hat{y}_t$ *and* μ_t separately is to provide further tests on the nature of retrospective voting in presidential elections. Our results on the growth equation have already rejected the model of competence. Thus, in our model rational voters should *not* be retrospective on the economy. This would imply that both coefficients on the two components of growth are zero: $\psi_4 = \psi_5 = 0$. On the contrary, a finding that these two coefficients are equal and positive ($\psi_4 = \psi_5 > 0$) would endorse a naïve retrospective voting model. In fact, this result would imply that the electorate simply looks at pre-electoral growth to judge the incumbent's performance; there is no attempt to distinguish expected growth (given military mobilizations, past shocks, etc.) from current shocks to growth. Finally, suppose that we find that both coefficients are positive but different. A difference in these coefficients would imply that the electorate is doing something a bit more sophisticated when voting than just looking at GNP growth in the election year. A finding that the electorate is trying to disentangle various components of growth might be the basis for a sort of rational retrospective voting. It is worth repeating, however, that even a finding of a difference between two coefficients would *not* endorse our specific model of rational retrospective voting based on competence.[14]

We also estimate a restricted version of this equation where military mobilization is left out:

$$v_t^p = \psi_0 + \psi_1 r_t + \psi_2 v_{t-2}^{bm} + \psi_4 \hat{y}_t + \psi_5 \mu_t + \varphi_t^p \qquad (9.10)$$

This specification implies that there is no direct "rally 'round the flag" effect although military mobilization would still influence elections indirectly, via its effect on economic growth.

Our specification differs from some (Erikson (1989)) past work on presidential voting since it does not include any direct measure of the popularity of the incumbent president or comparative evaluations of the two candidates. These measures are typically constructed from opinion poll data collected a few months or weeks prior to the election or immediately after the election. In our model, personality effects are relegated to the error term φ_t^p while the lagged House vote tracks changes in the partisan preferences of the electorate. While measures of individual candidate

---

[13]Note that the right-hand side of the expression for $\hat{y}_t$ contains the structural parameters γ and not their estimates. This is because the voters are assumed to know the parameters of the model. In the actual estimations, of course, $\hat{y}_t$ is estimated using the estimated values of the γ parameters and of the disturbance μ_{t-1}.

[14]Note that the error term φ in (9.9) does not appear in (9.3). Consequently, (9.3) and (9.9) constitute a recursive system. The recursive structure is preserved when we add congressional voting.

effects would be desirable, the standard measures (questions of data availability prior to 1948 apart) are subject to simultaneity bias. That is, it is difficult to know if voter likes and dislikes about candidates are cause or effect of voting decisions. Consequently, we do not include survey based measures in our specification.

For our specification where equation (9.8) has been augmented by lagged House vote, military mobilization, and growth, it is still possible to test for incumbency bias and a bias toward one of the parties, but the test must be conditioned on values of the right-hand side variables.

House elections

Our first specification for on-year House elections is identical to our specification for presidential elections, except that we augment the equation by including the presidential vote shock, φ^P. This implements the idea in our formal model and in Kramer (1971) that there is a random preference shock that is common to both presidential and congressional races. Kramer (1971) introduced this common shock as a model of coattails. In our formal model, the shock to presidential and House elections should be identical, since both arise from the random variable a, which perturbs voter preferences. However, since the shocks on both equations may contain candidate specific effects that are outside our formal models, we allow for independent shocks in both equations and expect λ_6, the coattail parameter, to be less than one. Following Kramer (1971), we assume no feedback from congressional shocks to the presidential race. The resulting equation is:

$$v_t^{hp} = \lambda_0 + \lambda_1 r_t + \lambda_2 v_{t-2}^{hm} + \lambda_3 mm_t + \lambda_4 \hat{y}_t + \lambda_5 \mu_t + \lambda_6 \varphi_t^p + \varphi_t^{hp} \quad (9.11)$$

$$t = 1916, 1920, 1924, \ldots, 1988$$

Coattails may be more pervasive, however, than indicated simply by correlated shocks. It is possible that all the benefit the White House incumbent's congressional ticket derives from military mobilization and economic growth occurs because mobilization and growth help in the presidential race, which then spills over into the House contest. In this case, the instrumented presidential vote should carry all the information contained in the mobilization and growth measures.[15] The estimated equation would become:

$$v_t^{hp} = \lambda_0 + \lambda_1 r_t + \lambda_2 v_{t-2}^{hm} + \lambda^* \hat{v}_t^p + \lambda_6 \varphi_t^p + \varphi_t^{hp}$$

---

[15] We thus implement, without simultaneity bias, the specification of Erikson (1990). This author checked only whether the presidential vote carried the economic effects; we check also for military mobilization.

where

$$\hat{v}_t^p = v_t^p - \varphi_t^p$$

and v_t^p is given by either (9.9) or (9.10).

Alternatively, it is possible, and this is our empirical finding, that the economy and military mobilizations have insignificant influence on the House vote and that partisan bias is also insignificant, leaving the only linkage between the presidential vote and the on-year House vote to be, in line with our theoretical model, the shock φ_t^p. For this case, we estimate the restricted model:

$$v_t^{hp} = \lambda_0 + \lambda_2 v_{t-2}^{hm} + \lambda_6 \varphi_t^p + \varphi_t^{hp} \tag{9.12}$$

Note that, although there is no partisan bias variable (r) in (9.12), differential voting that would, *ceteris paribus*, lead to split tickets is still predicted when $\psi_1 \neq 0$ in (9.10). A positive value for ψ_1 implies that the Republicans do better in presidential elections than in congressional elections.

Our first specification for the midterm House vote is identical in form to the presidential equation:

$$v_t^{hm} = \kappa_0 + \kappa_1 r_t + \kappa_2 v_{t-2}^{hp} + \kappa_3 mm_t + \kappa_4 \hat{y}_t + \kappa_5 \mu_t + \varphi_t^{hm} \tag{9.13}$$

$$t = 1918, 1922, 1926, \ldots, 1986$$

Note that, in the absence of a simultaneous election of the president, this equation, unlike the on-year equation, does not include a presidential vote shock.[16]

However, our theoretical model predicts no effect of military mobilization or growth. Since the lagged House vote reflects the on-year House cutpoint, there also may be no need to include r_t, the Republican bias parameter. These considerations lead to estimating the simple equation:

$$v_t^{hm} = \kappa_0 + \kappa_1 v_{t-2}^{hp} + \varphi_t^{hm} \tag{9.14}$$

We have a midterm cycle if the predicted midterm vote is less than the on-year vote. This is guaranteed if both $\kappa_0 < 0$ and $\kappa_1 < 1$. More generally, we would have a predicted midterm effect if:

$$v_{t-2}^{hp} - \hat{v}_t^{hm} = (1 - \kappa_1) v_{t-2}^{hp} - \kappa_0 > 0 \tag{9.15}$$

The econometric procedure for estimating the model is described in Alesina, Londregan, and Rosenthal (1993). Readers with training in econometrics can note that the system of unrestricted equations (9.9), (9.11), (9.13),

---

[16]Recall that all vote variables are defined with respect to the party holding the White House. For example, if the presidential elections in year $t-2$ shift the presidency from the Republicans to the Democrats, the $t-2$ House vote on the left-hand side of (9.11) will be the Republican House vote while it will be the Democrat House vote on the right-hand side of (9.13).

and (9.3) was estimated using maximum likelihood. Restricted estimates were than produced using Rothemberg's (1973) optimum minimum distance technique.

9.6 ESTIMATION RESULTS

The results for each of the four equations in our model are presented in tables 9.3–9.6. The column marked "(1)" in each table contains the results for the simultaneous estimation of the unrestricted versions of each equation, namely (9.3), (9.9), (9.11), and (9.13).[17] For the voting equations, there is also a column "(2)", which shows estimates for the restricted equations ((9.10), (9.12), or (9.14)) when the other voting equations are still unrestricted. Finally, in all tables, column "(3)" shows the joint estimation of the restricted version of the model (equations (9.3), (9.10), (9.12), and (9.14)).

Growth

The estimates of the coefficients of the growth model (see table 9.3) are very similar to, thus confirmatory of, the single equation estimates described in section 9.3. All coefficients are statistically significant, in both the unrestricted and system restricted estimations, at the 5 percent level.[18] With respect to the single equation estimates in table 9.2, the inflation surprise coefficient estimates in table 9.3 are slightly smaller in magnitude and slightly less precisely estimated, but still statistically significant.[19] The estimate of ρ indicates that the effect of the lagged shock, μ_{t-1}, is approximately half the effect of the current shock, μ_t. This estimate is similar to Nelson and Plosser's (1982) estimate of the MA(1) representation of annual GNP. The three shock variances of different types of year are not significantly different.

In years other than the second of each presidential term, all the explanatory power of right-hand side variables is in the military mobilization variable, since the variable *pe* is zero. Military mobilization accounts for about 30 percent of the variation in GNP in the fourth year of a presidential term and 44 percent in the first and third years of each term. In midterm election years, *pe* also plays a role; *pe* and *mm* jointly account for nearly two-thirds of the variation in second-year GNP growth. Partisan

---

[17]Recall from section 7.4 that the growth equation is estimated with a standard MA(1) process that allows for heteroskedasticity.

[18]One-tail tests were used, as is appropriate.

[19]The lesser precision of the estimates in table 9.3 partly reflects the estimation of three shock variances (one for each type of year) rather than the single variance of table 9.2. The use of three variances was purely a matter of computational ease.

Table 9.3. *The growth equation*

Variable	Coefficient	(1) Unrestricted	(3) System Restricted	
Constant	γ_0	3.254 (4.46)	3.214 (4.42)	
Partisan Effect	γ_1	-1.700 (-1.88)	-1.698 (-1.91)	
Military Mobilization	γ_2	3.027 (5.86)	3.087 (6.90)	
Lagged Growth Shock	ρ	0.518 (5.12)	0.484 (3.96)	
Type of Year		Residual Variance	Std. Error of Estimate	R^2
Non-election Years	$\sigma^2_{\mu n}$	13.502	3.254	0.437
Midterm Election Years	$\sigma^2_{\mu m}$	21.704	7.453	0.657
Presidential Election Years	$\sigma^2_{\mu p}$	19.377	6.336	0.300

Note: t-statistics in parentheses. The restricted estimates are computed using Rothemberg's (1973) Optimum Minimum Distance technique, which does not produce fresh estimates of the variables.

effects are substantial. The mean growth rate is 3.1 percent. The second year effect is estimated to be growth of 4.9 percent under Democrats and only 1.5 percent under Republicans. Overall, about 51 percent of the variation in annual GNP growth rates is accounted for by the military mobilization and partisan surprises.

Both military mobilizations and partisan inflation surprises have their origins in politics. These results thus support a basic theme of the volume: *the interconnection of politics and economics is sufficiently strong that the study of capitalist economies cannot be solely the study of the interplay of market forces.*

Voting

Conversely, economics has a manifest influence on politics. Perhaps the major impact of economics on politics appears more in the long-term distribution of policy preferences among voters than in the short-term variations in voting behavior captured by the parameter estimates. Economic interests are, as we emphasized in chapter 2, fundamental to partisan politics. These interests have a major influence on political preferences, including the growth–inflation trade-off in our model. Another impact of economics is manifest in retrospective voting on economic performance. We examine the interplay of retrospective voting, presidential coattails, partisan bias, and lagged effects in our discussion of the voting equations.

Presidential elections

Our results for presidential elections can be summarized as follows. First, growth in the year of the election yields strong benefits to incumbents. Second, the naïve retrospective voting assumption behind these benefits survives a statistical test. Third, military mobilization has no "rally 'round the flag" effect on presidential voting other than the effect that is transmitted by the effect of mobilization on growth. Fourth, independent of growth, incumbents are advantaged. Fifth, there is a strong tilt in favor of the Republicans in presidential elections. The estimates are presented in table 9.4.

The effect of economic growth on presidential elections is captured by the estimated coefficients on instrumented growth and the current growth shock. In the system restricted estimates, every additional percentage point of GNP growth is estimated to tack on 0.8 percent to the incumbent party's vote. Even larger impacts arise in the other specifications. With naïve retrospective voting, the coefficients on instrumented (forecast) growth and the current shock would be equal, i.e., $\psi_4 = \psi_5$. In the unrestricted model,

Table 9.4. *Presidential vote shares equation*

Variable	Coefficient	(1) Unrestricted	(2) Equation Restricted	(3) System Restricted
Constant	ψ_0	5.622 (0.54)	5.981 (0.58)	12.209 (1.28)
Republican Incumbent	ψ_1	10.365 (5.37)	10.362 (5.39)	8.842 (7.22)
Previous House Vote	ψ_2	0.743 (3.82)	0.739 (3.82)	0.692 (3.70)
Military Mobilization	ψ_3	-.406 (-0.17)	—	—
Expected Growth Rate	ψ_4	1.636 (3.21)	1.590 (3.92)	0.795 (3.68)
Current Growth Shock	ψ_5	1.139 (5.47)	1.140 (5.48)	1.174 (5.84)
Residual Variance	σ_p^2	13.601 (3.07)	—	—
		$R^2 = 0.764$		

Note: See note to Table 9.3.

the null hypothesis of equality cannot be rejected at conventional levels ($t = -0.96$). A similar result holds in the system restricted model ($t = 1.32$). Thus retrospective voting occurs even though we failed to find evidence that administrations make a difference in economic performance. In summary, our rejection of the competence model, together with these results on the effect of pre-electoral growth on presidential elections, imply a rejection of the rational retrospective voting assumption, as incorporated in our model.

Voters do not appear to "rally 'round the flag": the coefficient on military mobilization is insignificant. Military mobilization helps incumbents only insofar as mobilization produces growth in the economy. This result contrasts with research on presidential popularity (Mueller (1973)) which claims a direct short-run effect from wars.

Incumbents not only benefit from growth, whatever its origin, they also benefit simply from being incumbents. The reader may recall that even though, for reasons of tractability, incumbency advantage was not explicitly considered in our theoretical model, it certainly does not contradict our conceptual framework. If there were no incumbency bias, as explained in the preceding section, the sum of the predicted vote for a Republican incumbent and the predicted vote for a Democrat incumbent should equal 100. We tested this hypothesis using the unrestricted estimation and evaluating all variables at their sample means. The sum turns out to be 105.59. (The average incumbent vote would be half this or 52.8 percent.) The t-ratio for the test of the null hypothesis is 2.12, implying rejection at the standard 5 percent level.[20] Note that this finding of a substantial bias to the incumbent party holds even though we include those years when the incumbent president did not seek re-election.

Our theoretical model does allow for a bias to one party if that party is closer to the median voter. Our results indicate that party to be the Republicans. The very precisely estimated ψ_1 coefficient shows that Republicans, in the unrestricted case, *ceteris paribus*, average 10 percent more of the popular vote than Democrats. If the House vote had been split 50–50 in the previous midterm vote and if there were no military mobilization, our estimates would show the Republicans retaining the White House with 53.1 percent of the presidential vote, even in the presence of zero growth. A severe recession, with negative growth over 2 percent, would be needed to swing the election to the Democrats. In contrast, zero growth for the same scenario but with a Democrat incumbent would lead to a Republican landslide. The Democratic incumbent would receive only 42.8 percent of the popular vote.

The 10 percent Republican bias has to be tempered by the fact that the Democrats have had a majority in the House of Representatives in every

---

[20]Using the system restricted estimates, the sum is 107.69 and the t-ratio is 2.80.

election from 1932 onwards where a Republican has sought re-election. Nonetheless, the Democratic majorities have to be very large indeed before the Republican bias is canceled. When the Democrats have received about 57 percent of the previous House vote, the Republican bias is canceled; the presidential vote forecast would be the same for an incumbent of either party.

Voting for the House in on-years

For the years in which the House and the president are simultaneously elected, our basic findings (see table 9.5) are the following. Presidential coattails play an important role in House races but only through the shock term. The effect of the economy on presidential elections does not carry over to congressional races. Similarly, military mobilizations fail to have effects on on-year House races, either directly or, as in the case of presidential voting, indirectly via their effect on the economy. Unlike presidential elections, where there was a significant bias in favor of Republicans, neither party is significantly advantaged per se in House elections. But there is a highly significant effect of the lagged vote, as witnessed by the prolonged Democratic dominance of the House of Representatives.

Table 9.5. *On-year House vote equation*

Variable	Coefficient	(1) Unrestricted	(2) Equation Restricted	(3) System Restricted
Constant	λ_0	3.637 (0.48)	7.855 (1.20)	7.809 (1.20)
Republican Incumbent	λ_1	1.345 (0.98)		
Previous House Vote	λ_2	0.886 (6.42)	0.860 (6.56)	0.860 (6.56)
Military Mobilization	λ_3	1.567 (0.92)	—	—
Instrumented Growth	λ_4	0.554 (1.49)	—	—
Current Growth Shock	λ_5	0.032 (0.20)	—	—
Presidential Vote Shock	λ_6	0.547 (5.20)	0.534 (8.21)	0.531 (8.16)
Residual Variance	σ_{hp}^2	2.841		
	$R^2 = 0.905$			

Note: See note to Table 9.3.

Three observations indicate that partisan bias (λ_1), military mobilization (λ_3), and the economy (λ_4 and λ_5) are not important determinants of House elections. First, note that none of the coefficients of these variables has a magnitude that exceeds 1.5 times its standard error. Second, the magnitude of the partisan bias coefficient in the unrestricted on-year House equation is less than $\frac{1}{8}$ of the magnitude of the corresponding coefficient in the presidential equation. Similarly, the growth coefficients are less than $\frac{1}{4}$ the corresponding magnitude; indeed the coefficient on the current growth shock is (insignificantly) negative. Third, a statistical test strongly supports dropping all four coefficients.[21]

The absence of a significant effect for growth echoes recent work by Erikson (1990), who included both the current presidential vote and the current growth rate in a single equation estimation of House voting and found that the coefficient on growth was insignificant. Our analysis confirms this result in a context that both accounts for possible simultaneity bias and extends the sample from the postwar period back to 1916.

Our simultaneous approach discloses that it is not the entire presidential vote but simply the vote shock that has an effect on the House vote. Every point that the presidential candidate gains because of effects not captured by the growth variables is estimated to produce (in either equation restricted or system restricted models) a little more than half a point for his or her congressional ticket. This effect is very precisely estimated, with a t-statistic exceeding 8. The large impact of the presidential vote shock is consistent with the common shock **a** to preferences in our theoretical model. In on-year elections, there is, in the aggregate, an important shock that shifts voters to the same side of both the presidential and congressional cutpoints. The large value of the coefficient (0.53) suggests that our theoretical model appropriately captures an important effect in on-year elections.

The fact that the coefficient is not 1 suggests that, unlike in our theoretical model, the voters have some information on the realization of the shock. In this case, it is natural not to observe a complete transmission, namely the coefficient on the shock should be smaller than 1. In fact, the voters, rather than tilting fully in their congressional vote to the party favored for the presidency, would tilt only partially as a result of balancing behavior. Moreover, the significant residual variance in the House equations means that our theoretical model could be improved by allowing for uncorrelated sources of variation in presidential and House voting.

Our theoretical model of presidential and congressional voting reflects our basic hypothesis that voters pursue moderate policies by means of institutional balancing. This implies significant split-ticket voting in on-year elections if the parties are not symmetrically located about the ideal point

---

[21]The χ^2_4 statistic is 6.63.

of the median voter. The difference in the partisan bias coefficients in tables 9.4 and 9.5 suggests that there will be important differences in the aggregate support for the two parties in presidential and congressional races when there is an incumbent Republican president. However, the difference in the presidential and congressional percentages will also depend on the other variables in the model. To study this question, therefore, we developed figure 9.1. This figure assumes that there is a Republican president and that the economy grows at its forecast level of 3.2 percent in the fourth year of the term. It assumes no current growth shocks or vote shocks. The figure plots the presidential vote, the contemporaneous House vote, and the subsequent midterm vote against values of the previous midterm House vote that range from 40 percent to 60 percent Republican. The estimated presidential vote is always substantially greater than the estimated House vote. The gap would increase were the economy growing faster than average and shrink were the economy growing more slowly than average, but a severe recession would be needed for the Republicans, when they hold the White House, to actually fare worse in presidential elections than in elections for the House of Representatives.

At the forecast growth rate of 3.2 percent one can also detect a substantial, even though less than in the Republican case, aggregate split vote when the Democrats are in power as long as they hold a majority in the House. But here the pattern is reversed relative to the case of a Republican president,

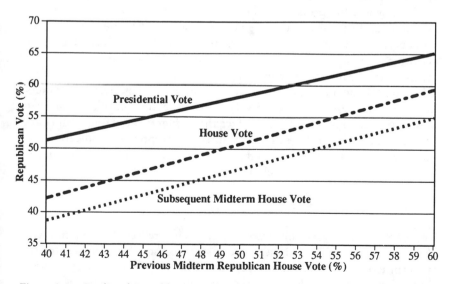

Figure 9.1. Predicted Republican vote with Republican incumbent president. The vote depends on the previous midterm House vote. The plots assume there are no shocks to growth or voting.

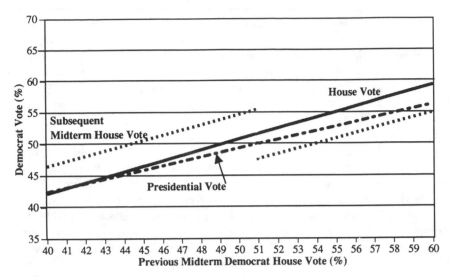

Figure 9.2. Predicted Democratic vote with Democratic incumbent president. The vote depends on the previous midterm House vote. The plots assume there are no shocks to growth or voting.

since the Democrats are disadvantaged in presidential elections. In figure 9.2, which makes the same assumptions as figure 9.1 except for the shift in incumbency, the presidential line now lies generally below the on-year House line. Even when the Democrats hold the White House, their presidential candidates should run behind their House slate. This poor performance is not the result of Democrats having negative coattails. On the contrary, the result is an interesting implication of institutional balancing. When the Democrats control the House of Representatives, the voters, knowing that the Democrats are very likely to retain control, punish their presidential candidates. Thus, the fact that Jimmy Carter ran behind the congressional ticket in 1976 cannot be directly interpreted as indicating that Carter was a weak candidate who had no coattails. According to our model, Carter was expected to run behind his ticket.

The midterm House vote

Figures 9.1 and 9.2 also illustrate the balancing reflected in the midterm cycle. The midterm line is based on our system restricted estimates for the midterm House vote shown in table 9.6. In figure 9.1, the midterm vote is always substantially below the on-year vote, since the Republicans are always forecast to retain the White House when they have over 40 percent of the previous House vote and normal growth occurs. In figure 9.2, the

Table 9.6. *Midterm elections House vote equation*

Variable	Coefficient	(1) Unrestricted	(2) Equation Restricted	(3) System Restricted
Constant	κ_0	1.398 (0.20)	-1.422 (-0.22)	-1.418 (-0.22)
Republican Incumbent	κ_1	0.240 (0.21)	—	—
Previous House Vote	κ_2	0.939 (7.63)	0.950 (8.18)	0.950 (8.18)
Military Mobilization	κ_3	-0.369 (-0.34)	—	—
Instrumented Growth	κ_4	0.090 (0.78)	—	—
Current Growth Shock	κ_5	0.181 (0.60)	—	—
Residual Variance	σ^2_{hm}	4.753 (2.99)	—	—
	$R^2 = 0.792$			

Note: See note to Table 9.3.

midterm vote is only below the on-year vote when the Democrats are strong enough at the previous midterm to retain control of the White House. For low values of the previous midterm vote, the line flips since the Democrats lose the White House but console themselves with midterm gains.

As can be seen most readily in figure 9.1, the midterm equation estimates differ substantially from those of the on-year estimates, even when the presidential shock is zero. In on-years, the predicted vote is very close to the previous on-year vote. There is no "presidential penalty" in on-years consistent with our theoretical model. This observation contrasts with the substantial loss that occurs at midterm.[22]

Like the on-year House vote, at midterm, none of the variables have significant coefficients except the lagged House vote. (See table 9.6.) A test fails to reject the hypothesis that the coefficients other than the constant and the lag are all zero.[23] Moreover, presidential coattails do not enter at midterm. Therefore, we estimated the restricted version of the model which includes only a constant and a lag. This parallels the theoretical model in that the economy and military mobilization do not enter but differs from it in the retention of the lag.

[22]For both equations, one can find a slight but statistically insignificant effect of regression to the mean.

[23]The test statistics is χ^2_4 with a value of 1.824 and a p-value of 0.768.

The midterm cycle illustrated in figures 9.1 and 9.2 clearly emerges. The predicted loss, calculated from equation (9.15), is always greater than zero. This loss ranges from 3.5 percent to 4.4 percent, depending on how well the president's party had done in the on-year House elections. For the entire range of actual on-year House votes, the loss is statistically significant since the estimated loss always exceeds twice the estimated standard deviation. The percentage of the electorate that potentially, depending on the identity of the presidential winner, shifts votes at midterm, is roughly double the predicted loss or about 8 percent. This is very close to our estimates in chapter 6 that were based on disaggregated data. The midterm House estimates thus strongly support the theoretical model.

9.7 THE DYNAMICS OF THE AMERICAN POLITICAL ECONOMY

Our empirically preferred model of the political economy comes from the system restricted estimates; that is, equations (9.3), (9.10), (9.12), (9.14) estimated jointly. Our results can be nicely summarized by looking at the steady-state dynamics of our system. What would happen if all the shocks vanished, that is, if all the random variables in the model were permanently set to zero? Would the system settle down to a consistent pattern of alternation in power or would there be a tendency for one party to rule forever?

To investigate these questions, we simulated the system, with the additional proviso that military mobilizations were always set at zero. Thus, the only source of variation is the endogenous variables of growth and election results. But because of the lagged effects of the House vote and incumbency bias in presidential elections, the dynamics are very complicated. To study them, one can begin with one party in office and an initial value for the past House vote in immediately past midterm elections. Equation (9.3) then gives the growth rate for a presidential year. The growth rate and the House vote are then substituted in (9.10) to obtain the presidential vote. The presidential vote and the past House vote are then substituted into (9.12) to obtain the on-year House vote. The winner of the presidency and (9.3) then determine the growth rate for the next four years. The on-year House vote is then substituted into (9.14) to obtain the midterm House vote. One is then ready for the next set of calculations for a four-year period. The process is repeated indefinitely.

When the process is iterated thousands of times we find, regardless of the starting values chosen, that the system settles down to a 36-year cycle, shown in figure 9.3. The length of cycles is very sensitive to parameter estimates, but the qualitative properties stated below are not.

The cycling results from the cumulative effects of midterm losses. Each midterm loss costs the party of the incumbent a larger share of the vote

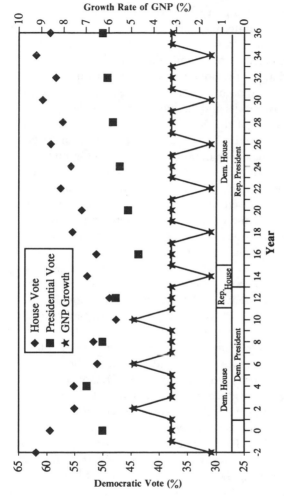

Figure 9.3. The long-run political-economic cycle. The graph shows steady-state behavior where there are no shocks to growth or voting. The cycle in growth results from the cycle in presidential voting. The cycle in presidential voting results from the cycle in legislative voting. The cycle in legislative voting results from the midterm cycle and lagged legislative voting.

than it wins back two years later. The longer a party retains control of the White House, the greater the cumulative erosion of its congressional delegation. Voters engage in more balancing as time progresses. Because the presidential vote is an increasing function of the lagged House vote, erosion of support for the incumbent party's House delegation in turn leads to a reduced presidential vote. Eventually, the presidential vote falls to a point where the incumbent's party loses the White House.

To see the process operate, we start the cycle, in figure 9.3, by picking year "0" as one of a presidential election. There is divided government, with the House dominated by the Democrats, who have a 62 percent share of the House elected at the previous midterm elections in year "−2". The economy is growing at its natural rate of 3.2 percent. The strength of the Democrats in the House results in their winning the presidency in a squeaker, with less than 51 percent of the vote. Regression to the mean results in a slight drop in the Democratic House share, which falls to 60 percent. In the second year of the new Democratic administration, growth accelerates to 4.9 percent. In spite of these good economic results and in accordance with the balancing hypothesis, the Democrats suffer a midterm reversal in the House elections and their share falls to 55 percent. The Democrats nonetheless win a second and third term and maintain unified government. But their House share continues to fall, particularly at midterm, so that by year 10, the Republicans gain control of the House as the Democratic share of the House vote falls to 48 percent. This leads to a brief two year period (mimicking the 80th Congress) of divided government with a Democratic president. Reflecting the renewed Republican House strength, the presidential elections of year 12 allow the Republicans to return to the White House. In the second year of their administration, growth falls to 1.5 percent. Although government is immediately divided under the Republicans at the first midterm election (year 14), they hold onto the White House for six consecutive elections. Finally, in year "36", the Democrats recapture the presidency. Year "36" reproduces year "0", so a cycle is achieved.

The feature of a 12-year period of Democratic control of the Presidency in the cycle is not the result of early landslide presidential victories, as occurred in 1932 and 1936. The Democrats persist for 12 years because they enter with a very strong House delegation resulting from the cumulative effects of midterm balancing over a prolonged period of Republican control of the executive. Indeed, if we simulate the model starting with the Democratic congressional share of 57 percent that was produced by the 1936 election, we find that the Republicans regain control of the White House in 1944, after which the simulation (even though the steady-state vote values are not reached immediately) always has 24 years of Republican rule followed by 12 years for the Democrats.

In summary, the Republicans control the White House for 24 years of each 36-year cycle, reflecting the bias in their favor. They are balanced by Democratic control of the House, for 32 of 36 years. Divided government is pervasive, occurring in 24 of the 36 years. There is, however, an important asymmetry. Democratic presidents have a sympathetic Congress in all but 2 of their 12 years in power; in contrast, Republican presidents face a hostile Congress for all but 2 of their 24 years in the White House. If unified government is important to policy initiatives, to step outside the model for a moment, the Democrats may be better positioned to initiate change.

A significant finding from the cycle is that the estimates are not overly influenced by the cumulative effects of the shock of the Depression and the military mobilization of World War II. The five consecutive Democratic presidential victories from 1932 to 1948 left the Democrats in control of the White House for 38 of the 74 years in our sample. Nonetheless, the estimates suggest that several Democratic victories were outliers in a system oriented to the Republicans. Similarly, one can argue that the estimates were not overly influenced by the presidential vote shocks of the Bull Moose candidacy, which led to Wilson's being in office at the start of our sample, and Watergate, which was perhaps instrumental in Carter's narrow victory.

The cycle also re-emphasizes our findings with respect to coattails and the midterm effect. Neither effect was apparent in the marginal distributions in table 9.1. In the long-run steady-state cycle, the Democrats always run behind their congressional ticket when they win the presidency and the Republicans always run ahead. In fact, Republican presidential candidates can run as much as 9 points ahead when they win and the Democrats can run as much as 10 points behind. When aggregated, the effects cancel and there is only a three-point average difference between the on-year presidential vote and on-year House vote, as seen in table 9.1.[24]

9.8 STRUCTURAL MODELS VERSUS FORECASTING

In this section, we compare our results to previous research, beginning with the voting studies, and then conclude with studies on the economic cycle.

The most cited estimates of economic voting in presidential elections are those by Fair (1978, 1982, 1988). Our work differs significantly in inspiration

---

[24]The reader may have further noted that, while in the marginal distributions, we observe only a 0.7 percent difference between the on-year and midterm House votes, our estimated effect is on the order of 3 and 4 percent. Again, this is a matter of the offsetting biases. On the three occasions when the Democrats gain control of the presidency in the steady-state cycle, the on-year House vote for the incumbent Republicans is quite low, about 40 percent in all three cases. At the next midterm elections, the Democrats are the incumbents, with a midterm vote for the incumbent party of 55 to 56 percent. (Thus, they in fact lose about 4 percent relative to the preceding on-year.) These swings result in there being little net difference in the average on-year and midterm votes for the incumbent's party.

and methodology from Fair's, and our results are also quite different. To begin with, our econometric specification is strictly tied to a theoretical model, built upon well-specified theoretical assumptions. Our goal is to test a theoretical model. Fair's objective is, instead, to produce a model of short-run forecasting; thus he makes several choices of specification which have no theoretical foundations but have the sole purpose of improving the fit by maximizing the R^2 of the regression. Not surprisingly, therefore, Fair's (1988) R^2 is higher than ours: 0.88 against 0.76. Such a high R^2 is obtained by making two theoretically unfounded specification choices. The first one is to add a linear time trend as a regressor. The second one is to include a dummy variable DEPR that marks whether the incumbent president is running for re-election.[25]

The use of the DEPR variable, while obviously good for forecasting, introduces simultaneity bias. Until the passage of the 22nd Amendment, every president was free to seek re-election. And every president who has not served for six years is still free to seek re-election. The decisions not to run of Truman in 1952 and Johnson in 1968 may have reflected knowledge of their chances; the announcements were made only in March of the election year. The other side of the coin is furnished by Truman's decision to run in 1948. His victory was one of our major forecast errors. He did better than our model predicted, given the status of the economy in 1948, the overall bias against Democrats, and Republican control of the 80th Congress. But Truman may well have had "inside information" on the presidential vote shock and elected to run. Consequently, Fair's error for this election is smaller than ours.

An important difference between our results and Fair's concerns the "long run" predictions of the two models. Fair finds a statistically significant linear trend in favor of the Democratic party. This implies that, in the long run, the Democratic party is expected to always win the presidency. On the contrary, our model predicts, both in the "short" and "long" run, alternation in office and a frequent occurrence of "divided government".

Where we agree with Fair, and many other authors, is on the effect of the economy on presidential elections. Our (restricted) coefficient of 0.80 on the GNP growth rate is within one standard deviation of Fair's (1988) estimate of 1.01. It is also similar in magnitude to Erikson's (1990) estimate on real income growth. The response of presidential vote to recent economic performance is clearly highly robust to model specification.

Another robust result is that the economy is not important in congressional elections. Using postwar data, Chappell and Suzuki (1990) report statistically significant results, but far weaker effects for Congress than for

---

[25]Fair may also obtain a better fit because he uses GNP growth over the second and third quarters rather than annual growth.

the presidency. Erikson (1990) concludes that the effect of the economy on congressional races is nearly entirely the consequence of presidential coattails. Our results are similar to Erikson's in a context that is free from the possible simultaneity bias of his estimator.

Our results on the economy can be summarized in two points. First, we do not find evidence of a pre-electoral surge in growth as predicted by Nordhaus's "political business cycle" model. This result confirms earlier findings for the United States by McCallum (1978), Hibbs (1987), Alesina (1988b), and Beck (1992). Alesina and Roubini (1992) present similar rejections of the Nordhaus model for other industrial democracies.[26] Second, we do find strong evidence of a "short-lived" partisan cycle, even in our sample starting back in 1915.

Our partisan results are consistent with earlier findings on different (i.e., shorter) samples by Alesina and Sachs (1988), Chappell and Keech (1988), Alesina (1988b), and Beck (1992). We have extended this earlier literature on several dimensions. In particular, our results on growth are obtained in a model in which, unlike in the cited literature, electoral results are endogenous. We have also extended the sample and controlled for military mobilizations.

As far as the widely cited work by Hibbs (1977, 1987) is concerned, we concur with it on one dimension and we disagree on another. We concur with Hibbs on the existence of partisan effects in macroeconomic policy. We disagree with him on the degree of persistence of partisan policies on the economy. While Hibbs (1987) claims that these effects are relatively permanent we emphasize that they are transitory.

9.9 RATIONAL RETROSPECTIVE VOTING

Before concluding this chapter it is useful to comment on our findings on rational retrospective voting. The model of administrative competence with the associated formalization of rational retrospective voting has been rejected rather unambiguously. On the other hand, our investigation of a possible difference between the predicted and the unpredicted components on growth as determinants of voting could not reject naïve retrospective voting. *The American electorate pays too much attention to the pre-electoral state of the economy to be consistent with our model of "rational retrospective voting".*

[26]Haynes and Stone (1987) claim to have found evidence of the Nordhaus "political business cycle" on GNP growth in the U.S. A careful reading of their paper, however, casts serious doubts about such a claim. In fact, they find such "evidence" only for Republican administrations. This result, in contrast to these authors' interpretation, is consistent with the model of the political cycle used in this book, rather than with the Nordhaus model.

A key question is then the following: should future research cast aside rationality when modelling retrospective voting on the economy?

We believe that the answer is "not quite" for at least three reasons. First of all, as we emphasized in the introduction of this chapter, the hypothesis of rational retrospective voting is rejected jointly with other assumptions underlying the model in which rationality is imposed. For example, and most importantly, we were forced to make, both for theoretical and econometric reasons, the strong assumption of competence affecting the economy through an MA(l) dynamic structure. Different dynamic stochastic models might lead to different findings. Second, there are only seven changes in the party holding the presidency in our sample period. Thus, the conclusions about covariances can only be viewed as tentative, because of the very few degrees of freedom. Third, we have tried to gain information about competence by analyzing the error structure in the growth time series. Using the error structure is always a relatively poor substitute for direct observation. Perhaps the voters know more than is indicated by the econometric estimates.

Indeed, understanding what the voters know and when they know it is essential to further progress in developing models of voter behavior. The model that we have tested rests on a tenuous assumption, namely that voters are able to learn competence, albeit with a one-period delay, and are able to learn current growth immediately. In contrast, assume, as seems at least as likely as this hypothesis, that the voters never succeed in distinguishing exogenous shocks from administrative competence. But say the voters believe that the performance of the economy depends on preventing the administration from shirking. The voters adopt the strategy of always punishing for poor economic performance. As a result, no administration shirks for fear of being punished, and the performance of the economy depends solely on exogenous shocks. In this scenario, retrospective voting is *rational*, yet we would find no evidence of variations in competence in the growth time series.

A related issue concerning voter rationality (or lack thereof) is the degree of forgetfulness. Namely it is often argued that the American electorate has a short memory: only the state of the economy immediately before an election matters. For example, Fair (1988) argues that the time horizon which matters in presidential elections is not even one year, but only two quarters before the election. A conclusion which is often drawn from this kind of evidence is that, since the American electorate forgets the past so easily, it cannot satisfy any rationality condition.

Things are, however, not so simple. Consider, for example, the first Reagan administration. In 1981–82 this administration experienced the worst recession in the postwar period (see table 7.1). In 1984, instead, growth was very high and president Reagan was re-elected with a landslide.

This outcome can be interpreted in two ways. One view holds that the electorate had already forgotten in 1984 the recession of 1982; thus the American voter is shortsighted and forgetful. The second view argues that it was rational not to punish Reagan for the 1981–82 recession. In fact, the recession was the expected result of partisan politics. The voters always *expect* low inflation and a downturn at the beginning of Republican administrations. The general point is that even the observation of short voter memory is not a definite rejection of rationality.

In summary, our results are consistent with naïve retrospective voting: a "rational" electorate should not pay so much attention to short-run economic growth as the American voters do. However, formal tests of rationality are complex and not always conclusive. Therefore we feel that our results should not shut the door on further theoretical and empirical research on rational retrospective voting.

9.10 CONCLUSIONS

Our empirical analysis has been successful on two crucial points which are the core of our theoretical framework. The first is that the polarization of the two major parties results in elections having important partisan effects on the economy. The second is that presidential and congressional elections are linked by the balancing effort of the electorate. The estimate of a bias toward Republicans in presidential elections and an offsetting bias to Democrats in on-year congressional elections supports the basic theoretical notions concerning balancing, split tickets, and divided government. The midterm cycle appears as a further instance of balancing.

We have largely confirmed and extended the results of Alesina and Sachs (1988), Chappell and Keech (1988), and Alesina (1988b) on the impact of elections of the economy, of Alesina and Rosenthal (1989) and Erikson (1990) on the midterm congressional cycle, and of Erikson (1989, 1990) on the impact of the economy on presidential and congressional elections. Military mobilizations affect voting by influencing the economy and hence presidential voting which in turn influences on-year congressional voting. Unlike earlier work, our estimation of a system of equations addresses endogeneity bias; moreover, our estimation holds for 1915 onward rather than simply the postwar period as most of the previous literature.

Even though our empirical results support the bulk of our theory, there are troubling findings that need to be addressed. Two, discussed at greater length in the introduction, are the persistence of seemingly naïve retrospective voting and the persistence of a midterm cycle even when preceded by predictable presidential landslides. Another is the bias to incumbent parties contained directly in the estimates of the presidential vote equation and in the highly significant role played by the lagged House vote in all equations.

Incumbency is clearly important in American politics; our empirical results confirm this fact. The incumbency advantage is not inconsistent with moderating behavior, as argued particularly in chapter 6. However, our theoretical model does not explicitly incorporate it; this is certainly an important extension to our theoretical work.

In summary, we have presented a unified rational choice model of national elections and the macroeconomy. The empirical tests of the model led, on the one hand, to rejection of rational retrospective voting but, on the other, to strengthened support for rational responses to electoral uncertainty via both the midterm electoral cycle and the partisan business cycle. Reconciling these contrasting results on rationality is an excellent topic for future theoretical and empirical research. While we sense we have built a better mousetrap, many dragons are still to be slain.

Appendix to chapter 9

Data used in the four-equation model

Year	GNP growth	Vote for Incumbent's Party		Incumbent	Lagged House Vote for Incumbent's Party	Military Mobilization
		President	House			
1914	-2.358					
1915	6.637			D		.005566
1916	7.279	51.626	48.881	D	50.338	.002502
1917	-.548			D		.448063
1918	5.053		45.096	D	48.881	2.183333
1919	1.080			D ·		-1.684615
1920	-1.146	36.190	37.957	D	45.096	-.800154
1921	-2.388			R		.034373
1922	5.708		53.600	R	62.043	-.111212
1923	12.430			R		-.024705
1924	2.919	65.259	57.709	R	53.600	.008089
1925	2.424			R		-.011167
1926	6.289		58.428	R	57.709	-.007165
1927	0.962			R		-.001215
1928	1.190	58.789	57.162	R	58.428	-.000899
1929	5.849			R		.001133
1930	-9.887		54.129	R	57.162	-.001417
1931	-8.894			R		-.004033
1932	-14.406	40.825	43.126	R	54.129	-.007715
1933	-2.124			D		-.001951
1934	7.384		56.184	D	56.874	.001152
1935	7.793			D		.002584
1936	13.219	62.487	58 476	D	56.184	.029214
1937	4.878			D		.014939
1938	-4.576		50.815	D	58.476	.006607
1939	7.593			D		.006399
1940	7.563	54.974	52.967	D	50.815	.091453
1941	16.263			D		1.003405
1942	17.220		47.662	D	52.967	1.511431

Appendix to chapter 9 (*cont'd*)

Year	GNP growth	Vote for Incumbent's Party		Incumbent	Lagged House Vote for Incumbent's Party	Military Mobilization
		President	House			
1943	16.664			D		3.753306
1944	7.863	53.776	51.706	D	47.662	1.659954
1945	-1.886			D		.388996
1946	-21.117		45.272	D	51.706	-6.516724
1947	-2.792			D		-1.048673
1948	3.862	52.326	53.241	D	45.272	-1.112196
1949	.027			D		.096378
1950	8.194		50.041	D	53.241	-.119999
1951	9.842			D		1.143288
1952	3.826	44.623	50.156	D	50.041	.210787
1953	3.929			R		-.088670
1954	-1.340		47.272	R	49.844	-.194568
1955	5.408			R		-.257535
1956	2.033	57.746	48.797	R	47.272	-.107784
1957	1.658			R		-.035572
1958	-.770		43.603	R	48.797	-.138855
1959	5.676			R		-.085531
1960	2.198	49.890	45.029	R	43.603	-.037640
1961	2.573			D		-.018176
1962	5.172		52.327	D	54.971	.153052
1963	4.025			D		-.078579
1964	5.201	61.345	57.502	D	52.327	-.026456
1965	5.631			D		-.033866
1966	5.621		51.327	D	57.502	.207652
1967	2.817			D		.125370
1968	4.064	49.593	50.922	D	51.327	.068315
1969	2.410			R		-.060610
1970	-.293		45.775	R	49.078	-.211919
1971	2.780			R		-.187811
1972	4.858	61.813	47.335	R	45.775	-.200681
1973	5.068			R		-.043546
1974	-.540		41.323	R	47.335	-.052222
1975	-1.265			R		-.025662
1976	4.771	48.930	42.754	R	41.323	-.030416
1977	4.561			D		-.012734
1978	5.158		54.322	D	57.246	-.015770
1979	2.448			D		-.025719
1980	-.166	44.711	51.286	D	54.322	-.000148
1981	1.917			R		.004588
1982	-2.582		43.782	R	48.714	.001910
1983	3.510			R		-.002841
1984	6.559	59.155	47.220	R	43.782	-.002072
1985	3.295			R		-.003170
1986	2.807		45.005	R	47.220	-.001156
1987	3.311			R		0
1988	3.803	53.939	45.998	R	45.005	0

10

---

*Partisan economic policy and divided government
in parliamentary democracies*

10.1 INTRODUCTION

Partisan cycles in economic policy and institutional balancing are not a
uniquely American phenomenon. On the contrary, the ideas developed in
this volume with specific reference to the United States have a much broader
appeal, and illuminate the political economy of other democracies. In
different institutional settings political and economic variables interconnect
in different ways, but this chapter argues that the concepts of polarization,
balancing, and partisan cycles can explain important aspects of the political
economy of parliamentary democracies.

First of all, long periods of divided government are hardly an American
monopoly. On the contrary, in parliamentary democracies cases of unified
government are rare. Laver and Shepsle (1990) appropriately define a
government to be unified "whenever a single party both forms the political
executive and commands a majority in the legislature". In the period
1945–82 fewer than 15 percent of the governments of parliamentary
democracies satisfied this definition.[1] All the other governments were not
unified: at least two parties were needed to participate either in the
government or in the parliamentary majority supporting the government.
Therefore, if one views coalition government as an example of division of
power, divided government is the norm rather than the exception. Based
upon this observation, Fiorina (1991) argues that Downs (1957) overplays
the contrast between the American two party system and European coalition governments: divided government in America and coalition governments in Europe have much more in common than it would appear at first
sight.

In addition, coalition government is not the only possible form of power
sharing: an additional one is the balancing of different levels of government.

---

[1]Strom (1984) and Laver and Shepsle (1991).

243

Regional, state, provincial, and municipal governments may all differ from the national government in their political composition and orientation, so that a large fraction of the citizens of a country really face two (or more) ideologically different administrations. Such situations are far from unusual in Germany (Brady, Lohmann, and Rivers (1992)), France, Italy, and elsewhere. In the United States, divided government occurs at the state level as well, and may interact with the institutional balancing at the national level (Fiorina (1992), Alesina, Fiorina, and Rosenthal (1991)).

Finally, the case of France is probably the closest to the United States, because the president, as well as the legislature, is directly elected by the citizens. Twice, from 1986 to 1988 and since 1993, the legislative elections have produced a right-of-center government while a Socialist president remained in office. These periods of *cohabitation* are similar to divided government in the United States.[2] In Portugal, also, a popularly elected president has come from a different party than the prime minister, whose selection reflects national legislative elections.

Once established that division of government is the norm rather than the exception, the next question is whether division of power balances polarized parties. Thus, we begin by asking whether political parties are polarized and policy motivated in economically developed democracies. Addressing this question in detail would require a volume in itself, but to make a very long story very short, we argue that the answer is yes. We agree with Laver and Schofield's (1990) view that one cannot explain the observed pattern of coalition government dynamics with a pure "office-seeking" assumption. On the contrary, "ideology" and partisan forces have to play an important role. With specific reference to economic policy, recent research[3] has shown that economic performance in other nations echoes the evidence on the United States that was presented in chapters 7 and 9. Specifically, the "rational partisan theory" which we found so successful for the United States is also appropriate for a large number of industrial democracies. Similarly the absence of evidence supporting an opportunistic cycle of growth and unemployment is, once again, not a peculiarity of the United States but a very general observation.

In summary, divided governments and partisan politics in general, and partisan economic cycles in particular, are the norm rather than the exception in parliamentary democracies. The final step, which is more difficult, is to argue that the electorate uses institutional balancing and division of power to purposely moderate policy outcomes.

Formal empirical research on this point is just in its embryonic stage.

---

[2] For a dissenting opinion see Pierce (1991).

[3] Alt (1985), Lewis-Beck (1988), Alesina (1989), Paldam (1989a, b), Alesina and Roubini (1992), Alesina, Cohen, and Roubini (1992, 1993).

Brady, Lohmann, and Rivers (1992), for instance, find evidence in the German case which is similar to the balancing midterm cycle in the United States. In Germany, the chancellor and the cabinet, that is, the executive arm of the national government, is chosen by the directly elected lower house of the legislature. Seats in the upper house of the German legislature are not directly elected but filled by Land (state) governments. Brady, Lohmann, and Rivers (1992) document how votes swing in Land elections to the parties which are not in the national government.

This chapter is organized as follows. Section 10.2 reviews the literature on partisan economic policy in parliamentary democracies. Section 10.3 discusses coalition governments and minority governments as examples of divided governments. Section 10.4 addresses the issue of partisan differences between sub-national and national governments. Section 10.5 examines the recent experience in France as the closest approximation of the United States case. The last section concludes.

10.2 PARTISAN CYCLES IN PARLIAMENTARY DEMOCRACIES

The United States is not the only country experiencing partisan cycles of GNP growth, unemployment, and inflation: these cycles are common in other democracies, particularly those with either a pure two-party system or with "two blocks" of parties.

In his seminal paper on partisan business cycles, Hibbs (1977) argued that in parliamentary democracies social democratic parties (and, more generally, parties of the political left) are associated with permanently lower unemployment and permanently higher inflation than parties of the right. However, Alt (1985) observed that partisan differences in the unemployment rate are not permanent but tend to occur only for a short period immediately after a change of government. Since Alt analyzed thirteen economies which are both small (relative to the United States) and open to international trade, he included the effects of international business cycles and world trade on unemployment. An example illustrates why this point is so important. The Socialist Francois Mitterand was elected president of France in May 1981 exactly at the beginning of a worldwide downturn, which culminated in the deep American recession of 1982. The French economy grew, but at a rate below 2 percent in the eighteen months which followed the election. This growth rate was not very high if taken in isolation, leading to questions about the partisan effect. However, compared to those of its major trading partners, the French growth rate was one of the highest for the period: this relatively high rate supports the partisan theory.

Alesina (1989) and, especially, Alesina and Roubini (1992) systematically test several political business cycles models of growth, unemployment, and inflation in a sample of eighteen democracies for the last thirty years. They find widespread support for the "rational partisan theory". Partisan differences in real GNP growth and unemployment are short lived. Although transitory, these differences are substantial; Alesina and Roubini (1992) calculate that eighteen months after a change of government toward the left, the rate of growth of GNP is about 2.6 percent higher than it would be after eighteen months following a change of government toward the right. This value is the average for eight countries with either a pure two-party system or a "two-block" system.[4] The analogous figure for the entire sample of eighteen democracies is about 1.8 percent. As for unemployment, the similar comparison between the aftermath of a left- or a right-wing change in government reveals a difference of about 3 percentage points in the unemployment rate. Inflation is typically higher with left-wing governments than with right-wing governments. Alesina and Roubini (1992) calculate that inflation has been about 2.5 percent higher with the left in office.[5]

These results on growth, unemployment, and inflation in industrial democracies are supportive of the "rational partisan theory" presented for the Unites States in chapter 7.

On the contrary, the same authors (Alesina and Roubini (1992)) find virtually no evidence in the growth and unemployment time series that supports the "opportunistic" political business cycle à la Nordhaus. GNP growth does not appear to be unusually high (and unemployment unusually low) in the period immediately preceding an election. Once again, the same result found for the United States holds in other industrial democracies.

An interesting difference between the United States and almost all the other OECD democracies concerns the timing of elections. The occurrence of elections at irrevocably fixed dates in the United States is an exception, rather than a rule. In fact, in most countries the executive can call early elections. This option is frequently used. Ito (1990) notes that the possibility of calling early elections may generate a different form of opportunistic behavior. The executive can call general elections when, for whatever reason, the economy is doing well: there is no need to manipulate the economy if the date of elections can be chosen at an appropriate time. Ito (1990) presents favorable evidence for this hypothesis for Japan, but Alesina, Cohen, and

[4]These countries are: the United States, the United Kingdom, France, Germany, Australia, New Zealand, Sweden, and Canada.

[5]This figure refers to an average for the eight countries mentioned in the previous footnote, and for the sample 1971–87. This sample captures the period of floating exchange rates in which inflation rates in different countries were not as closely linked to each other by the fixed rate system, prevalent in the pre-1971 period. The same figure for the sample period 1960–87 is slightly smaller.

Roubini (1993) fail to find any supportive evidence in any other country.[6]

In summary, the evidence for an "opportunistic cycle" on growth is as weak in OECD democracies as it is in the United States.

Alesina, Cohen, and Roubini (1992, 1993) confirm the absence of an opportunistic cycle in the "real" economy in OECD economies, but, parallel to the evidence presented by Tufte (1978) for the United States, they find some evidence of manipulations of monetary and fiscal policy instruments before elections. More precisely, they find that the government budget tends to be relatively loose in election years, and, to some extent, monetary policy relatively expansionary. However, these authors note that these political cycles on monetary and fiscal policy instruments are rather small and fairly irregular. These short term (and not very large) budget cycles are consistent with "rational" versions of the opportunistic cycle, as in Rogoff and Sibert (1988) and Rogoff (1990). According to these models, a rational electorate uncovers and punishes opportunistic behavior that is very overt, frequent, and extensive. Thus, only occasional short term budget and monetary manipulations are politically feasible rather than cycles of growth and unemployment extending over several years.

Finally, Lewis-Beck (1988) confirms that economic conditions strongly influence electoral results in parliamentary democracies. High growth, low unemployment, and low inflation are good news for incumbent governments and their parties. Empirical results with regard to the economy's influence on voting behavior vary across countries. In certain countries and time periods certain economic variables may be more important than others in influencing voting, but the basic proposition that the state of the economy in the period immediately preceding an election is important for voting behavior is generally supported by the evidence.[7]

In summary, the reader will have noted the remarkable similarity between other OECD democracies and the United States. *The United States is not an exception: its political cycles are very similar to those of many other industrial democracies.*

The important distinction is not between the United States and the other industrial democracies, but between two-party or "two-blocks" systems and large coalition governments. In fact, Alesina and Roubini (1992) find that partisan cycles are common in countries either with a two party system (United States, United Kingdom, New Zealand, Australia) or with clear right and left "blocks" (for instance, France, Germany, and Sweden) where

---

[6]Evidence is hard to find partly because early elections are also called when the economy is doing poorly but there is little hope of an improvement in the short term. A circumstance of this type appears to underlie Spanish Prime Minister Gonzales's call for early elections in 1993.

[7]See Lewis-Beck (1988) and the vast empirical evidence surveyed in that volume.

it is relatively easy to identify changes of governments from left to right and vice versa. In contrast, partisan cycles cannot be easily detected in countries typically run by large coalition governments, such as Italy, Belgium, or Austria. *A fortiori*, partisan cycles have not been observed in countries such as Japan, where one party held power for forty years, and there was, until 1993, little expectation of opposition success.

In proportional electoral systems, which often necessitate coalition government, sharp changes in economic policy are less frequent than, say, in the United Kingdom with the alternation in office of Conservative and Labor Parties. Can we then conclude that coalition governments bring more stability in economic policymaking? In some sense the answer is yes, because coalition governments avoid sharp partisan changes. On the other hand, coalition governments may bring "gridlock" and legislative inaction. In chapter 1, we stated that we would not make the costs of inaction a major focus of this book. It is nonetheless important to point out that recent theoretical (Alesina and Drazen (1991), Spolaore (1992)) and empirical (Roubini and Sachs (1989a, b) and Grilli, Masciandaro, and Tabellini (1991)) research suggests that when coalitions become too large and fragmented, they are associated with undesirable economic outcomes, such as large budget deficits. Each member of a coalition government has, in practice, a "veto power" which can be used to prevent the imposition of a fiscal burden on a specific constituency or group. As a result, coalition governments experience much difficulty in adopting "tough" budget measures.[8] Coalition governments do not necessarily *create* budget deficits, but once the deficits build up (for instance as a result of adverse economic shocks which reduce tax revenues), they delay the adjustment. This situation is modelled as a "war of attrition" in Alesina and Drazen (1991), who argue that fiscal stabilizations are delayed until the countervailing vetoes of different political groups are overcome, because further delays are too costly. Spolaore (1992) shows that the length of the delay in fiscal adjustment is increasing in the number of members of the coalition government.

The empirical results of Roubini and Sachs (1989a, b) are consistent with this "war of attrition" model. They show that, after the 1973–74 oil shock, countries led by large coalition (or minority coalition) governments had much more trouble adjusting than single-party governments or two-member coalition governments. The two countries with the highest debt to GNP ratios are Belgium and Italy: both countries have proportional representation and have always had (in the last twenty years) large and unstable coalition governments.

In summary, one can identify a trade-off: Majoritarian electoral systems

---

[8]See Alt and Lowry (1992) and Poterba (1992) for similar discussions concerning state governments in the United States.

with single party governments create partisan cycles but ensure relatively swift action and quick fiscal adjustments when needed. Coalition governments ensure "moderation" by avoiding partisan cycles, but create status quo biases and delays in the adoption of necessary fiscal adjustment programs.[9] This trade-off between single-party and coalition governments is essentially the same discussion (perhaps magnified) which is taking place in the United States over not only the pros and cons of divided versus unified government but also the dispersal of power, within Congress, from the party leadership to the heads of committees and subcommittees.

10.3 COALITION GOVERNMENTS

The previous section has established that partisan politics is important and that the degree of policy polarization and partisan cycles depends upon the structure of coalitions. In this section we further investigate the analogy between coalition governments in parliamentary democracies and divided government in the United States.

In parliamentary democracies with coalition governments, one can identify two types of division of political control. The first "involves separate and distinctive partisan control of legislative and executive powers" (Laver and Shepsle (1991), p. 252). The second involves power sharing between members of a coalition government which holds the executive and a majority in the legislature.

A typical example of the first type of division of power is minority governments with a single party holding the executive. In this case, the party holding the executive needs to find additional legislative support to pass and implement legislation. In this situation, the preferences of the party holding the executive *and* the composition of the legislature determine policy, as in our model of the United States.

Single party minority governments are the most directly comparable cases of divided government in parliamentary democracies with the United States case. A socialist government obtaining some support from center parties is analogous to Ronald Reagan's relying on defections from "Boll Weevil" Democrats. This type of government is not rare: according to Strom (1984), almost 25 percent of governments in a sample of parliamentary democracies for the period of 1945–82 were single party minority governments.[10]

---

[9]For example, only in 1993 did Italy adopt a modest fiscal adjustment plan after at least a decade since the debt problem had become obvious to every observer. In contrast, the United Kingdom, which had its own economic difficulties, never had a debt problem in the post-1973 period.

[10]Minority governments are, on average, more short lived than majority governments. Thus, if rather than the number of governments, one would count "years in office" the share of minority governments would be much lower but still not insignificant.

The typical example of the second kind of division of power is a coalition government with a majority in the legislature. In this case the coalition government does not need outside legislative support to form a majority, but compromise within the coalition implies shared control. Strom (1984) reports that half of the governments in his sample described above are of this type.

More generally, the two types of power sharing (executive–legislative division of control, and within-coalition division) often coexist for several reasons. First, one observes cases of "multiparty minority governments" (about 13 percent of the cases, according to Strom (1984)). These are governments which require intra-executive coalition bargaining *and* additional legislative support to govern. Second, even a coalition government with a majority in the legislature may have to be concerned with the minority parties. This argument parallels our comparison of "proportional" versus "majoritarian" models in chapter 3: it does make a difference whether the ruling coalition has a legislative majority of 51 percent or of 85 percent. To put it differently, whether a government is "viable" (i.e., can effectively govern) depends upon the composition of the legislature (Laver and Schofield (1990)). Third, the relative weight in the intra-party bargaining at the executive level is strongly influenced by the composition of the legislature. For instance, a minority member of the coalition government, given the composition of the legislature, may hold a credible threat of breaking the coalition and joining a feasible alternative one. In this situation, the minority member of the coalition government may obtain a disproportionate weight at the bargaining table.[11] For this reason, Laver and Schofield (1990) note that one should not expect that the median preferences within the government prevail all the time. The policy outcome will depend upon the composition of the legislature, as in our model. Fourth, there may be more than two influential parties, even in "majoritarian" systems. For example, during the first *cohabitation* in France, the Gaullist Prime Minister, Jacques Chirac, had not only to deal with a Socialist president but also to maintain a coalition with the traditional right (Giscard) in the legislature (Tuppen (1991)).

In summary, division of power is the norm rather than the exception. In Strom's (1984) sample, unified government is observed in less than 15 percent of the cases.[12] Outside of the United Kingdom, it is extremely rare to observe a single party government with a legislative majority.

---

[11]The small religious parties in Israel and the Socialist Party in Italy until 1993 are two good examples.

[12]As argued in note 10, simple party majority governments may last longer, on average, than coalition governments (Grilli, Masciandaro, and Tabellini (1991)). Thus, in terms of years in office, the share of single party majority governments in higher. This type of government is, in any case, much less frequent than coalition governments.

The next question is how do the voters participate in creating divided government? Can we claim, as we did for the United States, that the electorate, in the aggregate, sees division of power as a device to achieve policy moderation?

Downs (1957) emphasized a sharp distinction between voting behavior in two-party and multi-party systems. He argues that the voters have a much easier time in two-party systems: they simply cast their ballot for the party they prefer, hoping that this party will get a majority and govern. On the other hand, Downs (1957) claims that in multi-party systems with coalition governments, the voters are under pressure to behave irrationally and have a much harder time figuring out how their vote will translate into a governing coalition. In fact, given a certain distribution of shares and seats, different coalition governments may emerge.

Fiorina (1991) convincingly challenges Downs on this point by arguing that in the United States the voters face the possibility of "coalition government" as in multi-party parliamentary democracies; thus, if the American electorate considers that policy outcomes are the results of the interaction between the executive and the legislature, it may not have an "easier" time than the electorate of parliamentary democracies. Specifically, this volume has shown how the rational voter in the United States must be "conditionally sincere" rather than "unconditionally sincere". That is, when voting in, say, the legislative elections the voter has to take into account the expected result of the presidential election. A rational voter is required to do more than simply vote in every election for his favorite party, no matter what. The following simple example hints that in a multi-party parliamentary regime, the voters may behave in ways which resemble the American voter of this volume.

Consider a three-party system, in which the three parties are located in a segment $[0, 1]$. Party L locates at $\frac{1}{4}$; party C at $\frac{1}{2}$; and party R at $\frac{2}{3}$, as in

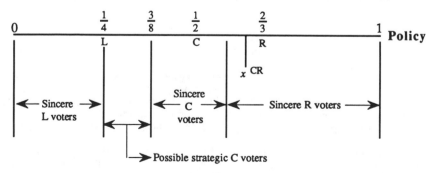

Figure 10.1. A three-party system. If the voters expect a center-right government dominated by R, leftists have an incentive to support the center party, C.

figure 10.1. If the voters are uniformly distributed on the $[0, 1]$ segment and vote "sincerely" party L obtains $\frac{3}{8}$ of the vote, party C $\frac{5}{24}$, and party R $\frac{5}{12}$.

Suppose that, for whatever reason, it is expected that with this distribution of shares, the C and R parties would form a majority coalition. The policy outcome of this coalition would be located somewhere in between $\frac{1}{2}$ and $\frac{2}{3}$, which are the two ideal policies of parties C and R respectively. Let us say that the policy outcome is point x^{CR} in figure 10.1; this point is closer to $\frac{2}{3}$ since party R has a larger share than party C.[13]

Consider now the voters with ideal points below but close to $\frac{3}{8}$, which is the point equidistant between the ideal policies of parties L and C. Under an assumption of sincerity, these voters choose L. However, if they switch to C, they can reinforce the more "moderate" member of the center–right coalition and move the policy outcome x^{CR} toward the left. In other words, these voters choose to "moderate" the coalition by being strategic, in the sense that they do *not* vote for the party with the ideal point closer to their own.[14]

The behavior of these voters is similar to the American "moderating" voters of this volume. The left voters who vote C are reminiscent of the left-of-center voters in our model who vote R for the legislature to balance the expected D president. In both cases, these voters choose a party which is *not* the closest to their ideal point in order to balance the policy outcome of the coalition government.

The preceding discussion is not even close to a fully specified model. We did not even begin to address the issue of how coalitions are formed in three- or more party systems, and how the voters would behave given how coalitions are formed.[15] However, the simple point that we have made here is that in multi-party systems, the voters have a strong incentive to be "strategic" in the sense of keeping an eye on how to balance a coalition rather than voting purely on the basis of which party offers the preferred platform.

Casual observations suggest that this type of "strategic" voting is not un-

---

[13]Note, however, that this may not in fact happen: party C can threaten to join Party L in an alternative coalition; this threat would impose policy closer to party C's ideal policy.

[14]If it is absolutely certain that the governing coalition will be CR, then every voter on the left of $\frac{1}{2}$ would want to vote C. However, with some uncertainty about electoral outcomes, as in chapter 4, this result would not hold. Alternatively, one may argue that a strong opposition may also influence policy from the legislative floor. Therefore, the most extreme left voters might choose to vote L even though they expect their party to be out of the government.

[15]See Austin-Smith and Banks (1988) for a formal model of three-party systems. In a series of papers Laver and Shepsle (1990, 1991) have studied the allocation of cabinet chairs in multiparty legislatures. This problem has also been addressed by Laver and Schofield (1990), who also model voter behavior.

common. In electoral campaigns center–right parties often target extreme right-wing voters with the message that, rather than wasting a vote on the extreme right, these voters should reinforce the moderate right, which may have to bargain in a coalition government with the moderate left.[16] Alternatively, with similar argument Socialist parties have pursued the Communist electorate.[17] A more precise estimate of the extent and characteristics of this strategic and balancing vote is beyond the scope of this chapter, but it is an excellent topic of future research.

In summary, this section has made the point that if one looks closely, the American two-party system is much closer to a multi-party system than what is usually thought. The two key features which these systems have in common are: (i) policymaking by compromise between two (or more) parties; (ii) the incentive for voters to influence this compromise by an appropriate choice in the ballot box.

10.4 SUB-NATIONAL GOVERNMENTS AS BALANCING INSTITUTIONS

In most democracies, the everyday life of the citizens is influenced not only by the national government but by various regional, state, provincial, cantonal, county, municipal, or other form of sub-national government. The allocation of power between national and sub-national governments varies greatly from country to country. At one extreme one finds Germany, characterized by a Federalist system in which the Land (state) governments have much autonomy from the national government. Somewhere in between is Italy, where reform in the 1970s substantially enhanced regional autonomy (Putnam, 1993). At the opposite extreme one finds France, with a very centralized system of government. In cases where sub-national units have substantial power and autonomy, voters can moderate the policies of the national government by tilting to the opposition parties in sub-national elections. This strategy may result in different parties predominating in different levels of government.

However, the simple observation that sub-national governments are not controlled by the same parties as the national governments is not necessarily an indication of balancing behavior. Even if all voters were voting sincerely for their most preferred party, non-identical governments could result because of the distribution of the electorate into geographic units; the national majority is not necessarily the majority of the majorities in the

---

[16]An example is the Christian Democratic Party in Italy, pursuing, until 1993, the conservative electorate voting for the Social Movement (MSI).

[17]The Italian (until 1993) and French Socialist Parties are good examples.

units.[18] Non-identical governments could also result because the units used different electoral systems than are used in national elections.

Balancing in sub-national elections thus cannot be inferred by simply comparing, for example, who is in power in Bonn (or Berlin) to who is in power in Munich or Hamburg. Balancing behavior requires that some of the voters who have favored the parties running the national government systematically turn against them in sub-national elections. Since national and sub-national elections are typically *not* held at the same time, the kind of balancing behavior described above resembles the American midterm cycle. Furthermore, the signalling interpretation of the midterm cycle (chapter 6) is quite appropriate for sub-national balancing. Observers often interpret a setback in sub-national elections of the parties in office at the national level as a negative "confidence vote" on the national government. Significant defeats in these elections may send a strong signal for change at the national level. This signalling effect may be important even in countries where the actual autonomy and legislative power of sub-national institutions are limited.

A similar argument based upon signalling is often mentioned with reference to the European Parliament, whose members are elected in the twelve nations comprising the European Economic Community. The European Parliament, at least thus far, has had a very limited influence in important legislative matters. Since opposition parties, from the Labor party in Britain to the National Front in France, have done well in these elections, it may well be the case that the European elections are used by the electorate of various countries to express approval or disapproval of their own national governments.

A careful empirical study of moderating electoral behavior in various countries requires the specification of appropriate statistical models with joint estimation of the outcomes of sub-national and national elections. The work would be similar to the joint model of presidential and congressional elections we presented in chapter 9, but the actual specification and implementation of the statistical model should take into account country specific instructional features: the same model would probably *not* be appropriate for all parliamentary democracies.

In a recent paper, Brady, Lohmann, and Rivers (1992) study moderating behavior in West Germany for the period 1961–1989. They convincingly argue that West Germany is a particularly appropriate case to study for several reasons. First, Land (state) governments have substantial autonomy from the national government; thus they provide a meaningful "balance of power". Second, and this is peculiar to Germany, the Land select members

---

[18]The problem is analogous to the possibility, in the United States, that a majority winner in the Electoral College may differ from the plurality winner in the popular vote.

of the Bundesrat, one of the two legislative chambers. (The other one, the Bundestag, is directly elected by the people with a "corrected" proportional system). Therefore, the Land elections can balance the national government in three ways: (i) by creating different legislative majorities at the Land level, alternative to the national government; (ii) by "signalling", with an electoral downturn of the parties in office at the national level; (iii) by reinforcing the opposition parties in the Bundesrat.

Brady, Lohmann, and Rivers (1992) point out that the federal structure and, we may add, the opportunities for balancing and moderation, were deliberate constitutional choices dictated by the catastrophic experience of the excessively centralized Third Reich.

They begin by noting that the previous literature on German elections has concluded that "it is almost a law that the governing coalition at the national level loses votes in the Land elections following the national election – only to be reelected with a relatively high vote share in the subsequent national election". This observation closely resembles the American midterm cycle.

Brady, Lohmann, and Rivers (1992) then present a statistical analysis of national and Land elections. They focus upon three determinants of voting behavior: party identification, based upon psychological or other "structural" factors, retrospective voting, and moderating behavior. The results concerning the third determinant of voting are those most relevant for us, but it is worth mentioning that they find much support for retrospective voting, in line with our and others' results for the United States.[19]

They find a very close relationship between the preceding national election and the subsequent Land election. The incumbent party at the national level consistently loses votes in Land elections. This finding is robust to several statistical tests and survives when other determinants of voting behavior are controlled for. The authors conclude that their results on moderating behavior in Germany are very consistent with our findings on the United States.

Studies for other countries along the lines of this paper by Brady, Lohmann, and Rivers (1992) are not available yet. A very fruitful area of research in comparative voting behavior would be a more systematic look at moderating behavior in several industrial democracies.

Sub-national balancing does seem to be prevalent elsewhere. For example, the leader of Portugal's Socialists, Antonio Guterres, tried to enhance his party's chance in recent local elections by claiming the outcome would not

---

[19]This result contradicts earlier literature cited by Brady, Lohmann, and Rivers (1992), which reported a relatively small retrospective voting in German elections.

have much effect on national politics in contrast to the tactics of the Social Democrats, the party of the prime minister. (Thus, the rhetoric dwelt on something like the α parameter in previous chapters.) Guterres claimed, "Aware that they face an overwhelming defeat, the Social Democrats are trying to convince the country that the municipal election could affect the stability of the government in the hope that this will play in their favor."[20]

10.5 THE FRENCH COHABITATION

From 1986 to 1988 and in 1993 France was led by a Socialist President and had a legislative majority, a government, and a prime minister all belonging to the center–right coalition of the Gaullists (RPR) and Conservatives (UDF). Can this *cohabitation* be interpreted as the French version of "divided government"? A strongly affirmative answer to this question was provided by Andre Fontaine in the first issue of *Le Monde* appearing after the elections of June 5, 1988, which marked the end of the first *cohabitation* period:

...one ought to ask why, after Francois Mitterand was elected by such a wide margin, he wasn't able to find more of the French prepared to give him the solid majority he would need to govern...

Another factor, which might, ought to, have had a role, relates to a fairly widespread distrust of the men and parties who contend for power, resulting from the feeling – so justified – that, relative to the great challenges of the end of this millennium, the internal quarrels of the French are really suicidal. This feeling was the basis of the popularity of *cohabitation*, making hegemony by either the right or the left impossible and constraining them to a minimum of cooperation in the national interest. Something similar takes place in America, with its system of checks and balances and its goal of having a bipartisan foreign policy. Another example is Portugal where the çitizens have elected, over a brief period in the last few years, a rightist legislature, a leftist president, Mario Soares, and, again, after it was dissolved, a rightist legislature.[21]

This section argues that, with qualifications, Fontaine's endorsement of *cohabitation* as balancing is correct.

In the Fifth French Republic, the President is directly elected and *shares* with the Prime Minister and his government the executive power. Given that the president and the legislature are chosen in separate elections, the possibility of divided control immediately arises. The right won the first presidential election in 1965 and held the presidency until 1981. These victories were twice "moderated" by extremely close legislative elections in 1967 and 1973 that were almost won by a Socialist–Communist alliance.

---

[20]Quoted by Peter Wise in "Portugal Socialists sense party victory", *Financial Times*, December 13, 1993.
[21]June 7, 1988. Authors' translation.

The legislative elections of 1988, called by President Mitterand immediately following his presidential victory, also can be viewed as moderating in that they produced a less than expected score for the left (Hoffman, 1988). These "close calls", in addition to the two *cohabitation* periods, suggest that there is a substantial middle-of-the road electorate in France that seeks to balance the left and right coalitions. In contrast, Pierce (1991) argues that the French political establishment has always viewed *cohabitation* as an aberration; they view American divided government as a workable situation but *cohabitation* as a disaster.

Pierce's main arguments are two. The first relies on the institutional differences between France and the United States. The second one emphasizes differences in party behavior and in the degree of ideological polarization.

The institutional argument holds that, unlike in the United States, executive power is split under *cohabitation*. In fact, the prime minister and the government belong to a different party than the president's. Pierce (1991) also notes that the French constitution is somewhat ambiguous about exactly how the executive power is split between the prime minister and the president.[22] This led to a conflictual rather than cooperative atmosphere between Mitterand, the president, and Chirac, the prime minister, in the 1986–88 period. However, the subsequent *cohabitation* with Balladur now seems considerably smoother than the earlier experience with Chirac.

The second difference is that while the two American parties are used to compromise and cooperation, the two French blocks are not, because they are more ideologically polarized. As a result, Pierce argues, *cohabitation* resulted in a conservative government with a Socialist president who maintained his influence only on a set of very specific issues, mostly in foreign policy. Mitterand and Chirac did not share power by reaching compromises on policy. Instead, Mitterand could unilaterally decide on some issues, while Chirac could do the same on different issues.

These observations are certainly well taken; nevertheless we do feel that the similarities between the French and the American cases of divided government are more striking than the differences. First, the newness of *cohabitation* does not mean that it will fail to be institutionalized. In the wake of the overwhelming victory of the right in the 1993 legislative elections, Chirac, at this time the leading contender of the right for the next presidential election, called for President Mitterand to resign. But other politicians on the right, including the new prime minister, Edouard Balladur, were considerably more circumspect in their public pronouncements. In the end, Mitterand

---

[22]For instance, Pierce (1991) notes constitutional ambiguities on the issue of supreme control of the armed forces.

remained in office, even after massive public rejection of Socialist performance in office. Second, as Tuppen (1991) pointed out, the president, by failing to sign legislation, can impose delays on even the domestic policies of the legislative majority. Third, the presidential office provides a significant forum for influencing public opinion. For example, Mitterand did not hesitate to criticize, after the very first Council of Ministers meeting of the Balladur government, the positions of the new "law and order" Interior Minister, Charles Pasqua. In January of 1994, Mitterand urged Balladur to show more concern with unemployment. Fourth, even if policy is formed by a division of power rather than compromise, an overall moderation may result. One may think of a left foreign policy and a right domestic policy as more moderate than a right policy in both areas. Indeed, the situation where the president and the prime minister have *de facto* jurisdictions is precisely the perspective that Laver and Shepsle (1991), in a companion piece to Pierce's, use to characterize parliamentary coalitions as a form of divided government.

10.6 CONCLUSION

Partisan policies, party polarization, divided government, and moderating behavior of voters are not uniquely American: *the United States is not exceptional*. On the contrary, we found remarkable similarities between the United States and other industrial democracies. In order to identify these similarities, one has to take account of important institutional differences. But once one looks beyond these differences, one can identify common trends and common forces at work.

First, we reviewed recent comparative research that shows that partisan cycles do not occur only in the United States. On the contrary they are quite common in other democracies. The crucial distinction on this point is not between the United States and all the others, but between two-party or two-block systems versus systems with large (and unstable) coalition governments.

Second, retrospective voting is a general phenomenon. Once again, the United States is no exception.

Third, office-oriented political business cycles (Nordhaus (1975)) are also absent in other democracies.

Fourth, divided government is very common. Coalition governments in parliamentary democracies have much in common with divided government in the United States.

Fifth, the American electorate is not the only one that moderates by means of institutional balancing. We focused on Germany and France to make this point; further research on other countries should be forthcoming.

The empirical evidence on partisan cycle in OECD democracies is quite systematic and robust. Laver and Shepsle (1990, 1991, 1992) and Schofield (1993) are making important progress in analyzing government formation in parliamentary democracies, from a "rational choice" perspective. Some scattered evidence of moderating behavior and "midterm cycles" has been reported for other countries. There is enough here to begin thinking about how everything fits together. In the first nine chapters of this book we have developed a general model of the political economy of the United States. In this chapter we hope that we have provided enough evidence that similar research projects are feasible for other countries as well. Once again, the United States is not unique.

REFERENCES

Alesina, A. 1987. Macroeconomic Policy in a Two-Party System as a Repeated Game. *Quarterly Journal of Economics* 102: 651–78.

————. 1988a. Credibility and Policy Convergence in a Two-Party System with Rational Voters. *American Economic Review* 78: 796–806.

————. 1988b. Macroeconomics and Politics, in *NBER Macroeconomic Annual 1988*, Cambridge, MA: MIT Press, 11–55.

————. 1989. Inflation, Unemployment and Politics in Industrial Democracies. *Economic Policy* 8: 55–98.

Alesina, A., and G. Carliner, eds. 1991. *Politics and Economics in the Eighties*, Chicago: University of Chicago Press and National Bureau of Economic Research.

Alesina, A., G. Cohen, and N. Roubini. 1992. Macroeconomic Policy and Elections in OECD Economies. *Economics and Politics* 4: 1–30.

————. 1993. Electoral Business Cycles in Industrial Democracies. *European Journal of Political Economy* 23: 1–25.

Alesina, A., and A. Cukierman 1990. The Politics of Ambiguity. *Quarterly Journal of Economics* 105: 829–50.

Alesina, A., and A. Drazen. 1991. Why Are Stabilizations Delayed? *American Economic Review* 82: 1170–88.

Alesina, A., M. Fiorina, and H. Rosenthal. 1991. Why Are There So Many Divided Senate Delegations? Cambridge, MA: National Bureau of Economic Research, Working Paper No. 3663.

Alesina, A., and V. Grilli. 1992. The European Central Bank: Reshaping Monetary Politics in Europe. In M. Canzoneri, V. Grilli, and P. Masson, eds. *Establishing a Central Bank: Issues in Europe and Lessons from the US.* London: Cambridge University Press and CEPR, 43–77.

————. 1993. On the Feasibility of a One-Speed or a Multi-Speed European Monetary Union. *Economics and Politics* 5: 145–66.

Alesina, A., J. Londregan, and H. Rosenthal. 1993. A Model of the Political Economy of the United States. *American Political Science Review* 87: 12–33.

Alesina, A., and H. Rosenthal. 1989. Partisan Cycles in Congressional Elections and the Macroeconomy. *American Political Science Review* 83: 373–98.

References

————. 1991. A Theory of Divided Government. Pittsburgh: Carnegie Mellon University, GSIA Working Paper.

————. 1992. Spatial Competition, Divided Government, and Political Polarization in the Context of Moderating Institutions. Paper presented at the Annual Meeting of the American Political Science Association.

Alesina, A., and N. Roubini. 1992. Political Cycles in OECD Economies. *Review of Economic Studies* 59: 663–88.

Alesina, A., and J. Sachs. 1988. Political Parties and the Business Cycle in the United States, 1948–84. *Journal of Money, Credit, and Banking* 20: 63–82.

Alesina, A., and S. Spear. 1988. An Overlapping Generations Model of Political Competition. *Journal of Public Economics* 37: 359–79.

Alesina, A., and L. Summers. 1993. Central Bank Independence and Macroeconomic Performance: Some Comparative Evidence. *Journal of Money, Credit, and Banking* 25: 151–62.

Alt, J. 1985. Political Parties, World Demand, and Unemployment: Domestic and International Sources of Economic Activity. *American Political Science Review* 79: 1016–40.

Alt, J., and A. Chrystal. 1983. *Political Economics*. Berkeley: Berkeley University Press.

Alt, J., and R. Lowry. 1992. Divided Government and Budget Deficits: Evidence for the States. Cambridge, MA: Harvard University. Unpublished.

Atkinson, A., and J. Stiglitz. 1980. *Lectures in Public Economics*. New York: McGraw Hill.

Aumann, R. 1959. Acceptable Points in General Cooperative *n*-Person Games. In A.W. Tucker and R. D. Luce, eds. *Contributions to the Theory of Games*, Vol. 4 (Annals of *Mathematics Studies*, 40). Princeton: Princeton University Press.

Austen-Smith, D. 1981. Party Policy and Campaign Costs in a Multi-Constituency Model of Electoral Competition. *Public Choice* 37: 389–402.

Austen-Smith, D., and J. Banks. 1988. Elections, Coalitions, and Legislative Outcomes. *American Political Science Review* 82: 407–22.

————. 1989. Electoral Accountability and Incumbency. In P. C. Ordeshook, ed. *Models of Strategic Choice in Politics*. Ann Arbor: University of Michigan Press, 121–48.

————. 1990. Stable Governments and the Allocation of Policy Portfolios. *American Political Science Review* 84: 891–900.

Ball, L., and G. Mankiw. 1992. Asymmetric Price Adjustment and Economic Fluctuations. Cambridge, MA: National Bureau of Economic Reserach, Working Paper # 4089.

Balke, N. S., and R. J. Gordon. 1989. The Estimation of Prewar Gross National Product: Methodology and New Evidence. *Journal of Political Economy* 97: 38–92.

Banks, J. S., and R. K. Sundaram. 1993. Adverse Selection and Moral Hazard in a Repeated Election Model. In W. A. Barnett et al., eds. *Political Economy: Institutions, Competition, and Representation*. Cambridge, UK: Cambridge University Press, 295–311.

Baron, D. P., and J. Mo. 1993. Campaign Contributions and Party–Candidate Competition in Services and Policies. In W. A. Barnett et al., eds. *Political*

261

References

Economy: Institutions, Competition, and Representation. Cambridge, UK: Cambridge University Press, 313–54.

Barro, R. 1991. Comments on McCubbins. In A. Alesina and G. Carliner, eds. *Politics and Economics in the Eighties.* Chicago: University of Chicago Press and National Bureau of Economic Research, 111–22.

Barro, R., and D. Gordon. 1983. Rules, Discretion, and Reputation in a Model of Monetary Policy. *Journal of Monetary Economics* 12: 101–22.

Beck, N. 1982. Parties. Administrations, and American Macroeconomic Outcomes. *Amercian Political Science Review* 76: 83–94.

————. 1992. The Shape of the Electoral Cycle. La Jolla: University of California at San Diego. Unpublished.

Benoit, J. P., and V. Khrisna. 1985. Finitely Repeated Games. *Econometrica* 53: 905–22.

Bernhardt, M. D., and D. Ingberman. 1985. Candidate Reputations and the 'Incumbency Effect'. *Journal of Public Economics* 27: 47–67.

Bernheim, D., B. Peleg, and M. Whinston. 1987. Coalition Proof Nash Equilibria. *Journal of Economic Theory* 42: 1–12.

Black, D. 1958. *Theory of Committees and Elections,* Cambridge, UK: Cambridge University Press.

Blanchard, O., and S. Fischer. 1989. *Lectures on Macroeconomics.* Cambridge, MA: MIT Press.

Boylan, R. J., J. Ledyard, and R. McKelvey. 1990. Political Competition in a Model of Economic Growth. Pasadena: California Institute of Technology. Unpublished.

Brady, D., S. Lohmann, and D. Rivers. 1992. Party Identification, Retrospective Voting and Moderating Elections in a Federal System: West Germany 1961–1989. Stanford, CA: Stanford University. Unpublished.

Brody, R. A., and B. I. Page. 1973. Indifference, Alienation, and Rational Decisions. *Public Choice* 25: 1–18.

Bruno, M., and J. Sachs. 1985. *The Economics of Worldwide Stagflation.* Cambridge, MA: Harvard University Press.

Cahoon, L. S., M. J. Hinich, and P. C. Ordeshook. 1978. A Statistical Multidimensional Scaling Model Based on the Spatial Theory of Voting. In P. C. Wang, ed. *Graphical Representation of Multidimensional Data.* New York: Academic Press, 243–78.

Cain, B., J. Ferejohn, and M. Fiorina. 1987. *The Personal Vote: Constituency Service and Electoral Independence.* Cambridge, MA: Harvard University Press.

Calvert, R. 1985. Robustness of the Multidimensional Voting Model: Candidates' Motivations, Uncertainty, and Covergence. *American Journal of Political Science* 29: 69–95.

Calvert, R., and J. A. Ferejohn. 1983. Coattail Voting in Recent Presidential Elections. *American Political Science Review* 77: 407–16.

Cameron, D. R. 1978. The Expansion of the Public Economy: A Comparative Analysis. *American Political Science Review* 72: 1243–61.

Campbell, J. Y., and N. G. Mankiw. 1987. Are Output Fluctuations Transitory? *Quarterly Journal of Economics* 102: 857–79.

Chappell, H. W., and W. R. Keech. 1988. The Unemployment Consequences of Partisan Monetary Policy. *Southern Economic Journal* 55: 107–22.

References

Chappell, H. W., and M. Suzuki. 1990. Aggregate Fluctuations for the U. S. Presidency, Senate, and House. Columbia: University of South Carolina. Unpublished.

Chilton, J. 1989. Pre-election Polling as a Cheap Talk Game. Columbia: University of South Carolina. Unpublished.

Cohen, G. 1993. Pre and Post Electoral Macroeconomic Fluctuations. Cambridge, MA: Harvard University. Unpublished doctoral dissertation.

Coleman, J. S. 1971. Indirect Processes Governing Party Positions in Elections *Public Choice* 11: 35–60.

Converse, P. E. 1964. The Nature of Belief Systems in Mass Publics. In D. Apter, ed. *Ideology and Discontent*. New York: Free Press, 206–61.

——. 1966. The Problem of Party Distances in Models of Voting Change. In M. K. Jennings and L. H. Ziegler, eds. *The Electoral Process*. Englewood Cliffs, NJ: Prentice-Hall, 175–207.

Coughlin, P., and S. Nitzan. 1981. Electoral Outcomes with Probabilistic Voting and Nash Social Welfare Maxima. *Journal of Public Economics* 15: 113–22.

Cox, G. W., and S. Kernell. 1991. *Divided Government*. Boulder, CO: Westview Press.

Cox, G. W., and M. D. McCubbins. 1991. Divided Control of Fiscal Policy. In G. W. Cox and S. Kernell, eds. *Divided Government*. Boulder, CO: Westview Press, 155–75.

——. 1993. *Legislative Leviathan: Party Government in the House*. Berkeley: University of California Press.

Cukierman, A. 1984. *Inflation, Stagflation, Relative Prices, and Imperfect Information*. Cambridge, UK: Cambridge University Press.

——. 1992. *Central Bank Strategy, Credibility and Independence*. Cambridge, MA: MIT Press.

Cukierman, A., S. Edwards, and G. Tabellini. 1992. Seignorage and Political Instability. *American Economic Review* 82: 537–56.

Cukierman, A., and A. Meltzer. 1986. A Positive Theory of Discretionary Policy, the Cost of Democratic Government, and the Benefits of a Constitution. *Economic Inquiry* 24: 367–88.

Denzau, A., and R. Mackay. 1983. Gatekeeping and Monopoly Power of Committees. *American Journal of Political Science* 27: 740–61.

Diamond, P. 1965. National Debt in a Neoclassical Growth Model. *American Economic Review* 55: 1125–50.

Downs, A. 1957. *An Economic Theory of Democracy*. New York: Harper and Row.

Enelow, J., and M. Hinich. 1984. *The Spatial Theory of Voting*. Cambridge, UK: Cambridge University Press.

——, eds. 1990. *Advances in the Spatial Theory of Voting*. Cambridge, UK: Cambridge University Press.

Erikson, R. 1988. The Puzzle of Midterm Loss. *Journal of Politics* 50: 1012–29.

——. 1989. Economic Conditions and the Presidential Vote. *Amercian Political Science Review* 83: 67–76.

——. 1990. Economic Conditions and the Congressional Vote: A Review of the Macrolevel Evidence. *American Journal of Political Science* 34: 373–99.

Fair, R. 1978. The Effects of Economic Events on Votes for Presidents. *Review of Economics and Statistics* 60: 159–72.

References

————. 1982. The Effect of Economic Events on Votes for President: 1980 Results. *Review of Economics and Statistics* 64: 322–25.

————. 1988. The Effect of Economic Events on Votes for President: 1984 Update. *Political Behavior* 10: 168–79.

Farquharson, R. 1962. *Theory of Voting*. New Haven: Yale University Press.

Feddersen, T. 1992. A Voting Model Implying Duverger's Law and Positive Turnout. *American Journal of Political Science* 36: 938–62.

————. 1993. Coalition-Proof Nash Equilibria in a Model of Costly Voting Under Plurality Rule. Evanston: Northwestern University. Unpublished.

Fenno, R. 1978. *Home Style*. Boston: Little, Brown.

Ferejohn, J. 1986. Logrolling in an Institutional Context: The Case of Food Stamps. In G. C. Wright, Jr., et al., eds. *Congress and Policy Change*. New York: Agathon Press, 223–53.

Ferejohn, J., and M. Fiorina. 1974. The Paradox of Not Voting: A Decision-Theoretic Analysis. *American Political Science Review* 68: 525–36.

Ferejohn, J., and C. Shipan. 1990. Congressional Influence on Bureaucracy. *Journal of Law, Economics, and Organization* 6, 1–20.

Fiorina, M. 1974. *Representatives, Roll Calls, and Constituencies*. Lexington, MA.: D. C. Heath.

————. 1981. *Retrospective Voting in American National Elections*. New Haven: Yale University Press.

————. 1988. The Reagan Years: Turning to the Right or Groping Toward the Middle. In B. Cooper et al., eds. *The Resurgence of Conservatism in Anglo-American Democracies*. Durham: Duke University Press.

————. 1989. *Congress: Keystone of the Washington Establishment*, 2nd edition. New Haven: Yale University Press.

————. 1990. An Era of Divided Government. In G. Peele et al., eds. *Developments in American Politics*. Oxford: Oxford University Press, 324–54.

————. 1991. Coalition Governments, Divided Governments, and Electoral Theory. *Governance: An International Journal of Policy and Administration* 4: 236–49.

————. 1992. *Divided Government*. New York: Macmillan.

Fischer, S. 1977. Long Term Contracts, Rational Expections, and the Optimal Money Supply Rule. *Journal of Political Economy* 85: 191–206.

Frey, B., and F. Schneider. 1978. An Empirical Study of Politico-Economic Interaction in the United States. *Review of Economics and Statistics* 60: 174–83.

Frieden, J. 1991. Greenbacks, Gold, and Silver: The Politics of American Exchange-Rate Policy, 1870–1973. CIBER Working Paper 91–04. Los Angeles: University of California, Los Angeles.

Friedman, M. 1968. The Role of Monetary Policy. *American Economic Review* 58: 1–17.

Friedman, M., and A. Schwartz. 1971. *A Monetary History of the United States*. Princeton: Princeton University Press.

Fudenberg, D., and J. Tirole. 1991. *Game Theory*. Cambridge, MA: MIT Press.

Gelman, A., and G. King. 1990. Estimating Incumbency Advantage without Bias. *American Journal of Political Science* 34: 1142–64.

References

Giavazzi, F., and A. Giovannini. 1989. *Limiting Exchange Rate Flexibility: The European Monetary System*. Cambridge, MA: MIT Press.

Gilligan, T. W., and K. Krehbiel. 1989. Asymmetric Influence and Legislative Rules with a Heterogeneous Committee. *American Journal of Political Science* 33: 459–90.

Golden, D., and J. Poterba. 1980. The Price of Popularity: The Political Business Cycle Reexamined. *American Journal of Political Science* 24: 694–714.

Gray J. A. 1978. On Indexation and Contract Length. *Journal of Political Economy* 86: 1–18.

Greenberg, J. 1979. Consistent Majority Rules over Compact Sets of Alternatives. *Econometrica* 47: 627–736.

———. 1989. Deriving Strong and Coalition-Proof Nash Equilibria from an Abstract System. *Journal of Economic Theory* 49: 195–202.

———. 1990. *The Theory of Social Situations: An Alternative Game-Theoretic Approach*. Cambridge, UK: Cambridge University Press.

Greenberg, J., and K. A. Shepsle. 1987. The Effect of Electoral Rewards in Multiparty Competition with Entry. *American Political Science Review* 81: 525–37.

Grilli, V., D. Masciandaro, and G. Tabellini. 1991. Political and Monetary Institutions and Public Finance Policies in the Industrial Democracies. *Economic Policy* 13: 342–92.

Hammond, T. H., and J. H. Fraser. 1983. Baselines for Evaluating Explanations of Coalition Behavior in Congress. *Journal of Politics* 45: 635–56.

Hammond, T., and G. Miller. 1987. The Core of the Constitution. *American Political Science Review* 81: 1155–74.

Hansen, S., T. R. Palfrey, and H. Rosenthal. 1987. The Relationship Between Constituency Size and Turnout: Using Game Theory to Estimate the Cost of Voting. *Public Choice* 52: 15–33.

Harvrilesky, T. 1987. A Partisan Theory of Fiscal and Monetary Regimes. *Journal of Money, Credit, and Banking* 19: 677–700.

———. 1993. *The Pressures on Monetary Policy*. Norwell, MA: Kluwer Academic Publishers.

Haynes, S., and J. Stone 1987. Should Political Models of the Business Cycle Be Revived? Working Paper No. 8716. Eugene: University of Oregon.

Heckman, J. N., and J. M. Synder, Jr. 1992. A Linear Factor Model of Roll Call Voting. Chicago: University of Chicago. Unpublished.

Hibbs, D. 1977. Political Parties and Macroeconomic Policy. *American Political Science Review* 71: 1467–87.

———. 1987. *The American Political Economy: Electoral Policy and Macroeconomics in Comtemporary America*. Cambridge, MA: Harvard University Press.

———. 1992. Partisan Theory after Fifteen Years. *European Journal of Political Economy* 8: 361–74.

Hinich, M. 1977. Equilibrium in Spatial Voting: The Median Voter Result Is an Artifact. *Journal of Economic Theory* 16: 208–19.

Hinich, M., and P. C. Ordeshook 1969. Abstention and Equilibrium in the Electoral Process, *Public Choice* 7: 81–106.

References

Hoffman, S. 1988. The Big Muddle in France. *New York Review of Books* 35 (No. 13): 52–6.

Hotelling, H. 1929. Stability in Competition. *Economic Journal* 39: 41–57.

Ingberman, D. E., 1994. Incumbent Reputations and Ideological Campaign Contributions in Spatial Competition. *Formal Theories of Politics II: Mathematical and Computer Modeling*, Special issue of *Mathematical and Computer Modeling*, Forthcoming.

Ingberman, D. E., and H. Rosenthal. 1994. Median Voter Theorems for Divisible Governments. Princeton: Princeton University. Unpublished..

Ingberman, D. E., and J. J. Villani. 1993. An Institutional Theory of Divided Government and Party Polarization. *American Journal of Political Science* 37: 429–71.

Ingberman, D. E., and D. A. Yao. 1991. Presidential Commitment and the Veto. *American Journal of Political Science* 35: 357–89.

Ito, Takatoshi. 1990. The Timing of Elections and Political Business Cycles in Japan. *Journal of Asian Economics* 1: 135–46.

Jacobson, G. 1990a. *The Electoral Origins of Divided Government*. Boulder, CO: Westview Press.

————. 1990b. Does the Economy Matter in Midterm Elections? *American Journal of Political Science* 34: 400–4.

————. 1991. The Persistence of Democratic House Majorities. In G. W. Cox and S. Kernell, eds. *Divided Government*. Boulder, CO: Westview Press. 57–84.

Kernell, S. 1991. Facing an Opposition Congress: The President's Strategic Circumstance. In G. W. Cox and S. Kernell, eds. *Divided Government*. Boulder, CO: Westview Press, 87–112.

Kiewiet, D. R. 1983. *Microeconomics and Micropolitics*. Chicago: University of Chicago Press.

Kiewiet, D. R., and M. D. McCubbins. 1991. *The Logic of Delegation*. Chicago: University of Chicago Press.

Kiewiet, D. R., and M. Udell. 1991. Back to the Beginning: A Reconsideration of the Electoral Effects of Short-term Economic Fluctuations. Presented at the annual meeting of the Midwestern Political Science Association, Chicago.

Kiewiet, D. R., and L. Zeng. 1993. An Analysis of Congressional Career Decisions, 1947–86. *American Political Science Review* 87: 928–41.

King, G., and A. Gelman. 1991. Systemic Consequences of Incumbency Advantage in Congressional Elections. *American Journal of Political Science* 35: 110–38.

Kramer, G. 1971. Short-term Fluctuations in U.S. Voting Behavior, 1896–1964. *American Political Science Review* 65: 131–43.

————. 1973. On a Class of Equilibrium Conditions for Majority Rule. *Econometrica* 41: 285–97.

Krehbiel, K. 1988. Spatial Models of Legislative Choice. *Legislative Studies Quarterly* 13: 259–319.

————. 1992. *Information and Legislative Organization*. Ann Arbor: University of Michigan Press.

Kydland, F., and E. Prescott. 1977. Rules Rather than Discretion: The Inconsistency of Optimal Plans. *Journal of Political Economy* 85: 473–90.

References

Laver, M., and N. Schofield. 1990. *Multiparty Government*. Oxford: Oxford University Press.

Laver, M., and K. A. Shepsle. 1990. Coalitions and Cabinet Government. *American Political Science Review* 84: 873–90.

————. 1991. Divided Government: America Is not 'Exceptional'. *Governance: An International Journal of Policy and Administration* 4: 250–69.

Lepper, S. 1974. Voting Behavior and Aggregate Policy Targets. *Public Choice* 18: 67–82.

Ledyard, J. 1984. The Pure Theory of Large Two-candidate Elections. *Public Choice* 44: 7–41.

Lewis–Beck, M. 1988. *Economics and Elections: The Major Western Democracies*. Ann Arbor: University of Michigan Press.

Lindbeck, A. 1976. Stabilization Policies in Open Economies with Endogenous Politicians. *American Economic Review*. Papers and Proceedings, 1–19.

Lohmann, S. 1992. The Optimal Degree of Commitment: Credibility Versus Flexibility. *American Economic Review* 82: 273–86.

Londregan, J. B., and T. Romer. 1993. The Polarizing Personal Vote. In W. A. Barnett et al., eds, *Political Economy: Institutions, Competition, and Representation*. Cambridge, UK: Cambridge University Press, 355–78.

Loomis, M., and K. T. Poole 1992. Last-term Behavior of Members of Congress. Pittsburgh: Carnegie Mellon University. Unpublished.

Lott, J. R., Jr., and S. G. Bronars 1993. Times Series Evidence on Shirking in the U.S. House of Representatives. *Public Choice* 76: 125–50.

Lucas, R. E., Jr. 1972. Expectations and the Neutrality of Money. *Journal of Economic Theory* 4: 103–24.

McCallum, B. 1978. The Political Business Cycle: An Empirical Test. *Southern Economic Journal* 44: 504–15.

McCarty, N., and K. T. Poole. 1992. The Spatial Mapping of Congressional Candidates and Contributors. GSIA WP 1992–46. Pittsburgh: Carnegie-Mellon University.

McCubbins, M. D. 1991. Party Governance and US Budget Deficits: Divided Government and Fiscal Stalemate. In A. Alesina and G. Carliner, eds. *Politics and Economics in the Eighties*. Chicago: University of Chicago Press and National Bureau of Economic Research, 83–111.

McKelvey, R. D. 1976. Intransitivities in Multidimensional Voting Models and Some Implications for Agenda Control. *Journal of Economic Theory* 12: 472–82.

————. 1979. General Conditions for Global Intransitivities in Formal Voting Models. *Econometrica* 47: 1085–1112.

McKelvey, R. D., and P. C. Ordeshook. 1985. Elections with Limited Information: A Fulfilled Expectations Model Using Contemporaneous Pool and Endorsement Data as Information Sources. *Journal of Economic Theory* 36: 55–85.

Mankiw, G. 1985. Small Menu Costs and Large Business Cycles: A Macroeconomic Model of Monopoly. *Quarterly Journal of Economics* 100: 529–39.

————. 1990. Optimal Collection of Seignorage: Theory and Evidence. NBER Working Paper. Cambridge, MA: National Bureau of Economic Research.

————. 1992. *Macroeconomics*. New York: Worth Publishers.

Mankiw, G., J. Miron, and D. Weil. 1990. The Adjustment of Expections to a Change

References

in Regime: A Study of the Founding of the Federal Reserve. *American Economic Review* 77: 358–74.

Mankiw, G., and D. Romer. 1991. *New Keynesian Macroeconomics*. Cambridge, MA: MIT Press.

Matthews, S. 1989. Veto Threats: Rhetoric in a Bargaining Game. *Quarterly Journal of Economics* 104: 347–69.

Mayhew, D. R. 1991. *Divided Government: Party Control, Lawmaking, and Investigations, 1946–1990*. New Haven: Yale University Press.

Meltzer, A. M., and S. F. Richard. 1981. A Rational Theory of the Size of Government. *Journal of Political Economy* 89: 914–27.

Milesi-Ferretti, G., 1991. *Dynamic Models of Strategic Policy Making* Cambridge, MA: Harvard University. Unpublished doctoral dissertation.

Minford, P. 1985. Interest Rates and Bonded Deficits in a Richardian Two-Party Democracy. London: CEPR Discussion Paper No. 79.

Moe, T. M. 1985. Control and Feedback in Economic Regulation: The Case of the NLRB. *American Political Science Review* 79: 1094–116.

Mueller, J. E. 1973. *Wars, Presidents and Public Opinion*. New York: Wiley.

Nelson, C. R., and C. T. Plosser. 1982. Trends and Random Walks in Macroeconomic Time Series. *Journal of Monetary Economics* 10: 139–62.

Nordhaus, W. 1975. The Political Business Cycle. *Review of Economic Studies* 42: 169–90.

Ordeshook, P. C. 1986. *Game Theory and Political Theory*. Cambridge, UK: Cambridge University Press.

Paldam, M. 1979. Is There an Electoral Cycle? A Comparative Study of National Accounts. *Scandinavian Journal of Economics* 81: 323–42.

————. 1989a. Politics Matter After All: Testing Alesina's Theory of RE Partisan Cycles. Aarhus University Working Paper.

————. 1989b. Politics Matter After All: Testing Hibbs' Theory of Partisan Cycles. Aarhus University Working Paper.

Palfrey, T. R. 1984. Spatial Equilibrium with Entry. *Review of Economic Studies* 51: 139–56.

Palfrey, T. R., and H. Rosenthal. 1985. Voter Participation and Strategic Uncertainty. *American Political Science Review* 79: 62–78.

Persson, T. 1991. Politics and Economic Policy. Lecture presented at the X Latin American Meeting of the Econometric Society, Punta del Este, Uruguay, August 28–30, 1991.

Persson, T., and G. Tabellini. 1990. *Macroeconomic Policy, Credibility, and Politics*. Chur, Switzerland: Harwood Academic Publishers.

Petrocik, J. 1990. Divided Government: Is It All in the Campaigns? In G. W. Cox and S. Kernell, eds. *Divided Government*. Boulder, CO: Westview Press, 13–38.

Phelps, E. 1973. Inflation and the Theory of Public Finance. *Swedish Journal of Economics* 74: 67–82.

Pierce, R. 1991. The Executive Divided Against Itself: Cohabitation in France, 1986–1988. *Governance: An International Journal of Policy and Administration* 4: 270–94.

Poole, K. T. 1981. Dimensions of Interest Group Evaluation of the U.S. Senate, 1969–78. *American Journal of Political Science* 25: 49–67.

References

————. 1984. Least Squares Metric, Unidimensional Unfolding. *Psychometrika* 79: 311–23.

————. 1991. Least Squares Metric, Unidimensional Scaling of Multivariate Linear Models. *Psychometrika*, 86: 123–49.

Poole, K. T., and R. S. Daniels. 1985. Ideology, Party, and Voting in the U.S. Congress, 1959–80. *American Political Science Review* 79: 373–99.

Poole, K. T., and T. Romer. 1993. Ideology, "Shirking", and Representation. *Public Choice* 77: 185–96.

Poole, K. T., and H. Rosenthal. 1984a. U.S. Presidential Elections 1968–1980: A Spatial Analysis. *American Journal of Political Science* 28: 283–312.

————. 1984b. The Polarization of American Politics. *Journal of Politics* 46: 1061–79.

————. 1985. The Political Economy of Roll-Call Voting in the 'Multi-Party' Congress of the United States. *European Journal of Political Economy* 1: 45–58.

————. 1986. The Dynamics of Interest Groups Evaluation of Congress. GSIA Working Paper 3-86-87. Pittsburgh: Carnegie Mellon University.

————. 1987. Analysis of Congressional Coalition Patterns: A Unidimensional Spatial Model. *Legislative Studies Quarterly* 12: 55–75.

————. 1991a. Patterns of Congressional Voting. *American Journal of Political Science* 35: 228–78.

————. 1991b. The Spatial Mapping of Minimum Wage Legislation. In A. Alesina and G. Carliner, eds. *Politics and Economics in the 1980s.* Chicago: University of Chicago Press and National Bureau of Economic Research, 215–46.

————. 1993a. The Enduring 19th Century Battle for Economic Regulation: The Interstate Commerce Act Revisited. *Journal of Law and Economics* (forthcoming).

————. 1993b. Spatial Realignment and the Mapping of Issues in American History. In W. H. Riker, ed. *Agenda Formation.* Ann Arbor: University of Michigan Press, 13–39.

Popkin, S. 1991. *The Reasoning Voter: Communication and Persuasion in Presidential Campaigns.* Chicago: University of Chicago Press.

Popper, K. 1959. *The Logic of Scientific Discovery.* New York: Basic Books.

Poterba, J. 1992. State Responses to Fiscal Crises: 'Natural Experiments' for Studying the Effects of Budgetary Institutions. Cambridge, MA: Massachusetts Institute of Technology. Unpublished.

Powell, G. B., Jr. 1991. 'Divided Government' as a Pattern of Governance. *Governance: An International Journal of Policy and Administration* 4: 231–35.

Putnam, R. D. 1993. *Making Democracy Work: Civic Traditions in Modern Italy.* Princeton: Princeton University Press.

Rabinowitz, G. 1976. A Procedure for Ordering Object Pairs Consistent with the Unidimensional Unfolding Model. *Psychometrika* 45: 349–73.

Riker, W. H. 1980. Implications from the Disequilibrium of Majority Rule for the Study of Institutions. *American Political Science Review* 74: 432–46.

Riker, W. H., and P. C. Ordeshook 1968. A Rational Calculus of Voting. *American Political Science Review* 62: 25–42.

Roemer, J. 1992. A Theory of Class Differentiated Politics in an Electoral Democracy. WP 384, Department of Economics. Davis: University of California, Davis.

References

Rogoff, K. 1985. The Optimal Degree of Commitment to an Intermediate Monetary Target. *Quarterly Journal of Economics* 100: 1169–90.

————. 1987. A Reputational Constraint on Monetary Policy. Special issue of *Journal of Monetary Economics*, Carnegie–Rochester Conference Series on Public Policy 24: 115–65.

————. 1990. Political Budget Cycles. *American Economic Review* 80: 1–16.

Rogoff, K., and A. Sibert. 1988. Elections and Macroeconomic Policy Cycles. *Review of Economic Studies* 55: 1–16.

Romer, C. 1989. The Prewar Business Cycle Reconsidered: New Estimates of Gross National Product, 1869–1908. *Journal of Political Economy* 97: 1–37.

Romer, C., and D. Romer. 1989. Does Monetary Policy Matter—a New Test in the Spirit of Friedman and Schwartz. In O. Blanchard and S. Fischer, eds. *NBER Macroeconomic Annual*. Cambridge, MA: MIT Press.

Romer, T., and H. Rosenthal. 1978. Political Resource Allocation, Controlled Agendas, and the Status Quo. *Public Choice* 33: 27–43.

————. 1979a. The Elusive Median Voter. *Journal of Public Economics* 12: 143–70.

————. 1979b. Bureaucrats vs. Voters: On the Political Economy of Resource Allocation by Direct Democracy. *Quarterly Journal of Economics* 93: 563–87.

Romer, T., and B. Weingast. 1991. Political Foundations of the Thrift Debacle. In A. Alesina and G. Carliner, eds. *Politics and Economics in the 1980s*. Chicago: University of Chicago Press and National Bureau of Economic Research, 175–209.

Rosenthal, H., and S. Sen. 1973. Electoral Participation in the French Fifth Republic. *American Political Science Review* 67: 29–54.

Rothemberg T. J. 1973. *Efficient Estimations with A Priori Information*. Cowles Foundation Monograph No. 23. New Haven: Yale University Press.

Roubini, N., and J. Sachs. 1989a. Political and Economic Determinants of Budget Deficits in the Industrial Democracies. *European Economic Review* 33: 903–33.

————. 1989b. Government Spending and Budget Deficits in the Industrialized Countries. *Economic Policy* 8: 99–132.

Sargent, T., and N. Wallace. 1975. Rational Expectations, the Optimal Monetary Instrument and the Optimal Money Supply Rule. *Journal of Political Economy* 83: 241–54.

Schofield, N. 1993. Party Competition in a Spatial Model of Coalition Formation. In W. Barnett et al., eds. *Political Economy: Institutions, Competition, and Representation*. Cambridge, UK: Cambridge University Press, 135–74.

Selten, R. 1975. Reexamination of the Perfectness Concept for Equilibrium Points in Extensive Games. *International Journal of Game Theory* 4: 25–55.

Shepsle, K. A. 1972. The Strategy of Ambiguity: Uncertainty and Electoral Competition. *American Political Science Review*, 66: 555–68.

————. 1986. The Positive Theory of Legislative Institutions: An Enrichment of Social Choice and Spatial Models. *Public Choice* 50: 135–78.

Shepsle, K. A., and R. N. Cohen 1990. Multiparty Competition, Entry, and Entry Deterrence in Spatial Models of Elections. In J. Enelow and M. Hinich, eds. *Advances in the Spatial Theory of Voting*. Cambridge, UK: Cambridge University Press, 12–45.

References

Shepsle, K. A., and B. R. Weingast. 1987. The Institutional Foundations of Committee Power. *American Political Science Review* 81: 85–104.

Snyder, J. M., Jr. 1990. Campaign Contributions as Investments: The U.S. House of Representatives 1980–1996. *Journal of Political Economy* 98: 1195–227.

———. 1991. The Dimensions of Constituency Preferences: Voting on California Ballot Propositions, 1974–1990. Chicago: University of Chicago. Unpublished.

Spolaore, E. 1992. Policy Making Systems and Economic Efficiency: Coalition Governments versus Majority Governments. Unpublished.

Stewart, C. J., III. 1990. Lessons from the Post–Civil War Era. In G. W. Cox and S. Kernell, eds. *Divided Government*. Boulder, CO: Westview Press.

Strom, K. 1984. Minority Governments in Parliamentary Democracies: The Rationality of Nonwinning Cabinet Solutions. *Comparative Political Studies* 17: 199–227.

———. 1985. Party Goals and Government Performance in Parlimentary Democracies. *American Political Science Review* 79: 738–54.

———. 1990. *Minority Government and Majority Rule*. New York: Cambridge University Press.

Sundquist, J. 1983. *Dynamics of the Party System*. Washington, DC: The Brookings Institution.

Taylor, J. 1979. Staggered Wage Setting in a Macro Model. *American Economic Review* 69: 108–13.

Tobin, J. 1972. Inflation and Unemployment. *American Economic Review* 62: 1–18.

Tovey, C. 1991. The Instability of Instability. Monterey, CA: Naval Postgraduate School. Unpublished.

Tufte, E. B. 1978. *Political Control of the Economy*. Princeton: Princeton University Press.

Tullock, G. 1991. Duncan Black: The Founding Father. *Public Choice* 71: 125–28.

Tuppen, J. 1991. *Chirac's France*. New York: St. Martin's.

Weingast, B. R. 1984. The Congressional-Bureaucratic System: A Principal-Agent Perspective (with Application to the SEC). *Public Choice* 44: 147–92.

———. 1993. Institutions and Political Commitment: A New Political-Economy of the Civil War Era. Stanford, CA: Stanford University. Unpublished.

Wittman, D. 1977. Candidates with Policy Preferences: A Dynamic Model. *Journal of Economic Theory* 14: 180–89.

———. 1983. Candidate Motivation: A Synthesis of Alternatives. *American Political Science Review* 77: 142–57.

———. 1990. Spatial Strategies When Candidates Have Policy Preferences. In J. Enelow and M. Hinich, eds. *Advances in the Spatial Theory of Voting*. Cambridge, U K: Cambridge University Press, 66–98.

Index

Alesina, A., 4n, 8n, 10, 11, 13n, 14, 14n, 17, 24n, 27n, 29n, 30n, 31, 32, 33, 33n, 82, 90n, 101n, 122n, 127n, 129n, 130, 167n, 168n, 171n, 173n, 176n, 179, 180n, 182n, 183n, 184n, 187n, 188n, 190, 190n, 194n, 196, 199n, 200n, 204n, 206n, 208, 212, 214, 215n, 219, 222, 237, 239, 244, 244n, 245, 246–7, 248

Alt, J., 4n, 8, 13, 187n, 244n, 245, 248n

Atkinson, A., 167n

Austen-Smith, D., 41n, 252n

autoregressive moving average, 193

balancing, institutional
effect of midterm middle-of-the road voters, 83–6
effect on mobile parties, 11, 131–2
effect on policy and parties, 121–2
electorate use of, 244–5
with heterogeneous parties, 122–4
of presidential and congressional elections, 239
with staggered terms, 126
by sub-national governments, 253–6
See also checks and balances; cohabitation in government; divided government; midterm voting cycle; moderation; split-ticket voting

Balke, N. S., 210

Ball, L., 167n

Banks, J. S., 30n, 252n

Baron, D. P., 41n

Barro, R. J., 9n, 29n, 171, 173n

Beck, N., 4n, 190, 208, 237

Bernhardt, M. D., 19n, 136, 205

Bernheim, D., 82

Black, D., 16

Blanchard, O., 165n, 166

bliss points. See ideal policies

Bonars, S. G., 39n

Brady, D., 244, 245, 254, 255, 255n

Brody, R. A., 37

Bruno, M., 162n

business cycle. See partisan business cycle (Hibbs); political business cycle (Nordhaus); rational partisan business cycle (Alesina)

Cahoon, L. S., 37

Cain, B., 127, 210

Calvert, R., 10, 17, 19n, 26, 28, 29, 52n, 85

Calvert–Wittman model, 131, 133

Cameron, D. R., 210

Carliner, G., 188n

certainty models of voting, 51–71, 92, 122–7

Chappell, H. W., 186, 190, 208, 208n, 236, 237, 239

checks and balances
effect of institutional, 43
voter use of, 2, 5, 10, 43

Chilton, J., 49n,

Chrystal, A., 13, 187n

coalition governments
avoidance of partisan cycles in, 247–9
in parliamentary democracies, 8, 243–4, 249–50
political control in parliamentary democracies, 249
in three-party system, 251–3

coattail, presidential
effect of random preference shock analogous to, 104, 106
in on-year election outcomes, 85, 209, 221–2, 227–8, 230
reverse effect, 199–200

cohabitation in government, 244, 250, 256–8

Cohen, G., 4n, 180, 186n, 187n, 200n, 244n, 246–7

272

Index

Cohen, R. N., 41
Coleman, J. S., 40
competence, administrative
  effect of differences in government,
    6–7, 188–9, 220, 238
  expected in model of economic growth,
    191–5, 200, 213, 215–16
  information collection related to, 7,
    200–3
  model, 191–5, 206, 216
competition, party, 16–17
  See also equilibrium, party; party platforms
conditionally sincere voting model
  divided government in, 68–9
  equilibria in stable, 52, 76–82, 113–17
  occurrence of unified government, 69
conditional sincerity
  in both periods in uncertainty model,
    109–10
  condition when equilibrium not satisfied,
    55–6
  voter condition of, 50–1
  of voters in legislative elections, 59, 75,
    109–10
  of voters in presidential elections, 76,
    92, 109–10
Congress
  balance of presidential role by, 131
  circumstances for and effect of moderation
    by president, 121–4
  impact on public policy, 2, 13–14, 45–6, 189
  See also dimensionality of policy space,
    staggered terms of office
congressional elections
  adjustment path with staggered terms,
    126–7
  certainty in midterm, 2–3
  effect on economy, 4
  incumbency advantage, 137, 139, 205
  See also balancing, institutional; cutpoint;
    House elections; legislative elections
convergence of party platforms
  formal analysis of partial, 28–9
  partisan model of partial, 19–28
  in repeated electoral game, 31–2
  See also polarization
Converse, P. E., 34
coordination game, 49–50
  See also conditional sincerity
Coughlin, P., 16
Cox, G. W., 13, 35n, 45
Cukierman, A., 13, 24n, 30n, 33, 33n, 166,
  167n, 171n, 173n, 179, 191n
cutpoint
  defined, 53–4
cutpoint, legislative
  in generalized pivotal-voter theorem

with uncertainty, 90–1, 95–6
with heterogeneous parties, 123
in midterm elections with inflation policy,
  196
in on-year elections with inflation
  policy, 197
in pivotal-voter theorem with certainty,
  57, 77
cutpoint, presidential
  in certainty model, 65, 75
  equilibrium with uncertain outcome,
    92, 99–100
  in on-year elections with inflation
    and competence factor, 197
cutpoint, strategies in four-policy majoritarian
  model, 68

Daniels, R. S., 35, 40
data sources
  for measurement of midterm cycle,
    139–40
  for U.S. political economy model, 6,
    209–13
Denzau, A., 46n
Diamond, P., 32
dimensionality of policy space, 34–9
discount factor, 89, 124, 177
divided government
  conditions for occurrences of, 13–14, 45,
    63–5, 69, 103, 106
  effectiveness, 8–9
  as outcome of voter moderation, 2, 10
  in parliamentary democracies, 243–4
  as remedy to political polarization,
    44
  in uncertainty model, 102, 103
  United States, 235, 243–4
  See also coalition governments;
    cohabitation in government; minority
    governments
D-NOMINATE scaling procedure, 35–9
Downs, A., 1, 16, 243, 251
Drazen, A., 8n, 248

economic growth
  comparison of Democratic and Republican,
    7–8, 180–3
  with competent and incompetent
    administrations, 188–9
  effect on elections, 4, 197–8, 200
  estimates for United States, 181–3, 216–17,
    223–4
  international comparison, 245–6
  occurrence of fluctuations, 206
  party preferences for, 167–78
economic growth model

273

Index

Index

legislative elections
  voter behavior in uncertainty model, 95
  voter conditional sincerity in, 75
  See also congressional elections; cutpoint,
    legislative; House elections
Lepper, S., 208
Lewis-Beck, M., 4n, 200n, 244n, 247, 247n
Lohmann, S., 173n, 244, 245, 254, 255, 255n
Londregan, J., 14, 14n, 19n, 188n, 194n, 196,
  199n, 204n, 222
Loomis, M., 39, 39n
Lott, J. R., Jr., 39n
Lowry, R., 8, 244n
Lucas, R. E., Jr. 5, 162

McCallum, B., 4n, 190, 190n, 208, 237
McCarty, N., 39n, 40, 204n
McCubbins, M. D., 9, 9n, 35n, 45
Mackay, R., 46n
McKelvey, R. D., 46
macroeconomic policy
  distributional effects, 169–70
  fiscal and monetary, 161–3
  Republican and Democratic parties, 1
  time lag of effect, 180
majoritarian models
  conditionally and unconditionally sincere
    voting, 66–71
  four-policy outcome model, 67–70, 77–8
  partisan cycles, 248–9
  of political decision-making, 45–6
Mankiw, G., 6n, 163, 165n, 167n, 184,
  185, 212
Masciandro, D., 8n, 13n, 248, 250n
Matthews, S., 46n
Mayhew, D. R., 8, 9
median voter
  party behavior with bliss point unknown,
    17, 24–5
  party ideal points relative to, and
    divided government, 63–4
  party ideal points relative to, and
    equilibrium, 60–1
  policy choice in majoritarian models, 70–1
  in ties in institutional balancing model,
    58–9
median-voter theorem
  candidate convergence in, 16, 57
  comparison with pivotal-voter theorem,
    56
Meltzer, A., 179, 191n
midterm voting cycle
  absence in certainty model, 65–6
  balancing effect by voters, 83–6, 94,
    105–6, 239
  certainty of occurrence, 104–5

determinants of size of midterm effect, 103,
  104
institutional balancing in, 2–3
interaction with incumbency advantage,
  137–9, 145–9
loss of voters for party in White House,
  4, 102–3, 140–5
with presidential election uncertainty, 206
probability of reversal in uncertainty
  model, 119–20
signaling theory, 138, 153–9
systematic and unsystematic intertemporal
  variation, 145–51
See also balancing, institutional; elections,
  midterm; moderation; uncertainty
  model
Milesi-Ferretti, G., 185
military mobilization, 205, 214–15, 218–20,
  222, 225–8, 231, 239
Miller, G., 46n
Minford, P., 169
minority governments, 249–50
Miron, J., 6n, 212
Mo, J., 41n
moderation
  behavior coexistence with incumbency
    advantage, 127, 138
  behavior in West Germany, 254
  link between competence and legislative,
    199
  midterm cycle achievement, 159
  party promises of, 31
  of policies in parliamentary democracies,
    244–5
  of president by legislature, 188, 195
  See also balancing, institutional; checks and
    balances; polarization
Moe, T., 13
Moving Average (MA), 192–3, 201, 216–17,
  223, 238
Mueller, J. E., 226

Nelson, C. R., 193, 216, 223
neutrality result, 162–3
Nitzan, S., 16
Nordhaus, W., 11, 12, 164, 178, 200, 237n, 258

open seat predictions, 152–9
Ordeshook, P. C., 30, 37, 108, 207n
overlapping generations model, 32

Page, B. I., 37
Paldam, M., 200n, 244n
Palfrey, T. R., 41, 207n
parliamentary democracies
  divided government in, 243, 249–51

276

Index

Index

predictions (*cont.*)
  of national elections in terms of previous
    midterm vote, 229–32
preferences. *See* ideal policies; party platforms;
    party preferences; preference shock,
    random (a); voter preferences
preference shock, random (a)
  in both periods in uncertainty model,
    107–17
  in congressional districts, 141, 144, 149–51
  critical value in presidential elections, 115
  drawn in first period of uncertainty
    model only, 118
  effect on party platforms, 129
  effect on voting, 101, 104
  policy divergence with high values of, 132
  reversal of midterm cycle produced by,
    104–5, 119–20
  in uncertainty models with staggered terms,
    127
  in voting under uncertainty, 86–90,
    91–2, 95, 97
Prescott, E., 29n, 171
president
  ideal policity different than legislative
    delegation of same party, 122
  insensitivity of policy to degree of power
    of, 132
  moderation of Congress by, 122, 124
presidential elections
  candidates' ideological positions, 35–7
  effect on economy, 4
  effect on size of midterm cycle, 103
  equalibria with certain outcome, 60–2,
    99, 100–1
  equalibria with uncertain outcome, 99–100,
    112–18
  estimates in U.S. political economy model,
    225–7
  France, 245, 256
  occurrences of divided government in, 103
  uncertainty generates midterm cycle,
    124
  voter behavior in certainty model, 58–9
  voter behavior in uncertainty model,
    92, 95, 97
  voter conditional sincerity with discrete
    changes, 75–6
  voters' conditional sincerity in, 92
  voting equations, empirical models for U.S.,
    219–21, 236
  See also cutpoint; elections, on-year;
    incumbency (advantage); landslide
    victory, presidential; voting, retrospective
primary elections, 40
public policy
  benefits of inflation to policymaker, 168

Democrats better positioned to initiate
    change, 235
determinants in cohabitation (France),
    257–8
determinants of outcomes, 2
impact of Congress on formation, 195
See also ideal policies; macroeconomic
    polcy; policy outcomes
Putnam, R. D., 253

Rabinowitz, G., 37
rational choice approach, 3–4, 6, 71–2, 237–9,
    240
rational expectations
  assumption in model of the economy, 5–6,
    162–3, 166
  defined, 3
  in voting choices and behavior of economic
    agents, 3, 33, 201
rational partisan business cycle (Alesina)
  criticism of theory, 184–7
  in Democratic and Republican
    administrations, 4
  electoral uncertainty as cause of, 3, 163–4
  empirical evidence 180–4, 206, 217–18,
    223–4
  expectations and electoral uncertainty in,
    2, 174
  for parliamentary democracies, 244
  theory, 11, 171–8
regression to the mean
  to explain midterm cycle, 85
  in incumbency advantage model, 145–9
  in political-economic cycle, 234
  in uncertainty model, 104
repeated-election models, 30–4
Riker, W. H., 207n
Rivers, D., 244, 245, 254, 255, 255n
Roemer, J., 10, 17, 24n, 27n
Rogoff, K., 6n, 167n, 173n, 179, 189, 191n, 247
Romer, C., 6n, 180, 184, 210, 212, 214
Romer, D., 163, 167n, 180, 184, 214
Romer, T., 9n, 35n, 39, 39n, 46
Rosenthal, H., 1, 4n, 10, 14, 19n, 35, 36f, 37,
    37n, 39, 39n, 40, 46, 70, 82, 90n, 101n, 108,
    122n, 124, 127n, 129n, 130, 188n,
    190, 194n, 196, 199n, 204n, 206n, 207n,
    208, 210, 212, 219, 222, 239, 244, 253
Rothemberg, T. J., 223
Roubini, N., 4n, 8n, 180, 187n, 200n, 214, 237,
    244n, 245, 246–47, 248

Sachs, J., 4n, 8n, 162n, 167n, 168n, 176n, 180n,
    190, 208, 237, 239, 248
Sargent, T., 5, 162
scaling procedures, 35–7
Schneider, F., 187, 187n